Praise for H. W. Brands's

THE ZEALOT AND THE EMANCIPATOR

ONE OF *SMITHSONIAN* MAGAZINE'S BEST BOOKS OF THE YEAR

"[Brands] scrupulously narrates the relevant facts and trusts readers to form their own conclusions. . . . *The Zealot and the Emancipator* relates these familiar events skillfully." —*The Wall Street Journal*

"Featuring the riveting narrative sweep, sharp eye for detail, and original analysis we have come to expect from H. W. Brands, *The Zealot and the Emancipator* vividly illuminates the convulsive battles to fulfill the long-deferred American dream of freedom for all."
  —Harold Holzer, author of *The Presidents vs. the Press*

"Engaging. . . . Brands concludes his fast-paced book with a grand flourish, bringing the seemingly disparate legacies of Brown and Lincoln into sync." —Washington Independent Review of Books

"Fascinating. . . . This book is the work of a master historian at the top of his craft." —*New York Journal of Books*

"A skilled narrative writer, Brands offers a vivid account of the raid on Harper's Ferry and its aftermath." —*London Review of Books*

"An informative, absorbing and heartbreaking American story, the reverberations of which are still felt today."
  —*BookPage* (starred review)

"This volume is a worthy companion to Brands's earlier biographies of FDR, Benjamin Franklin, and other eminent Americans."
  —Michael Burlingame, author of *Abraham Lincoln: A Life*

"Your concept of the antebellum and Civil War eras will be reshaped by this masterpiece." —*The Archive*, "Best Biographies"

"Reveal[s] striking parallels between the elections of 1860 and 2020. The extreme polarization, violent rhetoric, distortions—we've been here before." —*The Austin Chronicle*

"Entertaining and insightful. . . . [Brands] provides essential historical context and intriguing insights into both men's characters and decision-making." —*Publishers Weekly*

"An outstanding dual biography." —*Kirkus Reviews* (starred review)

"A fascinating and wonderfully readable portrayal of the tensions between fiery militancy and determined but measured devotion in working toward a goal." —*Library Journal*

"Superb. . . . A fascinating, authoritative, carefully researched account. . . . Brands presents the portraits of these two giants, Brown and Lincoln, in such stark and affecting terms that we cannot help but be moved and jarred by this story of their lives, their times, their beliefs and their deaths." —Bookreporter.com

"Good books about history inform. Great books about history inform, enlighten, and entertain. [*The Zealot and the Emancipator*] does all three." —*The Blue Mountain Review*

"Given the present political climate, one cannot help but find parallels, lessons, and warnings in *The Zealot and the Emancipator*." —*Law & Liberty*

"Brands has written perhaps his most fluent book, a constantly engaging study of history and biography worthy of the model on which it is built: Plutarch's parallel lives." —*The University Bookman*

H. W. BRANDS
THE ZEALOT AND THE EMANCIPATOR

H. W. Brands holds the Jack S. Blanton Sr. Chair in History at the University of Texas at Austin. He has written more than a dozen biographies and histories, two of which, *The First American* and *Traitor to His Class*, were finalists for the Pulitzer Prize.

ALSO BY H. W. BRANDS

The Reckless Decade
T.R.
The First American
The Age of Gold
Lone Star Nation
Andrew Jackson
Traitor to His Class
American Colossus
The Murder of Jim Fisk for the Love of Josie Mansfield
The Heartbreak of Aaron Burr
The Man Who Saved the Union
Reagan
The General vs. the President
Heirs of the Founders

The
ZEALOT
→ and the ←
EMANCIPATOR

The
ZEALOT
→ and the ←
EMANCIPATOR

John Brown, Abraham Lincoln
and the Struggle for American Freedom

H. W. BRANDS

ANCHOR BOOKS
A Division of Penguin Random House LLC
New York

FIRST ANCHOR BOOKS EDITION, OCTOBER 2021

Copyright © 2020 by H. W. Brands

All rights reserved. Published in the United States by Anchor Books,
a division of Penguin Random House LLC, New York, and distributed in
Canada by Penguin Random House Canada Limited, Toronto.
Originally published in hardcover in the United States
by Doubleday, a division of Penguin Random
House LLC, New York, in 2020.

Anchor Books and colophon are registered
trademarks of Penguin Random House LLC.

Portraits of Frederick Douglass courtesy of the Art Institute of Chicago
and the National Portrait Gallery. "To Colored Men!" broadside courtesy
of the National Archives. All other images courtesy
of the Library of Congress.

The Library of Congress has cataloged the Doubleday edition as follows:
Names: Brands, H. W., author.
Title: The zealot and the emancipator : John Brown, Abraham Lincoln and
the struggle for American freedom / H. W. Brands.
Description: First edition. | New York : Doubleday, 2020. |
Includes bibliographical references and index.
Identifiers: LCCN 2019036370 (print) | LCCN 2019036371 (ebook)
Subjects: LCSH: Brown, John, 1800–1859. | Lincoln, Abraham, 1809–1865. |
Abolitionists—United States—Biography. | Presidents—United States—
Biography. | Antislavery movements—United States—History—19th
century. | Harpers Ferry (W. Va.)—History—John Brown's Raid, 1859. |
United States—History—Civil War, 1861–1865—Causes. | United States—
History—19th century.
Classification: LCC E451. B795 2020 (print) | LCC E451 (ebook) |
DDC 326/.80922 B—dc23
LC record available at https://lccn.loc.gov/2019036370
LC ebook record available at https://lccn.loc.gov/2019036371

Anchor Books Trade Paperback ISBN: 978-0-525-56345-7
eBook ISBN: 978-0-385-54401-6

Author photograph © University of Texas
Book design by Cassandra J. Pappas

www.anchorbooks.com

Printed in the United States of America
10 9 8 7 6 5 4 3 2 1

Contents

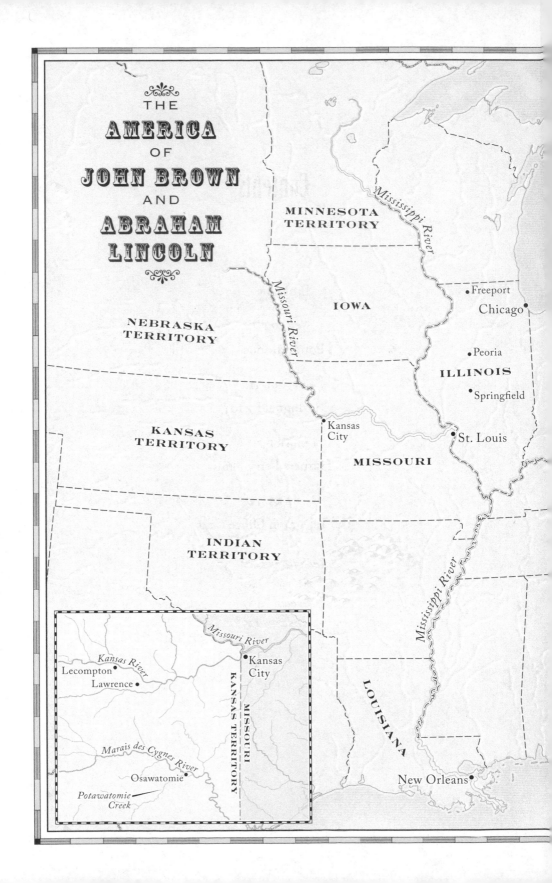

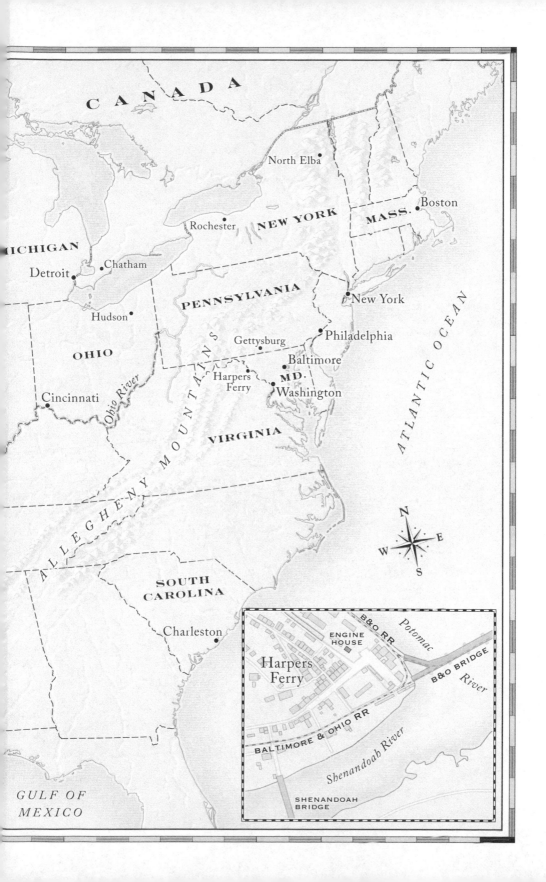

The
ZEALOT
⇾ and the ⇽
EMANCIPATOR

Prologue

THE PRISONER RAISED himself on his elbow and picked up his pen. The effort stabbed his side and stole his breath. "My Dear Wife, and Children Every One," he wrote. "I suppose you have learned before this by the newspapers that two weeks ago today we were fighting for our lives at Harpers Ferry."

John Brown shifted and tried to get comfortable. The wounds to his head had begun to heal, though they still looked a fright. But the gash in his side caused him searing pain. If he lay quietly and breathed softly, he could almost forget the saber thrust that had nearly killed him, yet the slightest shifting brought the bloody moment back. In all his life he had never spent so much time immobile. He supposed being in jail had its blessings.

That he was in jail and not in a grave was a minor miracle. John Brown believed in miracles. He believed in the God of the Old Testament, the author of miraculous sea partings and towering pillars of fire. The God of the New Testament, of quotidian wonders like multiplying loaves and fishes, he found less compelling. John Brown believed that God spoke to men. He believed God had spoken to *him*. God had commanded him to make war on the great wickedness of his country: slavery. John Brown had heeded the call and traveled to Kansas, where he had fought the agents of the slave power. He had come to Virginia to advance the struggle.

And now, in the waning autumn of 1859, he lay on a cot in a cell in Charles Town, the county seat for Harpers Ferry. He hadn't told his wife his plans; better she not know the risks he was taking. She would have heard eventually. Yet after what had happened, he assumed she had learned the news from the papers. She might not know she had lost two sons. In any case she should hear it from him. "During the fight Watson was mortally wounded," he wrote. "Oliver killed."

The pain of the writing compelled him to stop every few sentences. He would add more later.

ABRAHAM LINCOLN SHUDDERED on reading the news of John Brown's crime. From his law office in Springfield, Illinois, Lincoln had been plotting his return to public office. A decade had passed since his single term in Congress had ended, taking with it, apparently, his hopes of becoming someone important. He had talent; he *knew* he had talent. His mind was as sharp as the next man's, and sharper than that of anyone he knew with as little education as he had received. He could talk; he could amuse friends and persuade juries. He was a good lawyer, the best in Springfield—though he realized this wasn't saying a lot. A man of slighter ambition would have been content with how far he had come from the backwoods of his birth.

Or maybe it wasn't ambition per se. Perhaps the need to do something more, to win the praise of those around him, was his manner of fighting the melancholy that recurrently settled upon him and caused him to question whether life was worth living.

He had been making progress. His old political party, the Whigs, had gone to pieces amid the strife that was tearing the country apart. He had leaped from the wreck to a new party, the Republicans. He had traveled around Illinois speaking to Republican meetings large and small. He had locked horns with the Republicans' chief tormentor, Senator Stephen Douglas. He had carefully positioned himself among the Republicans on their defining issue: slavery. Not for Lincoln the uncompromising ultraism of those who demanded immediate abolition, or the moral absolutism of those who held that a "higher law" than the Constitution must govern the country on the slave question. No, Lincoln embraced the Constitution, fervently yet moderately, arguing that though it allowed the exclusion of slavery from the federal territories, it protected slavery in the states that chose to preserve it.

But now this. Lincoln knew that John Brown's assault on Harpers Ferry would be blamed on all Republicans. "Black Republicans," they were called by their opponents, for the darkness imputed to their motives and their solicitude for the welfare of black slaves. John Brown lent credence to the slur. He committed murder and treason, and tried to start a war of black slaves against white masters. And he did so, apparently, as part of a broad conspiracy against the South.

Lincoln wondered if Brown's extreme act had rendered moderation untenable. The South was closing ranks more tightly than ever against any challenge to its peculiar institution. Meanwhile many Northerners were making a hero of Brown, praising him for striking the blow against slavery their consciences told them *they* should have made.

Lincoln looked at the walls of his office. In the past few years he had been able to see beyond them. He had managed to push back the melancholy as he returned to political life. Now this. The walls closed in. The melancholy settled upon him once more. Lincoln's mother had taught him not to swear, but in his heart he was tempted to curse John Brown.

PART I

Pottawatomie

H OW DOES a good man challenge a great evil? How can a man of God confront the work of Satan?

John Brown remembered when he realized this was the fundamental issue of his life. He was sitting in a crowded church in Hudson, Ohio. He was surrounded by neighbors, but also by strangers who had come to the town to protest the killing of Elijah Lovejoy, an abolitionist preacher and publisher. Few in the assembly knew Lovejoy, and the shooting had occurred hundreds of miles away, in Illinois. But Hudson was a hotbed of abolitionism, and many that day could imagine that what had befallen Lovejoy might claim them. They gathered to praise him, to reassure themselves and to rededicate themselves to the cause of ridding their country of slavery.

John Brown was familiar to many in the group. Some had known him as a child. His father had moved the family from Connecticut, where John was born, to Ohio—"then a wilderness filled with wild beasts & Indians," he remembered many years later. "He was called on by turns to assist a boy five years older (who had been adopted by his Father & Mother) & learned to think he could accomplish *smart things* in driving the cows; & riding the horses," he wrote, speaking of himself in the third person. "Sometimes he met with rattle snakes which were very large; & which some of the company generally managed to kill."

His new home was a wonder. "After getting to Ohio in 1805 he was for some time rather afraid of the Indians, & of their rifles; but this soon wore off: & he used to hang about them quite as much as was consistent with good manners; & learned a trifle of their talk."

His father took up the tanning trade and taught his son the craft. Before long the boy was an expert. "He could at any time dress his own leather such as squirrel, raccoon, cat, wolf or dog skins; and also learned to make whip lashes: which brought him some change at times; & was of considerable service in many ways." Itchy feet that would mark his whole life appeared early. "At six years old John began to be quite a rambler in the wild new country finding birds and squirrels and sometimes a wild turkey's nest."

The narrator John Brown was telling his story to the son of a friend. The lad had inquired of Brown's biography, and Brown obliged. He included episodes of which he was not proud. "I must not neglect to tell you of a very *bad & foolish* habit to which John was somewhat addicted. I mean *telling lies;* generally to screen himself from blame; or from punishment. He could not well endure to be reproached; & I now think had he been oftener encouraged to be entirely frank, *by making frankness a kind of atonement* for some of his faults; he would not have been so often guilty in after life of this fault; nor have been obliged to struggle *so long* with *so mean* a habit." The struggle, he feared, wasn't over.

Struggle of another sort was less blameworthy. "John was *never quarrelsome;* but was *excessively* fond of the *hardest & roughest* kind of plays; & could *never get enough* of them. Indeed when for a short time he was sometimes sent to school the opportunity it afforded to wrestle, & snow ball & run & jump & knock off old seedy wool hats, offered to him almost the only compensation for the confinement & restraints of school." This attitude made an indifferent scholar. "He would always choose to stay at home & work hard rather than be sent to school."

He discovered a knack for self-reliance. "To be sent off through the wilderness alone to very considerable distances was particularly his delight; & in this he was often indulged so that by the time he was twelve years old he was sent off more than a hundred miles with companies of cattle; & he would have thought his character much injured had he been obliged to be helped in any such job."

At eight he lost his mother to what in those days was the most dangerous of maternal activities: childbearing. His father quickly remarried. John could find no fault in his stepmother, yet neither could he get close. "He never *adopted her in feeling,* but continued to pine after his own Mother for years." From the distance of half a century, he reflected, "This operated very unfavorably upon him; as he was both naturally fond of females &, withal, extremely diffident; & deprived him of a suitable connecting link between the different sexes; the want of which might under some circumstances, have proved his ruin."

He was twelve when America went to war with Britain—the second time, in 1812. His father provisioned the army with beef and enlisted young John to herd and drive the cattle to the camps. He became a pacifist as a result. "The effect of what he saw during the war was to so far disgust him with military affairs that he would neither train, *or drill;* but paid fines; & got along like a Quaker until his age finally has cleared him of military duty."

The experience changed him in another way. "He was staying for a short time with a very gentlemanly landlord since a United States marshal who held a slave boy near his own age very active, intelligent, and good feeling; & to whom John was under considerable obligation for numerous little acts of kindness. *The Master* made a great pet of John: brought him to table with his first company; & friends; called their attention to every little smart thing he *said or did,* & to the fact of his being more than a hundred miles from home with a company of cattle alone; while the *negro boy* (who was fully if not more than his equal) was badly clothed, poorly fed; *& lodged in cold weather;* & beaten before his eyes with iron shovels or any other thing that came first to hand. This brought John to reflect on the wretched, hopeless condition, of *Fatherless* & *Motherless* slave *children:* for such children have neither Fathers or Mothers to protect & provide for them. He sometimes would raise the question *is God their Father?*"

He continued to reflect as he grew older. The boy became a young man who was sober and spottily educated. "He never attempted to dance in his life; nor did he ever learn to know *one* of a pack of *cards* from *another.* He learned nothing of grammar; nor did he get at school so much knowledge of common arithmetic as the four ground rules." He sprouted rapidly in his mid-teens. "He became very strong & large of his age *&* ambitious to perform the full labour of a man; at almost any kind of hard work."

He was shy around those his own age, preferring the company of his elders. "This was so much the case; & secured for him so many little notices from those he esteemed; that his vanity was very much fed by it: & he came forward to manhood quite full of self-conceit; & self-confident; notwithstanding his *extreme* bashfulness." His siblings noticed; a younger brother called him "a king against whom there is no rising up." The narrator John Brown acknowledged the fault. "The habit so early formed of being obeyed rendered him in after life too much disposed to speak in an imperious or dictating way."

HE MARRIED at twenty to a woman as sober as he. They had seven children in a dozen years; she died just after the birth of the last. Two of the children themselves died young, but the others were strong and hearty. John Brown was a stern father, hoping to keep his children from falling into the bad habits he had learned at their age. The neighbors recalled the severity of the punishments he administered. One of his sons, Jason, remembered having a dream so vivid he thought it was real. He told his father, who said it was only a dream. When Jason insisted that it was true, his father thrashed him for lying. The boys were confused as to what was expected of them. Another son, Watson, later told his father, "The trouble is, you want your boys to be brave as tigers, and still afraid of you." A visitor to the homestead remarked that John Brown looked like an eagle. "Yes," said Watson, "or some other carnivorous bird."

Five years into the marriage Brown decreed that the family would move. The tanning business he operated in Hudson was thriving, and he had just built a new house for his growing family, but the itch was on him, and neither his wife, Dianthe, nor any of the children dared object. They landed in Richmond, in western Pennsylvania, where he channeled his restless energy and abundant strength into clearing twenty-five acres and building a new tannery. He became a model citizen of the district and in time its postmaster.

Richmond was where Dianthe died and John remarried. His second wife, Mary, was half his age, poor and unschooled. Her father was happy to marry her off. If she was daunted by the prospect of taking on Brown and his five children, she kept quiet about it. She did what was expected of her, minding the home and bearing children, lots of them. She had thirteen children in all, making a total of twenty for John Brown. Seven of Mary's children died early.

Yet they considered taking in more. The sympathy he had discovered for slaves at twelve was emerging slowly and uncertainly. "I have been trying to devise some means whereby I might do something in a practical way for my poor fellow-men who are in bondage," Brown wrote to his brother in 1834. "And having fully consulted my wife and my three boys"—the ones still at home—"we have agreed to get at least one negro boy or youth and bring him up as we do our own—viz., give him a good English education, learn him what we can about the history of the world, about business, about general subjects, and, above all, try to teach him the fear of God. We think of three ways to obtain one: First, to try to get some Christian slaveholder to release one to us. Second, to get a free one if no one will let us have one that is a slave. Third, if that does not succeed, we have all agreed to submit to considerable privation in order to buy one. This we are now using means in order to effect, in the confident expectation that God is about to bring them all out of the house of bondage."

The adoption of one black child was just the start. "I have for years been trying to devise some way to get a school a-going here for blacks," he told his brother. "I do think such advantages ought to be afforded the young blacks, whether they are all to be immediately set free or not. Perhaps we might, under God, in that way do more towards breaking their yoke effectually than in any other. If the young blacks of our country could once become enlightened, it would most assuredly operate on slavery like firing powder confined in rock, and all slaveholders know it well. Witness their heaven-daring laws against teaching blacks. If once the Christians in the free states would set to work in earnest teaching the blacks, the people of the slaveholding states would find themselves constitutionally driven to set about the work of emancipation immediately."

Brown could be better at dreaming than at doing. He and his wife never adopted a black child, and he never started a school. His wanderlust recurred, and he led the family back to Ohio, but to the hamlet of Franklin Mills rather than Hudson. Something about Brown kept him at a distance from neighbors. He wasn't unfriendly, in any overt way, but he formed no deep attachments. He would stay in one place for a time and then, without obvious reason or explanation, up stakes and move on. He moved in no consistent direction. Many in his day trended west, following the advancing frontier. But Brown moved east as often as west. His family, of course, went with him, and they learned to ask no questions. The model might have been one of the nomadic tribes of the Old Testament.

He shifted from herding cattle to tending sheep, which he hoped would bring him greater returns. He was vigilant and sensitive to the animals' needs, and his flocks grew. He had less luck with people. In the mid-1830s loose credit caused land prices to bubble, and Brown joined the speculation. A financial crisis in 1837 burst the bubble, catching many of the speculators short. Brown found himself deeply in debt. John Brown Jr. recalled the lesson his father learned from the experience, a lesson he shared with his son. "Instead of being thoroughly imbued with the doctrine of pay as you go," Brown said, "I started out in life with the idea that nothing could be done without capital, and that a poor man must use his credit and borrow; and this pernicious notion has been the rock on which I, as well as many others, have split. The practical effect of this false doctrine has been to keep me like a toad under a harrow most of my business life." Another son, Jason, later remarked, "It is a Brown trait to be migratory, sanguine about what they think they can do; to speculate; to go into debt; and to make a good many failures."

BROWN'S BANKRUPTCY FORCED a move back to Hudson, where his father still lived. And it was in Hudson where he discovered his life's mission. When Brown had left the town, slavery was an important issue in American politics but not one that dominated everything else. During the 1830s it achieved that dubious distinction. Two events triggered the change. In 1831 a slave called Nat Turner led a rebellion in southern Virginia that killed dozens of whites before being bloodily suppressed. The episode reminded Southern slaveholders that they sat atop a keg of powder. At any time other slaves might mimic Nat Turner and burst out murderously against their masters. The possibility of revolt had long inhabited the nightmares of slaveholders; now it filled their waking hours.

The second event was the decision of the British government to end slavery in the British empire. Abolition had already come to other countries: France and its empire, most of the New World republics that broke free from Spain. But Britain's decision to end slavery had a special effect on Americans, for Britain had introduced slavery to America in colonial days, and its law and practices were most akin to those in America. If the British could abolish slavery, thought both the friends and the foes of slavery in the United States, so could Americans.

Abolitionism became a growing force in American politics. William Lloyd Garrison founded *The Liberator,* a Boston paper that even its subscribers often judged intemperate in its treatment of slavery and slaveholders. Other papers appeared in other cities, including St. Louis, where Elijah Lovejoy denounced slavery with growing vehemence. It took courage to do so, for while New England abolitionists like Garrison were surrounded by people of similar views, Lovejoy operated in enemy territory—Missouri being a slave state. Lovejoy alienated his neighbors, some of whom were apologists for slavery, others who simply thought his agitation would harm the businesses and prospects of them all. Lovejoy's enemies smashed his printing presses repeatedly, eventually driving him across the Mississippi to Alton, in the free state of Illinois, where he launched a new abolitionist paper.

The move didn't save him. In November 1837 a crowd of slavery defenders attacked the building that housed Lovejoy's press. This time he fought back, opening fire on the attackers. In the exchange that followed, he was killed.

The news reached Hudson a short while later. The abolitionists in town could speak of nothing else. The excited discussion spilled over into the Thursday prayer meeting at the Congregational church Brown attended. He sat in the back of the room saying little but listening much. Finally, as the meeting drew to a close, he stood up. He raised his right hand, and in a determined tone that stuck in the memory of those present, declared, "Here, before God, in the presence of these witnesses, from this time I consecrate my life to the destruction of slavery."

ABRAHAM LINCOLN HAD no such epiphany and made no such declaration. Lincoln lacked Brown's unquestioning religious faith. Yet he confronted the same question Brown did: What was the moral man's obligation when faced with an immoral institution like slavery?

Lincoln knew slavery from his earliest days, as Brown did not. Lincoln was born in the slave state of Kentucky; his neighbors in Hardin County included hundreds of slaves. The Lincoln family owned no slaves, not least because Thomas Lincoln couldn't well afford them. Lincoln in later years spoke little about his father; what he said did the older man justice but no kindness. Recounting his ancestry, Lincoln arrived at his grandparents and their children. "Thomas, the youngest son, and father of the present subject, by the early death of his father, and very narrow circumstances of his mother, even in childhood was a wandering laboring boy, and grew up literally without education," Lincoln said. "He never did more in the way of writing than to bunglingly sign his own name."

Thomas Lincoln opposed slavery, partly for what it did to the slaves but also for what it cost non-slaveholding whites like himself. As visitors to the South often remarked, slavery demeaned manual labor, discouraging poor whites from improving their lot through their own toil. Thomas and Nancy Lincoln joined a sect that shared their antipathy toward slavery; when Lincoln was seven, his father moved the family across the Ohio River to free-state Indiana. "This removal was partly on account of slavery, but chiefly on account of the difficulty in land titles in Kentucky," Lincoln explained.

The region of Indiana Thomas selected was a wilderness. "He settled in an unbroken forest, and the clearing away of surplus wood was the great task ahead," Lincoln said. "A."—Lincoln himself—"though very young, was large of his age, and had an axe put into his hands at once; and from that till within his twenty-third year, he was almost constantly handling that most useful instrument—less, of course, in plowing and harvesting seasons." The family were hunters and gatherers, as well as farmers. The son was no Daniel Boone. "A. took an early start as a hunter, which was never much improved afterwards. A few days before the completion of his eighth year, in the absence of his father, a flock of wild turkeys approached the new log-cabin, and A., with a rifle gun, standing inside, shot through a crack, and killed one of them. He has never since pulled a trigger on any larger game."

Lincoln didn't like his father, though they shared certain traits. Neighbors commented that Lincoln acquired his storytelling skills from the older man. Lincoln's mother died when he was nine; Thomas remarried. A story recalled from his father had his second wife asking him whether he liked her or his first wife better. "Oh, now, Sarah," Thomas responded, in a style and tone any of Lincoln's adult acquaintances would have recognized. "That reminds me of old John Hardin down in Kentucky who had a fine looking pair of horses, and a neighbor coming in one day and looking at them said, 'John, which horse do you like best?' John replied, 'I can't tell. One of them kicks and the other bites and I don't know which is worst.'"

But Thomas detected energy and ambition in his son that reflected unfavorably on his own. He ridiculed Lincoln's efforts to improve himself; illiterate, he denied his son the chance at an education. "A. now thinks that the aggregate of all his schooling did not amount to one year," Lincoln recalled. "He was never in a college or academy as a student; and never inside of a college or academy building till since he had a law-license. What he has in the way of education, he has picked up. After he was twenty-three, and had separated from his father, he studied English grammar, imperfectly of course, but so as to speak and write as well as he now does. He studied and nearly mastered the six books of Euclid, since he was a member of Congress. He regrets his want of education, and does what he can to supply the want."

Thomas didn't beat his son, at least not beyond the norm of parents at the time. Perhaps Lincoln's size and strength protected him;

in any event Lincoln didn't mention physical blows. Except for one that came from a different source: "In his tenth year he was kicked by a horse, and apparently killed for a time." Yet he survived, well enough for his father to hire him out to neighbors, with the pay going to Thomas. The scheme was not unlike the hiring out of slaves, and Lincoln himself saw and felt the similarity. "I used to be a slave," he later said of that period.

THE GREAT ADVENTURE of Lincoln's youth was a river journey. "When he was nineteen, still residing in Indiana, he made his first trip upon a flat-boat to New-Orleans. He was a hired hand merely; and he and a son of the owner, without other assistance, made the trip. The nature of part of the cargo-load, as it was called, made it necessary for them to linger and trade along the Sugar Coast"—the stretch of the Mississippi where sugarcane enriched the planters—"and one night they were attacked by seven negroes with intent to kill and rob them. They were hurt some in the melee, but succeeded in driving the negroes from the boat, and then cut cable, weighed anchor and left."

The journey proceeded less eventfully for Lincoln and his partner. On this and a subsequent journey Lincoln visited New Orleans, where for the first time he witnessed the buying and selling of slaves on a commercial scale. Slave markets cast the institution of slavery in the harshest light, revealing the essential inhumanity of a system that allowed men, women and children to be bought and sold like cattle. Implausible accounts have Lincoln vowing, after witnessing the sale of a young woman—invariably described as "comely"—to deliver a blow against slavery one day. More likely the experience simply confirmed the distaste he already felt.

Thomas Lincoln moved the family again, when Lincoln was twenty-one. Their new residence was in Illinois, on the Sangamon River where the forest met the prairie. "Here they built a log-cabin, into which they removed, and made sufficient of rails to fence ten acres of ground, fenced and broke the ground, and raised a crop of sown corn upon it the same year," Lincoln recalled.

He tried his hand as a clerk in a store and mill at New Salem, Illinois. The business languished but Lincoln made friends. When the Black Hawk War broke out in 1832—resulting from a dispute over lands taken from the Sauk and other Indians—Lincoln enlisted. "A. joined a volunteer company, and to his own surprise, was elected captain of it. He says he has not since had any success in life which gave him so much satisfaction. He went the campaign, served near three months, met the ordinary hardships of such an expedition, but was in no battle."

Lincoln's success inspired him to try his hand at politics. "Returning from the campaign, and encouraged by his great popularity among his immediate neighbors, he, the same year, ran for the Legislature and was beaten—his own precinct, however, casting its votes 277 for and 7 against him."

The bug had bit. He tried again and was elected. A lawyer named John Stuart, of Springfield, was elected that same season, and during the campaign he had been impressed by Lincoln. He encouraged him to take up law. Lincoln heeded the suggestion. "He borrowed books of Stuart, took them home with him, and went at it in good earnest. He studied with nobody." During sessions of the legislature he put aside the books, but resumed his study at the sessions' end. In 1836 he satisfied the state's examiners that he was qualified to practice, and received his law license.

HE FELL in love. Ann Rutledge was four years younger than Lincoln and the daughter of the man who owned New Salem's inn, where Lincoln sometimes ate and slept. Ann drew the attention of visitors, including one man to whom she became engaged. But he departed on a long trip, and in his absence she struck up a friendship with Lincoln. The longer her fiancé stayed away, the better she liked Lincoln. Lincoln became thoroughly enamored of her. In time they agreed that if Ann could get out of her existing engagement, they would be married.

Then she was stricken ill, probably with typhoid fever. Her fiancé was nowhere in sight, and so it was Lincoln who sat by her bed. But not for long: Ann faded quickly and died.

Lincoln was crushed. He was generally awkward around women, but something in Ann Rutledge had calmed him and brought out his best. He never forgot her. Years later Lincoln received a visit from a friend from the New Salem days. The friend asked Lincoln if he had indeed loved Ann Rutledge, as people around the town recalled. "It is true; true indeed I did," Lincoln replied, according to the friend's recollection. "I loved the woman dearly and soundly. She was a handsome girl, would have made a good loving wife." Wistfully, Lincoln added, "I did honestly and truly love the girl and think often—often—of her now."

FREDERICK DOUGLASS WAS no less opposed to slavery than John Brown, and he was infinitely better informed on the subject. Douglass had been a slave in Maryland, where the temptation to escape was greater than for most slaves, because freedom was closer. A slave who slipped across the Mason-Dixon Line into Pennsylvania might make his way to Philadelphia, whose Quakers had been among the first groups in America to oppose slavery and who still provided shelter to fugitives from the South. Baltimore offered another escape point. The ships that sailed out of the harbor could hide stowaways, and the railroad that linked Maryland's commercial capital to the North tempted hitchhikers.

Yet precisely because freedom was so near and tempting, Maryland's slave owners watched their slaves closely. A slave who seemed tempted to flee might be sold to the Deep South, from which escape was all but impossible. Not least because it was so difficult, masters and overseers in the South were infamous for driving their slaves hard, often brutally. Many slaves from the upper South would rather die than be sold down the river, as the phrase went, referring to the Ohio and Mississippi.

Frederick Douglass was determined to escape all the same. He never knew the date of his birth—many slaves didn't—but it was around 1818. Douglass was unusual among slaves in knowing how to read and write. Part of his instruction came from the wife of a man his master had lent him to; part he conjured on his own after the man objected to his wife's instructing the boy. Literacy opened to him a world beyond the South, a world in which people with black skins need not be slaves. This revelation, which Southern slaveholders did their best to keep their slaves from discovering, made him start to reckon how *he* might become free.

The issue wasn't constantly pressing. Sometimes those who commanded him were comparatively humane, within the limits of the slave system. But others were beastly. A man named Covey was merciless. "We were worked in all weathers," Douglass recalled later. "It was never too hot or too cold; it could never rain, blow, hail, or snow, too hard for us to work in the field. Work, work, work, was scarcely more the order of the day than of the night. The longest days were too short for him, and the shortest nights too long for him. I was somewhat unmanageable when I first went there, but a few months of this discipline tamed me. Mr. Covey succeeded in breaking me. I was broken in body, soul, and spirit. My natural elasticity was crushed, my intellect languished, the disposition to read departed, the cheerful spark that lingered about my eye died; the dark night of slavery closed in upon me; and behold a man transformed into a brute!"

Yet a flicker of resistance remained in Douglass. Covey determined to beat it out of him. One day Douglass was in a stable, throwing hay down to the horses. "Mr. Covey entered the stable with a long rope," Douglass remembered. "And just as I was half out of the loft, he caught hold of my legs, and was about tying me. As soon as I found what he was up to, I gave a sudden spring, and as I did so, he holding to my legs, I was brought sprawling on the stable floor. Mr. Covey seemed now to think he had me, and could do what he pleased; but at this moment—from whence came the spirit I don't know—I resolved to fight; and, suiting my action to the resolution, I seized Covey hard by the throat; and as I did so, I rose. He held on to me, and I to him. My resistance was so entirely unexpected that Covey seemed taken all aback." Covey called to a slave hired from another master to help him subdue Douglass. The slave responded that he had been hired to work, not to fight. "He left Covey and myself to fight our own battle out. We were at it for nearly two hours. Covey at length let me go, puffing and blowing at a great rate, saying that if I had not resisted, he would not have whipped me half so much. The truth was, that he had not whipped me at all. I considered him as getting entirely the worst end of the bargain; for he had drawn no blood from me, but I had from him."

The denouement astonished Douglass. "The whole six months afterwards, that I spent with Mr. Covey, he never laid the weight of his finger upon me in anger. He would occasionally say, he didn't want to get hold of me again. 'No,' thought I, 'you need not; for you will come off worse than you did before.'" Yet Covey could have brought the law against Douglass. "It was for a long time a matter of surprise to me why Mr. Covey did not immediately have me taken by the constable to the whipping-post, and there regularly whipped for the crime of raising my hand against a white man in defense of myself. And the only explanation I can now think of does not entirely satisfy me; but such as it is, I will give it. Mr. Covey enjoyed the most unbounded reputation for being a first-rate overseer and negro-breaker. It was of considerable importance to him. That reputation was at stake; and had he sent me—a boy about sixteen years old—to the public whipping-post, his reputation would have been lost; so, to save his reputation, he suffered me to go unpunished."

The modest victory over Covey caused Douglass to consider something larger. He met a free black woman named Anna Murray who helped him plot his escape from bondage. She provided clothing, cash and advice. Douglass, posing as a sailor, with false identification, boarded a train bound north from Baltimore. The ruse worked, and without major incident he reached New York. "I have often been asked how I felt when I first found myself on free soil," he wrote later. The answer was simple yet profound. "A new world had opened upon me," he said. "I lived more in one day than in a year of my slave life."

Anna Murray joined him in New York, and the two were married. They were advised that he would be safer farther north, and they moved to Massachusetts, where he soon became a celebrated figure in the abolitionist movement. Escaped slaves were not unusual, but ones as handsome as Douglass and as eloquent as he proved to be were rare. He was persuaded to tell his story in lectures and in print; before long he was the face and voice of American abolitionism. He traveled to Britain, where he was lionized still more. British abolitionists weren't restrained by politics in the way American abolitionists sometimes were; they had no constitution protecting slavery, and they didn't worry about provoking a civil war in their country. They could indulge their moral preferences to their hearts' content. They couldn't get enough of Douglass. Some pooled resources to purchase his freedom from the Maryland master who still claimed ownership, after which Douglass was able to travel more freely around America.

IN 1847 DOUGLASS MET John Brown, in Springfield, Massachusetts. The meeting, and the impression Brown made, remained with Douglass ever after. "In person he was lean, strong, and sinewy, of the best New England mold, built for times of trouble and fitted to grapple with the flintiest hardships," Douglass wrote. "Clad in plain American woolen, shod in boots of cowhide leather, and wearing a cravat of the same substantial material, under six feet high, less than 150 pounds in weight, aged about fifty, he presented a figure straight and symmetrical as a mountain pine. His bearing was singularly impressive. His head was not large, but compact and high. His hair was coarse, strong, slightly gray and closely trimmed, and grew low on his forehead. His face was smoothly shaved, and revealed a strong, square mouth, supported by a broad and prominent chin. His eyes were bluish-gray, and in conversation they were full of light and fire. When on the street, he moved with a long, springing, race-horse step, absorbed by his own reflections, neither seeking nor shunning observation."

They shared a meal before Brown turned to business. "Captain Brown cautiously approached the subject which he wished to bring to my attention; for he seemed to apprehend opposition to his views." Brown had gathered that Douglass eschewed violence in confronting slavery. Brown did not. "He denounced slavery in look and language fierce and bitter, thought that slaveholders had forfeited their right to live, that the slaves had the right to gain their liberty in any way they could, did not believe that moral suasion would ever liberate the slave, or that political action would abolish the system."

Brown got more specific. "He said that he had long had a plan which could accomplish this end," Douglass recalled. "He said he had been for some time looking for colored men to whom he could safely reveal his secret, and at times he had almost despaired of finding such men, but that now he was encouraged, for he saw heads of such rising up in all directions. He had observed my course at home and abroad, and he wanted my cooperation."

Brown sketched his plan. Douglass, in his later description, added disclaimers that might have been his own rather than Brown's. "It did not, as some suppose, contemplate a general rising among the slaves, and a general slaughter of the slave masters. An insurrection he thought would only defeat the object, but his plan did contemplate the creating of an armed force which should act in the very heart of the South. He was not averse to the shedding of blood, and thought the practice of carrying arms would be a good one for the colored people to adopt, as it would give them a sense of their manhood. No people he said could have self-respect, or be respected, who would not fight for their freedom."

Brown showed Douglass a map and pointed to the Allegheny Mountains. "These mountains are the basis of my plan," he said. "God has given the strength of the hills to freedom; they were placed here for the emancipation of the negro race; they are full of natural forts, where one man for defense will be equal to a hundred for attack; they are full also of good hiding places, where large numbers of brave men could be concealed, and baffle and elude pursuit for a long time. I know these mountains well, and could take a body of men into them and keep them there despite of all the efforts of Virginia to dislodge them."

Brown laid out his strategy. "The true object to be sought is first of all to destroy the money value of slave property; and that can only be done by rendering such property insecure. My plan then is to take at first about twenty-five picked men, and begin on a small scale; supply them arms and ammunition, post them in squads of fives on a line of twenty-five miles, the most persuasive and judicious of whom shall go down to the fields from time to time, as opportunity offers, and induce the slaves to join them, seeking and selecting the most restless and daring."

Brown understood the need for secrecy. "He saw that in this part of the work the utmost care must be used to avoid treachery and disclosure," Douglass recounted. "Only the most conscientious and skillful should be sent on this perilous duty. With care and enterprise he thought he could soon gather a force of one hundred hardy men, men who would be content to lead the free and adventurous life to which he proposed to train them; when these were properly drilled, and each man had found the place for which he was best suited, they would begin work in earnest; they would run off the slaves in large numbers, retain the brave and strong ones in the mountains, and send the weak and timid to the North by the underground railroad; his operations would be enlarged with increasing numbers, and would not be confined to one locality."

Douglass asked how Brown's army would be supported. "He said emphatically he would subsist them upon the enemy. Slavery was a state of war, and the slave had a right to anything necessary to his freedom."

Douglass objected that Brown's project, far from loosing the grip of slavery upon the slaves, would tighten it. The very people Brown hoped to help would be harmed. "Suppose you succeed in running off a few slaves, and thus impress the Virginia slaveholder with a sense of insecurity in their slaves," Douglass said. "The effect will only be to make them sell their slaves further south."

Brown didn't deny it. "That will be first what I want to do," he said. "Then I would follow them up. If we could drive slavery out of *one county*, it would be a great gain; it would weaken the system throughout the state."

"But they would employ bloodhounds to hunt you out of the mountains," Douglass countered.

"That they might attempt," Brown granted. "But the chances are we should whip them, and when we should have whipt one squad, they would be careful how they pursued."

"But you might be surrounded and cut off from your provisions or means of subsistence," Douglass said.

Brown wasn't worried. "He thought that could not be done so they could not cut their way out," Douglass recorded. "But even if the worst came, he could but be killed, and he had no better use for his life than to lay it down in the cause of the slave."

Douglass offered a nonviolent approach, to no avail. "When I suggested that we might convert the slaveholders, he became much excited, and said that could never be. He knew their proud hearts and that they would never be induced to give up their slaves until they felt a big stick about their heads."

Writing years later, Douglass recalled the end of the conversation and the effect Brown had on him. "He observed that I might have noticed the simple manner in which he lived, adding that he had adopted this method in order to save money to carry out his purposes. This was said in no boastful tone, for he felt that he had delayed already too long and had no room to boast either his zeal or his self-denial. Had some men made such display of rigid virtue, I should have rejected it, as affected, false, or hypocritical, but in John Brown, I felt it to be as real as iron or granite. From this night spent with John Brown in Springfield, Mass., 1847, while I continued to write and speak against slavery, I became all the same less hopeful of its peaceful abolition. My utterances became more and more tinged by the color of this man's strong impressions."

→ 4 ←

ABRAHAM LINCOLN COULDN'T have afforded to be as categori-
cal about slavery as John Brown was, even if Lincoln's temperament had pointed him in that uncompromising direction. Not
long after being admitted to the practice of law, Lincoln moved to
Springfield to partner with John Stuart. Lawyers were thick in the
Illinois capital, and competition was fierce. Lincoln had to struggle to
keep the office in coal and ink. A full five years into the practice his
financial straits compelled him to decline an invitation to visit a friend
in Kentucky. "I do not think I can come to Kentucky this season," he
wrote. "I am so poor, and make so little headway in the world, that I
drop back in a month of idleness as much as I gain in a year's rowing."

Lincoln took the clients who walked in his door. Illinois courts
heard many cases involving slavery. The state lay across the Mississippi River from Missouri, and across the Ohio River from Kentucky,
and slave owners from both states frequently brought slaves with them
when they visited Illinois. Robert Matson did more than visit. His
roots were in Kentucky, but he owned a farm in Illinois. He made a
habit of bringing some of his Kentucky slaves to work on the farm for
limited periods, then shipping them back to Kentucky. Illinois law
winked at this practice, because it was exceptional enough to avoid
direct affront to the clause of the Illinois constitution forbidding slavery. In any event, most white citizens of Illinois shed few tears for
black slaves.

But Matson got careless. He valued the work of his black foreman
and decided to keep him in Illinois, effectively emancipating him. Yet
the foreman's wife and children remained slaves, at least in Matson's
view—and in the view of Matson's white housekeeper and mistress,

who conceived a jealous antipathy to the foreman's wife. On behalf of her paramour she threatened to send the wife and children back to Kentucky to be sold. The foreman acted first, spiriting his family into hiding with two local abolitionists. Matson thereupon sued the abolitionists for return of his property.

The abolitionists sought legal counsel. One of them, Hiram Rutherford, approached Lincoln. "I had known Abraham Lincoln several years, and his views and mine on the wrong of slavery being in perfect accord, I determined to hire him," Rutherford recalled. "I found him at the tavern sitting on the veranda, his chair tilted back against one of the wooden pillars, entertaining the bystanders and loungers gathered about the place with one of his irresistible and highly-flavored stories. My head was full of the impending lawsuit, and I found it a great test of my patience to await the end of the chapter then in process of narration. Before he could begin on another I interrupted and called him aside. I told in detail the story of my troubles, reminded him that we had always agreed on the questions of the day, and asked him to represent me at the trial of my case in court. He listened attentively as I recited the facts leading up to the controversy with Matson, but I noticed a peculiarly troubled look came over his face now and then, his eyes appeared to be fixed in the distance beyond me, and he shook his head several times as if debating with himself some question of grave import. At length, and with apparent reluctance, he answered that he could not defend me, because he had already been counseled with in Matson's interest, and was therefore under professional obligations to represent the latter unless released."

Rutherford reacted badly. "This was a grievous disappointment, and irritated me into expressions more or less bitter in tone," he said. "I remember retorting that 'my money was as good as anyone else's,' and although thoroughly in earnest I presume I was a little too hasty."

Rutherford soon rued his haste. Lincoln contrived to extricate himself from his obligation to Matson and thereupon told Rutherford he could represent him.

"But it was too late," Rutherford recounted. "My pride was up, and I plainly indicated a disinclination to avail myself of his offer."

So Lincoln, requiring some fee out of the suit, returned to Matson and took up his case, which was a weak one. "I remember well how he presented his side of the case," a professional colleague recounted. Lincoln told the court, "This, then, is the point on which this whole case turns: Were these negroes passing over and crossing the state, and thus, as the law contemplates, *in transitu*, or were they actually located by the consent of their master? If only crossing the state that act did not free them, but if located, even indefinitely, by the consent of their owner and master, their emancipation logically followed."

In fact, what Lincoln correctly identified as the crux of the case was the plaintiff's weakest argument, for it was apparent to nearly all—including the court—that Matson had intended to locate—that is, to domicile—the contested slaves in Illinois, and that only the wrath of his mistress had prompted him to send them back to Kentucky. The court ruled in favor of the slaves, who were thereby freed.

Hiram Rutherford recalled the denouement. "After the trial, which ended Saturday night, Matson left the country"—the region— "crossed the Wabash River on his way to Kentucky, evaded his creditors, and *never paid Lincoln his fee.*"

MARY TODD HAD a particular view of slavery. She had grown up in Kentucky surrounded by slaves and tended by servants in the Todd household. The face of the institution she observed was genteel and paternalistic, and she found in it little to object to.

Mary Todd met Lincoln after moving to Springfield from her parents' home in Lexington to that of her sister, who had married the son of a former governor of Illinois. Attractive, vivacious and educated in the manner of daughters of Southern gentry, she readily drew suitors. Stephen A. Douglas, a lawyer and a rising star of the Illinois Democratic party, was one. Abraham Lincoln, lawyer and Whig, was another. Mary Todd's family were Whigs. Perhaps this tipped her heart's balance toward Lincoln. Or maybe she saw promise not obvious to most in Springfield, who deemed Douglas the likelier to succeed.

Yet the path of love was convoluted. Some who knew Lincoln thought he still pined for Ann Rutledge. Others observed that he was simply inept around women. Lincoln proposed marriage to Mary Todd, then got cold feet. He asked to be released from his offer. Mary assented. Lincoln re-changed his mind; he once more wanted to tie the knot. His indecision affected everything he did, eventually causing acquaintances to wonder if he was losing his mind. "The doctors say he came within an inch of being a perfect lunatic for life," one remarked. "He was perfectly crazy for some time, not able to attend to his business at all. They say he does not look like the same person."

He never quite was. The couple were wed, but neighbors and friends failed to notice much affection between the two.

LINCOLN SEEMED SURER of himself in politics. He again won election to the state legislature, this time from Springfield, and added to his circle of Whig friends. His tenure in the Illinois assembly produced no landmark accomplishments for the state, but it did signal the position Lincoln would take in the politics of slavery. In 1837 he and a colleague, protesting what they considered an amoral position on slavery adopted by the assembly, offered a statement of their own views, which were firm but moderate. "They believe that the institution of slavery is founded on both injustice and bad policy, but that the promulgation of abolition doctrines tends rather to increase than to abate its evils," the two lawmakers said of themselves. They believed Congress had no power to interfere with slavery in the states, but did have power over slavery in the federal District of Columbia.

Lincoln's middle-of-the-road stance pleased Springfield's Whigs enough to win him nomination for Congress, and Springfield's voters sufficiently to elect him. He arrived in Washington in late 1847, amid the war between the United States and Mexico begun the previous year.

In the 1840s the American capital was a required stop on the tour of the many Europeans who came to the United States trying to make sense of the emerging phenomenon of democracy. Charles Dickens was disappointed. "It is sometimes called the City of Magnificent Distances," he wrote of Washington. "But it might with greater propriety be termed the City of Magnificent Intentions." Dickens observed the marks of the city's unfinished character: "spacious avenues that begin in nothing and lead nowhere; streets, mile-long, that only want houses, roads, and inhabitants; public buildings that need but a public to be complete; and ornaments of great thoroughfares, which only lack great thoroughfares to ornament." The city's incompleteness reflected a broader ambivalence about its reason for being. It had but one purpose, government, and that purpose was intermittent. "It has no trade or commerce of its own, having little or no population beyond the President and his establishment, the members of the legislature who reside there during the session, the government clerks and officers employed in the various departments, the keepers of the hotels and boarding-houses, and the tradesmen who supply their tables."

Dickens visited the Capitol. "The House of Representatives is a beautiful and spacious hall, of semi-circular shape, supported by handsome pillars," he wrote. "One part of the gallery is appropriated to the ladies, and there they sit in the front rows, and come in and go out as at a play or concert. The chair is canopied and raised considerably above the floor of the House, and every member has an easy chair and a writing desk to himself." After listening to some speeches, Dickens added, "It is an elegant chamber to look at, but a singularly bad one for all purposes of hearing."

The legislators themselves were a picturesque bunch. "They are striking men to look at, hard to deceive, prompt to act, lions in energy," he wrote. They were jealous of their honor and quick to resent insult. Dickens didn't personally witness any duels between lawmakers but was told on good authority that they happened regularly. He was initially puzzled by the lopsided, swollen cheeks he saw at nearly every desk. A glance at the floor resolved the mystery. "Both houses are handsomely carpeted, but the state to which these carpets are reduced by the universal disregard for the spittoon with which every honourable member is accommodated, and the extraordinary improvements on the pattern which are squirted and dabbled upon in every direction, do not admit of being described." Dickens noted the lack of marksmanship at disgustingly close range. "Several gentlemen called upon me who, in the course of conversation, frequently missed the spittoon at five paces, and one (but he was certainly short-sighted) mistook the closed sash for the open window at three."

———

LINCOLN DIDN'T CHEW tobacco. Mary Lincoln wouldn't have stood for it, and Mary accompanied him to Washington. They stayed at a boardinghouse a stone's throw from the Capitol. Mary was one of the few wives who accompanied their husbands to the capital for the congressional session, and she remained only weeks, soon put off by the lack of female company and the general uncouthness of the place. She wasn't universally appreciated by those she shared quarters with. "All the house—or rather all with whom you were on decided good terms—send their love to you," Lincoln wrote to Mary after she had left. "The others say nothing."

Lincoln made more friends than Mary did, being a friendlier sort. But he didn't make much of an impact. With most of his fellow Whigs, he distrusted James Polk, the Democratic president, and he challenged Polk's account of the origins of the war as growing out of an attack by Mexican troops against American troops on the American soil of Texas. What Polk called American soil, Lincoln told the House, was at best in dispute, with the evidence actually favoring Mexican ownership. "The country bordering on the east bank of the Rio Grande was inhabited by native Mexicans, born there under the Mexican government, and had never submitted to nor been conquered by Texas or the United States," he said.

Lincoln insisted that Polk substantiate his claims. The president must reveal the precise spot where the American blood had been spilled, and prove that this was American soil. "Let him answer, fully, fairly, and candidly," Lincoln said. "Let him answer with facts and not with arguments." If Polk could show that the spot was honestly American, Lincoln would support him. But if he couldn't or wouldn't, his failure would convict him of the grossest abuse of power. "Then I shall be fully convinced of what I more than suspect already, that he is deeply conscious of being in the wrong—that he feels the blood of this war, like the blood of Abel, is crying to Heaven against him."

Polk ignored Lincoln and his "spot resolutions," which never came to a vote of the House and won no honor for their author. In fact, in subsequent years Lincoln was ridiculed for his persistence in this bootless quest, with critics taunting him for his "spotty" record.

———

NOR DID ANOTHER Lincoln initiative gain traction. Upon the encouragement of Joshua Giddings, an Ohio Whig and a strong opponent of slavery, Lincoln and a colleague drafted a bill to abolish slavery in the District of Columbia. On Lincoln's part the measure grew out of his resolution in the Illinois legislature, and it reiterated the arguments he had made there. The Constitution gave the states control over slavery within their borders, but the federal district was Congress's own. Congress could abolish slavery there, and Lincoln thought it should.

Lincoln's measure called for gradual emancipation. Slaves currently in the district would remain slaves, but new slaves could not be brought into the district, and children born of slave mothers starting in 1850 would be free. Moreover, masters might emancipate their slaves and receive fair market value in compensation from the federal government.

There was a condition, though. Emancipation would not begin until it received the approval of voters in the district. If they disapproved, the project died. Lincoln didn't think this would be a problem. He told the House he had explained his bill to more than a dozen residents of the district. "There was not one but who approved," he said. "Every one of them desired that some proposition like this should pass."

The support was unsurprising. Slaves in Washington were personal servants, shop workers and others whose labor wasn't unlike that of free workers in Philadelphia, New York and Boston. The Washington slaves could become paid workers with no great jolt to the economy. Plantation slavery, the part of the slave system deemed essential to the Southern economy, didn't exist there. And Lincoln's proposal would allow Southerners to bring their personal slaves to Washington when they came on business or to visit, in the way Southerners could take their servants to Northern cities and states.

Even so, his bill went nowhere. Lincoln's own Whigs had other priorities. By no means were they all opposed to slavery, and many hoped their party would win the presidential election in 1848 behind the candidacy of a slaveholding hero of the war, Zachary Taylor. Lincoln yielded to political reality. "Finding that I was abandoned by my former backers and having little personal influence, I dropped the matter," he said later.

A DIFFERENT MEASURE addressing slavery came closer to approval, though it wasn't Lincoln's. Democrat David Wilmot of Pennsylvania proposed to exclude slavery from any territory acquired from Mexico in the war. The Wilmot Proviso won approval in the House of Representatives, where the North had a majority. It failed in the Senate, where the South wielded a veto. Its half success irked both sides: the South for the insult to slavery, the North for this new evidence of the power of the planters.

Lincoln's election to Congress had been part of a deal among Springfield Whigs to rotate in office. He kept his side of the bargain and stepped down when his two-year term ended. He didn't mean to retire from politics, but his return from Washington amounted to retirement. Although the Whigs' Taylor strategy indeed won them the presidency, it didn't prevent the party from fracturing over the slavery issue. Taylor proved to be the last elected Whig president, and after he suddenly died after a year in office, the party passed into eclipse—taking Lincoln, apparently, with it.

Making the best of things, he threw himself into the practice of law. Before long he was thinking that his political days were over. "His profession had almost superseded the thought of politics in his mind," he recalled of himself.

T HE REASON Frederick Douglass had met John Brown in Springfield was that Brown had once more grown restless. He moved the family to western Massachusetts, farther from slavery but closer to the center of the abolitionist movement. William Lloyd Garrison in Boston thundered louder than ever, assailing the Constitution as "a covenant with death and an agreement with Hell"—for sheltering slavery—and demanding its annulment, to be followed by a separation of the virtuous North from the sinful South. Yet Garrison disavowed violence, predicting that the end of slavery could come by peaceful methods. This seemed a non sequitur to many abolitionists, especially after Congress approved the Compromise of 1850, a package of laws addressing issues arising out of the recent war against Mexico. California, taken from Mexico, was admitted to the Union as a free state, tipping the sectional balance in Congress against the South; as compensation, the Fugitive Slave Act significantly enhanced the ability of Southern slave-catchers to capture fugitive slaves. Sheriffs and courts in the North, even private individuals, were dragooned into complicity in the seizure.

The Fugitive Slave Act outraged many in the North. William Lloyd Garrison naturally condemned it. Antislavery activists vowed popular resistance in order to prevent the law's enforcement. Frederick Douglass reconsidered his own nonviolent philosophy.

John Brown conjured something he called the League of Gileadites. Gilead was the Old Testament name for the mountainous territory east of the Jordan River. As Brown had explained to Douglass, he envisioned fugitive slaves and free blacks banding together for self-defense in the Alleghenies. But he would start by battling the new law in Massachusetts. "Nothing so charms the American people as personal bravery," he wrote, in what amounted to a charter for the league. Brown urged blacks to resist the fugitive law by force, including lethal force. "The trial for life of one bold and to some extent successful man, for defending his rights in good earnest, would arouse more sympathy throughout the nation than the accumulated wrongs and sufferings of more than three millions of our submissive colored population." And it would serve the one on trial. "No jury can be found in the Northern states that would convict a man for defending his rights."

Brown spelled out tactics. "Should one of your number be arrested, you must collect together as quickly as possible, so as to outnumber your adversaries who are taking an active part against you. Let no able-bodied man appear on the ground unequipped or with his weapons exposed to view; let that be understood beforehand. Your plans must be known only to yourself, and with the understanding that all traitors must die, wherever caught and proven to be guilty."

Steadfastness was essential. "Do not delay one moment after you are ready; you will lose all your resolution if you do. Let the first blow be the signal for all to engage; and when engaged do not do your work by halves, but make clean work with your enemies." Courage was crucial. "Let it be understood that you are not to be driven to desperation without making it an awful dear job to others as well as to you."

Brown was not above cynicism in this struggle. "After effecting a rescue, if you are assailed, go into the houses of your most prominent and influential white friends with your wives," he said. "That will effectually fasten upon them the suspicion of being connected with you, and will compel them to make common cause with you, whether they would otherwise live up to their profession or not. This would leave them no choice in the matter."

Again he commanded courage. "Hold on to your weapons, and never be persuaded to leave them, part with them, or have them far away from you. Stand by one another and by your friends while a drop of blood remains; and be hanged if you must, but tell no tales out of school. Make no confession. Union is strength."

Brown's words inspired more than forty black men and women to take the Gileadite pledge. But that was about all they did. The armed resistance Brown urged didn't appear, nor did the existence of the

Gileadites conspicuously disrupt the activities of slave-catchers in the Springfield area.

Still, the manifesto revealed the change occurring in Brown. The man who had once thought to shame the slaveholders into abolition by educating young blacks had become a promoter of violence against the agents of the slaveholders. He spoke of fighting to the last drop of blood; of executing traitors to the abolitionist cause; of falsely implicating reluctant whites. He hadn't yet volunteered to lead the armed campaign against slavery, but he was getting closer.

ABRAHAM LINCOLN ENDORSED the principle of the Fugitive Slave Act, if not the details of its implementation. The act was anchored in the Constitution, which Lincoln revered. The Constitution's Article IV declared, "No person held to service or labor in one State, under the laws thereof, escaping into another, shall, in consequence of any law or regulation therein, be discharged from such service or labor, but shall be delivered up on claim of the party to whom such service or labor may be due." The Fugitive Slave Act codified this constitutional mandate. Lincoln himself had written a version of the mandate into his proposal for emancipating the slaves of the District of Columbia.

The Fugitive Slave Act, moreover, was a legacy of Henry Clay, whom Lincoln esteemed as the model of everything a statesman should be. The Kentucky senator was the author of three great compromises that had held the Union together at critical moments: the Missouri Compromise of 1820, the South Carolina compromise of 1833, and the Compromise of 1850, which included the Fugitive Slave Act. When Clay died in 1852, Lincoln delivered a eulogy that detailed the careful balance Clay struck on the issue that vexed American democracy. "He ever was, on principle and in feeling, opposed to slavery," Lincoln said. Clay had long worked for emancipation in Kentucky, and hoped to see it in the country at large. "And yet Mr. Clay was the owner of slaves." Clay appreciated that emancipation was a practical issue as well as a moral one, and practical matters had to be acknowledged. "Cast into life where slavery was already widely spread and deeply seated, he did not perceive, as I think no wise man has perceived, how it could be at *once* eradicated, without producing a greater evil, even to the cause of human liberty itself."

In lauding Clay, Lincoln revealed his own views. "His feeling and his judgment, therefore, ever led him to oppose both extremes of opinion on the subject," he said of Clay, and of himself. The radical abolitionists—"those who would shiver into fragments the Union of these states, tear to tatters its now venerated Constitution, and even burn the last copy of the Bible rather than slavery should continue a single hour"—were no less dangerous to freedom than the Southern fire-eaters. In opposing both, Clay had served his country well. "Such a man the times have demanded, and such in the providence of God was given us," Lincoln said. Now that he was gone, the burden passed to his successors. "Let us strive to deserve, as far as mortals may, the continued care of Divine Providence, trusting that, in future national emergencies, He will not fail to provide us the instruments of safety and security."

LINCOLN WAS less enamored of Stephen Douglas, though Lincoln knew—and Clay himself would have admitted—that without Douglas, Clay's 1850 compromise might never have cleared Congress. Months into the struggle for the compromise, the energy of the aging Clay had faltered; when Clay stepped aside to recuperate, Douglas stepped forward to push the program the final yards to victory. Yet Lincoln wasn't inclined to honor Douglas. Douglas was a Democrat, for one thing. Lincoln knew enough of American politics to recognize that progress, however one defined it, came through the efforts of parties. Lincoln would always put Clay, the patron saint of the Whigs, above any Democrat, including Douglas.

There was a personal side to the story as well. Lincoln knew that Douglas had courted Mary Todd before she and Lincoln became engaged. Though Mary had chosen Lincoln, a tinge of the rivalry remained.

And then there was Douglas himself, an impressive fellow yet not a likable one. "He was a man of low stature, but broad-shouldered and big-chested," said Carl Schurz, a recent German immigrant who was assessing the lay of America's political land. "His head, sitting upon

a stout, strong neck, was the very incarnation of forceful combativeness; a square jaw and broad chin; a rather large, firm-set mouth; the
nose straight and somewhat broad; quick, piercing eyes with a deep,
dark, scowling, menacing horizontal wrinkle between them; a broad
forehead and an abundance of dark hair which at that period he wore
rather long and which, when in excitement, he shook and tossed defiantly like a lion's mane. The whole figure was compact and strongly
knit and muscular, as if made for constant fight."

Schurz didn't like Douglas but couldn't turn away. Schurz had
never seen or heard a more effective speaker. "His sentences were
clear-cut, direct, positive," he said. "They went straight to the mark
like bullets, and sometimes like cannon-balls, tearing and crashing.
There was nothing ornate, nothing imaginative in his language, no
attempt at 'beautiful speaking.'" Douglas could hit high; he could also
hit low. "It would be difficult to surpass his clearness and force of
statement when his position was right; or his skill in twisting logic or
in darkening the subject with extraneous, unessential matter when he
was wrong; or his defiant tenacity when he was driven to defend himself, or his keen and crafty alertness to turn his defense into attack, so
that, even when overwhelmed with adverse arguments, he would issue
from the fray with the air of the conqueror."

Douglas gave no quarter. "He was utterly unsparing of the feelings
of his opponents. He would nag and nettle them with disdainful words
of challenge, and insult them with such names as 'dastards' and 'traitors.' Nothing could equal the contemptuous scorn, the insolent curl
of his lip with which, in the debates to which I listened, he denounced
the anti-slavery men in Congress as 'the Abolition confederates,' and
at a subsequent time, after the formation of the Republican party, as
'Black Republicans.'" Truth was malleable to Douglas. "He would,
with utter unscrupulousness, malign his opponents' motives, distort
their sayings, and attribute to them all sorts of iniquitous deeds or
purposes of which he must have known them to be guiltless. Indeed,
Douglas's style of attack was sometimes so exasperatingly offensive
that it required, on the part of the anti-slavery men in the Senate, a
very high degree of self-control to abstain from retaliating."

No, Schurz didn't like Douglas, but he couldn't help respecting
him. "I have never seen a more formidable parliamentary pugilist."

———

THE PUGILIST HAD hoped not to have to battle over slavery again after the Compromise of 1850. "I have determined never to make another speech upon the slavery question," Douglas declared at the time. "And I will now add the hope that the necessity for it will never exist. I am heartily tired of the controversy, and I know the country is disgusted with it."

But he couldn't leave it alone. The fight for the 1850 compromise had taught Douglas how difficult the slavery question was, but it had also shown him how talented *he* was. Many called him the heir to Henry Clay in Congress. The mantle fit imperfectly, Douglas being a Democrat and Clay having been a Whig. Yet that very difference meant that Douglas might achieve something that had forever eluded Clay: the presidency. The Compromise of 1850 definitively split the Whigs; by Clay's death in 1852 they were demoralized and nearly defunct. The Democrats held together, giving them the inside track to the White House. As the leading Democrat in Congress, the most celebrated Democrat in the country, Douglas imagined himself sitting where Thomas Jefferson and Andrew Jackson, the patron saints of his party, had sat.

Which was what brought him back to the slavery question. The Compromise of 1850 had tied up all the loose ends of the slavery question. The states determined for themselves whether to allow or forbid slavery within their boundaries—no one disputed this. Congress, via the Missouri Compromise and now the Compromise of 1850, had ruled on slavery in the federal territories. The Fugitive Slave Act had strengthened the constitutional promise of interstate cooperation in the return of escaped slaves.

The 1850 compromise displeased all sides to some extent. Northerners felt tainted by the Fugitive Slave Act; Southerners resented the admission of free California. But neither side was *so* displeased as to seek to overturn the compromise, and the nation moved on.

Stephen Douglas looked forward to the Democratic convention of 1852, where he hoped to be rewarded with the party's nomination. During the convention's early rounds he led the balloting. But three other candidates split the vote with him, and in exhaustion the party turned to little-known Franklin Pierce, who easily won the general election.

Douglas handled the setback gracefully. He was a loyal Democrat and placed the party above any individual, he said. But he silently measured himself against Pierce and concluded that if merit counted, he—Stephen Douglas—should be president rather than Pierce. And he commenced calculating how to bring the rest of the party to the same conclusion.

His answer was to reopen the slavery question. The South was the birthplace of the Democracy, as the party called itself, and Southerners remained its most coherent bloc. They no longer possessed the numbers to make one of their own the party's nominee, but they could veto candidates they didn't like. Douglas determined to ingratiate himself to Southern Democrats.

Most Southerners had accepted the Missouri Compromise at the time of its negotiation in 1820. Their concession was the ban on slavery in the territories above the 36°30′ line. Few imagined slavery would ever be profitable there, and so they judged they weren't giving up much. But over time—and under attack by Northern abolitionists—Southerners began to chafe at the principle of the exclusion. They said they ought to have the same rights as Northerners in all the federal territories. And that included the right to take property, in their case including slaves, where they chose.

Stephen Douglas decided to give them that right. He wrapped his gift in a bill to provide a territorial government for Nebraska, a large region of the Louisiana Purchase above the Missouri Compromise line. Such a government was long overdue, Douglas declared. "To the states of Missouri and Iowa"—the region's next-door neighbors—"the organization of the Territory of Nebraska is an important and desirable local measure; to the interests of the Republic it is a national necessity," he said. A territorial government for Nebraska would allow the rapid development of America's western possessions. "The tide of emigration and civilization must be permitted to roll onward until it rushes through the passes of the mountains and spreads over plains and mingles with the waters of the Pacific," Douglas said. A territorial government would open the way to construction of railroads and telegraph lines to the Pacific. "No man can keep up with the spirit of this age who travels on anything slower than the locomotive and fails to receive intelligence by lightning."

Douglas understood that Southerners could hardly be expected to rally behind his Nebraska bill if the territory should remain off-limits to slavery. To bring them around, he proposed to repeal the Missouri Compromise. He realized this would be controversial; Northern opponents of slavery, considering the Missouri Compromise settled policy, would resist vehemently. A fellow legislator afterward recalled Douglas saying of repeal, "I know it will raise a hell of a storm."

Yet he went ahead. And he did so with no observable pangs of conscience. Douglas appealed to the guiding concept of democracy: that the voice of the people, if not necessarily the voice of God, is the voice that must direct public officials. The Missouri Compromise had denied settlers north of the 36°30′ line the right to determine for themselves whether to allow or forbid slavery. Douglas's Nebraska bill would restore this right. "The bill rests upon, and proposes to carry into effect, the great fundamental principle of self-government, upon which our republican institutions are predicated," he explained. "It does not propose to legislate slavery into the territories, nor out of the territories." By this time the bill had evolved to propose two territorial governments: one for Nebraska, the other for Kansas. Douglas continued, "It does not propose to establish institutions for the people, nor to deprive them of the right of determining for themselves what kind of domestic institutions they may have. It presupposes that the people of the territories are as intelligent, as wise, as patriotic, as conscientious as their brethren and kindred whom they left behind in the states."

"Popular sovereignty" was what Douglas called the concept of allowing settlers to determine the fate of the territories with respect to slavery. When the Nebraska bill became law as the Kansas-Nebraska Act, the measure killed the Missouri Compromise and replaced it with popular sovereignty.

Whether the law had won Douglas the Southern support he required to capture the next Democratic nomination remained to be seen. In the meantime it earned him the wrath of much of the North. Abolitionists called him the spawn of Satan; even moderate antislavery men shook their heads in dismay. At a stroke the Douglas measure overturned three decades of precedent between the two sides in the sectional dispute. Opponents of slavery had thought they had the evil institution contained by the Missouri Compromise line. But the line was now erased, and slavery could spread as far north as Canada. There seemed to be nothing the slaveholders wouldn't demand, and little they wouldn't get.

Douglas noted the uproar with wry resignation. "I could travel from Boston to Chicago by the light of my own effigy," he observed.

JOHN BROWN DIDN'T waste time on effigies; he preferred sub-stance to symbolism. From Massachusetts he moved his family to the Adirondack Mountains of New York, where antislavery phi-lanthropist Gerrit Smith had pledged land to start a colony of African Americans. North Elba, as the settlement was called, would show what blacks could do when their talents and energy were allowed to flourish. John Brown heard of the scheme and traveled to New York to meet Smith. He liked what he learned, and decided to relocate once again.

Life in North Elba was challenging. The winters were long and cold, the growing season short and uncertain. Yet hardship never daunted John Brown, and he pitched in and fashioned a new life. Richard Henry Dana Jr. had come to the attention of American read-ers with a memoir about California when it was still part of Mexico. *Two Years Before the Mast* inflamed James Polk's lust for California, which had contributed to his demand for war against Mexico. In 1849, Dana took a shorter journey, through the Adirondacks, where he discovered John Brown's new home. "The farm was a mere recent clearing," Dana wrote. "The stumps of trees stood out, blackened by burning, and crops were growing among them, and there was a plenty of felled timber. The dwelling was a small log-house of one story in height, and the outbuildings were slight. The whole had the air of a recent enterprise, on a moderate scale, although there were a good many neat cattle and horses. The position was a grand one for a lover of mountain effects; but how good for farming I could not tell."

The owner arrived some hours after Dana. "Late in the afternoon a long buckboard wagon came in sight, and on it were seated a negro man and woman, with bundles; while a tall, gaunt, dark-complexioned man walked before, having his theodolite and other surveyor's instruments with him, while a youth followed by the side of the wagon." The tall man was Brown, who supplemented the family income by part-time work as a surveyor. Brown stepped forward and greeted the visitors. "A grave, serious man he seemed, with a marked countenance and a natural dignity of manner," Dana said.

The visitors were asked to dinner. "We were all ranged at a long table, some dozen of us more or less, and these two negroes and one other had their places with us. Mr. Brown said a solemn grace." Dana noted that Brown addressed the negroes formally. "The man was 'Mr. Jefferson' and the woman 'Mrs. Wait.'" The two were recent arrivals from a place where they had been accorded less respect. "It was plain they had not been so treated or spoken to often before, perhaps never until that day, for they had all the awkwardness of field hands on a plantation."

The conversation with Brown impressed Dana and his friends. "We found him well informed on most subjects, especially in the natural sciences. He had books, and had evidently made a diligent use of them." The house was large for a cabin, with four rooms, but small for the crowd who lived there. "He seemed to have an unlimited family of children, from a cheerful, nice healthy woman of twenty or so, and full-sized red-haired son, who seemed to be foreman of the farm, through every grade of boy and girl, to a couple that could hardly speak."

Dana and his friends tried to pay for their meal. The eldest daughter, Ruth, managed the household, in the place of Brown's wife, Mary, who was ailing; Ruth consented to accept the cost of the food the visitors had consumed but nothing for her trouble. "We had some five-dollar bills and some bills of one dollar each," Dana recorded. "She took one of the one-dollar bills and went up into the garret, and returned with some change! It was too piteous. We could not help smiling, and told her we should feel guilty of highway robbery if we took her silver." She reluctantly acquiesced. "It was plain this family acted on a principle in the smallest matters."

———

FOR ALL THE APPEARANCE it presented to visitors, North Elba was a struggle for John Brown. Ruth recalled a winter day when her father nearly froze to death. He was returning from Springfield, where he still had business. He had found a ride most of the way but was left to cross the final mountain pass on foot, carrying his travel bag. "Before he came within several miles of home, he got so tired and lame he had to sit down in the road," Ruth said. "The snow was very deep, and the road but little trodden. He got up again after a while, went on as far as he could, and sat down once more. He walked a long distance in that way, and at last lay down with fatigue in the deep snow beside the path, and thought he should get chilled there and die." Another traveler approached but walked on past without seeing him. Brown concluded that the man was drunk. Thinking that if a drunkard could keep walking, so could he, Brown summoned his strength for a final push. With great effort he staggered to the house of a farmer named Scott. "Father could scarcely get into the house, he was so tired," Ruth recalled, evidently drawing on Brown's recollection or perhaps Scott's. Scott set Brown by the fire, gave him something to eat and eventually drove him the rest of the way by ox-drawn sled.

Brown never got comfortable in North Elba, committed though he was to the cause. Money was a constant problem. As Richard Dana had guessed, the mountains were indeed better for admiring than for farming, and Brown's efforts always came up short. In the early 1850s he shuttled back and forth between North Elba and Hudson, with continuing connections to Springfield. Much of the time he was trying to collect money owed to him, part of the time to postpone paying money owed *by* him.

Yet it wasn't just the money. He was searching for something, though he didn't know what. He was growing old. He had sired a large family. Most other men of his era and his position would have found that fulfilling. John Brown wanted more.

HE GOT IT in Kansas. Stephen Douglas had twinned Nebraska with Kansas in his bill to suggest that the former, filled with free farmers from Iowa, would develop into a free state, while the latter, attracting slaveholders from Missouri, would become a slave state. Popular sovereignty would yield a result satisfying to both sides.

He was disingenuous or naive. And because Stephen Douglas was anything but naive, disingenuousness was the only explanation. Kansas was the more appealing of the two territories on physical merits, and to Kansas the first settlers flocked. They raced and jostled to claim the choicest parcels of land for growing crops, the most convenient spots for siting towns. Jostling had been a feature of every new frontier in American history, but it had a novel aspect in Kansas. Popular sovereignty with respect to slavery meant that whichever side—proslavery or antislavery—put more of its people on the ground would determine the future for the state Kansas became. This was important to the prospective Kansans, of course, but not only to them. Kansas became a test of strength for the two sides in the national debate. The settling of Kansas provided the closest thing America had witnessed to a national referendum on slavery.

The two sides waged the contest with great vigor and little scruple. David Atchison, a Democratic senator from Missouri and the president pro tem of the Senate—which made him the acting vice president of the United States, following Millard Fillmore's promotion to the presidency on the death of Zachary Taylor—urged his fellow Missourians to do whatever it took to secure Kansas for slavery. "The people of Kansas, in their first elections, will decide the question whether or not the slaveholder is to be excluded, and it depends upon a majority of the votes cast at the polls," he told a crowd in western Missouri. Atchison asserted that the Yankee opponents of slavery were conspiring against the honest people of the South. He challenged Missouri to fight back. "If a set of fanatics and demagogues a thousand miles off can afford to advance their money and exert every nerve to abolitionize the territory and exclude the slaveholder, when they have not the least personal interest, what is your duty? When you reside in one day's journey of the territory, and when your peace, your quiet, and your property depend upon your action, you can, without an exertion, send five hundred of your young men who will vote in favor of your institutions. Should each county in the state of Missouri only do its duty, the question will be decided quietly and peaceably at the ballot box. If we are defeated, then Missouri and the other Southern states will have shown themselves recreant to their interests, and will deserve their fate."

The slavery men had the advantage at first. Missouri was next door to Kansas, giving Missourians a head start in the race there. And settlers from elsewhere typically passed through Missouri en route to Kansas, affording the Missourians a chance to hinder the progress of those from free states.

Missouri answered David Atchison's call to flood the polling places. In early voting for territorial offices, the turnout vastly exceeded the populations resident in the precincts, and many of the voters didn't even bother to spend the night in Kansas, returning at once to their Missouri homes. The bulging ballot boxes predictably favored the pro-slavery candidates, who proceeded to form a pro-slavery legislature that passed pro-slavery laws.

The laws were more extreme than anything on the books in the South. An "act to punish offences against slavery" decreed death as the penalty for disseminating abolitionist literature or merely speaking against slavery. The law was enforced by vigilante groups, in particular Missourians known as "border ruffians."

The opponents of slavery refused to be intimidated. Abolitionists organizing as emigrant-aid societies sponsored settlers who established communities devoted to the cause of freedom. Foremost was the town of Lawrence, some forty miles from the Missouri border. Underwritten by the New England Emigrant Aid Company, itself funded by abolitionist Amos Adams Lawrence of Massachusetts, the town waved its antislavery principles proudly. Three newspapers spread the good word of freedom; the Free State Hotel, the finest hostelry in Kansas, welcomed visitors and newcomers. After a trying first winter, the town grew rapidly and became a focus for free-state settlement in the surrounding area. The residents had bright hopes for their own future and that of Kansas, which would tip toward freedom if their efforts succeeded.

This was precisely what worried the slave-state men and their Missouri supporters. For months they harassed the inhabitants of Lawrence, threatening dire harm to persons and property. The tension built, and the ruffians grew full of themselves. A British traveler named Thomas Gladstone encountered a large gang of them after one of their excursions into Kansas. "I had just arrived in Kansas City, and shall never forget the appearance of the lawless mob that poured into the place," Gladstone wrote: "men, for the most part of large frame, with red flannel shirts and immense boots worn outside their trousers, their faces unwashed and unshaven." The hooligans were armed to the teeth with rifles, revolvers and bowie knives, and they swore a blue streak. "Looking around at these groups of drunken, bellowing, bloodthirsty demons who crowded around the bar of the hotel, shouting for drink, or vented their furious noise on the levee without, I felt that all my former experiences of border men and Missourians bore faint comparison with the spectacle presented by this wretched crew, who appeared only the more terrifying from the darkness of the surrounding night."

Gladstone had traversed several free states on the way to Missouri, and he perceived the difference in the cultures of North and South as reflected in the character of their inhabitants. That difference was magnified in Kansas, where free-state men and slave-state men lived within a few miles of each other. "Nowhere in America, probably, is the contrast between the Northern and the Southern man exhibited in so marked a manner as in Kansas," he wrote. "He who would see the difference between comfort and discomfort, between neatness and disorder, cleanliness and filth, between farming the land and letting the land farm itself, between trade and stagnation, stirring activity and reigning sloth, between a wide-spread intelligence and an almost universal ignorance, between general progress and an incapacity for all improvement or advancement, has commonly only to cross the border line which separates a free from a slave state. But he who would see these broad contrasts in a single view, the evidences of well-directed enterprise and intelligent energy mixed up with the ugly features of back-going and barbarity, should seek out Kansas, and make its strange varieties of inhabitants his study."

THOMAS GLADSTONE DIDN'T meet John Brown, but he might have met Brown's sons in Kansas had he known where to look. Five of the boys—grown men, in fact—had gone to Kansas in the early wave of emigrants. "During the years 1853 and 1854 most of the leading Northern newspapers were not only full of glowing accounts of the extraordinary fertility, healthfulness, and beauty of the Territory of Kansas, then newly opened for settlement, but of urgent appeals to all lovers of freedom who desired homes in a new region to go there as settlers, and by their votes save Kansas from the curse of slavery," John Brown Jr. recalled three decades later. John Brown Jr., Jason Brown, Owen Brown, Frederick Brown and Salmon Brown decided to leave Ohio for Kansas.

The boys had shown no greater ability than their father in the business of life; their accumulated property consisted chiefly of eleven head of cattle and three horses. Yet several of the cattle were a valuable breed, and so they took care to get them to Kansas safely. Owen, Frederick and Salmon bought steamer passage for themselves and the stock along the Great Lakes to Chicago. After wintering in Illinois, the three drove the animals overland to Kansas.

John Jr. and Jason, with their families, took a more direct route. They steamed down the Ohio River to the Mississippi, and up the Mississippi to St. Louis. In St. Louis they purchased two tents and some tools. They boarded another steamboat and ascended the Missouri River to Kansas City. The vessel was crowded with emigrants, mostly Southerners. "That they were from the South was plainly indicated by their language and dress; while their drinking, profanity, and display of revolvers and bowie-knives—openly worn as an essential part of their make-up—clearly showed the class to which they belonged, and that their mission was to aid in establishing slavery in Kansas," John recalled.

He wondered what he and the others had gotten themselves into. "A box of fruit trees and grape vines which my brother Jason had brought from Ohio, our plough, and the few agricultural implements we had on the deck of that steamer looked lonesome; for these were all we could see which were adapted to the occupations of peace. Then for the first time arose in our minds the query: Must the fertile prairies of Kansas, through a struggle at arms, be first secured to freedom before free men can sow and reap? If so, how poorly we were prepared for such work will be seen when I say that, for arms, five of us brothers had only two small squirrel rifles and one revolver."

The question lingered. As it did, a more pressing matter intruded. The scourge of westward emigration was cholera, which afflicted the choke points of travel where the surge of people overwhelmed the sanitation facilities. One of Jason Brown's sons contracted the disease at St. Louis; within hours of his first symptoms he was dead. Jason and John and the other family members buried the child by the riverside, at a hamlet called Waverly, where the boat had tied up for repairs.

They encountered Missouri's generic hostility toward free-state emigrants. "True to his spirit of hatred of Northern people," John recalled, "our captain, without warning to us on shore, cast off his lines and left us to make our way by stage to Kansas City, to which place we had already paid our fare by boat. Before we reached there, however, we became very hungry, and endeavored to buy food at various farm houses on the way; but the occupants, judging from our speech that we were not from the South, always denied us, saying, 'We have nothing for you.'"

Finally they reached their destination. "Arrived in Kansas, her lovely prairies and wooded streams seemed to us indeed like a haven of rest," John recounted. "Here in prospect we saw our cattle increased to hundreds and possibly to thousands, fields of corn, orchards, and vineyards." They set to work clearing the land, plowing the fields and sowing their crops. They lived in the tents, planning to put up houses before winter. They suffered the fever and chills of malaria. Their hay molded from summer's damp. Other settlers' cattle got into their corn. But such trials were the lot of farmers, and the Brown brothers took them in stride.

The political chicanery of Kansas was a different matter. The younger Browns witnessed the fraudulent first election of the territory. "There was no disguise, no pretense of legality, no regard for decency," John recalled. The ruffians, emboldened by the ballot coup, threatened bodily harm against any who challenged their dominance or questioned the slave future of Kansas.

John recalled his response and the ensuing result. "I wrote to our father, whose home was in North Elba, N.Y., asking him to procure and send to us, if he could, arms and ammunition, so that we could be better prepared to defend ourselves and our neighbors. He soon obtained them; but instead of sending, he came on with them himself,

accompanied by my brother-in-law Henry Thompson, and my brother
Oliver."

JOHN BROWN HADN'T intended to join his sons in Kansas. "If you
or any of my family are disposed to go to Kansas or Nebraska, with a
view to help defeat Satan and his legions in that direction, I have not
a word to say," he wrote to John before the latter set out. "But I feel
committed to operate in another part of the field." That other part of
the field was the colony in North Elba, where Mary and the younger
children remained. Perhaps Mary declared she'd had enough of moving; in any event there was no talk that she and the little ones would
go to Kansas. Brown naturally felt obliged to see to their welfare, and
his resources were insufficient to support them in New York while he
launched a new venture in Kansas.

But when he heard of the violence in Kansas and received John's
plea for arms, he couldn't resist. The battle for freedom was being
joined in the West, and he couldn't sit aside. He attended an antislavery convention in Syracuse, where he circulated John's letters. "John's
two letters were introduced, and read with such effect by Gerrit Smith
as to draw tears from numerous eyes in the great collection of people present," he wrote to Mary. And not only tears: "I received today
donations amounting to a little over sixty dollars—twenty from Gerrit Smith, five from an old British officer; others giving smaller sums
with such earnest and affectionate expressions of their good wishes as
did me more good than money even."

Yet the money was what made possible his decision to go to Kansas himself. Brown sold several cows and gave the money to Mary,
and using the money from Smith and the others, he bought a case of
rifles and some provisions, and with son Oliver headed for Kansas.
He reported to Mary on the trek. "I am writing in our tent about
twenty miles west of the Mississippi, to let you know that we are all
in good health and how we get along," he said. "We had some delay
at Chicago on account of our freight not getting on as we expected;
while there we bought a stout young horse that proves to be a very
good one, but he has been unable to travel fast for several days from
having taken the distemper." Brown hoped the animal would recover,

for they couldn't manage without him. "Our load is heavy, so that we have to walk most of the time; indeed, all the time the last day." They ate like travelers. "We fare very well on crackers, herring, boiled eggs, prairie chicken, tea, and sometimes a little milk. Have three chickens now cooking for our breakfast. We shoot enough of them on the wing as we go along to supply us with fresh meat. Oliver succeeds in bringing them down quite as well as any of us."

Passing through Missouri, Brown discovered in himself an aptitude for deception. The ruffians of the state were on the lookout for emigrants like Brown, especially ones transporting weapons. Brown passed himself off as a surveyor, and Oliver as his assistant. When they approached a group of men who looked as though they might cause trouble, Brown would get out his instruments and pretend to be running a line. Surveyors were welcome in the border regions, because they signified progress toward perfecting land titles. Brown would chat up the locals and continue on by. He and Oliver weren't stopped, and their baggage wasn't searched.

On arrival in Kansas they joined Brown's other sons on the Osawatomie River. The challenges of frontier life were in full view there. "We found our folks in a most uncomfortable situation, with no houses to shelter one of them, no hay or corn fodder of any account secured, shivering over their little fires, all exposed to the dreadful cutting winds, morning and evening and stormy days," Brown wrote to Mary. The exposure had taken its toll. "Fever and ague and chill-fever seem to be very general." His coming hadn't much improved the lot of the Brown colony. "We had, between us all, sixty cents in cash when we arrived."

Yet in another respect, things looked promising. "Last Tuesday was an election day with Free-State men in Kansas, and hearing that there was a prospect of difficulty we all turned out most thoroughly armed," Brown informed Mary. "But no enemy appeared, nor have I heard of any disturbance in any part of the Territory. Indeed, I believe Missouri is fast becoming discouraged about making Kansas a slave state, and I think the prospect of its becoming free is brightening every day."

WHILE THE Kansas-Nebraska Act propelled John Brown to Kansas, it pulled Abraham Lincoln back to politics. Stephen Douglas had seemed untouchable in Illinois after his handling of the Compromise of 1850; the majority Democrats in the Illinois legislature resoundingly reelected him to the Senate in 1852. Perhaps some head-turning effect of his popularity contributed to his audacity in overturning the Missouri Compromise in the Nebraska law, as the Kansas-Nebraska measure was often called. In any case, the controversy surrounding that decision gave Lincoln an opening to return to the political lists. As he recalled of himself for his biographer, "The repeal of the Missouri compromise aroused him as he had never been before."

William Herndon watched the stirring. Lincoln had exited his first law partnership, and then a second, before creating a third partnership, with Herndon, almost a decade his junior. Herndon had seen Lincoln retreat into the law; now he watched him regain the political spirit. "A live issue was presented to him," Herndon remarked about the Kansas-Nebraska law. "No one realized this sooner than he. In the office discussions he grew bolder in his utterances. He insisted that the social and political difference between slavery and freedom was becoming more marked; that one must overcome the other; and that postponing the struggle between them would only make it the more deadly in the end." Herndon remembered Lincoln saying, "The day of compromise has passed. These two great ideas have been kept apart only by the most artful means. They are like two wild beasts in sight of each other, but chained and held apart. Someday these deadly antagonists will one or the other break their bonds, and then the question will be settled." In another conversation Lincoln said of property in slaves, "It is the most glittering, ostentatious, and displaying property in the world, and now, if a young man goes courting"—in the South—"the only inquiry is how many negroes he or his lady-love owns. The love for slave property is swallowing up every other mercenary possession. Slavery is a great and crying injustice, an enormous national crime."

But Lincoln didn't run for office again, not yet. Instead he campaigned for Whig candidates around Illinois, which meant taking on Douglas, who was campaigning for Democratic candidates. At first in editorials in Whig newspapers, then in speeches delivered at a distance from Douglas, Lincoln assailed the repeal of the Missouri Compromise. Douglas ignored him, but Lincoln persisted, and eventually the two began speaking from the same platform. Political speeches in those days were high entertainment, especially away from Springfield, which heard speeches all the time. In October 1854, Douglas and Lincoln shared a stage in Peoria.

Douglas went first, as befitted the distinguished senator and the person making the positive argument for the new regime. Douglas attempted a filibuster against Lincoln, continuing so long that his listeners grew tired and hungry for their supper.

Lincoln listened patiently until his turn finally came. "It is now several minutes past five, and Judge Douglas has spoken over three hours," he observed to the crowd. "If you hear me at all, I wish you to hear me through. It will take me as long as it has taken him." He suggested a break to eat. Then they could regather. Lincoln added that he had agreed that Douglas should have the last word. "I suspected if it were understood that the Judge was entirely done, you Democrats would leave and not hear me," he explained, a slight smile on his face. "But by giving him the close, I felt confident you would stay for the fun of hearing him skin me."

The audience chuckled as they filed out. Most did indeed return to hear Lincoln make his case for the Missouri Compromise, lately repealed, and for the principle it represented. By this time defenders of the slave system lumped all opponents of any part of the system into a single category of abolitionism. Lincoln began by rejecting that taxonomy. "I wish to make and to keep the distinction between the *existing* institution, and the *extension* of it, so broad, and so clear that no honest man can misunderstand me, and no dishonest one successfully misrepresent me," he said. He cited Thomas Jefferson as the archetype of those who understood the distinction. A Virginian and a slaveholder, Jefferson nonetheless inspired the ordinance of 1787 that declared the original Northwest Territory off-limits to slavery. Jefferson understood that liberty, not servitude, was what would make America great. The development of the region from Ohio to Wisconsin had proven him right. "It is now what Jefferson foresaw and intended—the happy home of teeming millions of free, white, prosperous people, and no slave amongst them," Lincoln said.

The Missouri Compromise had built on Jefferson's vision, he continued. Lincoln wished that the entire Louisiana Purchase had been joined to the Union without slavery, but the institution already existed around New Orleans and again near St. Louis, and so it was allowed to continue there. But the largest part of the purchase was, like the old Northwest, preserved for freedom.

The Compromise of 1850 had brought California into the Union as a free state and been silent on slavery in the rest of the lands taken from Mexico. Again, Lincoln—and the other supporters of the Wilmot Proviso—had wished for more. But politics was the art of compromise, and compromise there was. Yet little was lost to slavery, for all parties to the bargain tacitly agreed that the arid regions of New Mexico and Utah would never sustain slavery.

The greatest feat of the Compromise of 1850 was that it effectively settled the question of slavery in the territories once and for all. This question had been the source of most of the friction between North and South since the founding of the republic; its settlement provided hope that the friction would ease and comity replace it.

"But *now* new light breaks upon us," Lincoln said sarcastically. "Now Congress declares this ought never to have been, and the like of it must never be again." Douglas and the others who supported the Kansas-Nebraska Act couldn't let the sleeping dog lie. They declared that the Missouri Compromise had contravened the liberty of slaveholders. "The sacred right of self-government is grossly violated by it!" Lincoln jeered. "That *perfect* liberty they sigh for—the liberty of making slaves of other people—Jefferson never thought of; their own father never thought of; they never thought of themselves, a year ago."

Partisans of slavery often charged their opponents with moral smugness. The charge wasn't always inaccurate. But Lincoln rejected it for himself and most in the North. "I have no prejudice against the Southern people," he said. "They are just what we would be in their situation. If slavery did not now exist amongst them, they would not introduce it. If it did now exist amongst us, we should not instantly give it up." Southerners frequently said that they hadn't invented slavery; it had been bequeathed to them, and they were doing their best to manage the inheritance. Lincoln didn't deny that this was a hard problem. "I surely will not blame them for not doing what I should not know how to do myself. If all earthly power were given me, I should not know what to do, as to the existing institution."

His first impulse, he said, would be to free all the slaves and send them to Liberia. But a moment's reflection revealed the impracticality of this. Most of the slaves knew nothing of Africa, and Africa nothing of them. "If they were all landed there in a day, they would all perish in the next ten days," Lincoln said. Nor were there ships to carry them to Africa. Perhaps in the long run, sending freed slaves to Africa would work, but not at once. Lincoln hoped it *would* work, for the alternatives were dismal. "Free them all and keep them among us as underlings? Is it quite certain that this benefits their condition?" Lincoln couldn't say it would. "What next? Free them, and make them politically and socially our equals? My own feelings will not admit of this; and if mine would, we well know that those of the great mass of white people will not. Whether this feeling accords with justice and sound judgment is not the sole question, if indeed, it is any part of it. A universal feeling, whether well or ill-founded, cannot be safely disregarded. We cannot, then, make them equals." Possibly some middle path would work, but only possibly. "It does seem to me that systems of gradual emancipation might be adopted," Lincoln said. "But for their tardiness in this, I will not undertake to judge our brethren of the South."

Yet the future of slavery in the states was not the issue. Lincoln made clear where he stood on slavery per se; it was a "monstrous injustice." But this was neither here nor there for the moment. The Constitution guaranteed states the right to decide on slavery within their own borders. The pressing issue was slavery in the territories. This was the well-settled issue Stephen Douglas had insisted on reopening. Douglas claimed that the public had demanded the reopening. Yet he had produced no evidence of such demand. "I conclude then that the public never demanded the repeal of the Missouri compromise," Lincoln said.

Douglas and the other repealers declared that equal justice to the South required that they be allowed to take their slaves into Nebraska and Kansas. "That is to say, inasmuch as you do not object to my taking my hog to Nebraska, therefore I must not object to you taking your slave," Lincoln paraphrased. This was logical only if there were no differences between hogs and slaves. But not even slaveholders defended this absurdity. The slaveholders had accepted a ban on the importation of slaves from overseas; there was no ban on the import of hogs. More recently the South had joined the North in declaring the Atlantic slave trade to be piracy, and to mandate death for violators. "Why did you do this? If you did not feel that it was wrong, why did you join in providing that men should be hung for it? The practice was no more than bringing wild negroes from Africa, to sell to such as would buy them. But you never thought of hanging men for catching and selling wild horses, wild buffaloes or wild bears." Slave dealers were treated as scum by genteel Southerners; no such disdain was exhibited toward horse dealers.

Allowing the extension of slavery, leading to the creation of new slave states, would magnify the voting advantage the Constitution had granted to slaveholders from the start. Slaves could not vote, but three-fifths of their number counted toward representation in the lower house of Congress. As a result, white Southerners wielded more power per person than white Northerners. Lincoln cited two states: South Carolina and Maine. Each had six representatives and therefore eight presidential electors. "In the control of the government, the two states are equals precisely." But Maine had more than twice as many white people as South Carolina. "Thus each white man in South Carolina is more than the double of any man in Maine."

Stephen Douglas had touted the Kansas-Nebraska Act as a Union-saving measure. "I, too, go for saving the Union," Lincoln said. "Much as I hate slavery, I would consent to the extension of it rather than see the Union dissolved, just as I would consent to any great evil to avoid a greater one." But the act was having just the opposite effect. "When it came upon us, all was peace and quiet. The nation was looking to the forming of new bonds of Union; and a long course of peace and prosperity seemed to lie before us. In the whole range of possibility, there scarcely appears to me to have been anything out of which the slavery agitation could have been revived, except the very project of repealing the Missouri compromise." Yet repeal had come. "And here we are, in the midst of a new slavery agitation, such, I think, as we have never seen before."

The race to determine the fate of Kansas was on. And it was shaping up far differently than Douglas had foretold. "Bowie-knives and six-shooters are seen plainly enough," Lincoln said. They would surely be used. He wondered where it all was leading. "Will not the first drop of blood so shed be the real knell of the Union?"

If the Missouri Compromise were not restored, democracy's fate would be grim, Lincoln declared. He saw the two sections of the country glaring at each other over the ruins of the compromise: "The South flushed with triumph and tempted to excesses; the North, betrayed, as they believe, brooding on wrong and burning for revenge. One side will provoke; the other resent. The one will taunt, the other defy; one aggresses, the other retaliates."

But if the compromise *were* restored—what then? "We thereby reinstate the spirit of concession and compromise, that spirit which has never failed us in past perils, and which may be safely trusted for all the future." Southerners should be able to see this as well as Northerners, for it would benefit both sections. "It would be worth to the nation a hundred years' purchase of peace and prosperity."

CHEERS FROM the Whigs in the audience greeted Lincoln's conclusion. The Democrats affected to be unimpressed. Stephen Douglas lit into him with the vigor his supporters expected, and their cheers outdid those of the Whigs for Lincoln. The Democrats proclaimed Douglas the day's victor.

But he himself was wary of Lincoln. Years later a Douglas friend, W. C. Gowdy, recounted having dinner with the senator the night before the Peoria debate. "After the evening meal Judge Douglas exhibited considerable restlessness, pacing back and forth on the floor of the room, evidently with mental preoccupation," Gowdy said. Gowdy asked Douglas what was on his mind. "It cannot be that you have any anxiety with reference to the outcome of the debate you are to have with Mr. Lincoln," he suggested. "You cannot doubt of your ability to dispose of him."

Douglas stopped his pacing. "Yes, Gowdy, I am troubled over the progress and outcome of this debate," he said. He had watched and measured Lincoln, and he knew what he was getting into. "I regard him as the most difficult and dangerous opponent that I have ever met."

Douglas wasn't misled by the applause he received at the next day's debate. He knew Lincoln had scored points. And he guessed Lincoln wouldn't go away.

L INCOLN HOPED to elevate his rivalry with Douglas to the Senate. His performance during the summer of 1854 prompted Springfield Whigs to nominate him for the state legislature, and though Lincoln showed little interest in the office, thinking his days as a mere state lawmaker were behind him, the voters of his district elected him.

He declined the honor. His eye was on the Senate. The Illinois legislature would choose a partner to Douglas in early 1855, and Lincoln feared that membership in the legislature would complicate if not preclude his selection.

He lobbied hard for the Senate seat, and he entered the legislative selection process as the favorite. On the first ballot he led all candidates, falling just five votes shy of a winning majority. But his momentum began to wane, and the position went to Lyman Trumbull, an antislavery Democrat.

A year earlier, Lincoln hadn't seen himself in politics at all. Then Stephen Douglas scuttled the Missouri Compromise, and Lincoln rejoined the fight, successfully enough to come within a handful of votes of election to the Senate. The failure, after getting so close, stung badly. "I never saw him so dejected," one of his allies remarked. "He said the fates seemed to be against him, and he thought he would never strive for office again."

HIS DISCOURAGEMENT didn't last. Ironically, it might have been Lincoln's deeper, background depression that snapped him out of his post-race funk, for he realized that the excitement of the attempt had pushed his chronic blues aside. William Herndon watched his partner closely during this period. "He was always calculating, and always planning ahead," Herndon recalled. "His ambition was a little engine that knew no rest. The vicissitudes of a political campaign brought into play all his tact and management and developed to its fullest extent his latent industry."

Lincoln had another reason to try again. Mary Todd Lincoln had chosen Lincoln over Stephen Douglas not least because she thought she saw more promise in him. But in the years since then, Douglas, not her husband, was the one whose career had flourished. Douglas was the lion of the Senate; his words and actions moved the country. He had an inside track to the White House. As for Lincoln, he remained a small-town lawyer. His shaggy-dog stories mortified Mary; his ill-fitting suits and homely appearance caused her to wonder what a girl who had grown up with money was doing with such a character. Hoping to make Mary happy—to give her reason to believe that her gamble on their marriage wasn't a dead loss—Lincoln determined to keep trying.

Yet discovering how and where to try was no easy task. The political ground was shifting beneath his feet. The slavery debate was tearing at both political parties, but while the Democrats had Stephen Douglas to hold them together, the Whigs had lost their bridge-builder, Henry Clay. They never found a substitute, and they fell into pieces. Lincoln became a man without a party.

Some Whigs joined the American, or Know-Nothing, party, which ranted in opposition to immigrants and Catholics. Some visited the antislavery Free Soil party. But most eventually reached the new Republican party, which knowingly took its name from the party of Thomas Jefferson, who had sought an end to slavery while appreciating the difficulty of getting there.

For many months Lincoln wasn't sure where he stood. "I think I am a Whig," he wrote to Joshua Speed, a friend, as late as August 1855. "But others say there are no Whigs, and that I am an abolitionist." Lincoln again denied the charge. "I now do no more than oppose the *extension* of slavery." He knew what else he was not. "I am not a Know-Nothing. That is certain. How could I be? How can anyone who abhors the oppression of negroes be in favor of degrading classes of white people? Our progress in degeneracy appears to me to be

pretty rapid. As a nation, we began by declaring that '*all men are created equal.*' We now practically read it 'all men are created equal, *except
negroes.*' When the Know-Nothings get control, it will read 'all men
are created equal, except negroes, *and foreigners, and Catholics.*' When
it comes to this I should prefer emigrating to some country where they
make no pretense of loving liberty—to Russia, for instance, where
despotism can be taken pure, and without the base alloy of hypocrisy."

Lincoln knew he and Speed—a Kentucky native like Lincoln, but
one who had moved back to Kentucky—didn't see eye to eye on slavery. In this letter Lincoln examined his own thinking as he explained
his position to his friend. "You suggest that in political action now,
you and I would differ," Lincoln wrote. "I suppose we would; not quite
as much, however, as you may think. You know I dislike slavery; and
you fully admit the abstract wrong of it. So far there is no cause of
difference. But you say that sooner than yield your legal right to the
slave, especially at the bidding of those who are not themselves interested, you would see the Union dissolved." Lincoln thought this a
false choice. "I am not aware that *anyone* is bidding you to yield that
right; very certainly *I* am not. I leave that matter entirely to yourself.
I also acknowledge *your* rights and *my* obligations, under the Constitution, in regard to your slaves. I confess I hate to see the poor creatures hunted down, and caught, and carried back to their stripes, and
unrewarded toils; but I bite my lip and keep quiet." Lincoln recalled a
steamboat trip he and Speed had taken from Louisville to St. Louis a
decade earlier. "You may remember, as I well do, that from Louisville
to the mouth of the Ohio there were, on board, ten or a dozen slaves,
shackled together with irons. That sight was a continual torment to
me; and I see something like it every time I touch the Ohio, or any
other slave-border. It is hardly fair for you to assume that I have no
interest in a thing which has, and continually exercises, the power of
making me miserable. You ought rather to appreciate how much the
great body of the Northern people do crucify their feelings in order to
maintain their loyalty to the Constitution and the Union."

Turning to the issue of the day, Lincoln continued, "I do oppose
the extension of slavery, because my judgment and feelings so prompt
me; and I am under no obligation to the contrary. If for this you and
I must differ, differ we must." Like Lincoln, Speed had condemned

the violence that attended the opening of Kansas to settlement, especially the hijacking of the territorial elections by the Missouri ruffians. Speed had gone so far as to advocate hanging the ringleaders. Lincoln thought this punishment extreme, but he shared Speed's anger. Yet he didn't think Speed had thought things through. "If Kansas fairly votes herself a slave state, she must be admitted, or the Union must be dissolved," Lincoln acknowledged. But what if the vote was unfair, skewed by the border ruffians, whom Speed wanted to hang? "Must she still be admitted, or the Union be dissolved? That will be the phase of the question when it first becomes a practical one."

And it was the fatal flaw in Stephen Douglas's popular-sovereignty formula, Lincoln judged. "I look upon that enactment not as a *law*, but as *violence* from the beginning," he told Speed, referring to the Kansas-Nebraska Act. "It was conceived in violence, passed in violence, is maintained in violence, and is being executed in violence. I say it was *conceived* in violence, because the destruction of the Missouri Compromise, under the circumstances, was nothing less than violence. It was *passed* in violence, because it could not have passed at all but for the votes of many members, in violent disregard of the known will of their constituents. It is *maintained* in violence because the elections since clearly demand its repeal, and this demand is openly disregarded."

Lincoln judged that Kansas was lost. "That Kansas will form a slave constitution, and, with it, will ask to be admitted into the Union, I take to be an already settled question, and so settled by the very means you so pointedly condemn," he said. So what was to be done? What would Lincoln do? "In my humble sphere, I shall advocate the restoration of the Missouri Compromise, so long as Kansas remains a territory, and when, by all these foul means, it seeks to come into the Union as a slave-state, I shall oppose it." Yet Kansas would be but one state; the Union would go on.

The problem was that the Democratic party had become beholden to the slave power, Lincoln said. Speed, a Democrat, had told Lincoln that if the Kansans made their state free by a fair vote, he as a Christian would rejoice. Lincoln thought such a statement meaningless. "All decent slave-holders *talk* that way, and I do not doubt their candor," he said. "But they never *vote* that way." Lincoln asked Speed to consider his own actions. "Although in a private letter or conversation you will express your preference that Kansas shall be free, you would vote for no man for Congress who would say the same thing publicly." Writ large, this was the condition of the Democratic party. "No such man could be elected from any district in any slave-state. You think Stringfellow & Co."—Benjamin Stringfellow was a leader of the Missouri ruffians—"ought to be hung, and yet at the next presidential election you will vote for the exact type and representative of Stringfellow. The slave-breeders and slave-traders, are a small, odious and detested class, among you, and yet in politics they dictate the course of all of you, and are as completely your masters as you are the masters of your own negroes."

IF LINCOLN WAS too radical for Joshua Speed, he was too conservative for William Herndon. The troubles in Kansas outraged and mobilized antislavery groups in Illinois, as elsewhere. "At Springfield we were energetic, vigilant, almost revolutionary," Herndon recalled. "We recommended the employment of almost any means, no matter how desperate, to promote and defend the cause of freedom." Not so Lincoln. "At one of these meetings Lincoln was called on for a speech. He responded to the request, counseling moderation and less bitterness in dealing with the situation before us. We were belligerent in tone and clearly out of patience with the government. Lincoln opposed the notion of coercive measures with the possibility of resulting bloodshed, advising us to eschew resort to the bullet."

Herndon recalled Lincoln's words: "Revolutionize through the ballot box, and restore the government once more to the affections and hearts of men by making it express, as it was intended to do, the highest spirit of justice and liberty. Your attempt, if there be such, to resist the laws of Kansas by force is criminal and wicked, and all your feeble attempts will be follies and end in bringing sorrow on your heads and ruin the cause you would freely die to preserve."

By Herndon's account, Lincoln's caution cooled the ardor of his radical friends. But it didn't prevent Lincoln from contributing to a free-Kansas fund Herndon and the others had raised.

On another occasion, too, Lincoln fought slavery with his money.

The free son of a black woman of Springfield had taken a job on a boat heading down the Mississippi to New Orleans. Upon reaching that city, he was thrown into prison. This wasn't an unusual fate; the "black code" in much of the South prescribed detention for free black visitors, lest their example of walking about unhindered and unowned put thoughts of freedom into the heads of black slaves. But the young man had failed to bring papers proving his freedom, and when his boat left for the return north, he remained in fetters. His mother appealed to Lincoln and Herndon, who took the case to the Illinois governor. The governor pleaded legal incapacity: Louisiana made its own laws. They then appealed to the governor of Louisiana, who less believably told them that the situation was beyond his control as well. Lincoln and Herndon feared that the young man might be sold into slavery to defray prison costs, and once sold, be lost forever. Despairing of winning his release by recourse to law, they took up a subscription among friends to purchase him. They forwarded the money to a New Orleans associate, and the young man was freed.

Lincoln's moderation was innate; his was not a passionate temperament. On the slavery question, Lincoln's moderation was also tactical. Stephen Douglas's decision to reopen the issue of slavery in the territories had revived Lincoln's political hopes; having had his hopes dashed before, he determined to move cautiously.

But caution was itself risky at a time when American politics was careening toward danger. On each side of the slavery debate, emotions were being deliberately inflamed to mobilize supporters against the other side. Northern abolitionists underwrote lectures by Frederick Douglass and others who could testify to the horrors of life under the lash; Southern defenders of slavery warned that the abolitionists were promoting slave rebellion and race-mixing.

Henry Ward Beecher made a habit of, and a handsome living by, stirring emotions. Beecher was a son of Lyman Beecher, a minister of Puritan persuasion who never found an unpopular cause he couldn't get behind. Henry Beecher followed his father to the pulpit but charted his own path from there. From the pulpit of his Plymouth Church in Brooklyn, Henry preached a gospel of love and opportunity, not justice and repentance; the good news of Beecher's Good Book was that God wanted men to be happy. And women, too: Beecher's church was crowded with women, not a few of whom vied for places near the front, where his loving eye might fall upon them. It did on several, and Beecher's reputation for ministering intimately to certain members of his flock added to the aura that came to surround him.

Bad fortune befell Plymouth Church in 1849 when the structure burned to the ground. But Beecher was wont to say that God intended men to find the good in the bad, and Beecher certainly did when, amid the rebuilding, Congress passed the Fugitive Slave Act. Henry Beecher, like all the Beechers—he had nine siblings—had been opposed to slavery from the cradle, but the new law gave him reason to oppose it more strenuously than ever. As he did, it brought larger crowds to his new church, expanded to accommodate them. By the mid-1850s Henry Beecher was the most famous clergyman in America. His printed sermons sold by the tens of thousands; his words were quoted in newspapers and journals; no visit to New York was complete until the visitor had taken the East River ferry to Brooklyn and walked the few blocks to hear the great man hold forth.

He never expounded to more widely noticed effect than in an 1856 sermon on Kansas. "A battle is to be fought," he began, in soothing tones that belied the subject. "If we are wise, it will be bloodless." His voice began to rise as he sketched the alternative. "If we listen to the pusillanimous counsels of men who have never shown one throb of sympathy for liberty, we shall have blood to the horse's bridles." Again softer: "If we are firm and prompt to obvious duty, if we stand by the men of Kansas, and give them all the help that they need, the flame of war will be quenched before it bursts forth, and both they of the West, and we of the East, shall, after some angry mutterings, rest down in peace." Harsher once more: "But if our ears are poisoned by the advice of men who never rebuke violence on the side of power, and never fail to inveigh against the self-defense of wronged liberty, we shall invite aggression and civil war."

Beecher recounted the violence already inflicted on Kansas by the minions of slavery. "At the hiss of an unscrupulous man"—David Atchison—"hordes of wild and indolent fellows that hang about the towns and cities of slave states as gigantic vermin rushed into Kansas, crushed the free and actual settlers at the polls, and by a wholesale fraud, not even denied or discouraged, reared up a legislature whose office it was to forge law for the benefit of slavery and for the extinction of liberty."

Thankfully, some brave defenders of freedom had traveled to Kansas too. These were actual settlers, men—with their women and children, in some cases—steeped in the American tradition of liberty and personal responsibility. They stood against the evildoers.

The struggle continued, Beecher said, even as he spoke, even as his listeners sat safely in their pews. "On the one side are representatives of civilization; on the other, of barbarism. On the one side stand men of liberty, Christianity, industry, arts, and of universal prosperity; on the other are the waste and refuse materials of a worn-out slave state population—men whose ideas of society and civilization are comprised in the terms: a rifle, a horse, a hound, a slave, tobacco, and whisky." The latter had no religion worth the name. "There is nothing but an annual uproarious camp-meeting where they get just enough religion to enable them to find out that the Bible justifies all the immeasurable vices and wrongs of slavery." The free-state men brought books, newspapers, schools, open minds. "The slave state men come without books—without enough education to read, if they had them—without schools or a wish for them. They come with statutes framed for making free thought a sin, free speech a penitentiary offence, a free press punishable with death if it in the least loosens the bonds of oppression."

Beecher's listeners were not on the battle lines of the struggle, but they had a role to play in this epic contest. What the Kansas heroes required were weapons, which any friend of freedom could help supply. These would make all the difference. "Arms and courage will inevitably secure an unbroken peace," Beecher said.

He quoted the Book of Revelation in describing the war that would come if those who claimed to love liberty failed to do their part. "And the second angel sounded, and as it were a great mountain, burning with fire, was cast into the sea; and the third part of the sea became blood." In his own voice he interpreted: "So will armed slavery be cast into Kansas. But will not these rivers of blood dash against the Alleghenies, and that fire flash along the line between the North and South?"

Beecher again appealed for donations. "Let them that have money now pour it out," he said. Time was of the essence. "What is done must be done quickly." There must be no holding back. "Funds must be freely given. Arms must be had, even if bought at the price mentioned by our Saviour: 'He that hath no sword, let him sell his garment and buy one.'"

———

HENRY BEECHER COULD speak at length; he could also compose epigrams, as when, asked how a man of the Bible could advocate sending weapons to Kansas, he replied that in the present case a single Sharps rifle was worth a hundred Bibles. Weapons henceforth dispatched to Kansas by antislavery groups were often dubbed Beecher's Bibles.

Yet Henry Beecher, for all his fame, wasn't even the most powerful abolitionist in the Beecher family. That honor went to his sister Harriet, who married a man named Stowe. And as Harriet Beecher Stowe she wrote the best-selling American novel of the nineteenth century, *Uncle Tom's Cabin*, which won more converts to the antislavery cause than all her brother's sermons—and all the words written and spoken by any other abolitionist.

She claimed no personal credit for the achievement, believing herself the agent of a higher power. She once told a friend she hadn't written *Uncle Tom's Cabin* at all.

"*What!*" the friend replied, astonished. "You did not write 'Uncle Tom'?"

"No," said Harriet Beecher Stowe. "I only put down what I saw."

"But you have never been at the South, have you?"

"No, but it all came before me in visions, one after another, and I put them down in words."

"Still," said the friend, "you must have arranged the events."

"No," said Stowe. "Your Annie"—the friend's daughter—"reproached me for letting little Eva die. Why, I could not help it. I felt as badly as anyone could. It was like a death in my own family, and it affected me so deeply that I could not write a word for two weeks after her death."

"And did you know that Uncle Tom would die?" the friend asked.

"Oh yes, I knew that he must die from the first, but I did not know *how*. When I got to that part of the story, I saw no more for some time. I was physically exhausted, too. Mr. Stowe had then accepted a call to Andover"—her husband, like her father and brother, was a minister—"and had to go there to find a house for the family." At her husband's urging, Harriet had gone with him and for a time was distracted by refurbishing and refurnishing a home. Uncle Tom, she thought, was the furthest thing from her mind. One busy morning was followed by midday dinner, after which she looked forward to a nap. "But suddenly arose before me the death scene of Uncle Tom with what led to it—and George's visit to him. I sat down at the table and wrote nine pages of foolscap paper without pausing, except long enough to dip my pen into the inkstand."

Just as she finished, Calvin Stowe awoke from *his* nap. "Wife, have not you lain down yet?" he asked.

"No, I have been writing, and I want you to listen to this, and see if it will do." She read, with tears streaming down her face at the pathos of the scene. He wept also.

"Do!" he said. "I should think it would do." He took the sheets from her, folded them carefully and sent them to her publisher, without a single revision or correction.

"I have often thought," Harriet Stowe concluded the story, "that if anything had happened to that package in going, it would not have been possible for me to have reproduced it."

Harriet Stowe's friend remembered this story and brought it up to her later, after publication of a new edition of *Uncle Tom's Cabin*, in the preface of which Stowe told of writing a sketch, many years earlier, of the death of a loyal slave. In the preface she said she had read the sketch to her children, who were deeply moved. This was the inspiration of Uncle Tom, Stowe told her new readers. The friend asked Stowe if there was a contradiction between the two versions.

"No," Harriet Stowe replied. "Both are true, for I had entirely forgotten that I had ever written that sketch, and I suppose I had unconsciously woven it in with the other."

Whatever the origins of Uncle Tom, *Uncle Tom's Cabin* became a sensation across the North and in other countries as well. Its affecting account of the saintly Tom, the angelic Eva and the sadistic Simon Legree left a deep impression on the minds and hearts of its millions of readers. Abraham Lincoln might or might not have said, on meeting Stowe, eighteen months after Fort Sumter, "So this is the little lady who made this big war," but the plausibility of the statement made it stick in literary lore.

CHARLES SUMNER WON far fewer friends to the antislavery cause than Harriet Beecher Stowe, but he made almost as many enemies of slavery's advocates as Henry Beecher. The senator from Massachusetts was a striking figure, tall and powerful, with a full mane of hair. He had attended the Boston Latin School as a young man, and when he entered politics, he littered his speeches with sufficient Latinisms to give his rotund delivery a Ciceronian air. For this reason, it jolted many listeners to hear Sumner descend to the most scurrilous mode of personal insult in attacking slavery and all who defended it.

In May 1856, Sumner outdid himself. During a five-hour speech spread over two days, the Republican lawmaker denounced the "crime against Kansas," as he called the Kansas-Nebraska Act and the events the law set in motion. It was a particularly lurid crime, Sumner said: "It is the rape of a virgin territory, compelling it to the hateful embrace of slavery; and it may be clearly traced to a depraved longing for a new slave state, the hideous offspring of such a crime."

Sumner dredged classical history for parallels to the corruption that had produced the travail of Kansas, but the worst from the days of Nero and Caligula "were small by the side of the wrongs of Kansas, where the very shrines of popular institutions, more sacred than any heathen altar, have been desecrated; where the ballot-box, more precious than any work in ivory or marble, from the cunning hand of art, has been plundered." Sumner glared about the Senate. "Are you against sacrilege?" he demanded. "I present it for your execration. Are you against robbery? I hold it up for your scorn. Are you for the protection of American citizens? I show you how their dearest rights have been cloven down, while a tyrannical usurpation has sought to install itself on their very necks!"

Sumner's recounting of recent history could have been delivered by Henry Beecher or Abraham Lincoln, so far as it traced the facts. Where Sumner left Beecher and Lincoln behind was in his characterization of the men he held responsible. Two in particular drew his wrath: Stephen Douglas and Andrew Butler, a Democratic senator from South Carolina.

Elaborating, Sumner called Douglas "the squire of slavery, its very Sancho Panza, ready to do all its humiliating offices." Douglas had delivered Kansas to the slave power, bound hand and foot. Or so he had attempted. Sumner dared him to follow up. "I tell him now that he cannot enforce any such submission. The senator, with the slave power at his back, is strong, but he is not strong enough for this purpose. He is bold. He shrinks from nothing. Like Danton, he may cry, '*l'audace! l'audace! toujours l'audace!*' but even his audacity cannot compass this work." Switching back to his classical theme, Sumner said of Douglas, "He may convulse this country with civil feud. Like the ancient madman, he may set fire to this temple of constitutional liberty, grander than the Ephesian dome; but he cannot force obedience to that tyrannical usurpation."

Andrew Butler was the Don Quixote to Douglas's Sancho Panza. A sponsor with Douglas of the Kansas-Nebraska Act, Butler was also a conspicuous representative of the South Carolina school of hair-trigger defensiveness on slavery. Sumner called Butler a blowhard and an ignoramus. "There was no extravagance of the ancient parliamentary debate which he did not repeat; nor was there any possible deviation from truth which he did not make, with so much of passion, I am glad to add, as to save him from the suspicion of intentional aberration." Sumner branded Butler a fool. "He cannot ope his mouth, but out there flied a blunder." Sumner ridiculed a Butler speech impediment, mocking the senator's "incoherent phrases discharged with the loose expectoration of his speech."

But it was the Don Quixote reference, in which Sumner returned to his sexual imagery, that got the attention of his audience. "The senator from South Carolina has read many books of chivalry, and believes himself a chivalrous knight," Sumner sneered. "Of course he has chosen a mistress to whom he has made his vows, and who, though ugly to others, is always lovely to him; though polluted in the sight of the world, is chaste in his sight—I mean the harlot Slavery. For her his tongue is always profuse with words. Let her be impeached in character, or any proposition made to shut her out from the extension of her wantonness, and no extravagance of manner or hardihood of assertion is then too great for this senator."

Butler was not in the Senate that day to hear Sumner's insults. But those present anticipated trouble. Stephen Douglas had a thick skin, yet he knew the trait wasn't universal among his colleagues. "That damn fool will get himself killed by some other damn fool," Douglas muttered of Sumner from the back of the chamber.

The other damn fool proved to be Preston Brooks, a South Carolina congressman and cousin of Butler. Brooks was closer in age and strength to Sumner than Butler was, and when he learned what Sumner had said of his compatriot and kinsman, he concluded he had to respond. The allegation that rankled most was the one that made slavery Butler's mistress. It was an open secret that slave owners forced themselves upon the women they owned; the many light faces among slave children were daily testament. Yet precisely because the secret was so open, it was denied with the utmost vigor by apologists for slavery. Preston Brooks was not going to let Charles Sumner get away with this insult.

Brooks weighed challenging Sumner to a duel. But judging that a duel would dignify the charges, he settled for caning his cousin's antagonist. He entered the Senate and approached Sumner's desk. Before Sumner realized what was happening, Brooks began beating him about the head and shoulders with his heavy, gold-capped cane. Sumner tried to get away but became entangled in the desk, which was attached to the floor. By the time Brooks was finished, Sumner was an unconscious bloody mess and so badly injured he would require years to recover.

Northerners were appalled by this violence on the very floor of the Senate. Southerners sent Brooks congratulations and offered replacements for his cane, which had broken from the force of the blows.

T HE VIOLENCE AGAINST Charles Sumner touched something in
John Brown he hadn't felt before. It arrived amid a change in
Kansas he hadn't expected. The struggle against slavery there had
been developing slowly, and in a manner that appeared to favor freedom. In December 1855, Brown wrote to Mary of a recent encounter
with the enemy. "About three or four weeks ago news came that a
Free-State man by the name of Dow had been murdered by a proslavery man by the name of Coleman, who had gone and given himself up
for trial to the proslavery Governor Shannon," he said. "This was soon
followed by further news that a Free-State man who was the only
reliable witness against the murderer had been seized by a Missourian
(appointed sheriff by the bogus legislature of Kansas) upon false pre-
texts, examined, and held to bail under such heavy bonds, to answer
to those false charges, as he could not give; that while on his way
to trial, in charge of the bogus sheriff, he was rescued by some men
belonging to a company near Lawrence; and that in consequence of
the rescue Governor Shannon had ordered out all the proslavery force
he could muster in the Territory, and called on Missouri for further
help." Two thousand men had answered the call and descended on
Lawrence. They demanded the surrender of the witness and of those
who had rescued him.

A smaller number of free-state men had responded and prepared
to resist. "A battle was hourly expected," Brown said. He and his sons
considered the matter, and five of them decided to go to the aid of the
Lawrence defenders. "We then set about providing a little corn-bread
and meat, blankets, and cooking utensils, running bullets and loading
all our guns, pistols, etc. The five set off in the afternoon, and after a

short rest in the night (which was quite dark), continued our march until after daylight next morning, when we got our breakfast, started again, and reached Lawrence in the forenoon, all of us more or less lamed by our tramp."

They discovered that negotiations had begun between Governor Shannon, for the slavery side, and the principals among the free-state men. A standoff accompanied the parley, and the residents of Lawrence used the time to erect earthworks against an attack. Eventually Shannon concluded that the town wasn't worth attacking. In exchange for receiving the witness, he called off the siege and sent the Missourians home.

"So ended this last Kansas invasion," Brown told Mary, "the Missourians returning with *flying colors,* after incurring heavy expenses, suffering great exposure, hardships, and privations, not having fought any battles, burned or destroyed any infant towns or Abolition presses; leaving the Free-State men organized and armed, and in full possession of the Territory; not having fulfilled any of all their dreadful threatenings, except to murder one *unarmed* man, and to commit some robberies and waste of property upon defenseless families, unfortunately within their power. We learn by their papers that they boast of a great victory over the Abolitionists; and well they may." But their boasts disguised the setback they had suffered. "Free-State men have only hereafter to retain the footing they have gained, and *Kansas is free,*" Brown wrote.

RETAINING THE FREE-STATE footing was no easy task. The winter of 1855–56 tested the endurance and faith of everyone in Kansas. "The weather continues very severe, and it is now nearly six weeks that the snow has been almost constantly driven, like dry sand, by the fierce winds of Kansas," Brown wrote in February. "Thermometer on Sunday and Monday at twenty-eight to twenty-nine degrees below zero. Ice in the river, in the timber, and under the snow, eighteen inches thick." The slavery partisans regained their confidence and renewed their harassment of the free-staters. "We have just learned of some new and shocking outrages at Leavenworth, and that the Free-State people there have fled to Lawrence, which place is again threatened with an attack. Should that take place, we may soon again be called upon to 'buckle on our armor,' which by the help of God we will do."

The slavery offensive escalated. "Camps were formed at different points along the highways and on the Kansas River, and peaceful travelers subjected to detention, robbery and insult," a free-state man recounted. "Men were stopped in the streets and on the open prairie, and bidden to stand and deliver their purses at the peril of their lives. Cattle, provisions, arms and other property were taken whenever found, without consent of the owners. Men were choked from their horses, which were seized by the marauders, and houses were broken open and pillaged of their contents."

The slavery men again invaded Lawrence. Their leader was David Atchison, who rode with a band calling itself the Kickapoo Rangers. "Boys, this day I am a Kickapoo Ranger, by God!" the now-former senator declared. "This day we have entered Lawrence with 'Southern rights' inscribed upon our banner, and not one damned abolitionist dared to fire a gun. Now, boys, this is the happiest day of my life. We have entered that damned town, and taught the damned abolitionists a lesson that they will remember until the day they die. And now, boys, we will go in again, with our highly honorable Jones"—the sheriff of the county, who provided respectable cover for the invasion—"and test the strength of that damned Free-State Hotel, and teach the Emigrant Aid Company that Kansas will be ours. Boys, ladies should, and I hope will, be respected by every gentleman. But when a woman takes upon herself the garb of a soldier, by carrying a Sharp's rifle, then she is no longer worthy of respect. Trample her under your feet as you would a snake!" Atchison looked around the group, and his voice grew more determined. "If one man or woman dare stand before you, blow them to hell with a chunk of cold lead," he demanded.

The slavery army responded with cheers. They rampaged through the town, scattering the residents, who ran for cover. They took hammers and axes to the presses and offices of the antislavery newspapers, smashing equipment, shattering furniture, ruining paper and other supplies. They positioned a small cannon, hauled to the town for the purpose, in front of the Free State Hotel and fired away. The first shot flew over the roof of the building. Subsequent shots penetrated the walls but left the structure standing. The invaders then decided to blow up the building. Piling kegs of gunpowder inside, they lit a fuse and ran. The powder went off, but still the building stood. Finally they applied torches to the wooden interior. Soon the building was a raging inferno. The mob cheered as the beams of the floors and roof crashed down.

As the fire burned itself out, leaving a smoking hulk, the ruffians helped themselves to personal effects the terrified residents had left in their flight. By evening the ruffians' triumph was complete, and they rode off, satisfied at the blow they had struck for slavery.

JOHN BROWN LEARNED of the sack of Lawrence at about the same time he heard of the bludgeoning of Charles Sumner. The two events dispelled any lingering illusions in Brown and other antislavery men that they were on the verge of victory. "We here have passed through an almost constant series of very trying events," Brown wrote to Mary. "We were called to go to the relief of Lawrence, May 22, and every man (eight in all), except Orson, turned out; he staying with the women and children, and to take care of the cattle. John was captain of a company to which Jason belonged; the other six were a little company by ourselves. On our way to Lawrence we learned that it had been already destroyed, and we encamped with John's company overnight. Next day our little company left, and during the day we stopped and searched three men."

Brown blamed the slavery marauders for the sack of Lawrence, but he also blamed the men of Lawrence itself for acting "in a very *cowardly* manner." He determined to put some spine into the free-staters. "On the second day and evening after we left John's men, we encountered quite a number of proslavery men, and took quite a number prisoners," he told Mary. "Our prisoners we let go; but we kept some four or five horses. We were immediately after this accused of murdering five men at Pottawatomie, and great efforts have since been made by the Missourians and their ruffian allies to capture us."

W HAT JOHN BROWN did not say in this letter, and what he
likely never told Mary, was that the accusation of murder of the
five men on Pottawatomie Creek was true. Brown had grown
frustrated, then infuriated, by the impunity of the slavery forces in
wreaking their violence, whether in Kansas or Washington. For the
breakdown of law and order in Kansas he blamed the Franklin Pierce
administration, which had given carte blanche to the slavery side. "A
number of United States soldiers are quartered in this vicinity for the
ostensible purpose of removing intruders from certain Indian lands,"
Brown wrote to Ohio congressman Joshua Giddings, whom he had
met. "It is, however, believed that the administration has no thought
of removing the Missourians from the Indian lands, but that the real
object is to have these men in readiness to act in the enforcement of
those *Hellish enactments* of the (so-called) Kansas Legislature, absolutely abominated by a great majority of the inhabitants of the Territory, and spurned by them up to this time." Brown had lost hope in
the federal government. "I confidently believe that the next movement
on the part of the administration and its proslavery masters will be to
drive the people here either to submit to those infernal enactments or
to assume what will be termed *treasonable grounds* by shooting down
the poor soldiers of the country with whom they have no quarrel
whatever." Brown made his warning clearer in his plea for help: "I
ask in the name of Almighty God; I ask in the name of our venerated
forefathers; I ask in the name of all that good or true men ever held
dear—will Congress suffer us to be driven to such 'dire extremities'?
Will anything be done?"

Giddings tried to calm Brown. "You need have no fear of the

troops," the congressman replied. "The President will never *dare* employ the troops of the United States to shoot the citizens of Kansas. The death of the first man by the troops will involve every free state in your own fate. It will light up the fire of civil wars throughout the North, and we shall stand or fall with you."

Yet Brown wasn't mollified, and neither were many of the other antislavery men in Kansas. A group of them gathered to protest the Pierce administration's support of the slavery side and to register their determination to resist the acts of the bogus Kansas legislature. "We utterly repudiate the authority of that legislature as a body emanating not from the people of Kansas but elected and forced upon us by a foreign vote," they declared. "We pledge to one another mutual support and aid in a forcible resistance to any attempt to compel us with obedience to those enactments."

They soon had something to resist. A judge appointed by the territorial legislature set up court at Dutch Henry's Crossing, where a pro-slavery settler named Henry Sherman—Dutch Henry, for his German (*deutsch*) origins—operated a ferry over Pottawatomie Creek. John Brown heard that the judge, Sterling Cato, had issued warrants for his arrest and the arrest of some of his sons. The charge was unclear, but the Browns were known to be antislavery men, and it involved one or more of the antislavery activities outlawed by the legislature. At the same time a large band of pro-slavery militia arrived in the area, presumably to enforce the warrants.

John Brown determined to investigate. "My father, in order to ascertain what their future purposes were, took his surveyors' instruments and flag men and chain men and run a line right into their camp," Brown's son Salmon recalled later. "I carried one end of the chain. At this time all the administration's surveyors were Southern sympathizers. That made us all hail fellows well met. They talked very freely. They said they came here to help the South first and themselves next, but there was one thing they would do—they would annihilate every one of those damned Browns, and they would stay with Judge Cato until every damned abolitionist was in hell."

Salmon Brown recalled the reaction of Brown and his crew. "We went home well nerved up for future action. They"—the slavery men—"did not know at that time that they were talking to old Puritan stock."

JOHN BROWN DECIDED to strike preemptively. A man named Henry Williams arrived in a camp of antislavery men that included Brown and his sons. "Williams knew everybody on the Pottawatomie," Salmon Brown recalled. "My father told him we were going back to Pottawatomie to break up Cato's court and get away with some of his vile emissaries before they could get away with us. 'I mean to steal a march on the slave hounds.'" Williams offered to provide names of Cato's abettors. Salmon Brown observed closely. "I stood within two feet of him while he wrote down the names of all the men that were killed," he said, referring to the Pottawatomie victims.

In the camp was a grindstone, which Brown and his sons put to use. "We ground up our broad swords on that grindstone," Salmon Brown said, referring to some archaic but deadly weapons his father had brought to Kansas. All in the camp understood what the broadswords were for. "We started off with the cheers of quite a crowd with their hats in the air, they knowing the purport of our mission."

The death squad consisted of John Brown; his sons Owen, Frederick, Salmon and Oliver; his son-in-law Henry Thompson; and a man named Theodore Weiner. For transport John Brown approached James Townsley, a free-state man who owned a lumber wagon. Townsley consented to help, though he later reconsidered. An observer of the preparations asked Brown himself to reconsider and exercise caution. Brown retorted vehemently, "Caution! Caution, sir! I am eternally tired of hearing that word *caution*. It is nothing but the word of cowardice."

The party set out. En route to the Pottawatomie settlement, they encountered riders coming the other way. One of the riders asked Brown's party what they were about. "They gave us no answer except that they were going to attend to very urgent business," the rider recalled. A second rider remembered John Brown voicing his indignation at the trespasses of the slavery men. "His manner was wild and frenzied, and the whole party watched with excited eagerness every word or motion of the old man," the second rider said. He added, "As I left them, he requested me not to mention the fact that I had met them."

Brown's party traveled through the night to a spot about a mile from the Pottawatomie settlement. At the edge of a wood they rested during the following day; the men were weary, and Brown insisted on waiting until night. "The reason for taking the night for our work was that it was impossible to take the men in the daytime," Salmon Brown explained.

Night fell. Brown waited a while longer. Finally, after ten o'clock, when the men on the killing list could be expected to be in bed, he led the group into the Pottawatomie hamlet. The first cabin they approached belonged to a pro-slavery man named James Doyle. Some dogs began barking loudly. "Old man Townsley went after the dogs with a broad sword, and he and my brother Fred soon had them all laid out," Salmon Brown said.

Mahala Doyle, the wife of James, remembered the terrifying moment. "We were all in bed, when we heard some persons come into the yard and rap at the door and call for Mr. Doyle, my husband," she told investigators. "This was about 11 o'clock on Saturday night of the 24th of May." James Doyle got up and went to the door. Without opening it, he asked what was wanted. One of Brown's men said they were looking for a man named Wilkinson. Would Doyle tell them where he lived? "My husband opened the door, and several came into the house, and said that they were from the army. My husband was a pro-slavery man. They told my husband that he and the boys must surrender, they were their prisoners. These men were armed with pistols and large knives. They first took my husband out of the house, then they took two of my sons—the two oldest ones, William and Drury—out, and then took my husband and these two boys, William and Drury, away. My son John was spared, because I asked them in tears to spare him. In a short time afterwards I heard the report of pistols. I heard two reports, after which I heard moaning, as if a person was dying; then I heard a wild whoop." And then silence. "My husband and two boys, my sons, did not come back any more," Mrs. Doyle ended her account.

Salmon Brown described the killings from the side of the killers. "The three Doyles were taken out of the house and a half mile or so away, and were slain with the broad swords," he said. "Owen Brown cut down one of them and another son"—likely Salmon himself, though he declined to admit it directly—"cut down the other and the old man Doyle."

Who fired the shots Mahala Doyle said she heard is unclear. Salmon Brown said no one besides his father fired a gun, but he also said, "Father never raised his hand in slaying these men." Conceivably John Brown shot one or more of the men after they were already dead. Or Salmon Brown was mistaken or lying. John Brown himself later said he did not kill anyone that night.

John Doyle, the son saved by his mother's tears, had nothing to offer about who did the killing, but he described the grisly result. "The next morning was Sunday, the 25th of May, 1856," he told investigators. "I went in search of my father and two brothers. I found my father and one brother, William, lying dead in the road, about two hundred yards from the house; I saw my other brother lying dead on the ground, about one hundred and fifty yards from the house, in the grass, near a ravine; his fingers were cut off; and his arms were cut off; his head was cut open; there was a hole in his breast. William's head was cut open, and a hole was in his jaw, as though it was made by a knife, and a hole was also in his side. My father was shot in the forehead and stabbed in the breast."

AFTER DISPATCHING the Doyles, the killers moved on. "We were disturbed by the barking of the dog," said Louisa Jane Wilkinson, the wife of Allen Wilkinson. "I was sick with the measles, and woke up Mr. Wilkinson, and asked if he heard the noise, and what it meant? He said it was only someone passing about, and soon after was again asleep."

But the dog resumed its barking. Louisa Wilkinson saw a shadow pass by the window and heard a knock at the door. "Who is it?" she asked. No one answered. She woke her husband. "Who is it?" he said.

This time came a reply: "I want you to tell me the way to Dutch Henry's."

Wilkinson started to answer through the door.

"Come out and show us."

Louisa grasped her husband and whispered to him not to go. He told the men outside that he couldn't find his clothes in the dark. He could give them directions from inside the house.

One of Brown's party, likely Brown himself, demanded that Wilkinson open the door. "If you don't open it, we will open it for you."

Wilkinson acceded, though his wife told him not to. "Four men came in, and my husband was told to put on his clothes," Louisa recalled. "They asked him if there were not more men about; they searched for arms, and took a gun and powder flask; all the weapon that was about the house. I begged them to let Mr. Wilkinson stay with me, saying that I was sick and helpless, and could not stay by myself. My husband also asked them to let him stay with me until he could get someone to wait on me; told them that he would not run off, but would be there the next day, or whenever called for."

John Brown pondered the request. "The old man, who seemed to be in command, looked at me and then around at the children"—the Wilkinsons had an eight-year-old and a five-year-old—"and replied, 'You have neighbors,'" Louisa recounted.

"So I have, but they are not here, and I cannot go for them," she answered.

"It matters not," said John Brown, who repeated his order that Wilkinson dress.

"My husband wanted to put on his boots and get ready, so as to be protected from the damp and night air, but they wouldn't let him," Louisa recalled. "They then took my husband away."

A minute or two later, Louisa thought she heard her husband's voice. But she couldn't be sure. She went to the door. Not a sound came from outside.

"Next morning Mr. Wilkinson was found about one hundred and fifty yards from the house, in some dead brush," Louisa said. "A lady who saw my husband's body said that there was a gash in his head and in his side; others said that he was cut in the throat twice."

Louisa added, still trying to understand what had happened, "My husband was a quiet man, and was not engaged in arresting or disturbing anybody. He took no active part in the pro-slavery cause, so as to aggravate the abolitionists; but he was a pro-slavery man."

THE KILLERS HAD one more call to make. Around two o'clock on the morning of May 25, James Harris and his wife heard a noise at their door, Harris later told investigators. "We were aroused by a company of men who said they belonged to the Northern army, and who were each armed with a sabre and two revolvers, two of whom I recognized, namely, a Mr. Brown, whose given name I do not remember, commonly known by the appellation of 'old man Brown,' and his son, Owen Brown."

John Brown and the others forced open the door. "They came in the house and approached the bed side where we were lying, and ordered us, together with three other men who were in the same house with me, to surrender; the Northern army was upon us, and it would be no use for us to resist." The three men were William Sherman, John Whiteman and a stranger whom Harris didn't know. "They had bought a cow from Henry Sherman and intended to go home the next morning," Harris said.

Brown and the others approached the bed where Harris and his wife remained. "Some had drawn sabres in their hands, and some revolvers. They then took into their possession two rifles and a Bowie knife, which I had there in the room—there was but one room in my house—and afterwards ransacked the whole establishment in search of ammunition."

Brown's party seized the man Harris didn't know and took him outside, apparently for questioning. He wasn't the one they were looking for. "He came back. They then took me out, and asked me if there were any more men about the place. I told them there were not. They searched the place but found none others but we four. They asked me where Henry Sherman was."

Harris said he was out looking for lost cattle.

"They asked if I had ever taken any hand in aiding pro-slavery men in coming to the Territory of Kansas, or had ever taken any hand in the last troubles at Lawrence, and asked me whether I had ever done the Free State party any harm or ever intended to do that party any harm; they asked me what made me live at such a place."

Harris replied that he hadn't done anyone harm. As to why he was in Kansas: "I then answered that I could get higher wages there than anywhere else." Whites in Missouri often complained about the low wages that resulted from competition with slaves. Harris hoped to do better in Kansas.

"Old Mr. Brown and his son then went into the house with me. The other three men, Mr. William Sherman, Mr. Whiteman, and the stranger were in the house all this time. After old man Brown and his son went into the house with me, old man Brown asked Mr. Sherman to go out with him, and Mr. Sherman then went out with old Mr. Brown, and another man came into the house in Brown's place."

Harris and the others in the house heard nothing for fifteen minutes. Then came a shot. The two men standing guard on the Harrises and the others left quickly.

"That morning about ten o'clock I found William Sherman dead in the creek near my house," James Harris said. "I was looking for Mr. Sherman, as he had not come back; I thought he had been murdered. I took Mr. William Sherman out of the creek and examined him. Mr. Whiteman was with me. Sherman's skull was split open in two places and some of his brains was washed out by the water. A large hole was cut in his breast, and his left hand was cut off except a little piece of skin on one side."

JASON BROWN HAD not accompanied his father and brothers on the killing mission to Pottawatomie Creek. He and John Brown Jr. were riding with a body of free-state militia. But the next morning they got wind of the slaughter. "A man rode up to us from the south, saying that five pro-slavery men had been killed on the Pottawatomie creek and horribly cut and mutilated, and that old John Brown and his party had done it," Jason recalled. He remembered being stunned by the report. "The thought that it might be true, that my father and his company could do such a thing was terrible, and nearly deprived me of my reason for the time."

He pulled himself together sufficiently to confront his father when John Brown's party returned to their camp. "I then asked him if he had anything to do with the killing of the pro-slavery men on the Pottawatomie."

John Brown looked his son in the eye. "I did not do it, but I approved of it," he said.

Jason objected that whoever did it, it was a wicked act and uncalled for.

"God is my judge, and the people of Kansas will yet justify my course," John Brown declared.

WHATEVER GOD THOUGHT of the murders, Kansas took a while to come around. The bloodletting shocked both sides in the quarrel. An officer of the U.S. cavalry, stationed at Fort Leavenworth and responsible for keeping the peace in Kansas, summarized much of the response. "No one can defend the action of the marshal's posse at Lawrence, in burning the hotel, destroying the printing-press, and other outrages; but no life was lost, no one was threatened or felt himself in danger," the major said. The reprisal was outrageously excessive. "Five men were taken out of their beds, their throats cut, their ears cut off, their persons gashed more horribly than our savages have ever done." He hoped the respectable class of free-state settlers would repudiate the Pottawatomie killings. "I cannot think that they countenance such acts."

The respectable class of settlers did indeed denounce the murders. "An outrage of the darkest and foulest nature has been committed in our midst by some midnight assassins unknown, who have taken five of our citizens at the hour of midnight from their homes and families, and murdered and mangled them in the most awful manner," said a resolution approved by a body of settlers gathered in the wake of the killings. To prevent a recurrence of the ghastly deed, the group resolved, "We will from this time lay aside all sectional and political feelings and act together as men of reason and common sense." They swore to oppose the virulent denunciations of one side against the other that had contributed to the violence. They would repudiate the armed militias, and they would work "to ferret out and hand over to the criminal authorities the perpetrators for punishment."

Henceforth John Brown was a wanted man. The others of his killing crew were wanted, too, but "Old Man Brown" was widely conceived to be the mastermind of murders and the most dangerous of the antislavery guerrillas in Kansas.

TWO OF HIS SONS felt the weight of the father's infamy first. Pro-slavery forces at once began searching for the Browns; they soon laid hands on John and Jason. Although John and Jason had *not* gone with their father that night, they were seized and treated harshly. "Brother Jason and I occupied a room which contained a bed and a small lamp-stand or table," John recalled of their detention. "Two others also occupied the room as guards. The early part of the night of this day had been spent by our guards at card playing at the little table. Jason, without removing his clothes, had lain down on the front side of the bed, and was in deep sleep. Occupying in like manner the side of the bed next the wall, at about midnight, as near as I can judge, I was awakened by the sudden opening of the outside door and the rushing in of a number of men with drawn bowie knives. Seizing the candle and saying, 'Which are they?' they crowded about our bed with uplifted knives. Believing that our time had come, and wishing to save Jason, still asleep, from prolonged suffering, I opened the bosom of his shirt and pointing to the region of his heart, said, 'Strike here.'"

Just then dogs started barking outside. The intruders, inferring the approach of someone, lost their desire to slay the Brown boys and scattered. John explained, "At Pottawatomie father had become to slave-holders and their allies in Kansas an omnipresent dread. Filled with forebodings of evil by day, he was the specter of their imaginings at night. Owing to that fear our lives were saved."

But their trials hadn't ended. "The next day we were placed in the custody of Captain Walker, of United States Cavalry, a Southerner who himself tied my arms back in such a manner as to produce the most intense suffering," John said. "Giving the other end of the rope to a sergeant, I was placed a little in advance of the column headed by Captain Walker, and to avoid being trampled by the horses which had been ordered to trot, I was driven at this pace in the hot sun to Osawatomie, a distance of about nine miles. The rope had been tied so tightly as to stop circulation. Instead of loosening the rope when we arrived at camp, a mile south of town, no change was made in it through that day, all of the following night, nor until about noon the next day. By that time my arms and hands had swollen to nearly double size, and turned black as if mortified."

The Brown brothers were eventually taken to Leavenworth and held as something between violators of the territorial laws and prisoners of war. The confusion about their status reflected a broader confusion about what was happening in Kansas. Had the affairs of Kansas been left to actual Kansas settlers, the murders on Pottawatomie Creek might have been handled as the crimes they were. But had the affairs of Kansas been left to the Kansans, John Brown wouldn't have been there, and neither would the other outsiders for whom Kansas was chiefly a piece in a larger contest. The South considered the killings cause for war, if not evidence of war itself. "WAR! WAR!" screamed a Missouri paper. "Eight Pro-Slavery Men Murdered by the Abolitionists . . . LET SLIP THE DOGS OF WAR!" Another Missouri paper demanded, "For every Southern man thus butchered, a decade"—ten—"of these poltroons should bite the dust." *DeBow's Review,* a New Orleans monthly then being published in Washington so its editor could moonlight in the Pierce administration, reprinted an assertion by some pro-slavery Kansans calling themselves the Law and Order party, asserting that "a state of civil war and insurrection exists among us." The review's editor urged Southern solidarity in the face of the outrages in Kansas. "The cause is one to which, without loss of a single day, every Southern man should contribute," he declared. "Those familiar with the state of affairs in Kansas *know* that it can only be abolitionized by the supineness of the people of this section, whose all is at stake in these contests."

JOHN BROWN DIDN'T at once see the papers calling for war, yet he girded for battle just the same. A week after the Pottawatomie killings, Brown learned that a band of Missourians had commenced his pursuit. He went to meet them, spoiling for a fight. "We started about 4 o'clock Sunday afternoon, going over the prairie without regard to any road, and continued the search until near midnight, which was very dark," Owen Brown recalled. "Then Father ordered a halt, and the horses to be picketed (we were all mounted)." They slept for two hours, and moved on. "Between daybreak and sunrise we noticed a man on horseback about a mile east of us. When we were within a half-mile of him he fired his gun and fled." John Brown took this as evidence the enemy was near.

Brown's party numbered fewer than a dozen; an accompanying free-state party, led by Samuel Shore, was perhaps twice as large. "On reaching the Black Jack oaks, Father ordered us to dismount and tie our horses to the trees," Owen continued. From there they advanced afoot. "On reaching the high ground where their guard had stood we could plainly see the Missourians' camp, a half-mile distant, with their tents and covered wagons drawn up in front, and a number of horses and mules picketed on the higher ground beyond. This camp (under command of Capt. H. C. Pate, as we found later) was on a point of land lying between two ravines, at this time dry." Henry Pate had been a leader at the sack of Lawrence; more recently he was the captor of Jason and John Brown Jr.

"Father ordered us to form a skirmish line, and Pate's men commenced firing at us," Owen Brown said. "When within rifle range Capt. Shore ordered his men to halt, and, though in a very exposed position, they bravely began in earnest to return the fire. Father directed us to reserve our fire, and to follow him in a diagonal direction into the larger ravine. Pate's men gave us the full benefit of their shooting, their bullets cutting the grass around us in a lively way. Though I do not think I was much scared, I noticed I felt very light on my feet, as if marching fast would be no effort."

Brown maneuvered his men across a low spot toward Pate's position. "Father placed us at short range, behind a natural bank in the bend of the ravine, so that their wagons afforded them no protection from our fire. During the time we were taking this position Capt. Shore kept up a constant firing, and by the time our men were located, he ordered his men to lie down and shoot from that position. At much shorter range we shot at any of Pate's men we could see, and into their tents." The fire from the free-staters drove the slavery men back into another ravine.

Sam Shore's fighters came up closer. "Carpenter, one of his men, had a Sharp's carbine, and rather recklessly exposing himself, in spite of warning, was soon badly wounded," Owen Brown said. "Henry Thompson, my brother-in-law, was so anxious to get a shot at them that he went higher up on the bank, and continued to shoot from there whenever he could see a man. I cautioned Henry, as I had Carpenter, that he was making too good a mark of himself, and that he ought to come back more below the bank. A few minutes later, while he was on his knees loading his gun, a musket ball hit him below the shoulder and passed under the shoulder blade. Falling, he rolled down the bank and lay there several minutes, the blood flowing freely. He then got up and saying, 'Boys, I'm going to do those fellows all the good I can while I live,' he resumed his firing from his former position. This he kept up until his whole left side was red with blood, when he fainted and fell again. One or two of Capt. Shore's men then took him away."

Both sides managed to find cover. The shooting continued sporadically for more than two hours. The sun rose higher and began to punish the combatants. "The heat by this time was intense, and we suffered much for want of water," Owen Brown said. "Some of Capt. Shore's men now left us, saying they were out of ammunition, and others went around to a high point of ground where they were not much exposed."

John Brown sought to keep his own fighters from retreating too. "Hold your ground, boys," he said, even as he gave the order to shoot the enemy's horses and mules, to prevent the Missourians' escape. Shore meanwhile confirmed that his men were out of ammunition. He asked Owen Brown if he thought they might retire from the field. "Perhaps it is best," Owen replied.

John Brown didn't like this answer. When he discovered that one of his own men had followed the example of Shore's fighters, he gave another order: "The first man that attempts to leave we will shoot." All stayed.

The outflanked Missourians had things worse. Several of Pate's men abandoned the field. Frederick Brown, who had been ordered by his father to remain with the horses, couldn't bear to miss the fight; now he galloped around the Missourians' camp, waving a sword and yelling, "Father, we have got them surrounded, and have cut off their communications." The Missourians fired at Frederick, but none of their bullets hit him.

The Missourians recognized that their position was untenable. A white handkerchief went up from their lines, attached to a ramrod. Not all the free-staters saw it, and some kept firing. The Missourians' commander, Pate, reiterated the message, seizing the white flag and stepping forward. "We are government officers sent out in pursuit of criminals," he declared. "You are fighting against the United States."

Owen Brown was the first to answer. "You are just the kind of government officers we want to fight—the kind that burned Lawrence, yes, and robbed and killed free-state men," he said.

John Brown hadn't seen the flag, but he noticed that the firing had ceased. Pate repeated to him what he had said to Owen. Brown replied, "If this is all you have to say, I have something to say to you. I demand of you an unconditional surrender."

Pate refused, whereupon Brown leveled his weapon at Pate, in plain sight of the other Missourians. Brown shouted at them what he had said to Pate.

One of the Missourians, Pate's second-in-command, replied, "We don't surrender unless our captain gives the order." The Missourians cocked their weapons and aimed at Brown.

Brown said to his men, "Put a dozen balls through the first man of them that shoots." Brown placed the muzzle of his Colt revolver almost against Pate's heart. "Give the order!" he demanded of Pate.

Pate hesitated but a moment. He gave the order.

The Battle of Black Jack was indecisive. Pate afterward claimed, not unreasonably, that Brown had violated the truce flag. And although Brown intended an exchange of Pate's surrendered fighters for free-state prisoners, including John and Jason, the arrival of a federal force compelled him to release the prisoners captured that day. His sons continued to languish.

Even so, Black Jack marked a turn in the struggle for Kansas. The violence to this point had been unorganized; Black Jack was the initial engagement of organized forces, one for slavery and the other against. In time some would call it the first battle of the Civil War.

AUGUST BONDI, an Austrian immigrant who, like many immigrants, found slavery simultaneously puzzling and appalling, was one of those who served with John Brown. He hadn't expected to take up arms against slavery, but he fell under Brown's spell. "He exhibited at all times the most affectionate care for each of us," Bondi later said of Brown. The men of Brown's company were often on short rations, chiefly pan bread and molasses, washed down with water drawn from Ottawa Creek, which ran near a camp they occupied during this period. "Nevertheless we kept in excellent spirits; we considered ourselves as one family, allied to one another by the consciousness that it was our duty to undergo all these privations to further the good cause; had determined to share any danger with one another, that victory or death might find us together."

Brown did the cooking, simple as it was. He said the blessing before each meal. "He was an orthodox Christian," Bondi recalled, adding, "Some of his sons were free-thinkers, regarding which he remarked that he had tried to give his children a good education, and now they were old enough to choose for themselves."

Brown lectured his men on the code of conduct for their cause. "Time and again he entreated us never to follow the example of the border ruffians, who took a delight in destruction; never to burn houses or fences, so often done by the enemy." As to killing: "Repeatedly he admonished us not to take human life except when absolutely necessary."

Bondi seems not to have asked the obvious question: Had it been necessary to kill the five men on Pottawatomie Creek? Rather, like the others drawn by Brown's stern charisma, he was willing to accept Brown's verdict on who should live and who die.

Bondi never before or after felt such kinship and purpose. "We were united as a band of brothers by the love and affection towards the man who with tender words and wise counsel, in the depths of the wilderness of Ottawa Creek, prepared a handful of young men for the work of laying the foundation of a free commonwealth."

JAMES REDPATH DIDN'T join John Brown's band of fighters; he carried a pen rather than a rifle. Yet he too felt Brown's magnetism. Redpath was another immigrant, from England, and he wrote for Horace Greeley's staunchly antislavery *New York Tribune*. He read about Brown after the Pottawatomie killings, and he went to investigate.

He rode slowly through a forested stretch along Ottawa Creek. He heard a rustling at one side of the trail. "Suddenly, thirty paces before me, I saw a wild-looking man, of fine proportions, with half-a-dozen pistols of various sizes stuck in his belt, and a large Arkansas bowie-knife prominent among them," Redpath recorded. "His head was uncovered; his hair was uncombed; his face had not been shaved for many months. We were similarly dressed—with red-topped boots worn over the pantaloons, a coarse blue shirt, and a pistol belt. This was the usual fashion of the times."

The wild man shouted at Redpath. "Hullo! You're in our camp," he said.

Redpath had learned American ways since coming to Kansas. He drew his Colt revolver and cocked it. "Halt! Or I'll fire!" he warned.

The man stopped. He looked closely at Redpath. He declared that he had seen him before, at Lawrence. He introduced himself as Frederick Brown, son of John Brown. He was carrying a pail and had come to the creek to fetch water. Satisfying himself that Redpath was no threat, he agreed to lead the reporter to Brown.

Redpath holstered his weapon and prepared to follow. Fred Brown plunged ahead. "He talked wildly, as he walked before me, turning round every minute, as he spoke of the then recent affair of Pottawatomie," Redpath wrote. "His family, he said, had been accused of it;

he denied it indignantly, with the wild air of a maniac." Fred worked himself into such a frenzy that Redpath had to say he would listen no more until he met John Brown. Fred shrugged and walked on. Redpath could tell they were nearing the camp by the challenges given them by gruff men standing sentry. Finally the trees parted.

"I shall not soon forget the scene that here opened to my view," Redpath recounted. "Near the edge of the creek a dozen horses were tied, all ready saddled for a ride for life, or a hunt after Southern invaders. A dozen rifles and sabers were stacked against the trees. In an open space, amid the shady and lofty woods, there was a great blazing fire with a pot on it; a woman, bare-headed, with an honest, sun-burnt face, was picking blackberries from the bushes; three or four armed men were lying on red and blue blankets on the grass; and two fine-looking youths were standing, leaning on their arms, on guard, nearby." One of the young men was Salmon Brown, then nineteen.

His father was busy. "Old Brown himself stood near the fire, with his shirt-sleeves rolled up and a large piece of pork in his hand," Redpath wrote. "He was cooking a pig. He was poorly clad, and his toes protruded from his boots. The old man received me with great cordiality." The others in the camp gathered around their leader and this stranger. "But it was for a moment only, for the Captain"—John Brown—"ordered them to renew their work." Before Redpath could ask the question at the top of his reporter's list, Brown preempted him. "He respectfully but firmly forbade conversation on the Pottawatomie affair."

Redpath didn't insist. He decided to observe camp life instead. "No manner of profane language was permitted," he noted. "No man of immoral character was allowed to stay, except as a prisoner of war." John Brown imposed—or conveyed—a kind of theocracy. "He made prayers in which all the company united, every morning and evening; and no food was ever tasted by his men until the Divine blessing had been asked on it. After every meal, thanks were returned to the Bountiful Giver. Often, I was told, the old man would retire to the densest solitudes, to wrestle with his God in secret prayer. One of his company subsequently informed me that, after these retirings, he would say that the Lord had directed him in visions what to do; that, for himself, he did not love warfare, but peace—only acting in obedience to the will of the Lord, and fighting God's battles for his children's sake."

Brown himself articulated his criteria for choosing followers. "I would rather have the small-pox, yellow fever and cholera all together in my camp than a man without principles," he told Redpath. "It is a mistake, sir, that our people make when they think that bullies are the best fighters, or that they are the men fit to oppose these Southerners. Give me men of good principles, God-fearing men, men who respect themselves; and with a dozen of them, I will oppose any hundred."

Redpath came away from the camp mightily impressed. "Never before had I met such a band of men," he said. "They were not earnest, but earnestness incarnate." Harking back to the English army of Oliver Cromwell, Redpath declared, "I had seen, for the first time, the spirit of the Ironsides armed and encamped." He added another thought, or rather prediction: "I had seen the predestined leader of the second, and holier American revolution."

WILLIAM PHILLIPS ENCOUNTERED John Brown later that summer. Brown spent the month of June tending to his wounded men, recruiting more fighters and dodging arrest by the territorial authorities. But by early July the camp life was chafing his activist spirit, and he decided to return to action. A free-state counterpart to the pro-slavery Lecompton legislature was scheduled to meet in Topeka; toward Topeka he directed his band.

At Lawrence, on the way, he met Phillips, another of Horace Greeley's reporters. The meeting served the purposes of both men. Phillips got an interview with the most notorious of the antislavery partisans; Brown had the opportunity to tell his story for national circulation. Brown didn't admit anything about the Pottawatomie killings, and Phillips didn't push him. Nor did Brown share what his future intentions were, not least because he didn't know. But otherwise he opened to Phillips in a way he had to no others.

"During the day he stayed with me in Lawrence I had my first good opportunity to judge the old man's character," Phillips recorded. "I had seen him in his camp, had seen him in the field, and he was always an enigma, a strange compound of enthusiasm and cold, methodic stolidity—a volcano beneath a mountain of snow." Phillips inquired of Brown's background and learned of Brown's peripatetic lifestyle. Brown delivered his opinions on military tactics. "He criticized all the arms then in use, and showed me a fine specimen of repeating-rifle which had long-range sights, and, he said, would carry eight hundred yards; but, he added, the way to fight was to press to close quarters."

Phillips discovered that he and Brown were traveling in the same direction; Brown asked him to wait until nightfall so that they could travel together. Brown didn't want to be on the road in daylight. Night came, and the company marched for several hours through the dark before Brown called a halt to eat and rest. The summer air had cooled; the grass was wet with dew. Brown offered Phillips a part of his own ration. "I was not at all hungry, and if I had been I doubt if I could have eaten it," Phillips recalled. "It was dry beef, which was not so bad; but the bread had been made from corn bruised between stones and then rolled in balls and cooked in the coal and ashes of the camp fire. These ashes served for saleratus"—a leaven.

Brown, observing Phillips's fastidiousness, said, "I am afraid you will hardly be able to eat a soldier's harsh fare."

Phillips acknowledged that he wasn't cut out for a soldier. (He later changed his mind, serving in the Union army during the Civil War and rising to the rank of colonel.)

The simple meal over, Brown and Phillips prepared to rest. "We placed our two saddles together, so that our heads lay only a few feet apart," Phillips recounted. "He spread his blanket on the wet grass, and, when we lay together upon it, mine was spread over us." The other men slept for the three hours Brown allotted them; Brown and Phillips talked. Or, rather, Brown did the talking, with Phillips simply prompting him from time to time. "I soon found that he was a very thorough astronomer, and he enlightened me on a good many matters in the starry firmament above us. He pointed out the different constellations and their movements. 'Now,' he said, 'it is midnight,' and he pointed to the finger marks of his great clock in the sky."

The two sides of Brown that Phillips had detected during the day grew more pronounced at night. "In his ordinary moods the man seemed so rigid, stern, and unimpressible when I first knew him that I never thought a poetic and impulsive nature lay behind that cold exterior," Phillips wrote. "The whispering of the wind on the prairie was full of voices to him, and the stars as they shone in the firmament of God seemed to inspire him."

Brown contrasted the stars with humans. "How admirable is the symmetry of the heavens, how grand and beautiful," he said. "Everything moves in sublime harmony in the government of God. Not so with us poor creatures. If one star is more brilliant than the others, it is continually shooting in some erratic way into space."

Brown turned to politics. "He discussed and criticized both parties in Kansas. Of the pro-slavery men he spoke in bitterness. He said that slavery besotted everything, and made men more brutal and coarse. Nor did the free-state men escape his sharp censure. He said that we had many noble and true men, but that we had too many broken-down politicians from the older states. These men, he said, would rather pass resolutions than act, and they criticized all who did real work. A professional politician, he went on, you never could trust, for even if he had convictions, he was always ready to sacrifice his principles for his advantage."

Brown reflected on the institutions of American life. "He thought society ought to be organized on a less selfish basis; for while material interests gained something by the deification of pure selfishness, men and women lost much by it. He said that all great reforms, like the Christian religion, were based on broad, generous, self-sacrificing principles. He condemned the sale of land as chattel, and thought that there was an infinite number of wrongs to right before society would be what it should be, but that in our country slavery was the 'sum of villainies,' and its abolition the first essential work. If the American people did not take courage and end it speedily, human freedom and republican liberty would soon be empty names in these United States."

TO HELP GIVE SUBSTANCE to his vision of a free America, Brown sharpened the discipline of his followers. He crafted a covenant for his men to sign, creating the "Kansas Regulars" and designating himself as their commander. "We severally pledge our word and our sacred honor to said Commander, and to each other," they promised. They would fight "for the maintenance of the rights and liberties of the Free-State Citizens of Kansas." They would be good and faithful soldiers. "We will observe and maintain a strict and thorough military discipline at all times."

Some thirty men took the pledge during August; from this time John Brown was commonly referred to as Captain Brown. He shortly found occasion to lead the Kansas Regulars into battle. He learned that a large pro-slavery force was marching in the direction of Osawatomie, a free-state stronghold. Their appearance and boasts declared that they intended to sack the town, as their comrades had sacked Lawrence three months earlier. Brown, whose frustration at being too slow to defend Lawrence had helped trigger the Pottawatomie murders, determined to prevent another such outrage.

Brown's company beat the slavery men to Osawatomie and awaited their arrival. Soon enough the slavery partisans came within rifle range, and in a first encounter Fred Brown was shot and killed. The loss of his son steeled John Brown's resolve but unnerved some of his men, as did the revelation that they were badly outnumbered. Brown ignored their fear and summoned them to battle. "Men, come on!" he shouted, rushing in the direction of the enemy.

They took up positions from which they could snipe at the attackers, and for a time held them at bay. But as the slavery side realized how few Brown's men were, their commander ordered a charge. Brown's fighters had never faced a charge, and they didn't wait to face this one. They scattered into the woods, leaving Osawatomie undefended.

The attackers had to decide between pursuing Brown's band and completing the job they had set for themselves. They chose the latter, deeming Brown's company too insignificant to bother chasing. Their commander later said that the battle at Osawatomie was no battle at all but "merely the driving out of a flock of quail." He also claimed, "We killed about thirty of them, among the number, *certain,* a son of Old Brown, and almost certain Brown himself." To this exaggeration he added an exculpation: "The boys would burn the town to the ground. *I could not help it.*"

John Brown, having been forced to retreat after his fleeing men, looked back upon the burning town. Jason Brown recalled tears rolling down his father's face. "God sees it," John Brown said. "I have only a short time to live—only one death to die, and I will die fighting for this cause. There will be no more peace in this land until slavery is done for. I will give them something else to do than to extend slave territory. I will carry the war into Africa."

PART II

Springfield

ABRAHAM LINCOLN WOULD have known what Brown meant, had he heard what Brown said about carrying the war to Africa. But Lincoln had battles of his own that season. He was campaigning for president—not for himself, but for John C. Frémont, the Republican standard-bearer. Frémont was dashingly handsome, with the exotic looks of his French-Canadian father; adventurously accomplished, as the leader of military explorations of the Far West; accidentally rich, after being swindled into an apparently worthless California tract that turned out to sit atop the Mother Lode of the gold rush; and politically connected, to Missouri senator Thomas Hart Benton, his father-in-law. Yet no one gave the Republican nominee much chance in his party's first try at the presidency. The South was solidly against him and every other Republican. The Democrats nominated James Buchanan, a Pennsylvanian whose sympathies ran southward.

The wild card in the race was Millard Fillmore, the former president, who received the nomination of the American party—the Know-Nothings. As Lincoln took up the cudgels for Frémont, he wielded them especially against Fillmore, who had even less chance of victory than Frémont but stole anti-Buchanan votes. "I understand you are a Fillmore man," Lincoln wrote to a Springfield neighbor. "If, as between Fremont and Buchanan, you *really* prefer the election of Buchanan, then burn this without reading a line further. But if you would like to defeat Buchanan, and his gang, allow me a word with you. Does anyone pretend that Fillmore can carry the vote of this state? I have not heard a single man pretend so. Every vote taken from Fremont and given to Fillmore is just so much in favor of Buchanan.

The Buchanan men see this; and hence their great anxiety in favor of the Fillmore movement. They know where the shoe pinches. They now greatly prefer having a man of your character go for Fillmore than for Buchanan, because they expect several to go with you, who would go for Fremont if you were to go directly for Buchanan."

Where Fillmore dodged the slavery issue, Lincoln bored in on it. "The question of slavery, at the present day, should be not only the greatest question, but very nearly the sole question," he declared in one of his many speeches for the Republican ticket. "The question is simply this: Shall slavery be spread into the new territories, or not? This is the naked question." The Democrats were trying to confuse things, Lincoln said. "Our adversaries charge Fremont with being an abolitionist. When pressed to show proof, they frankly confess that they can show no such thing. They then run off upon the assertion that his supporters are abolitionists." Lincoln didn't deny that abolitionists favored Frémont over Buchanan and Fillmore. But that didn't make abolitionists out of all Republicans, or even very many of them.

The Democrats denounced the Republicans as a threat to the country. "They tell us that the Union is in danger," Lincoln said. This was the pot calling the kettle black. "Who will divide it? Is it those who make the charge? Are they themselves the persons who wish to see this result?" The Union was not in danger, Lincoln assured his listeners. "All this talk about the dissolution of the Union is humbug—nothing but folly." Speaking for the Republicans and to the Democrats, he declared, "We *won't* dissolve the Union, and you *shan't*."

Lincoln's efforts failed to elect Frémont, but they stated the Republican case eloquently. And they marked Lincoln as one who could conceivably carry the banner in days ahead. He might have been excused for thinking of himself when he declared, at a Republican postmortem, "All of us who did not vote for Mr. Buchanan, taken together, are a majority of four hundred thousand. But in the late contest we were divided between Fremont and Fillmore. Can we not come together, for the future?"

It was a fair question, and the one on which Lincoln's hopes, no less than those of his party, hung. But for the moment he was faced with the humdrum of the office. In the spring of 1857 a Republican leader in Minnesota asked Lincoln to come to St. Paul to stump for the party. Lincoln begged off. "Having devoted the most of last year to politics, it is a *necessity* with me to devote this, to my private affairs," he explained.

He threw himself into his work, spending more time in the office and in court than for many months previous. He took pains to collect fees due him, as he hadn't always done. He was making up for lost ground but also preparing for the time when a political path might open for him. What William Herndon identified as the engine of his ambition had been reengaged; it wouldn't let him stand aside for long.

AS A YOUNG MAN, Roger Taney gave no sign of becoming the most notorious defender of slavery in the history of American jurisprudence. Indeed, the evidence pointed in the opposite direction. Taney practiced law in Frederick, Maryland, just below the Mason-Dixon Line, and was married to the sister of Francis Scott Key, an advocate for the legal rights of free blacks and the amelioration of the lot of slaves (and the lyricist of America's eventual national anthem). Taney joined Key and others in a legal-aid society that battled the kidnapping of free blacks into slavery. He meanwhile emancipated eleven slaves he had inherited, keeping only two who were, as he described them, "too old, when they became my property, to provide for themselves."

In a widely noted law case Taney took the part of a Methodist preacher charged with inciting slave rebellion by a sermon sharply critical of slavery. The client was unpopular, being an outsider, from Pennsylvania, and annoyingly self-righteous besides. Taney defended the preacher on free-speech grounds, but he went beyond the necessities of the case to indict slavery itself. He declared the institution a necessary evil, at best. "It was imposed upon us by another nation, while we were yet in a state of colonial vassalage," he said. "It cannot be easily or suddenly removed. Yet while it continues, it is a blot on our national character, and every real lover of freedom confidently hopes that it will be effectually, though it must be gradually, wiped away, and earnestly looks for the means by which this necessary object may be best attained. And until it shall be accomplished, until the time shall come when we can point, without a blush, to the language held in the Declaration of Independence, every friend of humanity will seek to lighten the galling chain of slavery and better, to the utmost of his power, the wretched condition of the slave."

Taney's argument persuaded the jury, which acquitted his client. Nor did his indictment of slavery harm his political advancement. He became Maryland's attorney general and then, after campaigning vigorously for Andrew Jackson, the attorney general of the United States. He took Jackson's side against the Bank of the United States, when that institution polarized the country. And upon the death of John Marshall, Jackson promoted Taney to chief justice of the Supreme Court.

For twenty years the Taney court had little to do with the slavery question, which embroiled the rest of American government but left the federal judiciary largely alone. The Constitution gave the states control over slavery within their borders. Since independence the Northern states had abolished slavery, to no particular complaint from the South. And few Northerners, beyond the most ardent abolitionists, who cited a higher law than the Constitution, claimed the right to command Southern states to end slavery there. As for slavery in the federal territories, that was a matter for Congress: first the Congress of the Articles of Confederation, with its 1787 ordinance banning slavery north of the Ohio River, and then the Congress of the Constitution, which had approved the Missouri Compromise, the Compromise of 1850 and the Kansas-Nebraska Act.

The slave question had surfaced in presidential politics most strikingly in the election of 1844, in which Democrat James Polk campaigned on a platform demanding the annexation of slave Texas. Presidential politics had shaped the Compromise of 1850, which was crafted with the potential veto of Zachary Taylor in mind. As things happened, Taylor suddenly died, and his successor, Millard Fillmore, was happy to accept what Henry Clay and Stephen Douglas produced. From that point forward, the slave question pervaded campaigns for presidential nominations and for the presidency itself.

But the judiciary remained aloof. State courts heard individual cases like those Roger Taney took part in, but on general policy judges and justices, especially of the federal government, deferred to the politicians. They did so, at any rate, until Chief Justice Taney took up slavery in the mid-1850s. Why he did so, and why then, wasn't easy to say. Taney had long hewed to the belief that the Supreme Court and its justices should stay out of politics. "I never speak upon political issues of the day in politics, nor in mixed companies, nor do I enter into any argument, or ever express an opinion to friends who I know differ from me," he replied to a Maryland congressman who had asked him to deny reports that he favored one candidate in a particular race. And he didn't intend to start. To do otherwise would injure the court's credibility.

Yet he *did* have views, and they changed over time, especially on slavery. Taney was a proud Southerner, though no longer a slaveholder, and he considered the South under assault by the North. His son-in-law inquired about his opinions on the campaign of 1856—in particular, what would happen should victory go to Republican Frémont or Know-Nothing Fillmore? Taney professed to hear the death knell of Southern liberty in the triumph of either. Secession would provide no answer; nor would it even occur. "How can the Southern states divide, with any hope of success, when in almost every one of them there is a strong and powerful party, acting in concert with the Northern Know Nothings, and willing to hold power from the North, if they may be enabled thereby to obtain the honors and offices of the general government and domineer in their own states," he wrote. "The South is doomed to sink to a state of inferiority, and the power of the North will be exercised to gratify their cupidity and their evil passions, without the slightest regard for the Constitution." True, there were voices in the South calling for armed resistance to Northern pretensions. "There are many bold and brave men at the South who have no vassal feeling to the North," Taney said. Some might attempt to fight. "But what can they do, with a powerful enemy in their midst? I grieve over this condition of things, but it is my deliberate opinion that the South is doomed, and that nothing but a firm united action, nearly unanimous in every state, can check Northern insult and Northern aggression."

Taney's gloom reflected something personal, too. In 1855 his wife and daughter were carried off by yellow fever. Taney's family had been his refuge from the storms of public life; this refuge was now denied him. He managed to order an inscription from David's lament over Saul and Jonathan to be chiseled upon their joint grave: "Lovely and comely in their life / Even in death they were not divided." But he was devastated. Friends wondered if he would be able to carry on.

IN THE SAME YEAR that Roger Taney joined the Supreme Court, Dred Scott traveled to Illinois. Scott was a black man, born into slavery in southern Virginia and transported by his owner to Alabama and then Missouri, where he was sold as a personal servant to an army doctor named John Emerson. The army regularly moved Emerson from post to post, and in 1836 it ordered him to a fort in Illinois. Dred Scott seems to have made no effort to claim his freedom while in Illinois, and he traveled on without recorded complaint to Wisconsin Territory, also free soil. There he married a woman named Harriet Robinson, another slave, who was sold by her owner to John Emerson. Emerson was transferred back to Missouri, but he left Dred Scott and Harriet in Wisconsin, hiring them out to fellow officers.

Emerson subsequently married Eliza Sanford and in 1840, four years after leaving Missouri with Dred Scott, sent for Scott, his wife and a daughter born to the couple. Dred Scott returned to Missouri, taking his wife and child with him. Three years later Emerson died, bequeathing the Scotts to his wife.

Dred and Harriet Scott in time decided to assert their freedom based on their residence in free territory. With the aid of lawyers not unlike the young Roger Taney, they sued their mistress. Missouri courts had formulated a "once free, always free" rule declaring that residence on free soil prevented a person transported to Missouri from being enslaved. But when the case appeared before the Missouri supreme court, that tribunal abandoned the old doctrine. "Times now are not as they were when the former decisions on this subject were made," the court explained. The Scotts were still slaves.

The Scotts turned to the federal court system. The case became *Dred Scott v. Sandford* after Mrs. Emerson transferred ownership of Dred Scott to her brother, and a clerk of the court misspelled Sanford's name. The federal district court in St. Louis ruled against Scott, who appealed to the Supreme Court.

Roger Taney was looking for a case that would give the Supreme Court a chance to rule on the issue that had tied the other branches of government in knots. He was also looking for something to ease his grief at the loss of his wife and daughter. Taney had been a Democratic political operative before becoming a judge, and he postponed a decision in the Dred Scott case until after Democrat James Buchanan was safely elected and inaugurated. Then he sallied into the midst of the fight.

In March 1857, Taney read the opinion of the court in the Dred Scott case. Taney was days from his eightieth birthday; though tall and lanky, he stooped when he walked, and his hand shook as he held the papers from which he spoke. He had outlived nearly all those who had known him in his days defending slaves; the audience in the court expected to hear from a Southerner and a Democrat. They weren't surprised when Taney and six other justices decided against Dred Scott and his family.

But many *were* surprised at the reasoning. Typically the Supreme Court decides cases on the narrowest grounds possible, setting broad precedents only when necessary. Taney had concluded that broad precedent on the slave question was quite necessary. Dred Scott's suit failed because Scott lacked standing to bring a suit in federal court, Taney said. Scott was not a citizen under the meaning of the Constitution. Nor were any other Africans or their descendants. "They had for more than a century before been regarded as beings of an inferior order, and altogether unfit to associate with the white race either in social or political relations, and so far inferior that they had no rights which the white man was bound to respect, and that the negro might justly and lawfully be reduced to slavery for his benefit," Taney read. Scott's lawyers had cited the egalitarian promise of the Declaration of Independence in their client's favor; Taney dismissed this. To be sure, Jefferson's immortal assertion about equality *seemed* to encompass "all men," as the words of the Declaration said. "But it is too clear for dispute that the enslaved African race were not intended to be included, and formed no part of the people who framed and adopted this declaration, for if the language, as understood in that day, would embrace them, the conduct of the distinguished men who framed the Declaration of Independence would have been utterly and flagrantly inconsistent with the principles they asserted, and instead of the sympathy of mankind to which they so confidently appealed, they would have deserved and received universal rebuke and reprobation." After all, Jefferson—and Washington and Madison and nearly every other Southern delegate to the Continental Congress—were slaveholders. Taney concluded from all this that Africans and their descendants in America, whether slaves or free blacks, were not citizens under the Constitution, and never could be.

Two decades earlier John Calhoun, amid a rising chorus of criticism from Northern abolitionists, had declared slavery not a necessary evil, as the young Roger Taney and most slaveholders had previously characterized it, but a "positive good." Calhoun argued that slavery uplifted Africans and their descendants, besides stabilizing Southern society. Calhoun's view gradually took hold among Southern whites, evidently including Taney, whose contribution to the ideology of white supremacy was his assertion in the Dred Scott case that blacks were a people apart, beyond the promise of the Declaration and the guarantees of the Constitution.

Yet Taney wasn't finished. He could have dismissed the case over Scott's lack of standing. But that wouldn't have served his larger purpose, which was to settle the issue of slavery in the territories once and for all. Taney, with many other Southerners by this time, deemed the Missouri Compromise to have been an infringement on Southern rights—namely, the property right of Southern slaveholders to take their slaves with them into the federal territories. Taney found warrant for his view in the Bill of Rights, which dealt chiefly, but not exclusively, with the rights of persons. "The rights of property are united with the rights of person, and placed on the same ground, by the fifth amendment to the Constitution, which provides that no person shall be deprived of life, liberty, and property, without due process of law," he wrote. "And an act of Congress which deprives a citizen of the United States of his liberty or property merely because he came himself or brought his property into a particular Territory of the United States, and who had committed no offence against the laws, could hardly be dignified with the name of due process of law." Taney continued, "Upon these considerations, it is the opinion of the court that the act of Congress which prohibited a citizen from holding and owning property of this kind in the territory of the United States north of the line therein mentioned is not warranted by the Constitution, and is therefore void."

This part of the decision was especially striking. Not only was it unnecessary to the verdict in the case, but it beat a dead horse—the Missouri Compromise—which had been put down by the Kansas-Nebraska Act. Yet the very lack of necessity for this ruling rendered Taney's meaning the more unmistakable. Congress had no power to bar slavery from the territories. The Republicans and other enemies of the South might froth and fume, but they were impotent to halt the spread of slavery.

ROGER TANEY'S RULING outraged every Republican in the land. It was bad enough, the Republicans said, that Congress had repealed the Missouri Compromise. But the repeal had not challenged the authority of Congress to legislate on slavery in the western territories; it had *reaffirmed* that authority. If Congress changed its mind and decided to reinstate the Missouri Compromise, and perhaps extend the ban on slavery to other western territories, it might do so. The Taney decision denied Congress this power. Taney had determined to end the debate on slavery in the western territories, and his decision appeared to do just that. Slavery might go into every territory. The Supreme Court had spoken; there was no more to be said.

In fact, there was *much* more to be said. The Dred Scott decision was only the second time in history that the Supreme Court had overturned a federal law. The other reversal occurred more than fifty years earlier. In that day the principle of judicial review had been novel, but the outcome of the case—*Marbury v. Madison*—favored the administration of Thomas Jefferson, who disputed the principle but didn't see fit to challenge the result. In the interim the principle had been vigorously disputed, by Andrew Jackson and Roger Taney, among others. The Supreme Court in 1819 had ruled that the Bank of the United States was constitutional; Jackson in 1832 vetoed a bill renewing the bank's charter, on grounds that it was *un*constitutional. "The Congress, the Executive, and the Court must each for itself be guided by its own opinion of the Constitution," Jackson explained in his veto message, written in part by Taney. "Each public officer who takes an oath to support the Constitution swears that he will support it as he understands it, and not as it is understood by others. It is as much the duty of the House of Representatives, of the Senate, and of the President to decide upon the constitutionality of any bill or resolution which may be presented to them for passage or approval as it is of the supreme judges when it may be brought before them for judicial decision. The opinion of the judges has no more authority over Congress than the opinion of Congress has over the judges, and on that point the President is independent of both."

Abraham Lincoln took a different tack in disputing the Supreme Court's authority in the Dred Scott case. Stephen Douglas had responded to the decision by declaring that all honest citizens must accept the court's decision as final, and that any who resisted it were enemies of democracy. Lincoln observed that Douglas had taken no such position on Jackson's veto of the bank bill, but rather had applauded the Democratic president's bold stroke. "It would be interesting for him to look over his recent speech, and see how exactly his fierce philippics against us for resisting Supreme Court decisions fall upon his own head," Lincoln said.

Inconsistency aside, Lincoln taxed Douglas for treating the Dred Scott verdict as the final word on the question of slavery in the territories. "Judicial decisions are of greater or less authority as precedents, according to circumstances," Lincoln said. Unanimous decisions commanded great respect, as did those that built on earlier decisions and were soundly rooted in historical fact. These conditions were absent in the Dred Scott case. The verdict was not unanimous but divided, 7 to 2. It continued no trend of decisions. And it was based on bad history—very bad history, Lincoln said. "Chief Justice Taney, in delivering the opinion of the majority of the Court, insists at great length that negroes were no part of the people who made, or for whom was made, the Declaration of Independence or the Constitution of the United States." This was simply wrong. "In five of the then thirteen states, to wit, New Hampshire, Massachusetts, New York, New Jersey and North Carolina, free negroes were voters, and, in proportion to their numbers, had the same part in making the Constitution that the white people had." Taney inferred from the present disabilities imposed on Negroes that things had always been so, or worse. This, too, was plainly false. In the early days of the republic, manumission was straightforward and often applauded; by the present decade it had become nearly impossible. "In those days, our Declaration of Independence was held sacred by all, and thought to include all; but now, to aid in making the bondage of the negro universal and eternal, it is assailed, and sneered at, and construed, and hawked at, and torn, till, if its framers could rise from their graves, they could not at all recognize it. All the powers of earth seem rapidly combining against him. Mammon is after him; ambition follows, and philosophy follows, and the theology of the day is fast joining the cry." The Supreme Court, in the Dred Scott case, had lent its weight to the oppression.

Lincoln didn't intend to resist the ruling of the court in the case—not that there was anything he or anyone else might effectively resist. But he hoped the court would change its mind. It might do so after reflecting on the criticism he and others offered. More likely, it would do so as a result of a change in personnel. Justices grew old and left the bench. New justices, unbeholden to the slave power, would interpret the Constitution differently.

Lincoln was speaking this day to an audience preparing for the Fourth of July. He asked his listeners to reflect on the Declaration of Independence. Of course its promise that all men were created equal was not part of the Constitution; the two documents were separate. But Lincoln deemed the Declaration no less a part of America's republican inheritance. Stephen Douglas had spoken shortly before Lincoln and had similarly taken the Declaration as his text. He had done so in defense of Roger Taney's ruling, especially the part contending that America's founders had not included Africans and their descendants among those to whom equality applied. Lincoln read from Douglas's speech: "They referred to the white race alone, and not to the African, when they declared all men to have been created equal. . . . They were speaking of British subjects on this continent being equal to British subjects born and residing in Great Britain. . . . The Declaration was adopted for the purpose of justifying the colonists in the eyes of the civilized world in withdrawing their allegiance from the British crown, and dissolving their connection with the mother country."

Lincoln asked his listeners to reflect on this interpretation. "Read that carefully over some leisure hour, and ponder well upon it," he said. "See what a mere wreck, a mangled ruin, it makes of our once glorious Declaration." In Douglas's reading, "all men" didn't mean anything close to all men. It exempted not only Negroes but white people living outside Britain and North America. "The French, Germans and other white people of the world are all gone to pot along with the Judge's inferior races," Lincoln said. "I had thought the Declaration contemplated the progressive improvement in the condition of all men everywhere." Not so, said Douglas. It was merely a phrase of convenience, drafted for a narrow political objective. "Why, that object having been effected some eighty years ago, the Declaration is of no practical use now—mere rubbish, old wadding left to rot on the battle-field after the victory is won," Lincoln chaffed Douglas.

Lincoln again referred to the approaching Fourth. "I appeal to all, to Democrats as well as others. Are you really willing that the Declaration shall be thus frittered away?—thus left no more, at most, than an interesting memorial of the dead past? thus shorn of its vitality, and practical value; and left without the *germ* or even the *suggestion* of the individual rights of man in it?"

LINCOLN CAUGHT himself. He realized he could fall into the trap Douglas had set when the senator, with most other Democrats, branded the Republicans as favoring entire equality between the races. Lurid images of white maidens compelled to marry hulking black men were often conjured in voters' minds and ascribed to the "Black Republicans."

Lincoln disavowed any such thing. "There is a natural disgust in the minds of nearly all white people to the idea of an indiscriminate amalgamation of the white and black races," he said. Lincoln didn't criticize this view or disclaim it for himself. But Douglas had gone too far. "He finds the Republicans insisting that the Declaration of Independence includes *all* men, black as well as white; and forthwith he boldly denies that it includes negroes at all, and proceeds to argue gravely that all who contend it does, do so only because they want to vote, and eat, and sleep, and marry with negroes! He will have it that they cannot be consistent else." Lincoln rejected this reasoning. "I protest against that counterfeit logic which concludes that, because

I do not want a black woman for a *slave* I must necessarily want her for a *wife*. I need not have her for either, I can just leave her alone. In some respects she certainly is not my equal; but in her natural right to eat the bread she earns with her own hands without asking leave of anyone else, she is my equal, and the equal of all others."

Lincoln elaborated on the equality identified in the Declaration. "I think the authors of that notable instrument intended to include *all* men, but they did not intend to declare all men equal *in all respects*. They did not mean to say all were equal in color, size, intellect, moral developments, or social capacity. They defined with tolerable distinctness in what respects they did consider all men created equal—equal in 'certain inalienable rights, among which are life, liberty, and the pursuit of happiness.'" The authors and signers of the Declaration were making a promise for the future as much as a claim on the present. "They did not mean to assert the obvious untruth, that all were then actually enjoying that equality, nor yet, that they were about to confer it immediately upon them. In fact they had no power to confer such a boon. They meant simply to declare the *right*, so that the *enforcement* of it might follow as fast as circumstances should permit. They meant to set up a standard maxim for free society, which should be familiar to all, and revered by all; constantly looked to, constantly labored for, and even though never perfectly attained, constantly approximated, and thereby constantly spreading and deepening its influence, and augmenting the happiness and value of life to all people of all colors everywhere."

Douglas had things precisely backward. "The assertion that 'all men are created equal' was of no practical use in effecting our separation from Great Britain," Lincoln said. "It was placed in the Declaration, not for that, but for future use. Its authors meant it to be—thank God, it is now proving itself—a stumbling block to those who in after times might seek to turn a free people back into the hateful paths of despotism. They knew the proneness of prosperity to breed tyrants, and they meant when such should reappear in this fair land and commence their vocation they should find left for them at least one hard nut to crack."

Douglas had expressed horror at the mixing of races by marriage and procreation. Lincoln shared this negative view. "Agreed for once—a thousand times agreed," Lincoln said. "There are white men enough to marry all the white women, and black men enough to marry all the black women; and so let them be married. On this point we fully agree with the Judge."

Yet Douglas didn't really believe what he said, Lincoln suggested. If anything, his defense of slavery *encouraged* racial amalgamation. "Let us see, in 1850 there were in the United States, 405,751 mulattoes," Lincoln said. "Very few of these are the offspring of whites and *free* blacks; nearly all have sprung from black *slaves* and white masters." Obviously slavery produced exactly the race-mixing that Douglas decried. And the policy of Douglas and the Democrats, of facilitating the spread of slavery into Kansas and the other territories, would yield more of the same. The Republicans, not the Democrats, were the true defenders of racial purity, Lincoln said. "If white and black people never get together in Kansas, they will never mix blood in Kansas. That is at least one self-evident truth." Lincoln conceded that some free blacks might move to Kansas. But he repeated that free blacks weren't the source of more than a slight fraction of the mixed-race offspring. Free blacks shared the disinclination to marry across race lines. Lincoln didn't use the word "rape," but his audience understood that it was the forcible relations between slave masters and slave women that produced the majority of mulattoes. "Slavery is the greatest source of amalgamation," he repeated.

What was the most potent *bar* to amalgamation? "The separation of the races is the only perfect preventive," Lincoln said. He cautioned that not all members of the Republican party favored separation. But most did. "I can say a very large proportion of its members are for it." Lincoln didn't distance himself from this group. "The chief plank in their platform, opposition to the spread of slavery," he continued approvingly, "is most favorable to that separation."

How would this be accomplished? "Separation, if ever effected at all, must be effected by colonization"—the transplanting of American Negroes to Africa or some other foreign land. The Republicans didn't explicitly support colonization. "The enterprise is a difficult one," Lincoln acknowledged. But *he* supported it, and he hoped he could bring his party around. "When there is a will there is a way, and what colonization needs most is a hearty will. Will springs from the two elements of moral sense and self-interest. Let us be brought to believe it is morally right, and, at the same time, favorable to, or, at least, not against, our interest, to transfer the African to his native clime, and we shall find a way to do it, however great the task may be."

JOHN BROWN WOULDN'T have guessed it, but the Battle of Osawatomie marked the beginning of the end of the armed struggle for Kansas. The Pierce administration, while sympathetic toward the slavery side, was embarrassed by the breakdown in public order in a territory that was supposed to be under the control of the federal government. To calm things, the administration turned to John Geary, a no-nonsense engineer of Scots-Irish descent, a decorated hero of the Mexican War, the iron-fisted mayor who had brought order to gold-rush San Francisco, and a physical giant of six and a half feet and more than 250 pounds. Geary reached Fort Leavenworth ten days after the burning of Osawatomie and decreed that all militia groups be disbanded. He visited Lecompton, the pro-slavery capital, and then Lawrence, the free-state center. "I desire to know no party, no section, no North, no South, no East, no West, nothing but Kansas and my country," he declared. By force of personality, and with the assistance of U.S. Army regulars, he gradually succeeded in imposing order on the troubled territory.

Yet order alone didn't answer the question that had started the troubles: Would Kansas be slave or free? The administration of James Buchanan left the question to a convention of Kansans, called by the pro-slavery territorial legislature to draft a constitution for the state Kansas should become. The convention met at Lecompton in the fall of 1857 and was packed with pro-slavery delegates who produced a document that guaranteed the future of slavery in Kansas. The document was referred to voters, but the free-state advocates boycotted. The pro-slavery side won handily. A second referendum, with broader participation, rejected the constitution. Buchanan nonetheless accepted the first, positive vote and sent the Lecompton constitution to Congress with the recommendation that it be the basis for the admission of Kansas to the Union.

STEPHEN DOUGLAS FELT skewered, and realized he had no one but himself to blame. In quiet moments, of which Douglas had few these days, he had to admit that his popular-sovereignty approach had blown up in his face. He had expected complaints from the likes of Abraham Lincoln, but he hadn't expected the civil war that broke out in Kansas. Douglas was cannily smart in the fashion required for success in politics, but he lacked the imagination to see into the souls of extremists like John Brown. Murder, cold-blooded murder! With medieval broadswords! And the burning of towns, and pitched battles—was this what popular sovereignty came to? Douglas didn't want to think so, but the evidence stared him in the face.

Nor had his policy prospered by even the most cynical standards. Douglas had hoped to unite the Democratic party—behind himself, naturally. Instead he had split the party almost as badly as the now-defunct Whigs had been split. Southern Democrats accepted the hijacking of Kansas politics by the Lecompton legislature and convention as slavery's due, but many Northern Democrats, who had wanted nothing more than never to have to think about slavery again, blamed Douglas for the Kansas violence that forced slavery upon their attention. Even Illinois Democrats, until now as loyal to Douglas as could be, showed signs of restiveness. They wouldn't forsake him for another Democrat, but they might stay away from the polls in sufficient numbers to allow his displacement by a Republican.

Douglas decided that strong measures were necessary. Since casting his lot with the Democrats in the days of Andrew Jackson, Douglas had made party loyalty an article of his political faith. Now he became an apostate. He broke with the Democratic president, Buchanan, over the Lecompton constitution, and he called on other Democrats to join him in his revolt.

"The Lecompton constitution is not the act of the people of Kansas," he declared in a letter for publication. "It does not embody the popular will of that Territory." The problem wasn't with popular sovereignty per se but with its flawed implementation in Kansas—or, rather, with its flawed interpretation by the president. The second vote, the negative one ignored by Buchanan, was the one that should be heeded. "With what show of justice or fairness can it be contended, in the face of this vote, that the people of Kansas do not, and have not, in the most solemn manner known to the laws, repudiated the Lecompton constitution as a wicked fraud upon their rights and wishes?" With none whatsoever, which was why, against the demands of the president, the Lecompton constitution "should be repudiated by every Democrat who cherishes the time-honored principle of his party and is determined, in good faith, to carry out the doctrine of self-government and popular sovereignty."

In private Douglas was even more scathing. He accused Buchanan of exploiting the Kansas question to discredit him personally. Douglas vowed to have his revenge. "By God, sir, I made Mr. James Buchanan," he said. "And by God, sir, I will unmake him." At a face-to-face meeting of the two men, Buchanan reminded Douglas of the precedent Andrew Jackson had established for dealing with opposition inside the Democratic party. "No Democrat ever yet differed from the administration of his own choice without being crushed," Buchanan said.

Douglas glared coldly back. "Mr. President," he replied, "I wish you to remember that Andrew Jackson is dead."

ABRAHAM LINCOLN OBSERVED the Democratic infighting with mixed emotions. "What think you of the probable '*rumpus*' among the Democracy over the Kansas constitution?" he wrote to Lyman Trumbull as the rift was developing. Douglas's stance had turned out to split *both* parties, with most Democrats adhering to the president out of party loyalty, and many Republicans joining Douglas on principle. Lincoln chose party over principle, although he explained it to himself otherwise. "I think the Republicans should stand clear of it," he told Trumbull of the Democratic fight. "Both the President and Douglas are wrong." Buchanan was more wrong, for selling out Kansas. But Douglas was wrong for being wily. Lincoln thought Douglas was trying to seduce Republicans and thereby weaken the Republican party. "From what I am told here"—Lincoln was writing from Chicago—"Douglas tried, before leaving, to draw off some Republicans on this dodge, and even succeeded in making some impression on one or two." Lincoln thought Republican solidarity was essential to the party's success on the big issues facing the country.

Or perhaps he was thinking of his own success. Any Republican alliance with Douglas might be good for Kansas, but it wouldn't be good for Lincoln. Douglas was coming up for reelection, and Lincoln hoped to unseat him. But to do so, he had to hold the antislavery vote. He needed to cast Douglas as the minion of the slaveholders and the enemy of freedom. All of a sudden Douglas was acting as though he had a conscience on the slave question. Lincoln doubted he had any such thing, but even if he did—*especially* if he did—Lincoln's prospects were bleak. Douglas was a great man in Illinois and shrewd enough to have done favors for every powerful interest in the state. Absent a conscience-driven revolt over slavery, Douglas would coast to reelection. His stance on the Lecompton constitution couldn't have been better calculated to forestall such a revolt.

Lincoln felt compelled to take bold action. Having made himself the most visible foe in Illinois of Douglas, he was the obvious choice for the state's Republicans to put forward against Douglas in the race for the Senate. As in most states prior to passage of the Seventeenth Amendment, the Senate race in Illinois in 1858 was actually a contest between parties. If the Democrats won a majority in the state legislature, that majority would make Douglas senator. If the Republicans won, Lincoln would replace him.

The Illinois Republicans, meeting in Springfield, did nominate Lincoln for the Senate, and he kicked off his campaign with an acceptance speech calculated to strike sparks. William Herndon had watched Lincoln draft the speech. "He wrote on stray envelopes and scraps of paper, as ideas suggested themselves, putting them into that miscellaneous and convenient receptacle, his hat," Herndon recalled. "As the convention drew near he copied the whole on connected sheets, carefully revising every line and sentence, and fastened them together, for reference during the delivery of the speech, and for publication." In fact, said Herndon, Lincoln didn't really need the copy for his delivery. "He had studied and read over what he had written so long and carefully that he was able to deliver it without the least hesitation or difficulty."

Lincoln knew the speech could make or break his campaign for the Senate, and perhaps whatever political career lay beyond the campaign. He needed to attract attention—to say something provocative. He was careful not to preempt himself. A political associate dropped by the office while Lincoln was crafting his message; the fellow asked Lincoln what he was writing. Lincoln responded vaguely that it was something he might speak or publish one day, but that he couldn't share it at present. There was a particular passage Lincoln wouldn't reveal, as he told the friend afterward in explaining his secrecy. "You would ask me to change or modify it, and that I was determined not to do. I had willed it so, and was willing if necessary to perish with it."

Lincoln often commenced speeches with a humorous anecdote, to loosen the crowd. Not on this day. He was dead serious. He got straight to the point, speaking slowly and emphasizing the key words with care. "If we could first know *where* we are, and *whither* we are tending, we could then better judge *what* to do, and *how* to do it," he said. He made clear he intended to campaign against the Kansas-Nebraska Act and its consequences. "We are now far into the fifth year since a policy was initiated with the avowed object and confident promise of putting an end to slavery agitation," he said. Stephen Douglas's policy—popular sovereignty—had done no such thing. "Under the operation of that policy, that agitation has not only not ceased, but has constantly augmented. In my opinion, it will not cease until a crisis shall have been reached, and passed."

The crisis was inevitable, Lincoln judged. Borrowing from the Gospel of Matthew, he declared, "A house divided against itself cannot stand."

Lincoln paused to let reporters get the line. He elaborated: "I believe this government cannot endure, permanently half slave and half free. I do not expect the Union to be dissolved—I do not expect the house to fall—but I *do* expect it will cease to be divided. It will become all one thing, or all the other. Either the opponents of slavery will arrest the further spread of it, and place it where the public mind shall rest in the belief that it is in course of ultimate extinction; or its advocates will push it forward, till it shall become alike lawful in all the states, old as well as new, North as well as South."

Lincoln's argument was red meat to both sides of the slavery debate. Southerners naturally heard it as a declaration of war against slavery, by the candidate of the avowedly antislavery party. Northerners interpreted it as an ominous prediction that the logic of the Dred Scott decision would open the doors to slavery everywhere.

Northerners, in particular Illinoisans, were his audience at the moment. Democrats among them, and likely some Republicans, would call him alarmist. The Dred Scott case dealt with the territories only; the states remained the masters of their fate on slavery.

Lincoln argued that he wasn't alarmist at all. He revisited recent events. At the beginning of 1854 slavery had been excluded from more than half the states by their own constitutions, and from most of the federal territories by congressional ban. But then came the Kansas-Nebraska Act, which repealed the congressional ban. "This opened all the national territory to slavery," Lincoln said. Defenders of the law, starting with Stephen Douglas, contended that it did nothing more than enshrine the principle of self-government. Lincoln denounced any such perversion of the sacred principle, saying that in the hands of Douglas it amounted to precisely this: "That if any one man choose to enslave another, no third man shall be allowed to object."

Even as the Douglas bill was moving through Congress, Lincoln continued, a law case came before the courts, brought by Dred Scott. The timing was convenient for the advocates of the law, in that it allowed them to dodge difficult questions on the constitutionality of popular sovereignty by declaring that the courts would have to decide. The case was still in the system at the time of the presidential election of 1856. The Democratic candidate won, but with a minority of the popular vote. Still, a win was a win, and the slavery cause benefited, for James Buchanan endorsed the opening of the territories to slavery. Shortly after Buchanan's inauguration, the Supreme Court delivered its decision in the Dred Scott case, giving Douglas, Buchanan and the slavery party all they could hope for. Whereupon the senator and the president declared that every good citizen must fall in line behind the court's decision.

This sequence of events was so convenient it suggested a conspiracy among the Democrats, Lincoln said. He drew an analogy. "When we see a lot of framed timbers, different portions of which we know have been gotten out at different times and places and by different workmen—Stephen, Franklin, Roger and James, for instance—and when we see these timbers joined together, and see they exactly make the frame of a house or a mill, all the tenons and mortices exactly fitting, and all the lengths and proportions of the different pieces exactly adapted to their respective places, and not a piece too many or too few—not omitting even scaffolding—or, if a single piece be lacking, we can see the place in the frame exactly fitted and prepared to yet bring such piece in—in such a case, we find it impossible to not *believe* that Stephen and Franklin and Roger and James all understood one another from the beginning, and all worked upon a common plan or draft drawn up before the first lick was struck." Lincoln's listeners caught his reference to Stephen Douglas, Franklin Pierce, Roger Taney and James Buchanan; some smiled even if they thought his argument overdrawn.

They weren't smiling when Lincoln extrapolated from the Dred Scott decision to a dire warning about slavery in the country at large. While the majority opinion of the Supreme Court in the case, and the separate concurring opinions, had declared that the Constitution did not permit Congress or the territorial legislatures to exclude slavery from the territories, they were silent on the obvious next question. "They all omit to declare whether or not the same Constitution permits a *state*, or the people of a state, to exclude it." Lincoln granted that the omission might have been an oversight. But given the neat fit of the timbers of the slave house Stephen and company had been constructing, it was a suspicious oversight. The same reasoning that led the Taney court to declare that slave owners could take their property to any territory might lead it to declare that slave owners could take their property to any *state*. Indeed, one of the associate justices, Samuel Nelson, appeared to lay the groundwork when he wrote, "Except in cases where the power is restrained by the Constitution of the United States, the law of the state is supreme over the subject of slavery within its jurisdiction." This might appear a nod to state supremacy, but the introductory clause was crucial. "In what cases the power of the states is so restrained by the U.S. Constitution is left an open question," Lincoln said. In just the same way the Kansas-Nebraska Act had left open the question of restraints upon the territories. "Put that and that together," Lincoln said, "and we have another nice little niche, which we may, ere long, see filled with another Supreme Court decision, declaring that the Constitution of the United States does not permit a *state* to exclude slavery from its limits."

This was the nightmare of all opponents of slavery: the reconquest of the North by the slave power. It might sound extreme, Lincoln admitted. But the undoing of the Missouri Compromise had sounded extreme before the Kansas-Nebraska Act and the Dred Scott decision. By land area, slavery had regained half the ground it had lost in the previous several decades. Regaining the rest appeared a matter of time. "Such decision is probably coming, and will soon be upon us, unless the power of the present political dynasty shall be met and overthrown." Moderate antislavery men, who had long thought time was on their side, needed to reconsider. "We shall lie down pleasantly dreaming that the people of Missouri are on the verge of making their state free; and we shall awake to the reality, instead, that the Supreme Court has made Illinois a slave state."

How could this awful outcome be averted? By Republicans banding together against the slave power. "Two years ago the Republicans of the nation mustered over thirteen hundred thousand strong," Lincoln said, referring to the election of 1856. Their numbers were growing. Lincoln looked to the race for Illinois senator—his own race—and to the contests beyond. "The result is not doubtful. We shall not fail. If we stand firm, we shall not fail. Wise councils may accelerate or mistakes delay it, but, sooner or later the victory is sure to come."

JOHN BROWN LEFT Kansas not long after the arrival of John Geary. Some observers of the Kansas scene surmised that Geary winked at Brown's departure, despite the murder charges trailing him. Kansas needed peace more than it needed justice; better that Brown be out of Kansas than in a Kansas jail, inspiring lynch mobs or rescue attempts.

Brown was happy to be gone. The peace that settled upon Kansas didn't suit his purposes; having taken up arms against slavery, he intended to keep fighting until slavery was vanquished. Kansas was no longer the place; "Africa," the slave South itself, would be the next, and final, battlefield.

Brown's rejection of anything but armed struggle informed a comment he made to one of his half sisters, living in Ohio. He hadn't seen her in years, but on his way east from Kansas he stopped at her house. She was antislavery, like all the Browns, but more interested in politics than he. "John, isn't it dreadful that Frémont should have been defeated and such a man as Buchanan put into office!" she said.

"Well, truly, as I look at it now, I see it was the right thing," Brown replied. "If Frémont had been elected, the people would have settled right down and made no further effort. Now they know they must work."

John Brown arrived in Boston in early 1857. He hoped to raise money for his continuing campaign, and to the armchair abolitionists of New England he was a great hero, the only authentic freedom fighter most of them had ever encountered. Frank Sanborn was smitten at first encounter. Fresh out of Harvard, imbued with the ideals of liberty, Sanborn worked for one of the many emigrant-aid societies that sprang up to assist the settlement of Kansas by free-state men. Brown took care to cultivate Sanborn, who might open the doors to others in Massachusetts. Sanborn responded by recommending Brown to his friends in the antislavery network. "'Old Brown' of Kansas is now in Boston, with one of his sons, working for an object in which you will heartily sympathize—raising and arming a company of men for the future protection of Kansas," Sanborn wrote to an abolitionist minister based in Worcester. "He wishes to raise $30,000 to arm and equip a company such as he thinks he can raise this present winter, but he will, as I understand him, take what money he can raise and use it as far as it will go. Can you not come to Boston tomorrow or next day and see Capt. Brown?" Sanborn added, "I like the man from what I have seen—and his deeds ought to bear witness for him."

What Sanborn didn't realize, because Brown took pains to disguise it, was that Brown's campaign for Kansas wouldn't take place in Kansas itself. His war had never been about Kansas per se; it was a struggle against slavery. And it was a struggle that would be won only in the homeland of slavery in the American South. Yet Brown realized that this was more than most of those from whom he sought money had bargained for. They were still thinking of Kansas, so he would let them think of Kansas. But he would use their money for his larger campaign.

Henry David Thoreau was a generation older than Frank Sanborn yet no less enamored of Brown. The famous transcendentalist recognized a kindred spirit in Brown, or thought he did. "A man of rare common-sense and directness of speech, as of action; a transcendentalist above all, a man of ideas and principles—that was what distinguished him," Thoreau recalled of Brown. "Not yielding to a whim or transient impulse, but carrying out the purpose of a life." Thoreau and the others wanted to hear war stories from Kansas; Brown rationed his responses. "He did not overstate anything, but spoke within bounds," Thoreau said. "I remember, particularly, how, in his speech here, he referred to what his family had suffered in Kansas, without ever giving the least vent to his pent-up fire. It was a volcano with an ordinary chimney-flue. Also referring to the deeds of certain Border Ruffians, he said, rapidly paring away his speech, like an experienced soldier, keeping a reserve of force and meaning, 'They had a perfect right to be hung.'" Brown was the opposite of a rhetorician, but that made him the more powerful speaker. "It was like the speeches of Cromwell compared with those of an ordinary king."

Brown's resolve was still more impressive. "When I expressed surprise that he could live in Kansas at all, with a price set upon his head, and so large a number, including the authorities, exasperated against him, he accounted for it by saying, 'It is perfectly well understood that I will not be taken,'" Thoreau recalled. Brown wasn't admitting to the Pottawatomie murders, but the suspicion that he was behind them sent shivers of excitement through his audience. Brown boasted of the deterrent effect in Kansas of his reputation. Often he had openly entered pro-slavery towns to transact business, he said, and no one had attempted to arrest him. "No little handful of men were willing to undertake it, and a large body could not be got together in season," he explained.

Brown stayed in private homes while in Boston; his comportment there enhanced the impression he made. "He used to take out his two revolvers and repeater every night before going to bed, to make sure of their loads, saying, 'Here are eighteen lives,'" one of his hosts remembered. To the lady of that house, Brown said, "If you hear a noise, put the baby under the pillow. I should hate to spoil these carpets, but you know I cannot be taken alive." Once he held the little girl up in one of his large hands, looked her in the eye and said, "When I am hung for treason, you can say that you used to stand on Captain Brown's hand."

Yet Brown had cause to believe that if the showdown came in Massachusetts, he wouldn't in fact be hanged. Theodore Parker, another of his sponsors, sketched for a friend, who happened to be a judge, how Brown might avoid both arrest and the gallows. "If I were in his position," Parker said, "I should shoot dead any man who attempted to arrest me for those alleged crimes"—the Pottawatomie murders. "Then I should be tried by a Massachusetts jury and be acquitted."

AMOS LAWRENCE WAS bowled over by Brown. "Captain John Brown, the old partisan hero of Kansas warfare, came to see me," the textile magnate and philanthropist wrote in his diary. "I had a long talk with him. He is a calm, temperate, and pious man, but when roused he is a dreadful foe." On the basis of this impression, Lawrence donated money to the Brown cause and promised more. "Enclosed please find twenty-five dollars toward the fund for the brave Captain John Brown, who may appropriately be called the 'Miles Standish' of Kansas," he wrote to a group collecting money for Brown. "Few persons know the character of this man, or his services; and he is the last one to proclaim his merits. His severe simplicity of habits, his determined energy, his heroic courage in time of trial, all based on a deep religious faith, make him a true representative of the Puritanic warrior." Lawrence noted that Brown's family required support while he was in the field. "It would afford me pleasure to be one of ten, or a smaller number, to pay a thousand dollars per annum till the admission of Kansas into the Union, for this purpose."

Shortly thereafter Lawrence gave Brown seventy dollars directly. "It is for your own personal use, and not for the cause in any other way than that," he explained. When Lawrence's challenge grant of support for Brown's family was quickly met by several friends, Brown suggested that the money be used to buy a better home and farm than his wife and younger children currently had in North Elba. Lawrence told Brown he needn't worry. "In case anything should occur while you are engaged in a good cause, to shorten your life, you may be assured that your wife and children shall be cared for more liberally than you now propose. The family of 'Captain John Brown of Osawatomie' will not be turned out to starve in the country, until liberty herself is driven out."

Many of those to whom Brown appealed professed to eschew violence; they sought assurance that what aid they gave him would be used defensively. "If you get the arms and money you desire," one asked, "will you invade Missouri or any slave territory?"

Brown refused to answer straightforwardly. "You all know me," he said. "You are acquainted with my history. You know what I have done in Kansas." In fact, they *didn't* know, about Pottawatomie, and Brown declined to enlighten them. He continued, "I do not expose my plans. No one knows them but myself, except perhaps one. I will not be interrogated; if you wish to give me anything, I want you to give it freely. I have no other purpose but to serve the cause of liberty."

Brown here wasn't providing cover to himself alone. He was protecting his sponsors, who could say, if the time came, that they didn't know of his plans for an invasion of the South. At least some of them apparently realized this; at any rate, he wasn't pressed on the issue.

Yet neither were they as open-handed as he wished. Brown's deception backfired when it came to fund-raising. While he let them think small, in terms of Kansas, he was thinking large, of the South. Their contributions suited the former but fell short of the latter. He might have blamed himself but instead blamed them. He left Boston and tossed a sneer over his shoulder. "Old Brown's *Farewell:* to the Plymouth Rocks; Bunker Hill Monuments, Charter Oaks, and Uncle Tom's Cabins," was the heading he put on his angry piece. "Has left for Kansas. Was trying since he came out of the territory to secure an outfit, or in other words the *means of arming and equipping thoroughly* his regular minute men, who are mixed up with the people of Kansas. And he leaves the States with a deep feeling of sadness, that after having exhausted *his own small means,* and with his *family and his* brave men, suffered hunger, nakedness, cold, sickness, and (some of them) imprisonment, with the most barbarous and cruel treatment, *wounds, and death;* that after lying on the ground for months, in the most unwholesome and sickly, as well as uncomfortable, places, with sick and wounded destitute of any shelter a part of the time, dependent in part on the care and hospitality of the Indians, and hunted like wolves; that after all this, in order to sustain a cause which *every Citizen of this 'Glorious Republic'* is under equal moral obligation to do (*and for the neglect of which he will be held accountable to God*), in which *every man, woman, and child of the entire human family* has a *deep and awful interest;* that when *no wages* are *asked* or *expected,* he cannot secure (amidst all the wealth, luxury, and extravagance of this *'Heaven exalted'* people) even the necessary supplies for a common soldier: 'How are the mighty fallen?'"

A different sort of man would have asked himself why he had failed to get his message across. John Brown wasn't that man. His failure simply strengthened his determination to carry his war to Africa. Others might forget that God would hold them accountable; John Brown did not.

ABRAHAM LINCOLN's Springfield speech caused the sensation he hoped for, and then some. Many of his allies thought he had taken things too far with his "house divided" imagery. William Herndon had known Lincoln was going to use the phrase and image, for Lincoln had read him the speech ahead of time. "It is true," Herndon said of the metaphor. "But is it wise or politic to say so?" Lincoln subsequently read the speech to an audience of a dozen close confidants. "Some condemned and not one endorsed it," Herndon said of the provocative line. Herndon recalled a member of the group spluttering about Lincoln's "damned fool utterance." The consensus was that it would frighten potential Republicans into the ranks of the Democrats. Yet Herndon, retrospectively claiming prescience, recalled telling his partner, "Lincoln, deliver that speech as read and it will make you president."

But it didn't seem likely to make him senator. Democrats were delighted at Lincoln's inflammatory rhetoric. "I had thought until recently that the Little Giant was dead in Illinois," one of them said, employing the nickname for the short Douglas, "until I saw the speech Mr. Lincoln made to the Republican convention in Springfield." This observer predicted that Lincoln's characterization of the struggle between slave states and free was entirely too extreme for Illinoisans and other westerners. The Democrats could use it to destroy Lincoln. "It is abolition and disunion so absolutely expressed that it should be made to burn Mr. Lincoln as long as he lives."

Lincoln knew his words would create a furor. But he claimed he couldn't have *not* spoken them. "I have never professed an indifference to the honors of official station; and were I to do so now, I should only make myself ridiculous," he scribbled a few weeks later in a note for a speech. "Yet I have never failed—do not now fail—to remember that in the Republican cause there is a higher aim than that of mere office." He remarked that opponents of slavery in Britain had labored for decades before achieving success. He allowed that success in America might take as long. "I cannot but regard it as possible that the higher object of this contest may not be completely attained within the term of my natural life. But I cannot doubt either that it will come in due time." And he wanted to be on the side of righteousness. "I am proud, in my passing speck of time, to contribute an humble mite to that glorious consummation, which my own poor eyes may not last to see."

All the same, Lincoln didn't employ the "house divided" language again. Once was enough. Yet he didn't retreat from the broader message of the speech: that the Democrats, led by Stephen Douglas, were engaged in a conspiracy to force slavery upon the whole nation. "I clearly see, as I think, a powerful plot to make slavery universal and perpetual in this nation," he jotted in another note. "The effort to carry that plot through will be persistent and long continued, extending far beyond the senatorial term for which Judge Douglas and I are just now struggling." Referring to his House Divided speech, he said, "In it I arrange a string of incontestable facts which, I think, prove the existence of a conspiracy to nationalize slavery. The evidence was circumstantial only; but nevertheless it seemed inconsistent with every hypothesis save that of the existence of such conspiracy. I believe the facts can be explained to day on no other hypothesis."

In public statements Lincoln feigned surprise at the stir he had caused. To a Chicago editor who had remarked on the force of his Springfield speech, Lincoln responded, "I am much flattered by the estimate you place on my late speech; and yet I am much mortified that any part of it should be construed so differently from anything intended by me." Choosing his words carefully, and avoiding the biblical reference, Lincoln went on, "The language, 'place it where the public mind shall rest in the belief that it is in course of ultimate extinction,' I used deliberately, not dreaming then, nor believing now, that it asserts, or intimates, any power or purpose to interfere with slavery in the states where it exists."

If Lincoln really thought the editor or anyone else would believe this disclaimer, he was reasoning more like a lawyer than a political candidate. His lawyerly logic would have run along lines asserting that the Southern states would eventually conclude that emancipation was in their own self-interest and would end slavery without external compulsion. But any politician would read the phrase and recognize that Southerners would see "ultimate extinction" as Lincoln's own plan for slavery.

So Lincoln belabored the point in his letter to the editor. "I have declared a thousand times, and now repeat that, in my opinion, neither the general government, nor any other power outside of the slave states, can constitutionally or rightfully interfere with slaves or slavery where it already exists. I believe that whenever the effort to spread slavery into the new territories, by whatever means, and into the free states themselves, by Supreme Court decisions, shall be fairly headed off, the institution will then be in course of ultimate extinction; and by the language used I meant only this."

Then Lincoln hedged again, and again. "I do not intend this for publication; but still you may show it to any one you think fit."

STEPHEN DOUGLAS WOULDN'T let Lincoln off so easily. He accused his opponent of preaching a war of North against South for the extinction of slavery. He asserted that Lincoln intended for federal law to run roughshod over state law. He denounced Lincoln for betraying the very Constitution he professed to hold so dear.

And in doing so, Douglas played into Lincoln's hands. Douglas was the incumbent and the favorite; he had no compelling reason to do anything that increased Lincoln's visibility. But each attack he made on Lincoln did just that. Lincoln, plausibly professing a desire to defend himself, challenged Douglas to a series of debates. "Will it be agreeable to you to make an arrangement for you and myself to divide time and address the same audiences during the present canvass?" he inquired in a note delivered to Douglas by a friend.

Douglas, doubtless cursing himself, initially demurred. "Recent events have interposed difficulties in the way of such an arrangement," he responded. Douglas said he and the Democratic party had worked out their campaign schedule so that Douglas could speak on the same bill as other Democratic candidates. There wouldn't be room for Lincoln.

"Besides, there is another consideration which should be kept in mind," Douglas continued. "It has been suggested recently that an arrangement had been made to bring out a third candidate for the U.S. Senate, who, with yourself, should canvass the state in opposition to me, and with no other purpose than to insure my defeat by dividing the Democratic party for your benefit." If Douglas agreed to debate Lincoln, he would have to debate the third candidate. This would be unfair. "He and you in concert might be able to take the opening and closing speech in every case."

Moreover, Lincoln should have asked earlier, Douglas said. Presumably Lincoln hadn't thought up this idea on the spur of the moment. Their paths had crossed already, or nearly so, on the campaign trail. Lincoln could have raised the issue then.

Yet after saying all this, Douglas consented to meet Lincoln. Having built Lincoln up by his denunciations, he could hardly do otherwise. He proposed one debate in each of the nine congressional districts of Illinois, except two where they had recently spoken separately. Douglas went so far as to specify a particular town in each district: Freeport, Ottawa, Galesburg, Quincy, Alton, Jonesboro and Charleston.

Lincoln didn't respond at once. Douglas's letter seems to have been slow in transit. Four days later, the two men sat down at the same dinner, Lincoln not knowing that Douglas had replied and Douglas puzzling why Lincoln, having suggested the debates in the first place, wouldn't take yes for an answer.

Some of the holdup might have been deliberate, on Douglas's part. Or so Lincoln inferred from reading Douglas's letter in a Chicago newspaper before he laid hands on the original. With Douglas's objections in the public domain, Lincoln felt compelled to answer them. To Douglas's statement that it had been "suggested" that a third candidate was waiting in the wings, Lincoln scoffed, "I can only say that such suggestion must have been made by yourself, for certainly none such has been made by me." To Douglas's complaint that Lincoln had tarried in making his proposal of debates, Lincoln disavowed any deviousness. "I can only say I made it as soon as I resolved to make it. I did not know but that such proposal would come from you; I waited respectfully to see." Lincoln certainly didn't expect Douglas to believe this, since Douglas had little to gain and much to lose from the debates. But if Douglas was going to start the debates in these letters, Lincoln wasn't going to back down.

Then, having matched Douglas's half-truths with dubious fractions of his own, he accepted the senator's plan. "I agree to an arrangement to speak at the seven places you have named," he said. "As to other details, I wish perfect reciprocity, no more."

THE DOUGLAS-LINCOLN debates—only later called the Lincoln-Douglas debates—were the highlight of the summer and early autumn in Illinois. Political campaigns were a reliable source of entertainment in nineteenth-century America, and this campaign promised to be more entertaining than most. The face-to-face format of the debates heightened the air of combat that surrounded every campaign. The contrast between the individuals—the pugnacious Little Giant versus the joke-telling Long Abe—couldn't have been more striking. The stakes were high; the fate of the country hinged on the issues the two men would discuss. One of the two might become the next president of the United States. Current odds favored Douglas, the most formidable figure in the party that had owned the White House for much of the century, but Lincoln was making a mark among the Republicans, whose national chances increased by the month. Newspapers from all over America sent correspondents to tip the papers' readers on the country's politics to come.

The first stop of the caravan was Ottawa, in north-central Illinois. The event was a boon to local businesses, which lodged and fed the ten thousand or so who doubled the town's population that day. Railroads appreciated the traffic, routing extra trains to carry the partisans of the two champions. Other spectators arrived by boat and barge, on the canal that antedated the railroad. Area farmers were less happy, for after the hotels filled, visitors camped out on whatever fields appeared vacant.

In late August the sun was still strong and the temperature high. The summer rains had stopped weeks earlier, and clouds of dust announced the approach of those who lived near enough to arrive by foot, horse and carriage on the day of the debate. Early arrivals got the best spots, which meant a standing place on the town square close to the platform. As for the platform, it had been constructed for the occasion, but not well. By the time it filled with all the local worthies who considered their presence necessary for the proceedings, their weight was too much for the underpinnings, and part of the structure crumpled.

STEPHEN DOUGLAS LED off. He traced the origin of the current dispute over slavery, and he blamed the party Lincoln currently represented. "Prior to 1854 this country was divided into two great political parties, known as the Whig and Democratic parties," Douglas said. "Both were national and patriotic, advocating principles that were universal in their application. An old-line Whig could proclaim his principles in Louisiana and Massachusetts alike. Whig principles had no boundary sectional line; they were not limited by the Ohio River, nor by the Potomac, nor by the line of the free and slave states, but applied and were proclaimed wherever the Constitution ruled or the American flag waved over the American soil." The Whigs and the Democrats had differed on numerous issues, to be sure—on a national bank, on the tariff, on federal support for roads and bridges. But they agreed on the slavery question. "The Whig party and the Democratic party jointly adopted the Compromise measures of 1850 as the basis of a proper and just solution of this slavery question in all its forms." Modestly eliding his own role in the 1850 compromise, Douglas credited Whig Henry Clay and Democrat Lewis Cass for its passage. His point was that it was a bipartisan measure. He added that the two parties had endorsed the compromise in their national platforms in 1852. "Thus you see that up to 1853–54, the Whig party and the Democratic party both stood on the same platform with regard to the slavery question. That platform was the right of the people of each state and each territory to decide their local and domestic institutions for themselves, subject only to the federal Constitution."

If members of the audience noticed that Douglas had inserted here his own interpretation of the Compromise of 1850, perhaps they forgave him, as one of the measure's authors. In fact the compromise did *not* give the people of each territory the right to decide on slavery for themselves; that right extended only to the new territories taken from Mexico. In the northern part of the Louisiana Purchase, the Missouri Compromise still forbade slavery.

Douglas plunged ahead. He explained how he had introduced what became the Kansas-Nebraska Act. He said it merely codified the popular-sovereignty principle of the Compromise of 1850. He noted that he had inserted language into the Kansas-Nebraska bill making the principle explicit: "It is the true intent and meaning of this Act not to legislate slavery into any State or Territory, or to exclude it therefrom, but to leave the people thereof perfectly free to form and regulate their domestic institutions in their own way, subject only to the Federal Constitution." The Kansas-Nebraska Act had received the bipartisan approval of Congress, revealing once again the broad acceptance of popular sovereignty.

And then the trouble started, Douglas said. Lincoln and others had conspired to dissolve the old Whig party, to join with some Democratic malcontents, and "to connect the members of both into an Abolition party, under the name and disguise of a Republican party." Douglas thereafter referred to Lincoln's party as the Black Republicans, to whom he ascribed wholly abolitionist views. Douglas read several planks of the platform of the first meeting of Illinois Republicans, in 1854, conveying their strongly antislavery opinions.

Loud applause from Lincoln's supporters interrupted Douglas as he read.

Douglas nodded knowingly. "Now, gentlemen, your Black Republicans have cheered every one of those propositions," he said. "And yet I venture to say that you cannot get Mr. Lincoln to come out and say that he is now in favor of each one of them." So Douglas put the questions directly. "I desire to know whether Mr. Lincoln today stands, as he did in 1854, in favor of the unconditional repeal of the Fugitive Slave law. I desire him to answer whether he stands pledged today, as he did in 1854, against the admission of any more slave states into the Union, even if the people want them. I want to know whether he stands pledged against the admission of a new state into the Union with such a Constitution as the people of that state may see fit to make. I want to know whether he stands today pledged to the abolition of slavery in the District of Columbia. I desire him to answer whether he stands pledged to the prohibition of the slave trade between the different states. I desire to know whether he stands pledged to prohibit slavery in all the territories of the United States, North as well as South of the Missouri Compromise line. I desire him to answer whether he is opposed to the acquisition of any more territory, unless slavery is prohibited therein."

This time it was the Democrats who cheered, believing their champion had put the challenger in a difficult spot.

Douglas said he wanted to get Lincoln on the record. Ottawa, the site of this debate, was in northern Illinois, the more antislavery part of the state. "I ask Abraham Lincoln to answer these questions, in order that, when I trot him down to lower Egypt"—the southern, pro-slavery part—"I may put the same questions to him. My principles are the same everywhere. I can proclaim them alike in the North, the South, the East, and the West. My principles will apply wherever the Constitution prevails and the American flag waves. I desire to know whether Mr. Lincoln's principles will bear transplanting from Ottawa to Jonesboro."

Douglas said he put the questions to Lincoln out of no personal disrespect. On the contrary, he had nothing but good feelings for him. "I have known him for nearly twenty-five years," Douglas said. "There were many points of sympathy between us when we first got acquainted. We were both comparatively boys, and both struggling with poverty in a strange land. I was a school-teacher in the town of Winchester, and he a flourishing grocery-keeper in the town of Salem." Douglas emphasized Lincoln's success, beyond what the evidence would bear. He explained how they had met in the state legislature. "He was then just as good at telling an anecdote as now. He could beat any of the boys wrestling, or running a foot-race, in pitching quoits or tossing a copper; could ruin more liquor than all of the boys of the town together; and the dignity and impartiality with which he presided at a horse-race or fist-fight excited the admiration and won the praise of everybody that was present and participated."

But since those good old days, Lincoln had turned abolitionist, Douglas said. As evidence he quoted from Lincoln's House Divided speech, laying stress on the passages that sounded the most extreme.

"I believe this government *cannot endure permanently half slave and half free*," Douglas read. "I do not expect the Union to be dissolved—I do not expect the house to fall; *but I do expect it will cease to be divided*. It will become all one thing, or all the other. Either the opponents of slavery *will arrest the further spread of it*, and place it where the public mind shall rest in the belief *that it is in the course of ultimate extinction*, or its advocates *will push it forward till it shall become alike lawful in all the States*,—old as well as new, North as well as South."

Again Lincoln's partisans cheered. "Good!" some shouted.

Again Douglas nodded knowingly. "I am delighted to hear you Black Republicans say 'good.' I have no doubt that doctrine expresses your sentiments, and I will prove to you now, if you will listen to me, that it is revolutionary and destructive of the existence of this government."

Douglas pointed out that America's founders had envisioned a nation half-free and half-slave. They had brought such a country into existence, and it had endured for seventy years. Was Lincoln wiser than they? The founders knew that the individual states understood their own interests best. "They knew that the laws and regulations which would suit the granite hills of New Hampshire would be unsuited to the rice plantations of South Carolina, and they therefore provided that each state should retain its own legislature and its own sovereignty, with the full and complete power to do as it pleased within its own limits, in all that was local and not national." Yet Lincoln proposed to ignore their insight and overturn their accomplishment.

Douglas cited Lincoln's criticism of the Dred Scott decision. "He says it deprives the negro of the rights and privileges of citizenship," Douglas asserted. "That is the first and main reason which he assigns for his warfare on the Supreme Court of the United States and its decision."

Douglas gazed around at his fellow Illinoisans. "I ask you, are you in favor of conferring upon the negro the rights and privileges of citizenship? Do you desire to strike out of our state constitution that clause which keeps slaves and free negroes out of the state, and allow the free negroes to flow in, and cover your prairies with black settlements? Do you desire to turn this beautiful state into a free negro colony, in order that when Missouri abolishes slavery she can send one hundred thousand emancipated slaves into Illinois, to become citizens and voters, on an equality with yourselves?" Douglas rephrased his question, and offered voting advice. "If you desire negro citizenship, if you desire to allow them to come into the state and settle with the white man, if you desire them to vote on an equality with yourselves, and to make them eligible to office, to serve on juries, and to adjudge your rights, then support Mr. Lincoln and the Black Republican party."

Douglas did not begrudge Lincoln's right to idiosyncratic views on race. "I do not question Mr. Lincoln's conscientious belief that the negro was made his equal, and hence is his brother," Douglas said. "But for my own part, I do not regard the negro as my equal, and positively deny that he is my brother, or any kin to me whatever." Lincoln liked to cite the Declaration of Independence, Douglas said. "He holds that the negro was born his equal and yours, and that he was endowed with equality by the Almighty, and that no human law can deprive him of these rights, which were guaranteed to him by the Supreme Ruler of the Universe." Douglas disputed Lincoln's theology. "I do not believe that the Almighty ever intended the negro to be the equal of the white man," he said. "If He did, He has been a long time demonstrating the fact. For thousands of years the negro has been a race upon the earth, and during all that time, in all latitudes and climates, wherever he has wandered or been taken, he has been inferior to the race which he has there met. He belongs to an inferior race, and must always occupy an inferior position."

This did not mean that the Negro must always be a slave. "By no means can such a conclusion be drawn from what I have said. On the contrary, I hold that humanity and Christianity both require that the negro shall have and enjoy every right, every privilege, and every immunity consistent with the safety of the society in which he lives. On that point, I presume, there can be no diversity of opinion. You and I are bound to extend to our inferior and dependent beings every right, every privilege, every facility and immunity consistent with the public good."

And what were the rights and privileges consistent with the public good? Douglas returned to the principle of popular sovereignty. "This is a question which each state and each territory must decide for itself," he said. He cited the example of Illinois. "We have provided that the negro shall not be a slave, and we have also provided that he shall not be a citizen, but protect him in his civil rights, in his life, his person and his property, only depriving him of all political rights whatsoever, and refusing to put him on an equality with the white man." Douglas added, "That policy of Illinois is satisfactory to the Democratic party and to me; and if it were to the Republicans, there would then be no question upon the subject. But the Republicans say that he ought to be made a citizen, and when he becomes a citizen he becomes your equal, with all your rights and privileges."

Douglas did not profess to dictate to other states. Maine allowed free Negroes to vote. That was Maine's prerogative. "I would never consent to confer the right of voting and of citizenship upon a negro; but still I am not going to quarrel with Maine for differing from me in opinion. Let Maine take care of her own negroes and fix the qualifications of her own voters to suit herself, without interfering with Illinois, and Illinois will not interfere with Maine."

Lincoln and the Republicans showed no such tolerance. "This doctrine of Mr. Lincoln, of uniformity among the institutions of the different states, is a new doctrine, never dreamed of by Washington, Madison, or the framers of this government," Douglas said. "Mr. Lincoln and the Republican party set themselves up as wiser than these men who made this government, which has flourished for seventy years under the principle of popular sovereignty, recognizing the right of each state to do as it pleased. Under that principle, we have grown from a nation of three or four millions to a nation of about thirty millions of people; we have crossed the Allegheny mountains and filled up the whole Northwest, turning the prairie into a garden, and building up churches and schools, thus spreading civilization and Christianity where before there was nothing but savage barbarism. Under that principle we have become, from a feeble nation, the most powerful on the face of the earth."

All this Lincoln would put at risk. Douglas refused to believe Illinois voters would let it happen. "If we only adhere to that principle, we can go forward increasing in territory, in power, in strength, and in glory until the Republic of America shall be the North Star that shall guide the friends of freedom throughout the civilized world.

And why can we not adhere to the great principle of self-government, upon which our institutions were originally based? I believe that this new doctrine preached by Mr. Lincoln and his party will dissolve the Union if it succeeds. They are trying to array all the Northern states in one body against the South, to excite a sectional war between the free states and the slave states, in order that the one or the other may be driven to the wall."

21

DOUGLAS WOULD HAVE continued, but the master of ceremonies signaled time. All faces turned toward Lincoln, who rose and looked about with what might have been a smile. "When a man hears himself somewhat misrepresented, it provokes him—at least, I find it so with myself," Lincoln said. "But when misrepresentation becomes very gross and palpable, it is more apt to amuse him."

Lincoln denied conspiring to break up the Whig party, and he disavowed the platform planks of the 1854 Republican convention to which Douglas had objected. "I never had anything to do with them," Lincoln said. He explained that he had not attended the convention, although he had been named to the committee and had been requested to come. "I refused to do so, and I never had anything to do with that organization. This is the plain truth."

As to Douglas's charge that he was an abolitionist, Lincoln denied it. He produced a copy of the speech he had given at Peoria in the wake of the passage of the Kansas-Nebraska Act, and prepared to read it.

"Put on your specs!" a voice shouted.

"Yes, sir, I am obliged to do so," Lincoln responded. "I am no longer a young man."

The length of Lincoln's extract tried the patience of the audience that day. But the gist was his denial at Peoria of being an abolitionist. "If all earthly power were given me, I should not know what to do, as to the existing institution," Lincoln quoted himself. "My first impulse would be to free all the slaves, and send them to Liberia—to their own native land. But a moment's reflection would convince me that whatever of high hope (as I think there is) there may be in this, in the long run, its sudden execution is impossible."

Lincoln denied Douglas's claim that he was a race leveler. "Anything that argues me into his idea of perfect social and political equality with the negro is but a specious and fantastic arrangement of words, by which a man can prove a horse chestnut to be a chestnut horse," Lincoln said. To make himself quite clear, he added, "I have no purpose, directly or indirectly, to interfere with the institution of slavery in the states where it exists. I believe I have no lawful right to do so, and I have no inclination to do so. I have no purpose to introduce political and social equality between the white and the black races. There is a physical difference between the two which, in my judgment, will probably forever forbid their living together upon the footing of perfect equality; and inasmuch as it becomes a necessity that there must be a difference, I, as well as Judge Douglas, am in favor of the race to which I belong having the superior position."

Yet Lincoln didn't wholly agree with Douglas in matters racial. In fact, they differed considerably. "There is no reason in the world why the negro is not entitled to all the natural rights enumerated in the Declaration of Independence—the right to life, liberty, and the pursuit of happiness," Lincoln said. "I hold that he is as much entitled to these as the white man. I agree with Judge Douglas he is not my equal in many respects—certainly not in color, perhaps not in moral or intellectual endowment. But in the right to eat the bread, without the leave of anybody else, which his own hand earns, he is my equal, and the equal of Judge Douglas, and the equal of every living man."

Lincoln realized that Douglas had scored points attacking his House Divided speech. He felt obliged to answer. He contended that America's founders themselves had placed slavery on the path to ultimate extinction by their ban on the import of slaves and their cordoning it out of the Ohio Valley. The founders had considered slavery a necessary evil; they hoped time would render it ultimately unnecessary and, for that reason, dispensable. It was Douglas who had spoiled their vision. "Lately, I think—and in this I charge nothing on the Judge's motives—lately, I think, that he, and those acting with him, have placed that institution on a new basis, which looks to the perpetuity and nationalization of slavery." Douglas had asked whether

Lincoln thought he was wiser than the founders; Lincoln threw the question back at Douglas. "I believe if we could arrest the spread"—of slavery—"and place it where Washington and Jefferson and Madison placed it, it *would be* in the course of ultimate extinction, and the public mind *would,* as for eighty years past, believe that it was in the course of ultimate extinction. The crisis would be past and the institution might be let alone for a hundred years, if it should live so long, in the states where it exists; yet it would be going out of existence in the way best for both the black and the white races."

Someone in the audience shouted, "Then do you repudiate popular sovereignty?"

"Let us talk about popular sovereignty," Lincoln responded. "What is popular sovereignty? Is it the right of the people to have slavery or not have it, as they see fit, in the territories?" This was not the reality, Lincoln said. "My understanding is that popular sovereignty, as now applied to the question of slavery, does allow the people of a territory to have slavery if they want to, but does not allow them *not* to have it if they *do not* want it." The Dred Scott decision made a mockery of popular sovereignty. "As I understand the Dred Scott decision, if any one man wants slaves, all the rest have no way of keeping that one man from holding them," Lincoln said.

Lincoln, likely as Douglas intended, wasted considerable breath refuting the exaggerations the senator had attributed to him. Eventually he returned to the charge that he was asserting a plot to impose slavery on all the states. Lincoln didn't deny the assertion, but he believed it had been misunderstood. "What is necessary to make the institution national?" he asked. "Not war. There is no danger that the people of Kentucky will shoulder their muskets, and, with a young nigger stuck on every bayonet, march into Illinois and force them upon us. There is no danger of our going over there and making war upon them. Then what is necessary for the nationalization of slavery? It is simply the next Dred Scott decision. It is merely for the Supreme Court to decide that no *state* under the Constitution can exclude it, just as they have already decided that under the Constitution neither Congress nor the territorial legislature can do it. When that is decided and acquiesced in, the whole thing is done."

Lincoln proceeded to elaborate on the Dred Scott reasoning, consuming several minutes of his allotted time. His logic was intricate and apparently hard for the audience to follow.

"Give us something besides Dred Scott!" a listener shouted.

"Yes; no doubt you want to hear something that don't hurt," Lincoln rejoined. He realized the moderator would be halting him soon; he hurried to the conclusion he had obviously written in advance. "Henry Clay, beau ideal of a statesman, the man for whom I fought all my humble life—Henry Clay once said of a class of men who would repress all tendencies to liberty and ultimate emancipation, that they must, if they would do this, go back to the era of our independence, and muzzle the cannon which thunders its annual joyous return; they must blow out the moral lights around us; they must penetrate the human soul, and eradicate there the love of liberty; and then, and not till then, could they perpetuate slavery in this country! To my thinking, Judge Douglas is, by his example and vast influence, doing that very thing in this community, when he says that the negro has nothing in the Declaration of Independence. Henry Clay plainly understood the contrary. Judge Douglas is going back to the era of our Revolution, and, to the extent of his ability, muzzling the cannon which thunders its annual joyous return. When he invites any people, willing to have slavery, to establish it, he is blowing out the moral lights around us."

John Brown dedicated himself to the struggle against slavery, which in the mid-1850s (the time of this photograph) was being waged by arms in Kansas.

Abraham Lincoln chose a different path: elective politics. A former Illinois state legislator and a one-term Whig member of Congress, Lincoln joined the new, antislavery Republican party in the 1850s in hopes of winning higher office.

This farm at North Elba in upstate New York was John Brown's home base.

Mary Brown learned to get along without her husband, who was absent more often than not. To her fell responsibility for raising the children, including these two.

While politics was Lincoln's ambition, his law practice kept a roof—in particular the roof of this Springfield house—over the heads of his family.

Mary Todd Lincoln had expected great things from her husband when they were wed; her ambitions for Lincoln amplified his own.

Frederick Douglass escaped from slavery in Maryland and became a powerful advocate of abolition—and an associate of John Brown's.

William Lloyd Garrison published *The Liberator*, the most prominent of the abolitionist journals.

Henry Ward Beecher preached abolition as part of his celebrated Brooklyn ministry.

Horace Greeley edited the *New York Tribune* and fancied himself a Republican kingmaker.

Philanthropist and reformer Gerrit Smith quietly funded John Brown's antislavery operations.

John Brown's participation in the murder of several proslavery settlers in Kansas in 1856 made him a wanted man, and life on the run took a toll on his health and appearance.

Dred Scott sued for his freedom from slavery; he lost, but the decision of the Supreme Court in the 1857 case proved a gift to Lincoln.

Roger Taney's troubled soul sought relief in the *Dred Scott* case, but the chief justice's opinion threw the nation into turmoil.

Democrat Stephen Douglas reopened the slavery debate in the 1850s and thereby afforded Abraham Lincoln a reentry into politics.

Although Lincoln lost his race for the Senate in 1858, his performance in debates against Stephen Douglas won him national recognition.

Brown's audacious raid on the federal arsenal at Harpers Ferry, Virginia, was launched in October 1859 from this rented farm across the Potomac River.

The raid misfired, leaving Brown and his men holed up in this engine house, where Brown and the other raiders not killed were captured.

The Southern press painted Brown as a tool of Satan, who in this image seems to smile his approval at Brown's bloody deeds.

In the North, Brown's bold stroke against slavery was viewed more favorably.
Following his conviction and hanging, he was treated as a martyr by abolitionists.

Amid the deepening division over slavery, Lincoln won the presidential election of 1860. Here he is being inaugurated.

Eleven Southern states, claiming fear for the future of slavery, and standing on their state's rights interpretation of the Constitution, seceded after Lincoln's election. Lincoln refused to let them go, and the cares of the ensuing Civil War aged him prematurely.

Although dead, John Brown was not forgotten. Union soldiers marched into battle singing "John Brown's body lies a-mouldering in the grave; his soul is marching on" (to the tune identified in this magazine illustration as "Glory Hallelujah").

Lincoln initially treated slavery and the defense of the Union as separate issues. But the war blurred the distinction, and he finally concluded that they could *not* be kept apart: that liberty and Union were inseparable. Here he reads a preliminary version of the Emancipation Proclamation to his cabinet.

Yet Lincoln didn't want to publish the proclamation until the Union won an important battlefield victory, lest emancipation be interpreted as an act of despair. That victory came at Antietam in September 1862.

TO COLORED MEN!

FREEDOM,
Protection, Pay, and a Call to Military Duty!

On the 1st day of January, 1863, the President of the United States proclaimed FREEDOM to over THREE MILLIONS OF SLAVES. This decree is to be enforced by all the power of the Nation. On the 21st of July last he issued the following order:

PROTECTION OF COLORED TROOPS.

"WAR DEPARTMENT, ADJUTANT GENERAL'S OFFICE, WASHINGTON, July 21.

"*General Order, No.* 233.

"The following order of the President is published for the information and government of all concerned:—

EXECUTIVE MANSION, WASHINGTON, July 30.

'"It is the duty of every Government to give protection to its citizens, of whatever class, color, or condition, and especially to those wh are duly organized as soldiers in the public service. The law of nations, and the usages and customs of war, as carried on by civilized powers, permit no distinction as to color in the treatment of prisoners of war as public enemies. To sell or enslave any captured person on account of his color, is a relapse into barbarism, and a crime against the civilization of the age.

'"The Government of the United States will give the same protection to all its soldiers, and if the enemy shall sell or enslave any one because of his color, the offense shall be punished by retaliation upon the enemy's prisoners in our possession. It is, therefore, ordered, for every soldier of the United States, killed in violation of the laws of war, a rebel soldier shall be executed; and for every one enslaved by the enemy, or sold into slavery, a rebel soldier shall be placed at hard labor on the public works, and continued at such labor until the other shall be released and receive the treatment due to prisoners of war.

'"ABRAHAM LINCOLN."'

'"By order of the Secretary of War.

'"E. D. TOWNSEND, Assistant Adjutant General."'

That the President is in earnest the rebels soon began to find out, as witness the following order from his Secretary of War:

"WAR DEPARTMENT, WASHINGTON CITY, August 8, 1863.

"SIR: Your letter of the 3d inst., calling the attention of this Department to the cases of Orin H. Brown, William H. Johnston, and Wm. Wilson, three colored men captured on the gunboat Isaac Smith, has received consideration. This Department has directed that three rebel prisoners of South Carolina, if there be any such in our possession, and if not, three others, be confined in close custody and held as hostages for Brown, Johnston and Wilson, and that the fact be communicated to the rebel authorities at Richmond.

"Very respectfully your obedient servant,

"EDWIN M. STANTON, Secretary of War.

"The Hon. GIDEON WELLES, Secretary of the Navy."

And retaliation will be our practice now—man for man—to the bitter end.

LETTER OF CHARLES SUMNER,
Written with reference to the Convention held at Poughkeepsie, July 15th and 16th, 1863, to promote Colored Enlistments.

BOSTON, July 13th, 1863.

"I doubt if, in times past, our country could have expected from colored men any patriotic service. Such service is the return for protection. But now that protection has begun, the service should begin also. Nor should relative rights and duties be weighed with nicety. It is enough that our country, aroused at last to a sense of justice, seeks to enrol colored men among its defenders.

"If my counsels should reach such persons, I would say: enlist at once. Now is the day and now is the hour. Help to overcome your cruel enemies now battling against your country, and in this way you will surely overcome those other enemies hardly less cruel, here at home, who will still seek to degrade you. This is not the time to hesitate or to higgle. Do your duty to our country, and you will set an example of generous self-sacrifice which will conquer prejudice and open all hearts.

"Very faithfully yours, "CHARLES SUMNER."

The Emancipation Proclamation, formalized on January 1, 1863, was accompanied by a call to the freedmen to join the Union army and help guarantee their liberty.

The war went slowly, even after emancipation, and Lincoln expected to lose his 1864 race for reelection. But a sudden turn of the military tide reversed the political mood, and Lincoln won comfortably. Here the crowd gathers for his second inauguration.

Frederick Douglass had been impatient, even furious, at Lincoln's slowness on slavery during the first part of the war. But by the time of Lincoln's second inauguration, which Douglass attended as an elder statesman of abolition, they were friends and allies.

Also in the inauguration crowd was John Wilkes Booth, an actor and angry Confederate sympathizer. Booth cast himself as Brutus to Lincoln's Julius Caesar.

Booth assassinated Lincoln in April 1865. The martyred president now sits on the National Mall.

John Brown, an earlier casualty in the struggle for freedom, lies at North Elba.

22

CARL SCHURZ KNEW Lincoln only by reputation before the debates with Douglas. Schurz had become a figure in Republican politics, speaking regularly among German immigrants. He had addressed a crowd in Chicago and was heading to Quincy to catch the next installment of the summer's traveling political show. "All at once, after the train had left a way station, I observed a great commotion among my fellow-passengers, many of whom jumped from their seats and pressed eagerly around a tall man who had just entered the car," he recalled. "They addressed him in the most familiar style: 'Hello, Abe! How are you?' and so on. And he responded in the same manner; 'Good evening, Ben! How are you, Joe? Glad to see you, Dick!'" Schurz looked to his traveling companion, who pointed and said, "Why, there's Lincoln himself!" The friend took Schurz forward and introduced him.

"I must confess that I was somewhat startled by his appearance," Schurz said of Lincoln. "There he stood, overtopping by several inches all those surrounding him. Although measuring something over six feet myself, I had, standing quite near to him, to throw my head backward in order to look into his eyes. That swarthy face with its strong features, its deep furrows, and its benignant, melancholy eyes, is now familiar to every American by numberless pictures. It may be said that the whole civilized world knows and loves it. At that time it was clean-shaven, and looked even more haggard and careworn than later when it was framed in whiskers. On his head he wore a somewhat battered 'stove-pipe' hat. His neck emerged, long and sinewy, from a white collar turned down over a thin black necktie. His lank, ungainly body was clad in a rusty black dress coat with sleeves that should have been longer; but his arms appeared so long that the sleeves of a 'store' coat could hardly be expected to cover them all the way down to the wrists. His black trousers, too, permitted a very full view of his large feet. On his left arm he carried a gray woolen shawl, which evidently served him for an overcoat in chilly weather. His left hand held a cotton umbrella of the bulging kind, and also a black satchel that bore the marks of long and hard usage. His right he had kept free for hand-shaking, of which there was no end until everybody in the car seemed to be satisfied. I had seen, in Washington and in the West, several public men of rough appearance; but none whose looks seemed quite so uncouth, not to say grotesque, as Lincoln's."

Lincoln apparently had been told that Schurz had been speaking for the Republican party to the Germans. "He received me with an off-hand cordiality, like an old acquaintance," Schurz recounted. "We sat down together. In a somewhat high-pitched but pleasant voice he began to talk to me, telling me about the points he and Douglas had made in the debates at different places, and about those he intended to make at Quincy on the morrow."

Schurz was struck by Lincoln's easy style. "I should have felt myself very much honored by his confidence, had he permitted me to regard him as a great man," Schurz said. "But he talked in so simple and familiar a strain, and his manner and homely phrase were so absolutely free from any semblance of self-consciousness or pretension to superiority, that I soon felt as if I had known him all my life and we had long been close friends." Schurz had noted the sound of laughter that surrounded Lincoln as he boarded the train and followed him into the car. Schurz now heard some of Lincoln's stories, which were interesting to Schurz chiefly for their effect on the teller. "He seemed to enjoy his own jests in a childlike way, for his unusually sad-looking eyes would kindle with a merry twinkle, and he himself led in the laughter; and his laugh was so genuine, hearty, and contagious that no one could fail to join in it."

They rode together all the way to Quincy, where Lincoln was offered a carriage to the home of a friend. He hoped to spend a quiet evening ahead of the debate. But the evening was far from quiet. The political circus was the biggest thing to hit Quincy since the circus itself, and the residents were making the most of it. Brass bands, one enlisted by each party, repeatedly struck up tunes for the rival champions. Residents and visitors to Quincy, again aligned by party, drank to the health of their heroes and sang their praises until far past midnight. Schurz got little sleep; he supposed Lincoln suffered too.

The audience was equally boisterous the next day. The Republicans shouted for Lincoln and against Douglas, and the Democrats responded in kind. Yet no one got angry or violent. "In spite of the excitement created by the political contest, the crowds remained very good-natured, and the occasional jibes flung from one side to the other were uniformly received with a laugh," Schurz said.

Lincoln had the opening and closing this day, Douglas the middle. Schurz, a public speaker himself, took notes of their performance. Lincoln's opening was lackluster. "It did not strike me as anything extraordinary, either in substance or in form. Neither had Mr. Lincoln any of those physical advantages which usually are thought to be very desirable, if not necessary, to the orator. His voice was not musical, rather high-keyed, and apt to turn into a shrill treble in moments of excitement; but it was not positively disagreeable. It had an exceedingly penetrating, far-reaching quality. The looks of the audience convinced me that every word he spoke was understood at the remotest edges of the vast assemblage. His gesture was awkward. He swung his long arms sometimes in a very ungraceful manner. Now and then he would, to give particular emphasis to a point, bend his knees and body with a sudden downward jerk, and then shoot up again with a vehemence that raised him to his tip-toes and made him look much taller than he really was—a manner of enlivening a speech which at that time was, and perhaps still is, not unusual in the West, but which he succeeded in avoiding at a later period."

Yet Lincoln's earnestness transcended his distracting delivery. "Even when attacking his opponent with keen satire or invective, which, coming from any other speaker, would have sounded bitter and cruel," Schurz said, "there was still a certain something in his utterance making his hearers feel that those thrusts came from a reluctant heart, and that he would much rather have treated his foe as a friend."

Schurz agreed with Lincoln's message, and as a Republican and fellow opponent of slavery he wanted Lincoln to win the debate. Yet he found himself worrying that Douglas, the veteran of years of debate in Congress and a master of all the arts of disputation, would chew Lincoln up. When Douglas rose to speak, Schurz's worries increased. "No more striking contrast could have been imagined than that between those two men as they appeared upon the platform," Schurz said. "By the side of Lincoln's tall, lank, and ungainly form, Douglas stood almost like a dwarf, very short of stature, but square-shouldered and broad-chested, a massive head upon a strong neck, the very embodiment of force, combativeness, and staying power." Schurz had first seen Douglas in the Senate years earlier, and he was curious to observe him in such a different setting. "On that stage at Quincy he looked rather natty and well groomed in excellently fitting broadcloth and shining linen," he said. "But his face seemed a little puffy, and it was said that he had been drinking hard with some boon companions either on his journey or after his arrival. The deep, horizontal wrinkle between his keen eyes was unusually dark and scowling. While he was listening to Lincoln's speech, a contemptuous smile now and then flitted across his lips, and when he rose, the tough parliamentary gladiator, he tossed his mane with an air of overbearing superiority, of threatening defiance, as if to say: 'How dare anyone stand up against me?'"

Schurz had disliked Douglas before; he now discovered that he detested him. "But my detestation was not free from an anxious dread as to what was to come," Schurz said. He feared the more for Lincoln as Douglas started to speak. "His voice, naturally a strong baritone, gave forth a hoarse and rough, at times even something like a barking, sound. His tone was, from the very start, angry, dictatorial, and insolent in the extreme. In one of his first sentences he charged Lincoln with 'base insinuations,' and then he went on in that style with a wrathful frown upon his brow, defiantly shaking his head, clenching his fists, and stamping his feet. No language seemed to be too offensive for him, and even inoffensive things he would sometimes bring out in a manner which sounded as if intended to be insulting; and thus he occasionally called forth, instead of applause from his friends, demonstrations of remonstrance from the opposition. But his sentences were well put together, his points strongly accentuated, his argumentation seemingly clear and plausible, his sophisms skillfully woven so as to throw the desired flood of darkness upon the subject and thus beguile the untutored mind, his appeals to prejudice unprincipled and reckless, but shrewdly aimed, and his invective vigorous and exceedingly trying to the temper of the assailed party. On the whole, his friends were well pleased with his performance, and rewarded him with vociferous cheers."

Douglas appeared to have prevailed. But then Lincoln spoke again. And to Schurz's not unbiased mind, he won the audience right back. "He replied to Douglas's arguments and attacks with rapid thrusts so deft and piercing, with humorous retort so quaint and pat, and with witty illustrations so clinching, and he did it all so good-naturedly, that the meeting, again and again, broke out in bursts of delight by which even many of his opponents were carried away, while the scowl on Douglas's face grew darker and darker."

Schurz would later see Lincoln deliver some of the great addresses in American history. He caught glimpses of that greatness on the stage at Quincy. "There was in his debates with Douglas, which, as to their form at least, were largely extemporaneous, occasionally a flash of the same lofty moral inspiration; and all he said came out with the sympathetic persuasiveness of a thoroughly honest nature, which made the listener feel as if the speaker looked him straight in the eye and took him by the hand, saying: 'My friend, what I tell you is my earnest conviction, and, I have no doubt, at heart you think so yourself.'"

23

A CROSS ILLINOIS the two men traveled, thrusting and parrying as they went. Before long they were repeating themselves, and repeating their repetitions. To many in each local audience their messages were fresh, but to those who followed the debates in the papers, the story grew old.

Occasionally something newsworthy surfaced. Ahead of the Freeport debate Douglas published a series of questions to Lincoln, trying to force him to choose between the moderate antislavery ground he favored and the more radical position of the Illinois Republican party. If Lincoln embraced the Republicans, he would lose votes of antislavery Democrats; if he distanced himself from his party, he would lose Republican votes.

The tactic had the disadvantage for Douglas of letting Lincoln prepare his answers ahead of time. Douglas was the quicker of the two on his feet; Lincoln the slower but steadier. Lincoln at Freeport read the questions and supplied his answers. Douglas had said, "I desire to know whether Lincoln today stands, as he did in 1854, in favor of the unconditional repeal of the Fugitive Slave law." Lincoln denied the premise and the conclusion. "I do not now, nor ever did, stand in favor of the unconditional repeal of the Fugitive Slave law." Douglas had written, "I desire him to answer whether he stands pledged today, as he did in 1854, against the admission of any more slave states into the Union, even if the people want them." Lincoln again denied both parts. "I do not now, nor ever did, stand pledged against the admission of any more slave states into the Union."

The examination continued, with Lincoln's answers echoing and refuting Douglas's questions. "I do not stand pledged against the admission of a new state into the Union, with such a constitution as the people of that state may see fit to make," Lincoln said. "I do not stand pledged to the prohibition of the slave trade between the different States. . . . I am impliedly, if not expressly, pledged to a belief in the right and duty of Congress to prohibit slavery in all the United States territories. . . . I am not generally opposed to honest acquisition of territory; and, in any given case, I would or would not oppose such acquisition, accordingly as I might think such acquisition would or would not aggravate the slavery question among ourselves."

Douglas listened with satisfaction. Lincoln appeared to be backing away from beliefs that many Illinois Republicans passionately held. Douglas knew the Republicans would have to turn out in record numbers to unseat him; Lincoln was giving them little reason to come to the polls.

Lincoln, realizing his disadvantage, launched a counteroffensive. He had prepared a list of questions of his own for Douglas to answer. One after the other Lincoln posed them to the senator. The most pointed demanded that Douglas explain what was left of popular sovereignty after the Dred Scott decision. "Can the people of a United States territory," Lincoln said, "in any lawful way, against the wish of any citizen of the United States, exclude slavery from its limits prior to the formation of a state constitution?"

Lincoln's question hung over the Freeport square while he finished his remarks; it hung there through Douglas's opening. Douglas understood the danger it posed, which was why he tried to dismiss it as one he had answered already—"a hundred times, from every stump in Illinois." Douglas's voice grew angry as he accused Lincoln of simply causing trouble. "Mr. Lincoln knew that I had answered that question over and over again. He heard me argue the Nebraska bill on that principle all over the state in 1854, in 1855, and in 1856, and he has no excuse for pretending to be in doubt as to my position on that question."

Yet Douglas recognized that he had to answer. And he realized he had no good answer. Lincoln was making him choose between popular sovereignty and the Dred Scott decision. No matter how he answered, he would alienate a large bloc of his party. If he chose popular sovereignty over the Dred Scott decision, he would anger the

South. If he chose the Dred Scott decision over popular sovereignty, he would lose much of the North.

He did what he could. "It matters not what way the Supreme Court may hereafter decide as to the abstract question whether slavery may or may not go into a territory under the Constitution," Douglas said. "The people have the lawful means to introduce it or exclude it as they please, for the reason that slavery cannot exist a day or an hour anywhere, unless it is supported by local police regulations. Those police regulations can only be established by the local legislature; and if the people are opposed to slavery, they will elect representatives to that body who will by unfriendly legislation effectually prevent the introduction of it into their midst. If, on the contrary, they are for it, their legislation will favor its extension. Hence, no matter what the decision of the Supreme Court may be on that abstract question, still the right of the people to make a slave territory or a free territory is perfect and complete."

SMITH ATKINS WAS an Illinois Republican who attended the Freeport debate. He afterward recalled meeting Lincoln ahead of the debate, in company with several other Lincoln partisans. "There was, in no sense, a consultation of Mr. Lincoln's supporters," Atkins said, "but in a general conversation that appeared to come about naturally, Mr. Lincoln read the questions he proposed to ask of Mr. Douglas." One of the questions was the one whether the people of a territory could exclude slavery in defiance of the Dred Scott ruling. "All of the prominent Republicans present who engaged in the conversation objected to Mr. Lincoln's asking that question of Mr. Douglas," Atkins recalled. "They argued that Mr. Douglas would, notwithstanding his unqualified endorsement of the Dred Scott case, answer that the people of a territory could exclude slavery by unfriendly legislation, and that Mr. Douglas would please the people by his answer, and would beat Mr. Lincoln for senator from Illinois."

Lincoln listened to the objections, Atkins remembered. But then he replied, "I don't know how Mr. Douglas will answer. If he answers that the people of a territory cannot exclude slavery, I will beat him.

But if he answers as you say he will, and as I believe he will, he may beat me for senator, but he will never be president."

Possibly Smith Atkins remembered things too well. Prescient statements eventually stuck to Lincoln like lint on his wool suit. Yet whether or not Lincoln said precisely what Atkins recalled him saying, the logic of the argument was sound. The Freeport Doctrine, as Douglas's formula was soon being called, had the effect its author anticipated in the Senate race against Lincoln. When Illinoisans went to the polls, they elected a majority of Democrats to the state legislature, who in turn elected Douglas to the Senate.

But the Douglas dodge enraged the South. Southern newspapers blasted the Freeport formula as a snare and a delusion; they called its author more dangerous to Southern interests than the most egregious abolitionist. If the South had anything to say about it, Stephen Douglas would indeed never be president.

As for Lincoln, he took the defeat philosophically. "The fight must go on," he wrote to an ally. "The cause of civil liberty must not be surrendered at the end of *one,* or even, one *hundred* defeats. Douglas had the ingenuity to be supported in the late contest both as the best means to *break down,* and to *uphold* the slave interest. No ingenuity can keep those antagonistic elements in harmony long. Another explosion will soon come."

PART III

Harpers Ferry

WHEN JOHN BROWN LEFT Boston in disgust at the lack of commitment among the abolitionists there, he reflexively headed back toward Kansas. He would take his war against slavery to the South, but his base was in Kansas. His followers, including his militant sons, were there; Kansas would be his springboard for whatever would follow.

Yet Kansas might also be a trap. John Brown and the other free-state fighters had done their job too well. The finagling over the Lecompton constitution left the future of Kansas in political limbo, but on the ground in the territory the antislavery settlers greatly outnumbered the pro-slavery ones. This wasn't entirely—or even mostly—the work of fighters like John Brown; the soil and climate of Kansas made it unsuited for the kind of plantation agriculture common in the South. Slavery had always been a long shot in Kansas, which was why the Missouri ruffians and the Pierce and Buchanan administrations had to work so hard to foster it there. The effect of Brown and his ilk was to enable Kansas to find its antislavery equilibrium.

But that very equilibrium meant Brown was no longer needed, or even wanted. Or, rather, he *was* wanted—for the Pottawatomie murders. And with law and order taking hold in Kansas, he might be arrested and tried for the crimes. John Brown Jr. warned his father against returning to Kansas, for precisely this reason. "It seems as though if you return to Kansas this spring I should never see you again," wrote the son, who had left the territory with his father. John feared that Kansans would show no gratitude for what Brown had done but would "hand you over to the tormentor." Perhaps John knew his father wouldn't be dissuaded by mere danger; perhaps he simply wanted to show his confidence in the old man, for he added, "I will not look on the dark side. You have gone safely through a thousand perils and hairbreadth escapes."

From Boston, Brown passed through Connecticut, stopping here and there to speak about Kansas. Charles Blair, a blacksmith—or "forger," as he called himself—heard Brown and was intrigued. Blair encountered Brown again the next morning. "He was exhibiting to a number of gentlemen who happened to be collected together in a druggist's store some weapons which he claimed to have taken from Captain Pate in Kansas," Blair recalled later. "Among them was a two-edged dirk, with a blade about eight inches long, and he remarked that if he had a lot of those things to attach to poles about six feet long, they would be a capital weapon of defense for the settlers of Kansas to keep in their log cabins to defend themselves against any sudden attack that might be made on them. He turned to me, knowing, I suppose, that I was engaged in edge-tool making, and asked me what I would make them for; what it would cost to make five hundred or a thousand of those things, as he described them."

Blair wasn't sure whether to take Brown seriously. "I replied, without much consideration, that I would make him five hundred of them for a dollar and a quarter a piece; or if he wanted a thousand of them, I thought they might be made for a dollar a piece," he said. But he couldn't commit himself until he looked further into the matter.

This was good enough for Brown. "He simply remarked that he would want them made," Blair said.

Blair still wasn't sure Brown was serious. "I thought no more about it until a few days afterwards," he said. "I did not really suppose he meant it."

Brown soon showed he did mean it. He asked Blair to fabricate a sample. Blair obliged, and Brown asked for a slight alteration that made the weapons easier to ship. Then Brown said he wanted a thousand.

Blair now had another reservation. He wondered whether Brown had the money to pay for the work. "Mr. Brown," he said, "I am a laboring man, and, if I engage in this contract with you, I shall want to know how I am going to get my pay."

"That is all right," Brown answered. "It is just that you should, and I will make it perfectly secure to you. I will give you one half the money, that is $500, within ten days; I will pay you the balance within thirty days, and give you ninety days to complete the contract."

Brown drew up the contract, and he and Blair signed it. Money proved a bit tighter than Brown had expected; for the first installment he was able to give Blair only $350. With this Blair purchased materials: wooden handles and iron for the blades. He set one of his men to forging the blades. Two weeks later Blair received another $200 from Brown, and the work proceeded.

But the promised balance—now of $450—did not appear within the thirty days specified. Instead Blair got a note from Brown saying, "If you do not hurry out but 500 of those articles it may, perhaps, be as well, until you hear again." Blair wasn't especially concerned. Other customers had been slow in paying. In any case, the handles for the weapons required seasoning before attachment to the blades, lest they shrink and come loose. Blair continued the work on the blades and let the handles dry.

During the following months, however, he neither heard from Brown nor received more money. Blair decided that business was business. "I stopped the thing right where it was, determining that I would not run any risk in the matter. I just laid it aside, and there it lay, the work in an unfinished state, the handles stored away in the store-house, the steel which I had purchased stored away in boxes, the few blades which I had forged laid away."

BROWN'S TRAVELS WERE complicated by the need to avoid arrest. "One of U.S. Hounds is on my track, and I have kept myself hid for a few days to let the track grow cold," he informed a friend. Fortunately for Brown, photography hardly existed, and no likeness of him circulated. As a result, using false names—Nelson Hawkins, Ian Smith—and care, he eluded his pursuers.

Illness also slowed him. Malaria was endemic to the Mississippi and Ohio valleys, and its "fever and ague" prostrated Brown for weeks at a stretch. Sometimes it affected his mental acuity. "I am much confused in mind, and cannot remember what I wish to write," he told his wife in one letter.

Between ill health and the calm that had settled over Kansas, Brown accomplished little for many months. He traveled about the Midwest to raise money, visiting Cleveland, Chicago, Milwaukee and other cities and towns where abolitionists congregated. He spent several weeks in Tabor, Iowa, regaining his strength and gathering loyalists around him. Most of the free-state men who had stood beside him in Kansas were Kansans; having kept Kansas out of slavery's grasp, they considered their work done. Brown now needed men who would follow him into the South.

As cold weather settled upon Iowa in the late autumn of 1857, making campaigning or even drilling difficult or impossible, Brown headed east once more.

"I am (praised be God!) once more in York State," he wrote to his wife from Rochester in January 1858. "Whether I shall be permitted to visit you or not this winter or spring, I cannot now say; but it is some relief of mind to feel that I am again so near you. Possibly, if I cannot go to see you, I may be able to devise some way for some one or more of you to meet me somewhere. The anxiety I feel to see my wife and children once more I am unable to describe." Yet duty called, and he hoped they could join him in committing to the higher cause. "Courage, courage, courage!—the great work of my life (the unseen Hand that 'guided me, and who has indeed holden my right hand, may hold it still,' though I have not known him at all as I ought) I may yet see accomplished (God helping), and be permitted to return, and 'rest at evening.'"

But home was hazardous for a man on the run. The authorities didn't know where Brown was, but they knew where he lived, and they kept a lookout for a man of his description in the vicinity of North Elba. He cautioned Mary against anything that might tip them off. "Do not noise it about that I am in these parts," he said, "and direct to N. Hawkins, care of Frederick Douglass, Rochester, N.Y."

Brown touched on a topic sensitive in the family. He had been trying to persuade his son-in-law Henry Thompson, who had been with him at Pottawatomie, to rejoin the company. Thompson had returned home, evidently having had enough of bloodshed. "O my daughter Ruth!" Brown wrote to Thompson's wife. "Could any plan be devised whereby you let Henry 'go to school' (as you expressed it in your letter to him while in Kansas), I would rather now have him 'for another term' than to have a hundred average scholars." Brown said he was sure some way could be devised whereby Ruth and her children could be supported while Henry was in the field. Yet he didn't want to push too hard. "God forbid me to flatter you into trouble!" he said to Ruth. "I did not do it before. My dear child, could you face such music if, on a full explanation, Henry could be satisfied that his family might be safe?" Brown acknowledged what he had put Ruth's mother through. "I would make a similar inquiry of my own dear wife; but I have kept her tumbling here and there over a stormy and tempestuous sea for so many years that I cannot ask her such a question."

Ruth considered Brown's plea. "Dear father, you have asked me rather of a hard question," she replied. "I want to answer you wisely, but I hardly know how. I cannot bear the thought of Henry leaving me again; yet I know I am selfish." It wasn't the danger so much as the separation she feared, she said. In fact she volunteered to join Henry with Brown's company. "Would my going be of any service to him or you? I should be very glad to be with him, if it would not be more expense than what we could do. I say *we;* could I not do something for the cause?"

Brown might have been willing to say yes. But Thompson would not. Ruth relayed his response to Brown: "Tell father that I think he places too high an estimate on my qualifications." And Thompson stayed home.

BROWN KEPT MOVING. "I am here with our good friends Gerrit Smith and wife, who, I am most happy to tell you, are ready to go in for a share in the whole trade," Brown wrote from Peterboro, New York, to his son John. The wealthy Smith was Brown's most consistent sponsor, and Brown was pleased for the continued support. He added, "I have still need of all the help I can possibly get, but am greatly encouraged in asking for it."

To stimulate help, Brown shared more about what the "whole trade" entailed. Frank Sanborn traveled to Peterboro to see Brown; he joined Brown, Gerrit Smith and one of Sanborn's college friends, Edwin Morton, who happened to be a tutor to Smith's children, at Smith's large house. "Here, in the long winter evening that followed, Brown unfolded for the first time to me his plans for a campaign somewhere in slave territory east of the Alleghenies," Sanborn recalled. "It was an amazing proposition—desperate in its character, wholly inadequate in its provision of means, and of most uncertain result. Such as it was, Brown had set his heart on it as the shortest way to restore our slave-cursed republic to the principles of the Declaration of Independence; and he was ready to die in its execution."

Sanborn and the others were skeptical and asked for specifics, not least because Brown was once more seeking money. "He laid before us in detail his methods of organization and fortification; of settlement in the South, if that were possible, and of retreat through the North, if necessary; and his theory of the way in which such an invasion would be received in the country at large."

Brown said he wanted candid responses to his plan. Yet when he heard them, he wasn't moved. "We listened until after midnight, proposing objections and raising difficulties," Sanborn recounted. "But nothing could shake the purpose of the old Puritan. Every difficulty had been foreseen and provided against in some manner; the grand difficulty of all—the manifest hopelessness of undertaking anything so vast with such slender means—was met with the text of Scripture: 'If God be for us, who can be against us?'"

Brown said preparations were well along. He needed but eight hundred dollars, although a thousand would be better. "With that he would open his campaign in the spring, and he had no doubt that the enterprise 'would pay,'" Sanborn related.

Once more Sanborn and the others cited the difficulties Brown would face. "But no argument could prevail against his fixed purpose; he was determined to make the attempt, with many or with few, and he left us only the alternatives of betrayal, desertion or support."

The group adjourned for the evening and met again the next day. "The discussion was renewed, and, as usually happened when he had time enough, Captain Brown began to prevail over the objections," Sanborn wrote. "We saw we must either stand by him or leave him to dash himself alone against the fortress he was determined to assault. To withhold aid would only delay, not prevent him."

That afternoon Sanborn met separately with Gerrit Smith. The two walked across the snowy hills of Smith's estate, discussing Brown's project. Smith agreed with Sanborn that they had no choice. "You see how it is," Smith said. "Our dear old friend has made up his mind to this course, and cannot be turned from it. We cannot give him up to die alone; we must support him." Smith said he would raise money for Brown in New York; Sanborn must do the same in Massachusetts. "I see no other way."

Sanborn nodded. "I had come to the same conclusion, and by the same process of reasoning," he said. He added, "It was done far more from our regard for the man than from hopes of immediate success."

Sanborn returned to Boston. A letter from Brown followed him. "My dear Friend," Brown wrote. "Mr. Morton has taken the liberty of saying to me that you felt half inclined to make a common cause with me. I greatly rejoice at this; for I believe when you come to look at the ample field I labor in, and the rich harvest which not only this entire country but the whole world during the present and future generations may reap from its successful cultivation, you will feel that you are out of your element until you find you are in it, an entire unit. What an inconceivable amount of good you might so effect by your counsel, your example, your encouragement, your natural and acquired ability for active service! And then, how very little we can possibly lose! Certainly the cause is enough to *live* for, if not to —— for."

Brown reflected on his own case. "I have only had this one opportunity, in a life of nearly sixty years; and could I be continued ten times as long again, I might not again have another equal opportunity. God has honored but comparatively a very small part of mankind with any possible chance for such mighty and soul-satisfying rewards." Brown anticipated success, even if it came at a cost. "I expect nothing but to endure hardness, but I expect to effect a mighty conquest, even though it be like the last victory of Samson. I felt for a number of years, in earlier life, a steady, strong desire to die; but since I saw any prospect of becoming a 'reaper' in the great harvest, I have not only felt quite willing to live, but have enjoyed life much, and am now rather anxious to live for a few years more."

RICHARD REALF WAS an Englishman of precocious literary talents, a poet published before he turned twenty. "I had been a protégé of Lady Noel Byron, widow of Lord Byron," he later said to investigators probing his connection to John Brown. "I had disagreed with Lady Noel Byron, on account of some private matters, which it is not necessary to explain here, but which rendered me desirous of finding some other place in which to dwell. Moreover, my instincts were democratic and republican, or, at least, anti-monarchical. Therefore I came to America."

Americans weren't interested in Realf's poetry, so he started writing for newspapers. The story of the day was the struggle for Kansas, and to Kansas he went. "I was residing in the city of Lawrence, Kansas, as a correspondent of the Illinois State Gazette, edited by Messrs. Bailhace & Baker," Realf continued. "I had been, and was, a radical abolitionist." John Brown, then in Tabor, Iowa, apparently read some of Realf's pieces and decided he might be useful. Brown sent one of his men, John Cook, to Lawrence to invite Realf to come to Tabor. Realf, curious, accepted the invitation.

The investigators asked Realf if Brown explained the purpose of the invitation.

"He stated that he purposed to make an incursion into the Southern states, somewhere in the mountainous region of the Blue Ridge and the Alleghenies," Realf replied.

What was the aim of the incursion?

"To liberate the slaves."

Did Brown explain how this was to be accomplished?

"Not at that time."

Did Realf enter into any agreement with Brown?

"Yes, sir."

Of what nature?

"I agreed to accompany him."

The investigators asked Realf what happened after this first meeting.

"From Tabor, where I myself first met John Brown and the majority of the persons forming the white part of his company in Virginia, we passed across the state of Iowa, until we reached Cedar county, in that state. We started in December, 1857. It was about the end of December, 1857, or the beginning of January, 1858, when we reached Cedar county, the journey thus consuming about a month of time. We stopped at a village called Springdale, in that county, where in a settlement principally composed of Quakers, we remained."

At Springdale, Realf and the others practiced at being soldiers. Brown soon left to travel east in search of funds to support them. He was absent for three months, returning in April 1858. Brown announced that the company was going to Canada. They made an odd group, some dozen men, mostly young but one much older, traveling for no reason they could reveal to those they encountered. Odder still was that they included a black man, Richard Richardson. And stranger yet, for that era, was that Richardson was treated just like the others.

One of the investigators queried Realf on this point. "Was Brown's intercourse with the negro of a character to show that he treated him as an equal and an associate?"

"It certainly was," Realf said. "To prove it, I will simply state that, having to wait twelve hours at Chicago, in order to make railroad connection from Chicago to Detroit, and to Canada, we necessarily had to breakfast and dine. We went into one of the hotels in order to breakfast. We took this colored man, Richardson, to table with us. The keeper of the hotel explained to us that it could not be allowed. We did not eat our breakfast. We went to another hotel, where we could take a colored man with us and sit down to breakfast."

"Where you could enjoy your rights, I suppose?"

"Yes, sir."

From Detroit the group crossed into Canada, halting at the town of Chatham. By this time the Underground Railroad had transported thousands of fugitive slaves to freedom in Canada, and among them Brown and his party were most welcome. They lodged at a hotel operated by a black man. From this hotel Brown discreetly circulated news of a convention to be held in Chatham for an important purpose.

Only when the small group had gathered did they learn what that purpose was. "John Brown, on rising, stated that for twenty or thirty years the idea had possessed him like a passion of giving liberty to the slaves," Realf recounted. "John Brown stated, moreover, that he had not been indebted to anyone for the suggestion of this plan; that it arose spontaneously in his own mind; that through a series of from twenty to thirty years it had gradually formed and developed itself into shape and plan. He stated that he had read all the books upon insurrectionary warfare which he could lay his hands upon—the Roman warfare; the successful opposition of the Spanish chieftains during the period when Spain was a Roman province; how with ten thousand men divided and subdivided into small companies, acting simultaneously, yet separately, they withstood the whole consolidated power of the Roman empire through a number of years." Brown described other insurrections, including that by slaves in Haiti against their white masters. "From all these things he had drawn the conclusion, believing, as he stated there he did believe, and as we all (if I may judge from myself) believed, that upon the first intimation of a plan formed for the liberation of the slaves, they would immediately rise all over the Southern states. He supposed that they would come into the mountains to join him, where he purposed to work, and that by flocking to his standard they would enable him (by making the line of mountains which cuts diagonally through Maryland and Virginia down through the Southern states into Tennessee and Alabama, the base of his operations) to act upon the plantations on the plains lying on each side of that range of mountains, and that we should be able to establish ourselves in the fastnesses, and if any hostile action (as would be) were taken against us, either by the militia of the separate states, or by the armies of the United States, we purposed to defeat first the militia, and next, if it were possible, the troops of the United States, and then organize the freed blacks."

The investigators asked where Brown expected to acquire assistance. Who were to be his soldiers?

"The negroes were to constitute the soldiers," Realf said. "John Brown expected that all the free negroes in the Northern states would immediately flock to his standard. He expected that all the slaves in the Southern states would do the same. He believed, too, that as many of the free negroes in Canada as could accompany him, would do so."

What would happen to the slaveholders?

"The slaveholders were to be taken as hostages, if they refused to let their slaves go. It is a mistake to suppose that they were to be killed; they were not to be. They were to be held as hostages for the safe treatment of any prisoners of John Brown's who might fall into the hands of hostile parties."

And the non-slaveholders?

"All the non-slaveholders were to be protected. Those who would not join the organization of John Brown, but who would not oppose it, were to be protected; but those who did oppose it, were to be treated as the slaveholders themselves."

Did Brown say anything else?

"John Brown said that he believed a successful incursion could be made; that it could be successfully maintained; that the several slave states could be forced (from the position in which they found themselves) to recognize the freedom of those who had been slaves within the respective limits of those states."

WITH THIS AS a preface, John Brown presented to the group a document he called a "Provisional Constitution and Ordinances for the People of the United States." They scratched their heads but kept silent as he read the preamble: "Whereas slavery, throughout its entire existence in the United States, is none other than a most barbarous, unprovoked, and unjustifiable war of one portion of its citizens upon another portion—the only conditions of which are perpetual imprisonment and hopeless servitude or absolute extermination—in utter disregard and violation of those eternal and self-evident truths set forth in our Declaration of Independence; therefore we, citizens of the United States, and the oppressed people who, by a recent decision of the Supreme Court, are declared to have no rights which the white man is bound to respect, together with all other people degraded by the laws thereof, do, for the time being, ordain and establish for ourselves the following Provisional Constitution and Ordinances, the better to protect our persons, property, lives, and liberties, and to govern our actions."

Brown didn't explain what territory the proposed government would claim, or what the government's relations to the existing federal and state governments would be. Instead he proceeded to the constitution's first article, which endorsed a radical form of equality. "All persons of mature age, whether proscribed, oppressed, and enslaved citizens, or of the proscribed and oppressed races of the United States, who shall agree to sustain and enforce the Provisional Constitution and Ordinances of this organization, together with all minor children of such persons, shall be held to be fully entitled to protection under the same."

Subsequent articles proclaimed three branches for the provisional government. The legislative branch would consist of a single house "composed of not less than five nor more than ten members." Brown was starting small. The executive branch would be headed by a president and a vice president. The judicial branch would consist of a supreme court manned by a chief justice and four associate justices, and of five circuit courts, one for each of the justices. The justices would be elected rather than appointed.

There was much more, to the sum of forty-eight articles. Brown's charter was designed for a war government, as indicated by article 32, which mandated a "fair and impartial trial" for any captured prisoner; and article 37, which decreed the death penalty for deserters, spies and saboteurs. Article 33 declared that slaveholders who voluntarily released their slaves should be "treated as friends, and not merely as persons neutral." Articles 40 through 44 forbade swearing, drunkenness, quarreling and fornication; ordered capital punishment for rape; authorized a bureau for repairing broken families; enjoined respect for the Sabbath; encouraged the open carrying of firearms by women as well as men; and banned the concealed carrying of weapons. Article 46 asserted, unconvincingly, the loyalty of Brown and his followers to the existing governments in the United States: "The foregoing articles shall not be construed so as in any way to encourage the overthrow of any state government, or of the general government of the United States, and look to no dissolution of the Union, but simply to amendment and repeal. And our flag shall be the same that our fathers fought under in the Revolution."

Not until this article was there any objection from the gathered group, who realized that they were the delegates to Brown's constitutional convention. The first forty-five articles were adopted unanimously and without discussion. The loyalty article rubbed one delegate the wrong way, and he moved to strike it out. But the motion failed to win a second, and the article was swiftly adopted, as were the remaining two, unanimously.

The constitution having been adopted, Brown was named commander in chief of the provisional regime's armed forces.

The group adjourned, with most still wondering what they had done.

ROWN HIT the road once more. From western Canada he traveled east, always seeking money. He met with six of his supporters who had formed a secret committee to fund his activities—Gerrit Smith, Frank Sanborn, Theodore Parker, Samuel Howe, George Stearns and Thomas Higginson. Smith supplied another endorsement, a new donation and a fresh disclaimer. "I have great faith in the wisdom, integrity, and bravery of Captain Brown," Smith wrote to Sanborn. "For several years I have frequently given him money toward sustaining him in his contests with the slave-power. Whenever he shall embark in another of these contests I shall again stand ready to help him; and I will begin with giving him a hundred dollars. I do not wish to know Captain Brown's plans; I hope he will keep them to himself."

Brown made a quick visit to North Elba, where he saw his wife and the children there, and looped west through Ohio and Illinois, finally reaching Kansas in late June. "We were at supper that day at a hotel in Lawrence," wrote James Redpath, the journalist who had visited Brown's camp on Ottawa Creek, "when a stately old man, with a flowing white beard, entered the room and took a seat at the public table. I immediately recognized in the stranger John Brown. Yet many persons who had previously known him did not penetrate his patriarchal disguise."

The disguise extended to his name, which he had changed once more, to Shubel Morgan. A recent uptick in violence in Kansas caused Brown to think there might be more fighting there. He wasn't averse to the possibility. Difficulties dogged his plans for an attack on the

South. An erstwhile member of Brown's entourage, Hugh Forbes, unhappy with Brown's leadership, had been spreading tales in Washington of what Brown had in mind. Brown's backers took fright and determined to rein him in. "It seems to me that under these circumstances Brown must go no further, and so I write him," said Gerrit Smith to Frank Sanborn. "I never was convinced of the wisdom of his scheme. But as things now stand, it seems to me it would be madness to attempt to execute it."

Letters, even from such a previously unquestioning supporter as Gerrit Smith, might not have stopped Brown from marching south. But Brown depended more than ever on the money of Smith and others, without which he couldn't go forward. Beyond money were weapons. The Kansas committees of Sanborn and his associates had purchased rifles and sent them west, intending that the guns be used in the self-defense of free-state settlers in Kansas. The rifles had *not* been intended for a war against one of the slave states. Moreover, while cash was hard to trace, guns left a trail of purchase and shipment, and that trail led back to those who had paid for them. Members of the committees now demanded that the weapons be kept out of the hands of Brown, who had been relying on them for his Southern campaign.

A recurrence of malaria additionally muddled Brown's plans. "Have been down with the ague since last date"—two weeks earlier— "and had no safe way of getting off my letter," he wrote to Frank Sanborn in August. "I had lain every night without shelter, suffering from cold rains and heavy dews, together with the oppressive heat of the days." A month later he hadn't fully recovered. "I am still very weak, and write with great labor," he informed his wife, in a letter unsigned lest it fall into the hands of the authorities.

He lay low in Kansas through the autumn. "My health is some improved since I wrote you last, but I still get a shake now and then," he said in December. Yet he hadn't lost sight of what he now took to be his true mission. "Am still preparing for my other journey."

THE INACTIVITY WORE on him. He determined to strike a blow for freedom, even if smaller than the insurrectionary war he envisioned.

A fugitive slave from Missouri approached Brown and asked for help. He, his wife and children, and another slave were to be sold down the river; could Brown help him?

Brown could and did, as he explained in a letter he sent to Horace Greeley, who published it in the *New York Tribune*. "Two small companies were made up to go to Missouri and forcibly liberate the five slaves, together with other slaves," Brown wrote. "We proceeded to the place, surrounded the buildings, liberated the slaves, and also took certain property supposed to belong to the estate." The slaves informed them that some of the property belonged not to the master but to a tenant on the plantation. "We promptly returned to him all we had taken," Brown said. "We then went to another plantation, where we found five more slaves, some property and two white men. We moved all slowly away into the Territory"—Kansas—"for some distance, and then sent the white men back."

Having rescued the slaves, Brown intended to guide them to permanent freedom in Canada. The task was daunting. Neither Brown nor the fugitives were dressed for the prairie winter. Frostbite afflicted the bare feet of the fugitives and the hands and ears of all the group. Kansas sheriffs and federal troops were on the lookout for the runaways and their abettors. To the charge of slave-stealing was added that of murder, for one of the members of the second company that went out with Brown had killed a man who resisted the liberation. The Underground Railroad extended into Kansas at this time, affording safe houses for Brown and his party, but between the houses, on the open road, they were conspicuous and vulnerable.

Yet Brown was intrepid, and his example inspired other antislavery men to join him for parts of the journey. One of them described a scrape with the law. "A short distance from our road was Muddy Creek, where the marshal, supposing our party must pass that way, stationed himself on the opposite side of the creek, with eighty armed men, for he had made careful preparations, knowing that it was no joke to attack old Brown. Captain Brown had with him only twenty-three white men, all told. He placed them in double file, in front of the emigrant wagons, and said, 'Now go straight at 'em, boys! They'll be sure to run.' In obedience to this order, we marched towards the creek, but scarcely had the foremost entered the water when the valiant marshal mounted his horse and rode off in haste. His men followed as fast as possible, but they were not all so lucky as he was in untying their horses from the stumps and bushes. The scene was ridiculous beyond description; some horses were hastily mounted by two men. One man grabbed tight hold of the tail of a horse, trying to leap on from behind, while the rider was putting the spurs into his sides; so he went flying through the air, his feet touching the ground now and then." Several of Brown's men were mounted; he ordered them to give chase. They returned with four prisoners and five horses. The latter were put to use for transport; the former were held as hostages. Brown lectured the hostages on the evils of slavery; when the party had passed the most dangerous stretch of that part of the journey, he released them, without their horses, to walk home.

Brown's company crossed out of Kansas in early February. "I am once more in Iowa through the great mercy of God," he wrote to Mary. "Those with me and other friends are well." Yet his Iowa friends at Tabor weren't so friendly now. The Taborites had been willing to support Brown's struggle against slavery when it took place in Kansas, but when Brown brought the struggle to Iowa, in the form of the fugitives, their fervor cooled. "While we sympathize with the oppressed and will do all that we conscientiously can to help them in their efforts for freedom," a resolution approved by their church meeting explained, "nevertheless we have no sympathy with those who go to slave states to entice away slaves and take property or life."

Brown got the hint and departed. Other communities were more welcoming. At Grinnell, named for Josiah Grinnell, Iowa's leading abolitionist, the reception couldn't have been more supportive. Brown, still irked at Tabor's standoffishness, sent back to that town a summary of what Grinnell had done for the cause: "1st. Whole party and teams kept for two days free of cost. 2d. Sundry articles of clothing given to captives. 3d. Bread, meat, cakes, pies, etc. prepared for our journey." There was more, including twenty-six dollars in cash and congratulations and encouragement on the work in hand.

Yet hurdles remained. Brown's reputation struck terror into the hearts of some who might have opposed him, as it had frightened the posse he scattered at Muddy Creek. But it seemed to embolden others, who thought that by capturing or killing him they could win a reputation of their own. One story related afterward told of an intemperate pro-slavery fellow haranguing a crowd about what he would do to that murdering, man-stealing abolitionist Brown if he ever laid eyes on him. He would shoot him on the spot, he vowed.

A bearded gentleman in the back of the crowd responded in a mild voice. "My friend, you talk very brave," he said. "And as you will never have a better opportunity to shoot Old Brown than right here and now, you can have a chance." He produced two revolvers from under his coat and offered one to the brave orator, telling him to fire at will.

The boaster grew pale as he realized who the man was. He turned his back and stalked away, leaving Brown to re-holster the pistols.

The journey from eastern Iowa to Chicago went more swiftly, courtesy of a railroad agent who let them ride in an empty boxcar. The agent pretended not to notice, and in fact refused payment lest he and the railroad be found complicit. "We might be held for the value of every one of those niggers," he said.

The penultimate leg of the flight, from Chicago to Detroit, was also by train, this time paid for with funds Brown gathered on the way. The journey concluded for the fugitives with a ferry ride to Windsor, Canada. Their number had grown from eleven to twelve when one of the women gave birth on the journey. In Canada they were safe, for British law governed Canada, and the British, once having been the great slave traders of the Atlantic world, had become arch abolitionists.

John Brown took satisfaction in the accomplishment. His career as a liberator had begun.

27

T HE FLIGHT to Canada with the fugitives enhanced Brown's
mystique. He once more visited the Boston area, again seeking
money. Bronson Alcott heard him address a group in Concord.
"He tells his story with surpassing simplicity and sense, impress-
ing us all deeply by his courage and religious earnestness," the old
transcendentalist wrote in his diary. "Our best people listen to his
words—Emerson, Thoreau, Judge Hoar, my wife; and some of them
contribute something in aid of his plans without asking particulars,
such confidence does he inspire in his integrity and abilities." Alcott
read between the lines of Brown's words. "The Captain leaves us much
in the dark concerning his destination and designs for the coming
months. Yet he does not conceal his hatred of slavery, nor his readiness to strike a blow for freedom at the proper moment. I infer it is
his intention to run off as many slaves as he can, and so render that
property insecure to the master. I think him equal to anything he
dares—the man to do the deed, if it must be done, and with the martyr's temper and purpose."

Brown certainly looked the part. "He is of imposing appearance,
personally," Alcott wrote: "tall, with square shoulders and standing;
eyes of deep gray, and couchant, as if ready to spring at the least rustling, dauntless yet kindly; his hair shooting backward from low down
on his forehead; nose trenchant and Romanesque; set lips, his voice
suppressed yet metallic, suggesting deep reserves; decided mouth;
the countenance and frame charged with power throughout. Since
here last he has added a flowing beard, which gives the soldierly air
and the port of an apostle. Though sixty years old, he is agile and alert,

and ready for any audacity, in any crisis. I think him about the manli-
est man I have ever seen."

WHEN FREDERICK DOUGLASS SAW John Brown, he too realized
something had changed. But it wasn't just the beard—and it wasn't,
Douglass thought, for the better. "From the time of my visit to him in
Springfield, Mass., in 1847, our relations were friendly and confidential," Douglass wrote of Brown. "I never passed through Springfield
without calling on him, and he never came to Rochester without calling on me. He often stopped over night with me, when we talked over
the feasibility of his plan for destroying the value of slave property,
and the motive for holding slaves in the border states." Brown's plan,
as Douglass remembered it, had been to establish a chain of safe spots
in the mountains that ran from Virginia to Canada. Small squadrons
of fighters would defend the safe places and the slaves who would,
on Brown's encouragement, run away to them. Via the safe refuges
the slaves would be transported to freedom, though some—many,
Brown hoped—would choose to join his small army and help wage
the struggle.

The plan had appealed to Douglass. "Hating slavery as I did, and
making its abolition the object of my life, I was ready to welcome any
new mode of attack upon the slave system which gave any promise
of success," he said. "I readily saw that this plan could be made very
effective in rendering slave property in Maryland and Virginia value-
less by rendering it insecure. Men do not like to buy runaway horses,
or to invest their money in a species of property likely to take legs and
walk off with itself." In the worst case, the plan would fail but would
publicize the lengths to which brave men were willing to go to fight
slavery. By that means, if not by the other, slavery would be rendered
less secure.

The plan hung fire while Brown dealt with the affairs of Kansas
and gathered support. Douglass saw Brown periodically, and certain
remarks Brown made caused Douglass to believe that the old man's
plans were changing. "Once in a while he would say he could, with
a few resolute men, capture Harper's Ferry, and supply himself with
arms belonging to the government at that place." Douglass didn't

know whether to take this seriously. "He never announced his intention to do so. It was, however, very evidently passing in his mind as a thing he might do. I paid but little attention to such remarks."

Not until the summer of 1859 did Douglass realize that Harpers Ferry had become the focus of Brown's attention. "John Brown wrote to me, informing me that a beginning in his work would soon be made, and that before going forward he wanted to see me, and appointed an old stone-quarry near Chambersburg, Penn., as our place of meeting. Mr. Kagi, his secretary, would be there, and they wished me to bring any money I could command, and Shields Green along with me." John Kagi was a twenty-four-year-old Ohioan who had met Brown in Kansas and quickly fallen under his spell. He was resourceful and obedient, and Brown made him secretary of war in his notional government. Shields Green was an escaped slave, from South Carolina, hardy and resourceful.

Brown was living under the name Ian Smith, and in this letter he posed as a miner. "He said that his 'mining tools' and stores were then at Chambersburg, and that he would be there to remove them," Douglass recounted. Douglass managed to raise a small amount of money, and with Shields Green he went to Chambersburg.

"I approached the old quarry very cautiously, for John Brown was generally well armed, and regarded strangers with suspicion," Douglass wrote. There was a bounty of thousands of dollars on his head, and Brown couldn't be too cautious. "As I came near, he regarded me rather suspiciously, but soon recognized me, and received me cordially. He had in his hand when I met him a fishing-tackle, with which he had apparently been fishing in a stream hard by; but I saw no fish, and did not suppose that he cared much for his 'fisherman's luck.' The fishing was simply a disguise, and was certainly a good one. He looked every way like a man of the neighborhood, and as much at home as any of the farmers around there. His hat was old and storm-beaten, and his clothing was about the color of the stone-quarry itself—his then present dwelling-place."

The four men—Brown, Douglass, Kagi and Green—sat down amid the rocks of the quarry. "The taking of Harper's Ferry, of which Captain Brown had merely hinted before, was now declared as his settled purpose, and he wanted to know what I thought of it."

Nothing good, as Douglass explained. "I at once opposed the measure with all the arguments at my command." The attack would be fatal to those who engaged in it and destructive of the prospects of freeing slaves. "It would be an attack upon the federal government, and would array the whole country against us."

Brown was neither surprised nor deterred by Douglass's dissent. "He did not at all object to rousing the nation," Douglass said. "It seemed to him that something startling was just what the nation needed. He had completely renounced his old plan, and thought that the capture of Harper's Ferry would serve as notice to the slaves that their friends had come, and as a trumpet to rally them to his standard. He described the place as to its means of defense, and how impossible it would be to dislodge him if once in possession."

Douglass couldn't match Brown for details, and he didn't try. But he remained convinced the plan was lunacy. "I told him, and these were my words, that all his arguments, and all his descriptions of the place, convinced me that he was going into a perfect steel-trap, and that once in he would never get out alive; that he would be surrounded at once and escape would be impossible."

Brown wouldn't budge. "He was not to be shaken by anything I could say, but treated my views respectfully, replying that even if surrounded he would find means for cutting his way out; but that would not be forced upon him; he should, at the start, have a number of the best citizens of the neighborhood as his prisoners and that holding them as hostages he should be able, if worse came to worse, to dictate terms of egress from the town."

Douglass began to question Brown's sanity. "I looked at him with some astonishment, that he could rest upon a reed so weak and broken, and told him that Virginia would blow him and his hostages sky-high, rather than that he should hold Harper's Ferry an hour." The failure of the attack would simply fasten the fetters of the slaves more tightly.

Brown still refused to yield. So did Douglass. "Our talk was long and earnest; we spent the most of Saturday and a part of Sunday in this debate—Brown for Harper's Ferry, and I against it; he for striking a blow which should instantly rouse the country, and I for the policy of gradually and unaccountably drawing off the slaves to the mountains, as at first suggested and proposed by him."

In time Douglass ran out of breath and arguments. He said he was going home, and he invited Shields Green to join him.

Brown made one more plea. "He put his arms around me in a manner more than friendly, and said: 'Come with me, Douglass; I will defend you with my life. I want you for a special purpose. When I strike, the bees will begin to swarm, and I shall want you to help hive them.'"

Douglass shook him off. "My discretion or my cowardice made me proof against the dear old man's eloquence—perhaps it was something of both which determined my course."

Douglass then looked to Shields Green. "When about to leave I asked Green what he had decided to do, and was surprised by his coolly saying, in his broken way, 'I b'leve I'll go wid de ole man.'"

28

W HEN ABRAHAM LINCOLN PREDICTED another explosion that would advance the cause of the Republican party, he was thinking of something like the Kansas-Nebraska Act or the Dred Scott decision. He was thinking of Stephen Douglas, not John Brown.

He had to think of his wife, too, and his children. Mary had borne Lincoln four sons. Robert turned fifteen amid his father's Senate campaign against Douglas. Willie was six and Tad four that season. Another son, Eddie, the second born, had died before his fourth birthday. Mary endorsed her husband's political ambitions; the idea of being married to a great man appealed to her more than ever. But growing boys had to eat and the family be cared for. Lincoln's campaign against Douglas had brought him recognition but cost him income; as after his previous failures, he needed to recoup lost financial ground. "I have been on expenses so long without earning anything that I am absolutely without money now for even household purposes," he wrote to a friend.

As before, he redoubled his efforts in his practice. At least he tried to. But his mind was elsewhere. "No man knows, when that presidential grub gets to gnawing at him, just how deep in it will get until he has tried it," Lincoln observed afterward. His need to concentrate on his practice furnished an excuse when he received unappealing invitations to speak. "It is bad to be poor," he responded to one such request. "I shall go to the wall for bread and meat, if I neglect my business this year as well as last. It would please me much to see the city, and good people, of Keokuk, but for this year it is little less than an impossibility."

Yet he never declined the invitations he liked, the ones that would advance his ambitions. No sooner had the votes been counted in the Senate election than he was plotting his party's course for 1860. "Douglas has gone South, making characteristic speeches, and seeking to re-instate himself in that section," Lincoln reported to Lyman Trumbull, the other Illinois senator. "The majority of the Democratic politicians of the nation mean to kill him," Lincoln continued, figuratively. "But I doubt whether they will adopt the aptest way to do it. Their true way is to present him with no new test, let him into the Charleston convention"—the Democrats' 1860 national convention— "and then outvote him, and nominate another. In that case, he will have no pretext for bolting the nomination, and will be as powerless as they can wish."

But Lincoln didn't think Douglas's enemies would take this tack. Southerners who reviled him for his Freeport formula of subverting the Dred Scott decision would try to force his hand. This would work to Douglas's benefit—and to the Republicans' peril. "If they push a slave code upon him, as a test, he will bolt at once, turn upon us, as in the case of Lecompton, and claim that all Northern men shall make common cause in electing him president as the best means of breaking down the slave power. In that case, the Democratic party go into a minority inevitably; and the struggle in the whole North will be, as it was in Illinois last summer and fall, whether the Republican party can maintain its identity, or be broken up to form the tail of Douglas' new kite." The former was the only viable course, Lincoln said. "The truth is, the Republican principle can in no wise live with Douglas; and it is arrant folly now, as it was last spring, to waste time and scatter labor already performed, in dallying with him."

If the Republicans could avoid the snare of cooperating with Douglas, the future was theirs, Lincoln judged. "You must not let your approaching election in Ohio so result as to give encouragement to Douglasism," Lincoln wrote to Salmon Chase, Ohio's Republican governor. "That ism is all which now stands in the way of an early and complete success of Republicanism."

Unity was crucial. Schuyler Colfax was a Republican congressman from Indiana; Lincoln wrote to him regretting that they had failed to meet on a recent visit by Colfax to Illinois. "Besides a strong desire to make your personal acquaintance, I was anxious to speak with you on politics, a little more fully than I can well do in a letter," Lincoln said. "My main object in such conversation would be to hedge against divisions in the Republican ranks generally, and particularly for the contest of 1860." What Lincoln feared most was the temptation of Republicans in different states to write platforms that played to local voters but divided the party as a whole. In New England, for instance, Republicans demanded repeal of the Fugitive Slave Act, to widespread approval there. But the same demand in other regions could be fatal to Republican hopes. "In these things there is explosive matter enough to blow up half a dozen national conventions, if it gets into them; and what gets very rife outside of conventions is very likely to find its way into them," Lincoln said. "What is desirable, if possible, is that in every local convocation of Republicans, a point should be made to avoid everything which will distract Republicans elsewhere." A failure to coordinate would weaken the party internally; it would also allow the Democrats to attack the party with more telling effect. This must not be allowed. "In a word, in every locality we should look beyond our noses; and at least say *nothing* on points where it is probable we shall disagree."

The Fugitive Slave Act especially worried Lincoln. "Please pardon the liberty I take in addressing you, as I now do," he wrote to Salmon Chase. "It appears by the papers that the late Republican state convention of Ohio adopted a platform of which the following is one plank, 'A repeal of the atrocious Fugitive Slave Law.'" Lincoln didn't presume to tell Ohioans their business, but he believed he had to speak for Republicans in other states, starting with Illinois. "This is already damaging us here. I have no doubt that if that plank be even *introduced* into the next Republican national convention, it will explode it. Once introduced, its supporters and its opponents will quarrel irreconcilably. The latter believe the U.S. constitution declares that a fugitive slave 'shall be delivered up'; and they look upon the above plank as dictated by the spirit which declares a fugitive slave 'shall not be delivered up.' I enter upon no argument one way or the other; but I assure you the cause of Republicanism is hopeless in Illinois if it be in any way made responsible for that plank. I hope you can, and will, contribute something to relieve us from it."

While one threat to Republican unity came from within the party, another came from outside. Members of the American party spoke of amalgamating with disaffected Democrats and willing Republicans in a minimally antislavery coalition. Lincoln at once protested. "Of course I would be pleased to see all the elements of opposition"—to slavery—"united for the approaching contest of 1860," he professed in a letter to one of the amalgamationists, Nathan Sargent. "But I confess I have not much hope of seeing it. You state a platform for such union in these words, 'Opposition to the opening of the slave-trade; & eternal hostility to the rotten Democracy.' You add, by way of comment, 'I say, if the Republicans would be content with this, there will be no obstacle to a union of the *opposition*.'" Lincoln declared Sargent's project absurd on its own terms. "Such a platform, unanimously adopted by a national convention, with two of the best men living placed upon it as candidates, would probably carry Maryland, and would certainly not carry a single other state. It would gain nothing in the South, and lose everything in the North."

Citing his own state, Lincoln declared, "Last year the Republicans of Illinois cast 125,000 votes; on such a platform as yours they cannot cast as many by 50,000." Lincoln was a Republican, and he would insist that the Republicans remain true to their bedrock principles. "Your platform proposes to allow the spread and nationalization of slavery to proceed without let or hindrance, save only that it shall not receive supplies directly from Africa," he told Sargent. "Surely you do not seriously believe the Republicans can come to any such terms." Sargent seemed to think his coalition would weaken the Democrats in the South; Lincoln thought this absurd, too. "If the rotten Democracy shall be beaten in 1860, it has to be done by the North; no human invention can deprive them of the South."

EVEN AS LINCOLN talked political strategy, he increasingly emphasized the moral element in Republican opposition to slavery. "Never forget that we have before us this whole matter of the right or wrong of slavery in this Union, though the immediate question is as to its spreading out into new territories and states," he told an audience in Chicago. "I do not wish to be misunderstood upon this subject of slavery in this country. I suppose it may long exist, and perhaps the best way for it to come to an end peaceably is for it to exist for a length of time. But I say that the spread and strengthening and perpetuation of it is an entirely different proposition. There we should in every way resist it as a wrong, treating it as a wrong, with the fixed idea that it must and will come to an end." This was the chief reason Republicans should resist making common cause with Democrats, and the party's chief hope for ultimate triumph. "If we do not allow ourselves to be allured from the strict path of our duty by such a device as shifting our ground and throwing ourselves into the rear of a leader"—Stephen Douglas—"who denies our first principle, denies that there is an absolute wrong in the institution of slavery, then the future of the Republican cause is safe and victory is assured."

After Douglas published an article in *Harper's Magazine* elaborating the agnosticism that underpinned his philosophy of popular sovereignty, Lincoln shook his head in redoubled determination. "This will never do," he said. "He puts the moral element out of this question. It won't stay out."

It certainly wouldn't if Lincoln had his way. "Slavery is wrong, morally and politically," he told an audience of Republicans in Cincinnati. "I desire that it should be no further spread in these United States, and I should not object if it should gradually terminate in the whole Union." He continued, "I think we want and must have a national policy in regard to the institution of slavery that acknowledges and deals with that institution as being wrong." Compromise on this point would be fatal. "Whoever desires the prevention of the spread of slavery and the nationalization of that institution yields all when he yields to any policy that either recognizes slavery as being right, or as being an indifferent thing. Nothing will make you successful but setting up a policy which shall treat the thing as being wrong."

Slavery was wrong for what it did to blacks; it was also wrong for what it did to whites. And because whites voted, while blacks did not, Lincoln took pains to stress what whites lost from slavery. Lincoln, with other Republicans, advanced an ideology of free labor, which decried slave labor but also stressed the dignity of the white working man. "I hold that if there is any one thing that can be proved to be the will of God by external nature around us, without reference to revelation, it is the proposition that whatever any one man earns with his hands and by the sweat of his brow, he shall enjoy in peace," Lincoln told his Cincinnati audience. "I say that whereas God Almighty has given every man one mouth to be fed, and one pair of hands adapted to furnish food for that mouth, if anything can be proved to be the will of Heaven, it is proved by this fact, that that mouth is to be fed by those hands, without being interfered with by any other man who has also his mouth to feed and his hands to labor with. I hold that if the Almighty had ever made a set of men that should do all the eating and none of the work, he would have made them with mouths only and no hands, and if he had ever made another class that he had intended should do all the work and none of the eating, he would have made them without mouths and with all hands. But inasmuch as he has not chosen to make man in that way, if anything is proved, it is that those hands and mouths are to be cooperative through life and not to be interfered with."

The dignity of white labor required that white workers not be restricted in where they could settle. "That they are to go forth and improve their condition is the inherent right given to mankind by the Maker," Lincoln said. "In the exercise of this right you must have room." The eastern states in America had largely filled up. "Where shall we go to?" He gazed out at his audience. "Where shall *you* go to escape from over-population and competition?" He supplied the answer: "To those new territories which belong to us, which are God-given for that purpose."

But if slavery got there first, white workers would find themselves competing with slave labor, and in that contest they would lose. Lincoln polled his listeners: "My good friends, let me ask you a question—you who have come from Virginia or Kentucky, to get rid of this thing of slavery—let me ask you what headway would you have made in getting rid of it, if by popular sovereignty you found slavery on that soil which you looked for to be free when you got there?" He knew the answer. "You would not have made much headway if you had already found slavery here, if you had to sit down to your labor by the side of the unpaid workman."

Lincoln reiterated that opposition to slavery, and in particular to its spread, was not mere philanthropy for blacks. It was crucial to the betterment of whites. "It is due to yourselves as voters, as owners of the new territories, that you shall keep those territories free."

LINCOLN'S DEVOTION to the antislavery cause impressed his hearers. The morning after his Cincinnati speech a local Republican called at Lincoln's hotel. "How would you feel if we nominated you for president?" he asked.

Lincoln wasn't ready to answer the question in public. He tried to laugh it off. "Just think of such a sucker as me as president!" he said. To a friend, Jesse Fell, he added, in a tone that was more of a lament, "Oh, Fell, what's the use of talking of me for the presidency, whilst we have such men as Seward, Chase and others, who are so much better known to the people, and whose names are intimately associated with the principles of the Republican party."

Fell answered that Lincoln was more electable than the others, precisely for being unknown.

Lincoln thought the matter over. "I admit the force of what you say, and admit that I am ambitious and would like to be president," he replied. He acknowledged the compliment in Fell's remarks. But he didn't think what Fell envisioned could happen. "There is no such good luck in store for me as the presidency."

Lincoln's modesty cloaked his shrewdness, which told him to duck the question of a presidential candidacy as long as possible. William Seward and Salmon Chase were strong figures who had held public office during the period since the slavery crisis had sharpened in 1850; each had left a trail of decisions for which he might be criticized. Lincoln's advantage was his lack of a trail; having held no office, he had no such record to defend. The longer he kept his head down, the better his chances when he finally stood up.

I N JULY 1859, John Brown traveled to Harpers Ferry. He called himself Isaac Smith and said he was looking for a farm to rent. John Unseld, who lived on the Maryland side of the Potomac River about a mile from the town, met Brown, Brown's sons Watson and Oliver, and Jeremiah Anderson on the road. "Good morning, gentlemen," Unseld recalled greeting them. "How do you do?" The equipment Brown and the others carried caused Unseld to think they were prospectors. "I suppose you are out hunting mineral gold and silver?" he suggested.

"No, we are not," Brown answered. "We are out looking for land. We want to buy land. We have a little money, but we want to make it go as far as we can." Brown asked what price land was selling for in the vicinity.

Unseld said it ran from fifteen to thirty dollars an acre.

"That's high," Brown said. "I thought to buy land here for about a dollar or two dollars per acre."

Unseld said Brown would have to go much farther west to find land that cheap. He suggested Kansas.

Unseld let Brown's party ponder their situation and proceeded on his errand into Harpers Ferry. Returning some hours later, he ran into the visitors again. Brown continued to express interest. "I have been looking round your country up here, and it is a very fine country, a very pleasant place, a fine view," Brown said. "The land is much better than I expected to find it; your crops are pretty good." He asked Unseld if any farms were for sale in the neighborhood.

Unseld directed him to a farm about four miles away, belonging to a family named Kennedy.

Brown took note, cautiously. "I think we had better rent awhile until we get better acquainted," he said. Given the high prices, he wanted to be sure he received value for his money.

Unseld said the Kennedys might rent their farm, especially if the renting could lead to a sale.

Brown asked directions; Unseld gave them. Unseld inquired how Brown intended to use the farm. The Kennedy place didn't have much fertile soil.

"My business has been buying up fat cattle, and driving them on to the state of New York, and selling them," Brown said. "We expect to engage in that again."

Unseld didn't have reason to doubt the explanation. They parted once more. Unseld encountered Brown a couple of times during the next several days, also on the road. The first time Brown said he had arranged to rent the Kennedy farm; the second time he offered to show Unseld the receipt for the rent he had paid.

Unseld shook his head. "I don't want to see the receipt," he said. "It is nothing to me." Unseld drew no particular inference from Brown's offer, and he was willing to accept Brown's story. The Kennedy farm lay on the main road four miles from Unseld's place, and five miles from Harpers Ferry, and each time Unseld ventured by the Kennedy place, he naturally looked to see what was going on. Brown was friendly. He said he had been a surveyor and had worked in New York, Ohio and as far west as Kansas. He said he prospected for minerals while out surveying. "I have a little instrument that I carry in my hand, about the size of a small bucket, that has a magnet that will tell where there is any iron ore," he said. "Sometimes I carry that; it has a needle to it; if the ore is in front of me the needle will point to it, and as I come there it will turn."

During August and September other members of Brown's company arrived at the Kennedy farm. They stayed in the two houses on the property and mostly kept out of sight lest the presence of a large group of single men draw suspicion. Brown enlisted one of his daughters and a daughter-in-law to cook and clean for the group and lend an air of normality.

Osborne Anderson was one of Brown's followers. Anderson was a black man, born free in Pennsylvania, who attended Oberlin College before moving to Chatham, Canada, to open a printing shop amid the black community there. He heard of the convention Brown called for his provisional constitution and decided to attend. On account of his facility with words he was made recording secretary of the convention, and in the course of the meeting he became a convert to Brown's project. He joined Brown at the Kennedy farm, traveling the last leg from the Pennsylvania-Maryland border under cover of darkness. In slave-state Maryland any unfamiliar and unsupervised black man was certain to attract attention.

Anderson found the farm and its lodgings suitably nondescript. "To a passer-by, the house and its surroundings presented but indifferent attractions," he recalled. "Any log tenement of equal dimensions would be as likely to arrest a stray glance. Rough, unsightly, and aged, it was only those privileged to enter and tarry for a long time, and to penetrate the mysteries of the two rooms it contained—kitchen, parlor, dining-room below, and the spacious chamber, attic, store-room, prison, drilling room, comprised in the loft above—who could tell how we lived at Kennedy Farm."

John Brown imposed a disciplined routine. Every morning he gathered the family—as he called the group—for prayer, which always concluded with a plea for those in bondage. "I never heard John Brown pray, that he did not make strong appeals to God for the deliverance of the slave," Anderson recounted. The praying done, Brown sent most of the men, especially Anderson and the handful of other blacks, into the loft for the day. "Few only could be seen about, as the neighbors were watchful and suspicious," Anderson said. "It was also important to talk but little among ourselves, as visitors to the house might be curious." Hidden in the loft, the men read a military manual Hugh Forbes had written before defecting, and they whispered among themselves, relating their biographies to one another. "But when our resources became pretty well exhausted, the ennui from confinement, imposed silence, etc., would make the men almost desperate." Relief came only at night. "We sallied out for a ramble, or to breathe the fresh air and enjoy the beautiful solitude of the mountain scenery around, by moonlight."

In early October, Brown traveled to Pennsylvania to coordinate with John Kagi, his second-in-command, who oversaw the transport of weapons to the Kennedy farm. These included the pikes Brown had ordered in Connecticut and finally paid for. While Brown was gone, the discipline among the men slipped. "The men at the farm had been so closely confined," Anderson said, "that they went about the house and farm in the day-time during that week, and so indiscreetly exposed their numbers to the prying neighbors, who thereupon took steps to have a search instituted in the early part of the coming week."

The slip forced Brown's hand. He had hoped to wait for more arrivals. With the score he had on hand, he could hardly strike terror into the slave South. But he wasn't sure any more were coming. Even some of those he had expected had suffered a change of heart. Now, learning that the suspicions of the neighbors had been stirred, he decided he had no choice.

On Sunday morning, October 16, he brought his men together. "He read a chapter from the Bible, applicable to the condition of the slaves, and our duty as their brethren, and then offered up a fervent prayer to God to assist in the liberation of the bondmen in that slaveholding land," Anderson recalled. "The services were impressive beyond expression. Every man there assembled seemed to respond from the depths of his soul, and throughout the entire day, a deep solemnity pervaded the place."

After breakfast Brown called the roll. A sentinel was stationed outside the door, and Brown let the men know that the time had come. He read the provisional constitution. Those who had not sworn allegiance to it before now did so. Orders were issued as to who would do what and how the men were to comport themselves. "Gentlemen, let me impress this one thing upon your minds," Brown said. "You all know how dear life is to you, and how dear your life is to your friends. In remembering that, consider that the lives of others are as dear to them as yours are to you. Do not, therefore, take the life of any one, if you can possibly avoid it. But if it is necessary to take life to save your own, then make sure work of it."

The balance of the day was filled with final preparations. At eight o'clock in the evening, after dark had completely fallen, Brown said, "Men, get on your arms. We will proceed to the Ferry."

THE COMPANY HEADED OFF. Brown drove a wagon loaded with weapons; the men marched behind him. No one spoke a word; to the eye of a casual observer the group might have been a funeral procession, except that the wagon bore pikes rather than a body.

At about ten thirty Brown's party reached the east end of the bridge from Maryland over the Potomac to Harpers Ferry. A watchman guarded the town at the west end. Perhaps hearing Brown's wagon, he hoisted a lantern and crossed the bridge toward the raiding party. Two of Brown's men, John Kagi and Aaron Stevens, aimed their rifles at him and demanded his surrender. He thought they were joking. He recognized Brown, though he knew him as Isaac Smith, and he couldn't imagine why Brown and his friends would want to take him prisoner. But they soon convinced him they were serious, and he handed over his gun and let himself be taken.

The raiders continued across the bridge into the town. Just beyond the bridge was the gate of the federal armory. The gate was locked, with a guard, Daniel Whelan, in the watch house behind the gate. "I heard the noise of their wagon coming down the street," Whelan recalled. "I advanced about three yards out from the watch-house door and observed the wagon standing facing the armory gate." Whelan thought the wagon belonged to his boss, the head watchman, and he walked toward the gate to greet him. But two of the strangers started picking at the padlock on the gate. "Hold on!" he said. They ignored him. Whelan then saw the rest of Brown's party. The raiders demanded he open the gate. He said he wouldn't. But he had ventured too close to the gate. One of the raiders reached through and grabbed him by the coat. "Five or six ran in from the wagon, clapped their guns against my breast, and told me I should deliver up the key," he recounted. He said he didn't have it.

Brown couldn't decide whether to believe him. He didn't want to shoot Whelan, if only because it would alert the town. So while several of his men kept their rifles leveled at Whelan, two others employed a crowbar and hammer and broke the lock.

Whelan felt helpless. "They all gathered about me and looked in my face," he said. "I was nearly scared to death with so many guns about me. I did not know the minute or the hour I should drop. They told me to be very quiet and still and make no noise or else they would put me to eternity."

Brown ordered his men to take control of the armory, starting with the watch house and the attached fire-engine house. The place was empty but for Whelan and a guard at the far end, three hundred yards away, and the task was swiftly accomplished.

Brown declared his purpose to Whelan and the other prisoner, the bridge sentry. "I came here from Kansas, and this is a slave state," Brown said. "I want to free all the negroes in this state. I have possession now of the United States armory. If the citizens interfere with me, I must burn the town and have blood."

MOST OF THE TOWN had slept through the minor commotion thus far. They proceeded to sleep while Brown sent small parties to secure the rifle factory, on the south side of the town, fronting the Shenandoah River; the arsenal, where finished weapons were stored; and the bridge over the Shenandoah River. In the process the raiders took a few more prisoners, to prevent their spreading the word of the operation. Brown ordered his men to cut the telegraph wires leading out of town, to extend the isolation.

By midnight Brown could congratulate himself on the success of the first stage of the operation. With fewer than twenty men he had seized the parts of the town that mattered for his purposes. No one had been killed, and almost no one knew what was happening. Nor would anyone find out until Monday morning, when the town would awake to discover Brown's liberation army in its midst.

He put the intervening hours to use. The point of the raid was only partly to acquire weapons; equally it was to alert the slaves in the area that their freedom was at hand—that it was in *their* hands if they would grasp it. No sooner had Brown secured the three positions in town than he sent some of his men into the Virginia countryside. Lewis Washington owned a farm and numerous slaves about five miles from Harpers Ferry. He was a great-grandnephew of George Washington, an associate of the Virginia governor, and an important man in that part of the state. He later recalled being roused from his sleep by a band of armed men. "They appeared at my chamber door about half past one o'clock in the morning," he said. "My name was called in an under tone, and supposing it to be by some friend who had possibly arrived late, and being familiar with the house, had been admitted in the rear by the servants, I opened the door in my night-shirt and slippers. I was in bed and asleep. As I opened the door there were four armed men with their guns drawn upon me just around me. Three had rifles, and one a large revolver. The man having a revolver held in his left hand a large flambeau"—torch—"which was burning." The man in charge of the group, Aaron Stevens, informed Washington that he was a prisoner.

Washington assessed the situation. "I observed that each man had two revolvers sticking in his belt in front besides the rifle," he recounted. They were too well armed simply to rob him, he thought. "Possibly you will have the courtesy to tell me what this means," he inquired of them.

Stevens answered, "We have come here for the purpose of liberating all the slaves of the South."

Washington couldn't decide if the men before him were insane. But he chose not to test them. He got dressed and prepared to do as they said.

John Cook, one of his captors, had learned that Washington owned a collection of antique weapons. He relayed the information to Stevens, who demanded that Washington reveal where they were. Washington showed them to a gun closet in his dining room. The raiders took out three guns, along with a sword said to have been presented to George Washington by Frederick the Great of Prussia.

Stevens wasn't satisfied with the haul. "Have you a watch?" he demanded.

"I have," Washington replied.

"Where is it?"

"It is on my person."

"I want it," Stevens said.

"You shall not have it," Washington answered.

"Take care, sir," Stevens warned. Changing the subject, he said, "Have you money?"

Washington said he did, and that Stevens shouldn't have it.

"Take care, sir," Stevens repeated.

"I am going to speak very plainly," Washington said. "You told me your purpose was philanthropic, but you did not mention at the same time that it was robbery and rascality." He told Stevens and the others that because they had him outgunned, they could forcibly divest him of his watch and money, but he wouldn't surrender them.

Stevens considered the situation. "I presume you have heard of Osawatomie Brown?" he said.

"No, I have not," Washington said.

"Then you have paid very little attention to Kansas matters."

Washington said he had become so disgusted by the news from Kansas that whenever he encountered a news article with the word "Kansas," he stopped reading.

"Well," said Stevens, in a tone Washington interpreted as self-important, "you will see him this morning."

The other raiders had been rounding up Washington's slaves. They located only three, the others being away on a Sunday night visiting family and friends on other farms. The raiders hitched up a carriage and a wagon. Stevens ordered Washington into the carriage, which Shields Green, the friend of Frederick Douglass, drove. The raiders, not knowing the horses or the livery, had fouled things up; Washington had to straighten them out. In the wagon were several of Washington's male slaves; the women were left behind. The slaves looked unhappy, Washington thought.

The two vehicles and the raiders set off in the direction of Harpers Ferry. Before long they passed a house belonging to a widow named Henderson. Aaron Stevens seemed ready to enter the house, but Washington told him that only the widow and her daughters lived there. "It would be an infamous shame to wake them up at this hour of the night," he said. Stevens grudgingly agreed.

Farther on they passed the property of John Allstadt. The raiders were not to be denied a second time. They removed a rail from Allstadt's fence and carried it toward the house. "I heard the jar of the rail against the door, and in a few moments there was a shout of murder and general commotion in the house," Washington recounted. "I thought first it was his servants hallooing murder, but he told me afterwards it was his daughters; finding this commotion going on, they put their heads out of the window and hallooed murder; one of these fellows drew his rifle on them and ordered them to go in and shut the window." Allstadt and his nineteen-year-old son, under guard, and several of his slaves, hardly more willing, were loaded in a wagon, and the whole contingent continued toward Harpers Ferry.

Washington gradually realized that Stevens had been truthful in talking of wanting to free the slaves. "Up to that time I supposed it was merely a robbing party who possibly had some room at the Ferry," he said. "I did not look on the thing as very serious at all until we drove to the armory gate, and the party on the front seat of the carriage said 'All's well,' and the reply came from the sentinel at the gate 'All's well.' Then the gates were opened and I was driven in and was received by old Brown."

John Brown greeted the prisoners cordially, considering the circumstances. "You will find a fire in here, sir," he told Washington, motioning to the armory's engine house. "It is rather cool this morning."

They went inside, and Brown explained to Washington why he had been arrested. "My particular reason for taking you first was that, as the aide to the governor of Virginia, I knew you would endeavor to perform your duty, and perhaps you would have been a troublesome customer to me," he said. "Apart from that, I wanted you particularly for the moral effect it would give our cause, having one of your name as a prisoner." Brown said he might not keep Washington for long. "It is too dark to see to write at this time, but when it shall have cleared off a little and become lighter, if you have not pen and ink, I will furnish them to you, and I shall require you to write to some of your friends to send a stout, able-bodied negro. I think after a while, possibly, I shall be enabled to release you, but only on the condition of getting your friends to send in a negro man as a ransom." Brown added, by way of warning, "I shall be very attentive to you, sir, for I may get the worst of it in my first encounter, and if so, your life is worth as much as mine."

WASHINGTON TOOK NOTE, and not with pleasure, that his slaves were treated as well as he. "They were brought in to the fire," he recalled. The engine house was a brick building about twenty-four feet square, divided in two by an interior wall, forming what the locals called the engine house proper and the watch house. The stove was in the watch house. Washington was led directly into the watch house to warm up; he was followed by his slaves. "They came in repeatedly to warm themselves," he recalled.

Washington also took note that his slaves were armed. Osborne Anderson had been in the party that seized Lewis Washington and John Allstadt and their slaves. Anderson's account of the night had the prisoners showing less composure than Washington's version did. "Col. Washington opened his room door and begged us not to kill him," Anderson wrote. Washington shivered with fear on learning he was going to be taken prisoner, Anderson said. "He stood as if speechless or terrified." He begged to be let alone. "You can have my slaves if you will let me remain," Anderson quoted him. Washington's plea failing, he lost his nerve. "The colonel cried heartily when he found he must submit," Anderson said.

He complained still more on being made to hand over his heirloom sword to Anderson, a black man. John Brown had given special orders on this point; when enforced by Aaron Stevens and John Cook, the order made Washington still more upset.

John Allstadt was equally flummoxed, Anderson related. "He went into as great a fever of excitement as Washington had done. We could have his slaves, also, if we would only leave him." When this was denied, he grew very anxious. "He hesitated, puttered around, fumbled and meditated for a long time." Only then did he accept the inevitable.

After Anderson helped deliver Washington and Allstadt to Harpers Ferry, he listened to Brown give orders to Aaron Stevens and one or two others. "Capt. Brown next ordered me to take the pikes out of the wagon in which he rode to the Ferry, and to place them in the hands of the colored men who had come with us from the plantations, and others who had come forward without having had communication with any of our party," Anderson said. The number of these latter—the slave volunteers—inspired intense interest and much debate before long; Anderson declined to offer a tally. But he made a point to stress that the idea for arming the slaves had been Brown's.

"It was out of the circumstances connected with the fulfillment of this order that the false charge against 'Anderson' as leader, or 'ringleader,' of the negroes grew," he wrote.

BY THE TIME the party with Lewis Washington and John Allstadt and their slaves returned to Harpers Ferry, the situation there had grown more complicated. The man scheduled to relieve the bridge watchman at the turn of the shift arrived; when he refused to surrender to Oliver Brown, he was shot. The bullet only nicked him, and he escaped. The sound of the shot awoke people nearby, and the man's story told confusedly of armed strangers in the town.

A bit before one thirty on the morning of Monday, October 17, the regular eastbound Baltimore & Ohio train rolled into the Harpers Ferry station. The wounded watchman informed the conductor that there were armed men on the bridge leading out of the town. The conductor, A. J. Phelps, held the train. While he did, Shephard Hayward, a free black man and the baggage master at the station, walked toward the bridge looking for the absent watchman. Hayward evidently hadn't heard about the raiders. He did hear a call to halt but instead turned around and headed back toward the station. One of the raiders, presumably thinking he was going to spread the alarm, shot him in the back.

John Starry was a physician who lived in Harpers Ferry. His residence was close to the railroad bridge. "About half past one o'clock, I heard a shot fired in the direction of the Baltimore & Ohio railroad bridge, the iron span of the bridge, and immediately afterwards a cry of distress, as if somebody had been hurt," Starry recalled. He leaped out of bed and went into the street. "When I got there I found the negro porter, Hayward, shot, the ball entering from behind, through the body, nearly on a line with the base of the heart, a little below it. He told me that he had been out on the railroad bridge looking for a watchman who was missing, and he had been ordered to halt by some men who were there, and, instead of doing that, he turned to go back to the office, and as he turned they shot him in the back. I understood from him that he walked from there to the office, and when I found him he was lying on a plank upon two chairs in the office."

Starry did what he could for Hayward, which wasn't much, and returned to the street. He saw strange men bearing rifles go into the armory. His curiosity and sense of civic responsibility caused him to look into the matter. "I went then to the armory gate, and before I got to the gate I called for the watchmen. I was ordered to halt. I did so, and inquired of the men who halted me what had become of the watchmen. I wanted to inquire why they allowed persons to go in and out of that gate, when they knew they were shooting down those whom they met in the street." Starry asked for two of the watchmen by name: Medler and Murphy. "The fellow told me that there were no watchmen there; that he did not know Medler or Murphy, but, said he, 'There are a few of us here.'" Starry didn't know what the stranger was talking about. He retreated yet didn't go home, instead lingering to find out what the invaders were up to. "That was about three o'clock, I suppose," he said. "I watched them from that time until daylight, sometimes very close to them, and sometimes further off. About four o'clock I heard a wagon coming down the street. I did not know what that meant, and I watched them as closely as I could. About five minutes after five o'clock, I saw a four-horse team driving over the Baltimore and Ohio railroad bridge." This was part of the procession coming from Lewis Washington's and John Allstadt's farms. "I did not know whose it was. In that wagon there were three men standing up in the front part, with spears in their hands, white men, and two were walking alongside armed with rifles. I did not see any negroes. I saw but these men. I understood afterwards there were negroes with them, but I did not see them."

MORNINGS COME LATE to Harpers Ferry, with the Maryland Heights above the east bank of the Potomac slowing the sunrise. As the sky lightened on that Monday morning, the Baltimore & Ohio train pulled out of the Harpers Ferry station. John Brown had decided to release it. Surprise had achieved all it could for him; the time had come to let the world understand that emancipation had begun. The train crossed the river and proceeded into Maryland. At the first opportunity conductor Phelps halted the train and telegraphed the news of the occupation of Harpers Ferry. "Express train bound east, under my charge, was stopped this morning at Harpers Ferry by armed abolitionists," he explained. "They have possession of the bridge and the arms and armory of the United States." The conductor told of the shooting of the baggage man. "The doctor says he cannot survive." He described the raiders: "They are headed by a man who calls himself Anderson and number about one hundred and fifty strong. They say they have come to free the slaves and intend to do it at all hazards. The leader of those men requested me to say to you that this is the last train that shall pass the bridge either east or west. If it is attempted, it will be at the peril of the lives of those having them in charge."

The telegram reached the railroad headquarters in Baltimore just before eight o'clock that morning. It wasn't initially believed. "Your dispatch is evidently exaggerated and written under excitement," responded W. P. Smith, the B&O train master. "Why should our trains be stopped by abolitionists, and how do you know they are such and that they number one hundred or more? What is their object? Let me know at once before we proceed to extremities."

"My dispatch was not exaggerated, neither was it written under excitement as you suppose," Phelps insisted in reply. "I have not made it half as bad as it is. The Captain told me that his object was to liberate all the slaves, and that he expected a reinforcement of 1500 men to assist him. Hayward, the negro porter, was shot through the body, and I suppose by this time is dead. The Captain also said he didn't want to shed any more blood."

Train master Smith, whose job was to keep the trains running, still didn't believe the conductor. In a wire to the station master at Wheeling, west of Harpers Ferry, Smith wrote, "Matter is probably much exaggerated and we fear it may injure us if prematurely published. Don't let our trains be interrupted."

AS THE TOWNSPEOPLE of Harpers Ferry awoke, word of the alien force in their midst passed from person to person and household to household. From within the armory Osborne Anderson observed the effect. "Daylight revealed great confusion, and as the sun arose, the panic spread like wild-fire," he recounted. "Men, women and children could be seen leaving their homes in every direction, some seeking refuge among residents and in quarters further away, others climbing up the hillsides and hurrying off in various directions, evidently impelled by a sudden fear which was plainly visible in their countenances or in their movements."

A few armory workers, unaware of the danger, walked into the grasp of the raiders and were taken prisoner. Before long no one was left who didn't know. And those who did know, exaggerated. "The spectators, about this time, became apparently wild with fright and excitement," Anderson wrote. "The number of prisoners was magnified to hundreds, and the judgment-day could not have presented more terrors, in its awful and certain prospective punishment to the justly condemned for the wicked deeds of a lifetime, the chief of which would no doubt be slaveholding, than did Capt. Brown's operations."

As the morning passed, the broader world began to respond. Conductor Phelps told others besides his boss what he had seen and heard; the tale grew more lurid as it changed hands. A news dispatch from Frederick, Maryland, to Baltimore declared, "Information has been received here this morning of a formidable negro insurrection at Harpers Ferry. An armed band of abolitionists have full possession of Harpers Ferry and the United States arsenal. . . . They are led by about two hundred and fifty whites, with a gang of negroes fighting for their freedom. . . . The leader told Conductor Phelps, of the Baltimore and Ohio Railroad train, that they *'were determined to have liberty, or die in the attempt.'*"

The alarm caused militia leaders in Maryland to summon their troops for action. Riders from Harpers Ferry informed towns on the Virginia side of the Potomac; Virginia companies mobilized as well.

"It was about twelve o'clock in the day when we were first attacked by the troops," Osborne Anderson recalled. John Brown had been preparing for this. "Capt. Brown was all activity, though I could not help thinking that at times he appeared somewhat puzzled." As the conflict drew near, he settled down. He strapped on the sword of George Washington and made ready to defy the forces of Washington's own state.

The Maryland militia reached Harpers Ferry first, and started across the Potomac bridge. Brown pulled his men from outlying positions into a firm center. "The troops are on the bridge, coming into town," he declared. "We will give them a warm reception." As the Marylanders approached, Brown counseled patience. "Be cool. Don't waste your powder and shot. Take aim and make every shot count." Brown's men were well armed, but Brown bore no gun, only the ceremonial sword. Yet he stood at the front, in plain view of the attackers.

They came off the bridge to within sixty yards of the armory gate. "Let go upon them!" shouted Brown. His men fired, felling several of the militia. His men reloaded; the Marylanders kept coming, albeit less confidently than before. Brown's men fired; more militia went down.

"From marching in solid martial columns, they became scattered," Anderson said of the Maryland militia. "Some hastened to seize upon and bear up the wounded and dying—several lay dead upon the ground." Anderson inferred that the militia had expected the raiders to disperse at the soldiers' approach; the fact that the raiders had held their ground and inflicted lethal damage compelled them to reconsider. "The consequence of their unexpected reception was, after leaving several of their dead on the field, they beat a confused retreat to the bridge." There they stayed, awaiting reinforcements.

The raiders suffered more from the sniping of townsmen than from the aborted assault of the militia. "Dangerfield Newby, one of our colored men, was shot through the head by a person who took aim at him from a brick store window on the opposite side of the street, and who was there for the purpose of firing upon us," Anderson related, still indignant years later. "Newby was a brave fellow. He was one of my comrades." Shields Green avenged Newby. "Green raised his rifle in an instant and brought down the cowardly murderer before the latter could get his gun back through the sash."

The raiders' position became more precarious at mid-afternoon, when the Virginia militia arrived. "Armed men could be seen coming from every direction," Osborne Anderson recalled. "Soldiers were marching and countermarching, and on the mountains a host of blood-thirsty ruffians swarmed, waiting for their opportunity to pounce upon the little band." After the new troops took up positions, the battle was resumed, with the raiders giving as good as they got. "Volley upon volley was discharged, and the echoes from the hills, the shrieks of the townspeople, and the groans of their wounded and dying, all of which filled the air, were truly frightful." Anderson, without citing evidence beyond his impression from behind the armory walls, later contended that the Virginians' losses were greater than they afterward let on. "The Virginians may well conceal their losses, and Southern chivalry may hide its brazen head, for their boasted bravery was well tested that day, and in no way to their advantage."

In fact the Virginians suffered few losses, for all the noise and shooting. Brown realized he and his men were trapped. "We will hold on to our three positions"—the armory, the arsenal and the rifle factory—"if they are unwilling to come to terms, and die like men," he declared.

WHAT BROWN EXPECTED by way of terms is unclear. Indeed, much about his thinking at this point is unclear. For one who had conducted himself and his followers with tactical acuity in Kansas, he floundered at Harpers Ferry. The only logic behind attacking Harpers Ferry rested in seizing its weapons and making an escape to the mountains. To try to hold the armory was madness. The position was surrounded by the Potomac and Shenandoah Rivers, which met within a stone's throw of the armory, and by Bolivar Heights, the elevation behind the town. Even if Brown's men could retain control of the Harpers Ferry ends of the bridges, they could never fight their way through the militia forces on the other sides. And the heights gave the militia ideal spots for pouring fire down upon Brown's position.

He seems to have expected that slaves in the area would learn of his bold stroke and rush to his side. The slaves, of course, were the ones to be supplied with the weapons, both the hundreds of pikes he brought with him and the guns he acquired from the armory. But how they were to reach him at Harpers Ferry, even if they wanted to, he never explained.

Brown's lieutenants believed the slaves were *not* supposed to reach them at Harpers Ferry. John Kagi, Brown's most able subordinate, understood that the operation made sense only if the raiders struck and escaped before the countryside was aroused. By messenger from the rifle works, which he had taken with two other raiders, Kagi pleaded with Brown to order the evacuation. But Brown refused, leaving Kagi and his comrades dangerously exposed.

John Starry, the doctor who spread the alarm, had watched the fighting from the town side. At about three in the afternoon, as the militiamen were driving closer to Brown's position in the armory, Starry informed them where they could find some more of the raiders. "I said to them that two or three of Brown's men were in Hall's works"—the rifle factory—"and if they wanted to show their bravery they could go there," he related.

An officer of the militia took the suggestion and directed his men's fire at the rifle shop. "At the first fire Kagi and the others who were with him in Hall's works went out the back way towards the Winchester railroad, climbed out on the railroad and into the Shenandoah River. There they were met on the opposite side by a party who were there and driven back again, and two of them were shot. Kagi was killed, and a yellow"—mulatto—"fellow, Leary, was wounded and died that night, and the yellow fellow Copeland was taken unhurt."

The other militiamen pressed their attack on Brown's central position. They drove the raiders out of the arsenal, throwing them back into the armory. Before long Brown lost most of that. The engine house was his final redoubt. Less than twenty-four hours after launching his long-planned war of liberation, Brown had effectively made himself and his surviving men prisoners.

Perhaps he was deluded into thinking the people of Virginia were like those of Kansas, where his audacity had more than once made up for his deficiency in numbers. But in Kansas he fought Missourians, for whom Kansas was a political cause, not their home. Nor in Kansas was he threatening to start a slave rebellion, the hoary nightmare of white Southerners. In Kansas his irregular forces fought irregulars; at Harpers Ferry he faced organized militias.

The fighting on Monday afternoon was sporadically cruel. Brown's men fired out from the armory and then from the engine house. Their accuracy was almost random, seeming to the townsfolk more like sniping or assassination than honest warfare. A prominent slave-holder, George Turner, had just arrived in the town when a bullet struck him in the neck and killed him. The popular mayor of Harpers Ferry, Fontaine Beckham, surveying the state of affairs in the town, was killed by another raider's bullet.

Brown's men suffered worse. As their position deteriorated, Brown tried to parley. He sent one of his men, William Thompson, with a hostage to seek a truce. When Thompson got close enough to the defenders to talk, several aimed their guns at him and threatened to blow off his head. Thompson gave up the hostage and was himself taken captive. Brown tried again, dispatching his son Watson and Aaron Stevens. The townsfolk ignored the truce flag the two carried, shooting both Watson Brown and Stevens. Watson staggered back to the engine house; Stevens was captured.

Some of the townsmen weren't content to take prisoners. Harry Hunter, a grandnephew of Mayor Beckham, later explained how he and another man burst into the hotel where Thompson and Stevens were being held. A woman put herself between them and Thompson, but they thrust her aside. "We then caught hold of him and dragged him out by the throat, he saying, 'Though you may take my life, eighty thousand will rise up to avenge me and carry out my purpose of giving liberty to the slaves.' We carried him out to the bridge, and two of us, leveling our guns in this moment of wild exasperation, fired, and before he fell a dozen more balls were buried in him. We then threw his body off the trestle work."

Hunter and the other man returned to the hotel to give Stevens the same treatment. They changed their minds when they got close. "We found him suffering from his wounds and probably dying. We concluded to spare him and start after others and shoot all we could find. I had just seen my loved uncle and best friend I ever had shot down by those villainous abolitionists, and felt justified in shooting any that I could find. I felt it my duty and had no regrets."

NIGHTFALL ON Monday evening silenced the guns. Brown understood he was surrounded, yet he remained defiant. The commander of the Virginia militia called on him to surrender; he responded with his terms. "In consideration of all my men, whether living or dead, or wounded, being soon safely in and delivered up to me at this point with all their arms and ammunition," Brown said, "we will then take our prisoners and cross the Potomac bridge, a little beyond which we will set them at liberty; after which we can negotiate about the government property as may be best. Also we require the delivery of our horse and harness at the hotel."

Brown's offer was rejected out of hand. He wasn't going to be allowed to leave Harpers Ferry with any hostages. If most of those in Harpers Ferry had their way, he wouldn't leave with his life.

Inside the engine house the night passed slowly. Oliver Brown and Watson Brown suffered badly from their wounds. Watson's hopes improved slightly when the captain of one of the Maryland militia companies allowed his unit's surgeon to go to the engine house and dress Watson's wounds. Oliver was soon beyond care. "In the quiet of the night young Oliver Brown died," one of the hostages recalled. "He had begged again and again to be shot, in the agony of his wound, but his father had replied to him, 'Oh, you will get over it,' and 'If you must die, die like a man.'" John Brown turned to speak with some of the prisoners. "Oliver Brown lay quietly over in a corner," the hostage continued. "His father called to him, after a time. No answer. 'I guess he is dead,' said Brown."

OUTSIDE THE ENGINE HOUSE John Brown's fate was being sealed. The president of the Baltimore & Ohio Railroad, less phlegmatic than his own train superintendent, had sent telegrams to the governor of Virginia and the president of the United States as soon as he heard of the troubles in Harpers Ferry. "The United States armory at Harpers Ferry is in the possession of rioters," he told James Buchanan. "The presence of United States troops is indispensable for the safety of government property and of the mails. A special train will be ordered to be in readiness for any troops ordered to be sent." He added, "The rioters are more than two hundred strong."

Buchanan accepted the offer and set the federal military in motion. The army had no troops at the capital, but there were some marines nearby. To command them, Buchanan chose an officer he and others in the military judged to be the country's most promising. Robert E. Lee was supposed to be in Texas fighting Comanches, but family matters had drawn him back to Virginia, to the plantation he and his wife had inherited from her father. Conveniently, the plantation lay hardly a mile from the White House, on a hill in Arlington overlooking the Potomac. Buchanan summoned Lee and ordered him to lead the marines against the insurrectionists at Harpers Ferry.

Lee chose as his adjutant a young cavalry officer named J. E. B. Stuart. The two caught a train at Washington that took them to the main B&O line west of Baltimore. The marines were already en route to Harpers Ferry; Lee ordered them to halt short of the town so he and Stuart could catch up. They did so, and with Lee in command the federal force continued to Harpers Ferry, arriving just before midnight.

Lee assessed the situation, soon learning that the number of the raiders was vastly exaggerated. They were a small group, and pinned in the engine house. His instinct was to attack at once. But his concern for the hostages caused him to wait until daylight, when it would be easier to distinguish the hostages from their captors.

"Their safety was the subject of painful consideration," Lee reported afterward, "and to prevent, if possible, jeopardizing their lives, I determined to summon the insurgents to surrender." His terms to the raiders were straightforward and implacable. "If they will peacefully surrender themselves and restore the pillaged property, they shall be kept in safety to await the orders of the President," Lee wrote in a note. He added, "Colonel Lee represents to them, in all frankness, that it is impossible for them to escape; that the armory is surrounded on all sides by troops; and that if he is compelled to take them by force he cannot answer for their safety."

To deliver the note, Lee turned to Jeb Stuart. The junior officer later recalled the moment. "I approached the door in the presence of perhaps two thousand spectators, and told Mr. 'Smith' that I had a communication for him from Colonel Lee," he said. Those outside the engine house still thought they were dealing with Isaac Smith, the one who had called himself a cattle buyer. "He opened the door about four inches, and placed his body against the crack, with a cocked car-bine in his hand." Stuart had served in Kansas during the troubles there; he suddenly identified the mastermind of the present insur-rection. "I recognized old Osawatomie Brown, who had given us so much trouble in Kansas," he said.

Brown tried to negotiate. "He presented his propositions in every possible shape, and with admirable tact, but all amounted to this— that the only condition on which he would surrender was that he and his party should be allowed to escape," Stuart recounted. "Some of his prisoners begged me to ask Colonel Lee to come to see him. I told them that he would never accede to any terms except those he had offered."

Lee had prepared for Brown's refusal to surrender. He ordered the marines to stand ready for a swift assault. "My object was, with a view of saving our citizens, to have as short an interval as possible between the summons and the attack," Lee explained afterward.

Israel Green was the marines' unit commander. "Colonel Lee gave me orders to select a detail of twelve men for a storming party, and place them near the engine-house in which Brown and his men had entrenched themselves," Green said. "I selected twelve of my best men, and a second twelve to be employed as a reserve." Green and Stuart agreed that the moment the parley failed, Stuart would step aside from the door and wave his hat. "I had my storming party ranged alongside of the engine-house, and a number of men were provided with sledge-hammers with which to batter in the doors," Green said.

"Suddenly Lieutenant Stuart waved his hat, and I gave the order to my men to batter in the door. Those inside fired rapidly at the point where the blows were given upon the door. Very little impression was made with the hammers, as the doors were tied on the inside with ropes and braced by the hand-brakes of the fire-engines, and in a few minutes I gave the order to desist. Just then my eye caught sight of a ladder, lying a few feet from the engine-house, in the yard, and I ordered my men to catch it up and use it as a battering-ram. The reserve of twelve men I employed as a supporting column for the assaulting party. The men took hold bravely and made a tremendous assault upon the door. The second blow broke it in. This entrance was a ragged hole low down in the right-hand door, the door being splintered and cracked some distance upward."

Green was the first one through the opening. His timing was fortunate. "Brown had just emptied his carbine at the point broken by the ladder, and so I passed in safely," he said. "Getting to my feet, I ran to the right of the engine which stood behind the door, passed quickly to the rear of the house, and came up between the two engines. The first person I saw was Colonel Lewis Washington," whom Green knew. "On one knee, a few feet to the left, knelt a man with a carbine in his hand, just pulling the lever to reload. 'Hello, Green,' said Colonel Washington, and he reached out his hand to me. I grasped it with my left hand, having my saber uplifted in my right, and he said, pointing to the kneeling figure, 'This is Osawatomie.'"

Brown turned toward Green and lifted his rifle. "Quicker than thought I brought my saber down with all my strength upon his head," Green said. "He was moving as the blow fell, and I suppose I did not strike him where I intended, for he received a deep saber cut in the back of the neck. He fell senseless on his side, then rolled over on his back. He had in his hand a short Sharp's cavalry carbine. I think he had just fired as I reached Colonel Washington, for the marine who followed me into the aperture made by the ladder received a bullet in the abdomen, from which he died in a few minutes." Green moved to deliver the coup de grâce. "As Brown fell I gave him a saber thrust in the left breast." But Green's weapon wasn't up to the task. "The sword I carried was a light uniform weapon and, either not having a point or striking something hard in Brown's accouterments, did not penetrate. The blade bent double."

Brown's life was spared by this accident. The fight for the engine house was almost over. "By that time three or four of my men were inside," Green said. "They came rushing in like tigers, as a storming assault is not a play-day sport. They bayoneted one man skulking under the engine, and pinned another fellow up against the rear wall, both being instantly killed. I ordered the men to spill no more blood. The other insurgents were at once taken under arrest, and the contest ended. The whole fight had not lasted over three minutes."

THE ASSAULT ON Harpers Ferry produced shock waves that rumbled around the region and country, with truth chasing rumor. "Insurrectionary Outbreak in Virginia," began the Richmond *Dispatch*. "The startling intelligence reached this city yesterday that an insurrectionary outbreak had occurred at Harper's Ferry, Sunday, and that negroes to the number of 500, aided by about 200 white men, the whole being under the command of a white captain, named Anderson, had seized the U.S. Arsenal at that place and captured the town itself." The newspaper quoted the alarmed telegram from the president of the Baltimore & Ohio Railroad to the governor of Virginia, and it described the military operations then set afoot. The paper went on to suggest that someone had been lax in Washington, citing an anonymous letter to the secretary of war predicting an attack on Harpers Ferry in mid-October. The letter warned that "abolitionists and negroes would seize the U.S. arsenal at Harper's Ferry." But the secretary had dismissed the warning as "so improbable" that it should be ignored.

Virginians were understandably excited about the events in their own state; the first reports suggested that the raid at Harpers Ferry was like the Nat Turner revolt a generation earlier, only worse—for being bigger, according to the numbers reported; better armed, after the capture of the arsenal; and led by white abolitionists, who presumably had support in the North.

Yet papers in other states were equally alarmed. "Fearful and Exciting Intelligence," proclaimed the *New York Herald* at the top of a ladder headline. "Negro Insurrection at Harpers Ferry / Extensive Negro Conspiracy in Virginia and Maryland / Seizure of the United

States Arsenal by the Insurrectionists / Arms Taken and Sent into the Interior / The Bridge Fortified and Defended by Cannon / Trains Fired into and Stopped—Several Persons Killed."

By the next day the *Herald* had caught its breath. "Who is Brown, the leader?" the paper demanded, in words approximated across the country. Facts were scarce. "Report has it that he was born in Kentucky," said the paper, which also pronounced him dead. Brown's trail through Kansas was traced, culminating in a confused and dismissive telling of Brown's motivation: "After the death of his first son, occasioned by the tortures and fatigue of his forced march, Brown swore vengeance on the pro-slavery party, and it was frequently observed by the most prudent of the free-State men that he was evidently insane on the subject." The paper went on to say in its own voice, "Captain Brown was fanatical on the subject of anti-slavery, and seemed to have the idea that he was specially deputed by the Almighty to liberate slaves and kill slaveholders."

Even the abolitionist press had reservations about Brown. William Lloyd Garrison's *Liberator* characterized the Harpers Ferry raid as "misguided, wild and apparently insane, though disinterested and well-intentioned." Garrison detested slavery with a passion second to none, but he still eschewed violence in seeking its demise. Brown's good intentions didn't change Garrison's mind, and Brown's mental imbalance, Garrison judged, didn't aid the abolitionist cause.

THE QUESTION OF Brown's sanity exercised nearly everyone involved in the slavery debate. Many Southerners had long deemed abolitionists mad for trying to overturn the South's beneficent institution, or if not certifiably mad, then hysterical in the lengths to which they took their false altruism. Other Southerners, though, reckoned that imputations of insanity would let the North off too easily. They contended that actions like Brown's were the all-too-logical consequence of allowing the abolitionists a place at the political table.

The Republican party had a special interest in Brown. From nothing in 1854 the Republicans had become the equals of the Democrats, whose lineage ran back to Thomas Jefferson. Their first presidential candidate, John Frémont, had come close to winning the White

House; their next candidate would have an even better chance, unless something unforeseen occurred.

Brown's attack on Harpers Ferry might be just that something. Republicans at once took cover. "We are damnably exercised about the effect of Old Brown's wretched fiasco in Virginia upon the health of the Republican party!" a Chicago Republican wrote to Abraham Lincoln. "The old idiot—the quicker they hang him and get him out of the way, the better." Republicans in Chicago were contending that Brown had nothing to do with them. "You see how we treat it," Lincoln's correspondent continued. "I hope we occupy the right ground."

Some Republicans had trouble getting out of the way. William Seward was the best known of the Republicans, having been a senator from New York for a decade, starting with the Whig party. Antislavery sentiments sat well with New York voters, and Seward had indulged himself on numerous occasions, including his first speech in the Senate, in which he bearded the lions of the Whig party, Henry Clay and Daniel Webster. Clay and Webster contended that the Constitution required what they were proposing as the Compromise of 1850; Seward rejoined that there was "a higher law than the Constitution." Seward's assertion didn't scuttle the compromise, yet it helped torpedo the Whig party. And it put him at the head of Republicans looking toward the White House as the 1860 election approached.

But it also made him vulnerable to charges that his "higher law" was exactly what extremists like John Brown appealed to, and that Seward would do to the Republicans what he had already done to the Whigs. Some in the party chafed at evidence that Seward was already awarding himself the nomination. "He has forgotten everything else, even that he is a senator and has duties as such," one of his Senate colleagues, a Maine Republican, asserted, adding that Seward affected "the airs of a president."

Seward's opponents allowed themselves to imagine that John Brown could save the party rather than wreck it, by denying Seward the nomination. "Since the humbug insurrection at Harper's Ferry, I presume Mr. Seward will not be urged," a Pennsylvania Republican wrote hopefully to Lincoln.

———

LINCOLN HIMSELF groaned on hearing the news from Harpers Ferry. It overtook him while he was touring Kansas, meeting and speaking to local Republicans. Some of his listeners knew Brown; all knew *of* him. Many admired him. To them Lincoln said, "John Brown has shown great courage and rare unselfishness." He could hardly have said less while seeking their support.

But neither could he say more if he hoped to convince Americans elsewhere that he stood for moderation and the rule of law. Lincoln deliberately distanced himself from Brown's actions, if not his motives or character. "No man, North or South, can approve of violence or crime," Lincoln said. Besides being wrong, Brown's raid would surely be unavailing. "It was, as all such attacks must be, futile as far as any effect it might have on the extinction of a great evil."

It couldn't have come at a worse time. The prospects of the Republican party had been improving by the month. So had Lincoln's own prospects.

And now this. Lincoln shook his head in dismay.

IN THE IMMEDIATE AFTERMATH of the storming of the engine house, there was no way to describe the Harpers Ferry raid other than as a wretched fiasco. Most of the raiders were dead or in custody; the few who had escaped before the storming, including Osborne Anderson, were on the run. The encouragement to slaves to flee their masters had failed utterly; those who joined Brown had been compelled to do so. Far from freeing them, Brown's quixotic venture seemed certain to fasten their chains tighter, as chains had been tightened after the Nat Turner rebellion.

Yet Brown was unrepentant. As the wounded were hauled out of the engine house, he was asked, "Are you Captain Brown of Kansas?"

"I am sometimes called so," he replied.

"Are you Osawatomie Brown?"

"I tried to do my duty there."

"What was your present object?"

"To free the slaves from bondage."

"Were there any persons but those with you now, connected with the movement?"

"No, there was no one connected with the movement but those who came with me." This was not true, but Brown wasn't going to implicate anyone his captors didn't already know about.

"Did you expect to kill people in order to carry your point?"

"I did not wish to do so, but you forced us to do it."

Brown's wounds at first appeared to be life threatening. This appearance, and some wishful thinking, accounted for the early reports that he was dead or dying. Israel Green's dress sword had lacerated Brown's scalp, causing his blood to flow freely and then clot in his hair and beard, lending him a gruesome mien. One of the marines had bayoneted him in the side, but the blade had struck no vital organs. The result was that though he couldn't move without pain, he could speak coherently—indeed forcefully.

From the moment of capture he began to impress his enemies. The governor of Virginia, Henry Wise, reached Harpers Ferry in time to interrogate the raiders after the taking of the engine room. "I immediately examined the leader, Brown, his lieutenant, Stevens, a white man named Coppie, and a negro from Canada," Wise subsequently reported to the Virginia legislature. "They made full confessions. Brown repelled the idea that his design was to run negro slaves off from their masters. He defiantly avowed that his purpose was to arm them and make them fight by his side in defense of their freedom, if assailed by their owners or anyone else; and he said his purpose especially was to war upon the slaveholders and to levy upon their other property to pay the expense of emancipating their slaves. He avowed that he expected to be joined by the slaves and by numerous white persons from many of the slave as well as the free states."

Brown's story shifted in the days after his capture, but what didn't change was the effect he had on his interrogators. "They are themselves mistaken who take him to be a madman," Henry Wise declared. "He is a bundle of the best nerves I ever saw cut and thrust and bleeding and in bonds. He is a man of clear head, of courage, fortitude and simple ingenuousness." Lewis Washington and the other hostages told Wise that Brown had treated them humanely; Wise saw no reason to question their testimony. "He inspired me with great trust in his integrity as a man of the truth," Wise said of Brown. "He is a fanatic, vain and garrulous; but firm, truthful and intelligent." Wise related what Lewis Washington had said of Brown, that he was "the coolest and firmest man he ever saw in defying danger and death. With one son dead by his side, and another shot through, he felt the pulse of his dying son with one hand and held his rifle with the other and commanded his men with the utmost composure, encouraging them to be firm and to sell their lives as dearly as they could."

Henry Wise wasn't alone in wanting to speak with Brown. James Mason was one of Virginia's senators; his home was but thirty miles from Harpers Ferry, and he couldn't resist the opportunity to stand up to his state's enemies. Charles Faulkner was a congressman who lived even closer. Clement Vallandigham, also a congressman, was from a district in Ohio barely more distant. A reporter for the *New York Herald* recounted a conversation between Brown and the three lawmakers, held in the crowded office of the armory, where Brown lay on the floor on some old bedding. The prisoner's compromised state couldn't disguise his vigor and strength of character, the reporter said. "He is a wiry, active man, and, should the slightest chance for an escape be afforded, there is no doubt he will yet give his captors much trouble. His hair is matted and tangled, and his face, hands, and clothes, all smouched and smeared with blood. Colonel Lee stated that he would exclude all visitors from the room if the wounded men were annoyed or pained by them, but Brown said he was by no means annoyed; on the contrary, he was glad to be able to make himself and his motives clearly understood. He converses freely, fluently and cheerfully, without the slightest manifestation of fear or uneasiness, evidently weighing well his words, and possessing a good command of language. His manner is courteous and affable, and he appears to make a favorable impression upon his auditory, which, during most of the day yesterday, averaged about ten or a dozen men."

Senator Mason wanted to know who was behind Brown's venture. Brown refused to give names.

"Can you tell us, at least, who furnished money for your expedition?"

"I furnished most of it myself," Brown lied. "I cannot implicate others. It is by my own folly that I have been taken. I could easily have saved myself from it had I exercised my own better judgment, rather than yielded to my feelings."

"You mean if you had escaped immediately?" asked Mason.

"No; I had the means to make myself secure without any escape, but I allowed myself to be surrounded by a force by being too tardy."

"Tardy in getting away?"

"I should have gone away, but I had thirty odd prisoners, whose wives and daughters were in tears for their safety, and I felt for them. Besides, I wanted to allay the fears of those who believed we came here to burn and kill. For this reason I allowed the train to cross the bridge, and gave them full liberty to pass on. I did it only to spare the feelings of those passengers and their families, and to allay the apprehensions that you had got here in your vicinity a band of men who had no regard for life and property, nor any feeling of humanity."

"But you killed some people passing along the streets quietly," Mason objected.

"Well, sir, if there was anything of that kind done, it was without my knowledge. Your own citizens, who were my prisoners, will tell you that every possible means were taken to prevent it. I did not allow my men to fire, nor even to return a fire, when there was danger of killing those we regarded as innocent persons, if I could help it. They will tell you that we allowed ourselves to be fired at repeatedly and did not return it."

A bystander in the room spoke up. "That is not so," he said. "You killed an unarmed man at the corner of the house over there"—he pointed—"and another besides."

Brown refused to yield. "See here, my friend, it is useless to dispute or contradict the report of your own neighbors who were my prisoners."

Mason returned to the matter of Brown's collaborators. "If you would tell us who sent you here—who provided the means—that would be information of some value."

"I will answer freely and faithfully about what concerns myself," Brown said. "I will answer anything I can with honor, but not about others."

Clement Vallandigham pressed this point harder. "Mr. Brown, who sent you here?"

"No man sent me here; it was my own prompting and that of my Maker, or that of the devil, whichever you choose to ascribe it to. I acknowledge no man in human form."

"Did you get up the expedition yourself?"

"I did."

Brown had been searched upon capture; his pockets had contained his provisional constitution.

"Did you get up this document?" demanded Vallandigham.

"I did. They are a constitution and ordinances of my own contriving."

"How long have you been engaged in this business?"

"From the breaking of the difficulties in Kansas. Four of my sons had gone there to settle, and they induced me to go. I did not go there to settle, but because of the difficulties."

"How many are engaged with you in this movement?" inquired James Mason. "I ask those questions for our own safety."

"Any questions that I can honorably answer I will, not otherwise," Brown repeated. "So far as I am myself concerned I have told everything truthfully. I value my word, sir."

"What was your object in coming?"

"We came to free the slaves, and only that."

One of the militia volunteers interjected, "How many men did you have?"

"I came to Virginia with eighteen men only, besides myself."

"What in the world did you suppose you could do here in Virginia with that amount of men?"

"Young man, I don't wish to discuss that question here."

"You could not do anything," the militiaman said.

"Perhaps your ideas and mine on military subjects would differ materially."

James Mason retook control of the questioning. "How do you justify your acts?"

"I think, my friend, you are guilty of a great wrong against God and humanity. I say that without wishing to be offensive. And it would be perfectly right in anyone to interfere with you so far as to free those you willfully and wickedly hold in bondage. I do not say this insultingly."

"I understand that," Mason answered.

"I think I did right, and that others will do right who interfere with you at any time and all times. I hold that the golden rule, 'Do unto others as you would that others should do unto you,' applies to all who would help others gain their liberty."

Lieutenant Jeb Stuart spoke up. "But you don't believe in the Bible," he said.

"Certainly I do," Brown answered.

James Mason asked what wages Brown paid his men.

"None," Brown replied.

"The wages of sin is death," quoted Jeb Stuart, a devout student of the Bible.

"I would not have made such a remark to you, if you had been a prisoner and wounded in my hands," Brown observed.

Mason asked Brown if all this talking was fatiguing him.

"Not in the least," Brown said.

Democrat Vallandigham wanted to know if Joshua Giddings, his Republican Ohio colleague, had been involved in Brown's raid. "Did you talk with Giddings about your expedition here?" he asked.

"I won't answer that," Brown said, "because a denial of it I would not make, and to make any affirmation of it I should be a great dunce."

A bystander raised the religious question again. "Do you consider this a religious movement?" he asked.

"It is, in my opinion, the greatest service a man can render to God," Brown said.

"Do you consider yourself an instrument in the hands of Providence?"

"I do."

"Upon what principle do you justify your acts?"

"Upon the golden rule," Brown repeated. "I pity the poor in bondage that have none to help them; that is why I am here—not to gratify any personal animosity, revenge or vindictive spirit. It is my sympathy with the oppressed and the wronged, that are as good as you and as precious in the sight of God."

"Certainly," said the bystander. "But why take the slaves against their will?"

Brown denied it. "I never did," he said.

"You did in one instance, at least."

Aaron Stevens, lying wounded beside Brown, now spoke. "You are right. In one case, I know the negroes wanted to go back."

Stevens was asked where he was from. Ohio, he said. Vallandigham asked him if he lived near Jefferson. Stevens started to answer, but Brown broke in. "Be cautious, Stevens, about any answers that would commit any friend," Brown said. "I would not answer that."

Stevens didn't. He rolled over, with a moan, and fell silent again.

The reporter for the *New York Herald* who was transcribing the conversation asked Brown if he had anything more he wanted the world to know about his deeds and motives.

"Only that I claim to be here in carrying out a measure I believe

perfectly justifiable, and not to act the part of an incendiary or ruffian, but to aid those suffering great wrong," Brown said. "I wish to
say, furthermore, that you had better—all you people at the South—
prepare yourselves for a settlement of that question that must come
up for settlement sooner than you are prepared for. The sooner you
are prepared the better. You may dispose of me very easily; I am
nearly disposed of now; but this question is still to be settled—this
negro question I mean—the end of that is not yet. These wounds were
inflicted upon me—both saber cuts on my head and bayonet stabs
in different parts of my body—some minutes after I had ceased firing and had consented to surrender, for the benefit of others, not for
my own."

Jeb Stuart vehemently denied Brown's assertion.

Brown brushed him aside. "I believe the major would not have
been alive—I could have killed him just as easy as a mosquito when
he came in—but I supposed he came in only to receive our surrender,"
he said. He added, "There had been long and loud calls of 'surrender'
from us—as loud as men could yell—but in the confusion and excitement I suppose we were not heard. I do not think the major, or any
one, meant to butcher us after we had surrendered."

Another officer asked Brown why he hadn't surrendered before the
attack.

"I did not think it was my duty or interest to do so," Brown replied.
"We assured the prisoners that we did not wish to harm them, and they
should be set at liberty. I exercised my best judgment, not believing
the people would wantonly sacrifice their own fellow-citizens, when
we offered to let them go on condition of being allowed to change our
position about a quarter of a mile. The prisoners agreed by vote among
themselves to pass across the bridge with us. We wanted them only as
a sort of guaranty of our own safety; that we should not be fired into.
We took them in the first place as hostages and to keep them from
doing any harm. We did kill some men in defending ourselves, but I
saw no one fire except directly in self-defense. Our orders were strict
not to harm anyone not in arms against us."

A townsman in the room asked, "Brown, suppose you had every
nigger in the United States, what would you do with them?"

"Set them free."

"To set them free would sacrifice the life of every man in this community."

"I do not think so," Brown said.

"I know it. I think you are fanatical."

"And I think you are fanatical," Brown rejoined. "Whom the gods would destroy they first make mad—and you are mad."

33

JOHN BROWN'S TRIAL began quickly but not without controversy. Virginia law mandated that if the appropriate court was in session, a trial had to begin. The court for Harpers Ferry, in nearby Charles Town, was soon to end its session; to fit John Brown's trial in, the proceedings had to commence within days.

This suited the Virginia authorities. Despite what they had heard from John Brown, they couldn't be sure his conspiracy wasn't larger than he had let on. In fact, they were fairly certain it *was* larger. On Brown's person and at the Kennedy farm they found letters and other documents linking Brown to his benefactors in the North. It wasn't unreasonable to suppose that if the abolitionist network could produce one John Brown, it might produce others.

Moreover, Governor Wise and other Virginia authorities caught wind that Northerners who supported Brown's cause, without perhaps any previous connection, were planning to break him out of jail. Some of Brown's free-state friends in Kansas were said to be coming to Virginia. The longer Brown lingered in custody, the more time the rescuers would have to organize.

Yet there were arguments for delay. The first was that the wounded Brown was in no position to stand trial. Indeed, he couldn't stand at all. He had been transported from Harpers Ferry to Charles Town lying in a wagon; similarly recumbent he passed the time in his jail cell. Brown's supporters sent letters to Wise saying the prisoner must be allowed to recover; Wise himself recognized the difficulty the prosecution might encounter convincing a jury—or the wider world—that the old man lying weak and bandaged on a cot in the courtroom had really presented a danger to the great Commonwealth of Virginia.

Weighing everything, Wise reckoned that the hazards of delay were larger than those of promptness. The proceedings commenced a week after the storming of the engine house. Brown and the four others captured with him, including Aaron Stevens, also wounded, and Shields Green, were brought before the court of Judge Richard Parker. Security was heavy. Several dozen deputies and militiamen surrounded the courthouse, with rifles and bayonets at the ready. Cannons placed in front of the courthouse threatened to blast anyone who tried to disturb the proceedings. The prisoners were manacled. "Brown seemed weak and haggard, with eyes swollen from wounds on the head," the reporter for the *New York Herald* observed.

The sheriff read the preliminary charges against the five: treason against Virginia and murder of the five townsmen killed in the raid. Judge Parker asked the prisoners if they had counsel.

Brown responded by protesting the legitimacy of the trial. "I did not ask for any quarter at the time I was taken," he said. "I did not ask to have my life spared. The governor of the state of Virginia tendered me his assurance that I should have a fair trial; and under no circumstances whatever will I be able to have a fair trial. If you seek my blood, you can have it at any moment, without this mockery of a trial. I have had no counsel. I have not been able to advise with any one. I know nothing about the feelings of my fellow-prisoners, and am utterly unable to attend in any way to my own defense. My memory don't serve me. My health is insufficient, although improving. There are mitigating circumstances that I would urge in our favor, if a fair trial is to be allowed us. But if we are to be forced with a mere form—a trial for execution—you might spare yourselves that trouble. I am ready for my fate. I do not ask a trial. I beg for no mockery of a trial—no insult—nothing but that which conscience gives, or cowardice would drive you to practice. I again ask to be excused from the mockery of a trial. I do not even know what the special design of this examination is. I do not know what is to be the benefit of it to the Commonwealth. I have now little further to ask, other than that I may not be foolishly insulted, only as cowardly barbarians insult those who fall into their power."

Judge Parker declined to respond to Brown's tirade, except to assign two local lawyers as counsel for the defense. One of the two,

Charles Faulkner, immediately attempted to decline the appointment, but his objection was overruled. The other, Lawson Botts, accepted the appointment without complaint and said he would do his best for the defense.

Brown was asked if *he* accepted the appointment. He didn't. "I have sent for counsel," he said. "I did apply, through the advice of some persons here, to some persons whose names I do not now recollect, to act as counsel for me, and I have sent for other counsel, who have had no possible opportunity to see me. I wish for counsel if I am to have a trial; but if I am to have nothing but the mockery of a trial, as I have said, I do not care anything about counsel. It is unnecessary to trouble any gentleman with that duty."

The attorney for the county responded, "You are to have a fair trial."

Brown didn't trust him. "I am a stranger here," he said. "I do not know the disposition or character of the gentlemen named. I have applied for counsel of my own, and doubtless could have them, if I am not, as I said before, to be hurried to execution before they can reach me. But if that is the disposition that is to be made of me, all this trouble and expense can be saved."

"The question is, do you desire the aid of Messrs. Faulkner and Botts as your counsel?" the county attorney insisted. "Please answer yes or no."

"They should exercise their own pleasure," Brown said. "I feel as if it were a matter of very little account to me."

A GRAND JURY WAS summoned to hear the evidence against the prisoners. The jury produced an indictment: for conspiring with slaves to produce an insurrection, for treason against the Commonwealth of Virginia, and for murder.

The defendants were asked how they pleaded. All said, "Not guilty." They asked to be tried individually. The court accepted the request and chose to try John Brown first.

Lawson Botts, for Brown, immediately asked for a delay. "I am instructed by Mr. Brown to say that he is mentally and physically unable to proceed with his trial at this time," Botts said. "He has heard today that counsel of his own choice will be here, whom he will, of course, prefer. He only asks for a delay of two or three days. It seems to me but a reasonable request, and I hope the court will grant it."

Judge Parker answered that waiting for counsel was no cause for delay, but physical disability in the defendant might be. He summoned the doctor who had been tending to Brown in jail. The doctor said Brown's injuries were not such as to impair his thinking or his hearing. The doctor saw no reason the trial shouldn't proceed. One of the guards at the jail volunteered that Brown talked quite freely and capably at the jail. Judge Parker denied postponement.

Selection of a jury occupied an afternoon. Brown attended on a cot. He lay with his eyes closed and a quilt drawn up to his chin, apparently oblivious to the proceedings. The potential jurors were asked whether they had already formed opinions about the guilt or innocence of the defendant, and whether they had moral scruples that would prevent their convicting a man on a charge that carried the death penalty. Twelve who satisfied the judge that they had not and did not were impaneled.

THE TRIAL PROPER began on Thursday morning, October 27. John Brown managed to walk across the street from the jail to the courthouse, but once in the courtroom he took to his cot and covered up. Observers noted that the swelling around his eyes had diminished.

Lawson Botts surprised the court by submitting a statement sent from one A. H. Lewis, a longtime resident of Akron, Ohio. "John Brown, leader of the insurrection at Harper's Ferry, and several of his family have resided in this county many years," Lewis's statement attested. "Insanity is hereditary in that family. His mother's sister died with it, and a daughter of that sister has been two years in a Lunatic Asylum. A son and daughter of his mother's brother have also been confined in the lunatic asylum, and another son of that brother is now insane and under close restraint. These facts can be conclusively proven by witnesses residing here, who will doubtless attend the trial if desired."

Botts said he had shown the statement to his client, who responded that in his father's family there was no insanity at all. Things were different among his mother's kin. "On his mother's side there have been repeated instances of it," Botts said Brown had told him. "Some portions of the statements in the dispatch he knows to be correct, and of other portions he is ignorant. He does not know whether his mother's sister died in the lunatic asylum; he is not apprised of the fact that another son of that brother is now insane and in close confinement. He also desires his counsel to say that he does not put in the plea of insanity, and if he has been at all insane he is totally unconscious of it, yet he adds that those who are most insane generally suppose that they have more reason and sanity than those around them."

At this point Brown demanded to speak for himself. Rising on his elbow, he said of the insanity plea, "I look upon it as a miserable artifice and pretext of those who ought to take a different course in regard to me, and I view it with contempt more than otherwise. As I remarked to Mr. Green"—an assistant to Botts—"insane persons, so far as my experience goes, have but little ability to judge of their own sanity; and, if I am insane, of course I should think I know more than all the rest of the world. But I do not think so. I am perfectly unconscious of insanity, and I reject, so far as I am capable, any attempt to interfere in my behalf on that score."

Lawson Botts let his client speak, then said that though the defense was not making an insanity plea, which might have required a delay in the proceedings to confirm the statement from Ohio, the defense *was* renewing its request for a delay, to allow additional lawyers to appear. A recent telegram revealed that at least one lawyer, a man named Lewis, was en route from the North, and the reluctant Botts, only too happy to step aside from his court-imposed duty, asked the court to give the man time to arrive. He repeated that his client was not making an insanity plea, but he was asking for a fair trial. He believed his trial would be fairer if he had the lawyers he liked.

Andrew Hunter, for the prosecution, resented the aspersions cast on the court by the suggestion that the trial wasn't fair in its present form. "What does he mean by wishing delay for the purpose of having a fair trial?" he demanded. "In a proper sense, and in the only sense in which it can be regarded by the court, it *is* a fair trial according to the laws of Virginia, and the safeguards against wronging the prisoner which these laws throw around him. If the prisoner's idea of a fair trial is to have it so shaped as to produce a fairness in his conception, outside of what the laws recognize, it becomes the duty of the counsel for the Commonwealth, and of the court, to resist any attempt of that kind." Hunter was skeptical of the information just sprung on the court. "We know not who this Mr. Lewis is. We know not whether he is to come here as counsel for the prisoner, or whether he wants to head a band of desperadoes. We have a right to believe the latter as well as the former. There had been time enough since the letter for northern counsel was mailed last Saturday, for it to reach him, and for him to arrive here ere this, if he had designed coming. It was fairly inferable that he did not intend to come, and the telegraph did not say he would come. But might it not be an attempt to gain time and learn the latest day when a rescue could be attempted?"

Charles Harding, also of the prosecution, offered a broader warning against tricks by the defense. He noted that the prisoner had professed to be unable to walk and insisted on being carried into court on a bed the previous day, yet at the end of the session had stood up and walked back to the jail unaided.

Judge Parker ordered that the trial move forward. If new counsel arrived, he or they could join the defense team then.

CHARLES HARDING OPENED for the prosecution by recounting in detail the deaths of the five men slain by the raiders. He told of the premeditated kidnapping of Lewis Washington and John Allstadt and their slaves. He cited Brown's provisional constitution to show that he had intended to create a government within the borders of the Commonwealth of Virginia. He read the Virginia laws on treason, on encouraging slaves to flee, and on murder, each punishable by death. He promised to prove beyond reasonable doubt all the charges against the prisoner.

The defense countered by focusing on the specifics of the laws the prisoner was charged with breaking. Virginia's treason law required proof that the accused intended to establish a separate and distinct government. Confessions to treason had to be given in open court to be admissible. Other evidence had to be supported by the testimony of two witnesses to the criminal act. On the matter of instigating the flight of slaves, the law said such instigation must have taken place in Virginia. Actions taken in Maryland didn't qualify, nor did actions taken on the federal property of the armory. The same considerations applied to the murder charges. Capital murder, moreover—for which death was the penalty—required premeditation. Members of the jury, the defense said, must bear all these facts in mind in considering the case before them. The burden of proof lay with the prosecution.

The prosecution began calling its witnesses. John Starry, the doctor, told of being awakened by the shot that proved fatal to porter Shephard Hayward. Conductor A. J. Phelps related the same events from his perspective.

On cross-examination, Phelps told of meeting John Brown, who had apologized for the killing of Hayward. "He said he was very sorry; it was not his intention that any blood should be spilled; that it was bad management on the part of the men in charge of the bridge." There would be no more killings if the people were peaceable. Brown added, "You doubtless wonder that a man of my age should be here with a band of armed men, but if you knew my past history you would not wonder at it so much."

The prosecution called Lewis Washington, who related his version of the events in question. On cross-examination, he explained that Brown had taken good care of the hostages. "We were kept in the rear engine house, and allowed to keep a safe position," he said. "There was no effort to endanger us; Brown's conduct was not rude or insulting toward us."

Witness testimony filled the rest of the day; the next morning the prosecution produced Brown's provisional constitution and a bundle of some fifty letters and papers. The sheriff, who had seen Brown's handwriting, was called to identify the papers as coming from the same source.

Brown interrupted to say he would spare the court the trouble. "I will face the music," he said. The documents were his.

Prosecutor Hunter wanted a more dramatic effect. He insisted on displaying the documents one by one. At each Brown said, "Yes, that is mine."

The prosecution summoned several more witnesses, who corroborated most of the facts asserted by the prosecutors but who nonetheless, under cross-examination, made Brown seem a decent fellow for a gun-toting abolitionist. One of the hostages, a worker at the armory, said, "Captain Brown told me his object was to free the slaves, and not the making of war on the people; that my person and private property would be safe; that his war was against the accursed system of slavery." This man had been seized on coming to work on Monday morning. Brown didn't want the man's family to worry, so he allowed him to return to his home, with an escort, and to eat a hot breakfast while there. This witness didn't take the slave uprising very seriously. "There were three or four slaves in the engine-house; they had spears, but all seemed badly scared."

WHEN THE DEFENSE had its turn, the witnesses said much the same thing about Brown the man. One after the other noted Brown's patience under duress and his refusal to inflict gratuitous violence. Prosecutor Hunter found the testimony tedious and beside the point; Brown's forbearance, he said, had "no more to do with this case than the dead languages."

Brown lay on his cot through all this, occasionally joining in the defense team's questioning. Then, after several witnesses for the defense were called but didn't appear, and the court made no attempt to find them, he got to his feet to register a protest. "May it please the court," he said, "I discover that, notwithstanding all the assurances I have received of a fair trial, nothing like a fair trial is to be given me, as it would seem. I gave the names, as soon as I could get at them, of the persons I wished to have called as witnesses, and was assured that they would be subpoenaed. I wrote down a memorandum to the effect, saying where those parties were; but it appears that they have not been subpoenaed as far as I can learn; and now I ask if I am to have anything at all deserving the name and shadow of a fair trial, that this proceeding be deferred until tomorrow morning; for I have no counsel, as I before stated, in whom I feel that I can rely, but I am in hopes counsel may arrive who will attend to seeing that I get the witnesses who are necessary for my defense. I am myself unable to attend to it. I have given all the attention I possibly could to it, but am unable to see or know about them, and can't even find out their names; and I have nobody to do any errand, for my money was all taken when I was sacked and stabbed, and I have not a dime. I had two hundred and fifty or sixty dollars in gold and silver taken from my pocket, and now I have no possible means of getting anybody to go my errands for me, and I have not had all the witnesses subpoenaed. They are not within reach, and are not here. I ask at least until tomorrow morning to have something done, if anything is designed; if not, I am ready for anything that may come up."

This effort seemed to require all the prisoner's energy. "Brown then lay down again, drew his blanket over him, and closed his eyes and appeared to sink in tranquil slumber," the *Herald* reporter on the trial observed.

Brown in fact did get legal help. Various attorneys sent by Brown's friends or traveling on their own hook arrived, alleviating the burden of his Virginia lawyers, who were happy to shed responsibility for a despised client bound for certain conviction.

The trial ran into the weekend. The prosecution didn't bother cross-examining any of the defense witnesses, so confident were they of the jury's support. The defense began its summary by reminding the jury that the burden of proof was on the prosecution and contending that the sum of the prosecution's evidence fell short of the standard for conviction. Judge Parker had hoped to finish the trial before Sunday, but the defense had more to say, and he didn't want to be accused of forcing a verdict. He recessed until Monday.

By then Brown looked better physically. "His health is evidently improving," the reporter remarked, before adding, "He was laid on a bed, as usual."

The defense reiterated that the burden of proof lay on the state. The prosecution, it said, had failed to clear the bar of reasonable doubt that Brown had committed treason, according to Virginia's law; that he had committed murder, with premeditation; and that he had, while within Virginia, conspired to encourage slaves to rebel.

The prosecution countered that treason was implicit in the provisional constitution drafted by the defendant. The attack on Harpers Ferry had obviously been premeditated, and the murder of five men was the result. As for inciting slave rebellion, if putting weapons in their hands wasn't incitement, nothing was.

THE PROSECUTION'S SUMMARY finished at half past one. The jury was sent out; it returned before two thirty. The *Herald* man who had faithfully followed the proceedings from the start described the end. "The crowd filled all the space from the couch inside the bar, around the prisoner, beyond the railing in the body of the court, out through the wide hall and beyond the doors," he wrote. "There stood the anxious but perfectly silent and attentive populace, stretching its neck to witness the closing scene of Old Brown's trial. It was terrible to look upon such a crowd of human faces, moved and agitated with but one dreadful expectancy—to let the eyes rest for a moment upon the only calm and unruffled countenance there, and to think that he alone of all present was the doomed one above whose head hung the sword of fate. But there he stood, a man of indomitable will and iron nerve, all collected and unmoved."

The clerk of the court spoke. "Gentlemen of the jury, what say you?" he asked. "Is the prisoner at the bar, John Brown, guilty or not guilty?"

"Guilty," said the foreman of the jury.

"Guilty of treason, and conspiring and advising with slaves and others to rebel, and murder in the first degree?" the clerk asked.

"Yes," said the foreman.

The reporter watched and listened. "Not the slightest sound was heard in the vast crowd as this verdict was thus returned and read," he recounted. "Not the slightest expression of elation or triumph was uttered from the hundreds present, who, a moment before, outside the court, joined in heaping threats and imprecations on his head; nor was this strange silence interrupted during the whole of the time occupied by the forms of the court. Old Brown himself said not even a word, but, as on any previous day, turned to adjust his pallet, and then composedly stretched himself upon it."

34

M**Y DEAR WIFE, and Children Every one," John Brown wrote on October 31. "I suppose you have learned before this by the newspapers that two weeks ago today we were fighting for our lives at Harpers Ferry." Brown related that Oliver Brown had been killed during the fighting and Watson Brown mortally wounded. "I received several sabre cuts in my head; & bayonet stabs in my body." He had been taken prisoner. "I have since been tried, & found guilty of treason, etc.; and of murder in the first degree. I have not yet received my sentence."

His conscience was clear and his soul at rest. "Under all these terrible calamities, I feel quite cheerful in the assurance that God reigns; will overrule all for his glory; and the best possible good. I feel *no* consciousness of guilt in the matter: or even mortification on account of my imprisonment; and irons; & I feel perfectly assured that very soon no member of my family will feel any possible disposition to blush on my account. Already dear friends at a distance with kindest sympathy are cheering me with the assurance that *posterity*, at least, will do me justice."

His wounds were improving. His jailer was an honest man. "You may rest assured that both *kind hearts* and *kind faces* are more or less about me, whilst thousands are thirsting for my blood."

He offered a benediction to his family and reminded them to put their faith in God. "He will never leave or forsake you, unless you forsake him." He urged them to practice Christian charity. "Never forget the poor nor think anything you bestow on them to be lost to you even though they may be as *black* as Ebedmelech the Ethiopian. . . .

Be sure to entertain strangers. . . . Remember them that are in bonds as bound with them."

The mails were irregular, and not for four days was he able to send this letter. Just before it went out, he penned a postscript: "Yesterday November 2d I was sentenced to be hanged on 2 December next. Do not grieve on my account. I am still quite cheerful. God bless you all."

JOHN BROWN'S SENTENCE had largely been determined when the jury rendered its guilty verdict. Each of the crimes for which he was convicted carried the death sentence. Yet Judge Parker asked Brown if he wished to speak before the sentence was announced.

Brown rose from his bed and faced the judge. "I have, may it please the court, a few words to say," he responded. "In the first place, I deny everything but what I have all along admitted, of a design on my part to free slaves. I intended certainly to have made a clean thing of the matter, as I did last winter when I went into Missouri, and there took slaves without the snapping of a gun on either side, moving them through the country, and finally leaving them in Canada. I designed to have done the same thing again on a larger scale. That was all I intended to do. I never did intend murder or treason, or the destruction of property, or to excite or incite the slaves to rebellion, or to make insurrection. I have another objection, and that is that it is unjust that I should suffer such a penalty. Had I interfered in the manner which I admit, and which I admit has been fairly proved—for I admire the truthfulness and candor of the greater portion of the witnesses who have testified in this case—had I so interfered on behalf of the rich, the powerful, the intelligent, the so-called great, or in behalf of any of their friends, either father, mother, brother, sister, wife, or children, or any of that class, and suffered and sacrificed what I have in this interference, it would have been all right, and every man in this court would have deemed it an act worthy of reward rather than punishment."

Brown looked around the room. "This court acknowledges, too, as I suppose, the validity of the law of God. I see a book kissed, which I suppose to be the Bible, or at least the New Testament, which teaches me that all things whatsoever I would that men should do to me, I should do even so to them. It teaches me further to remember them that are in bonds as bound with them. I endeavored to act upon that instruction. I say I am yet too young to understand that God is any respecter of persons. I believe that to have interfered as I have done, as I have always freely admitted I have done on behalf of His despised poor, is no wrong, but right. Now, if it is deemed necessary that I should forfeit my life for the furtherance of the ends of justice, and mingle my blood further with the blood of my children and with the blood of millions in this slave country whose rights are disregarded by wicked, cruel, and unjust enactments, I say let it be done."

He gazed around the courtroom again, pausing at Judge Parker. "Let me say one word further. I feel entirely satisfied with the treatment I have received on my trial. Considering all the circumstances, it has been more generous than I expected. But I feel no consciousness of guilt. I have stated from the first what was my intention, and what was not. I never had any design against the liberty of any person, nor any disposition to commit treason or excite slaves to rebel or make any general insurrection. I never encouraged any man to do so, but always discouraged any idea of the kind. Let me say also in regard to the statements made by some of those who were connected with me, I fear it has been stated by some of them that I have induced them to join me, but the contrary is true. I do not say this to injure them, but as regretting their weakness. Not one but joined me of his own accord, and the greater part at their own expense. A number of them I never saw, and never had a word of conversation with till the day they came to me, and that was for the purpose I have stated. Now, I am done."

THE COURTROOM WAS perfectly still while Brown spoke. Most of those present refused to accept Brown's version of events, which contradicted the evidence on which he had been convicted. But all admired his composure and courage in the face of imminent doom.

The judge broke the silence. He pronounced the sentence: hanging, in thirty days. The court was adjourned.

———

SOME OF BROWN'S SUPPORTERS hoped to stay the execution by springing him from jail. Several of his Kansas friends, weary of the peace that had settled over that territory, hoped to revive the old spirit by galloping to Brown's rescue. But two hurdles blocked their way. The first was the cordon of troops Governor Wise threw around the Charles Town jail. Wise had been embarrassed by the ease with which Brown had commenced the Harpers Ferry raid, and by the need for Virginia, a principal expositor of state self-sufficiency, to turn to the national government to subdue the raiders. He wasn't going to be embarrassed again. No one was allowed near the jail without authorization; every body of men was halted and interrogated miles away.

The second hurdle was Brown's refusal to countenance a rescue. The inactivity imposed by his wounds and the bars of his cell afforded Brown time to reflect on the outcome of the raid. The great act of his life had been a dismal failure. It hadn't freed a single slave; in all likelihood it would make the lot of the slaves worse. And now he was bound for the scaffold.

Yet Brown believed God worked in mysterious ways. God must have a plan for him still. If John Brown couldn't free the slaves in his life, perhaps he might free them in his death. In Kansas he had fought ferociously, like a man who didn't fear death but neither wanted to die. Now Brown came to embrace death. *This* was the end toward which God had been guiding his steps; *this* would be the great act of his life.

In the clearest terms Brown made would-be rescuers understand he would not permit a rescue. George Hoyt was one of the Northern additions to Brown's defense team; he was also a spy for some of those who wanted to free him. Hoyt hinted at a rescue; Brown "positively refused his consent to any such plan," Hoyt reported. Brown sealed his refusal by pledging to his jailer, the one who had been kind to him, that he would not attempt to escape.

HE MEANWHILE REASSURED his family that all was well. His wounds continued to heal, he said. His appetite was good. His jailer provided him with everything he needed and some nonessential niceties. "I am, besides, quite cheerful, having (as I trust) 'the peace of God, which passeth all understanding,' to rule in my heart, and the testimony (in some degree) of a good conscience that I have not lived altogether in vain. I can trust God with both the time and the manner of my death, believing, as I now do, that for me at this time to seal my testimony for God and humanity with my blood will do vastly more toward advancing the cause I have earnestly endeavored to promote, than all I have done in my life before." He hoped Mary and the children could accept this as he had come to accept it. "Remember, dear wife and children all, that Jesus of Nazareth suffered a most excruciating death on the cross as a felon, under the most aggravating circumstances."

Mary had indicated she wanted to visit him. He gently pushed her back. The journey would be expensive, and the money could be better spent on herself and the children. The journey, moreover, would subject her to scrutiny and criticism, from which he knew she shied. "The sympathy that is now aroused in your behalf may not always follow you. There is but little more of the romantic about helping poor widows and their children than there is about trying to relieve poor 'niggers.'" A visit would make the final separation harder. "The little comfort it might afford us to meet again would be dearly bought by the pains of a final separation. We must part; and I feel assured for us to meet under such dreadful circumstances would only add to our distress."

Yet pushing her away didn't come easily. "Oh, Mary! do not come, but patiently wait for the meeting of those who love God and their fellow-men, where no separation must follow."

His eyes were on the future victory, and so must hers be. "I cannot remember a night so dark as to have hindered the coming day, nor a storm so furious and dreadful as to prevent the return of warm sunshine and a cloudless sky."

She read his letters but still wanted to see him before he died. She said she could bear the scrutiny, and others offered to bear the expense. His resistance weakened. "If you feel sure that you can endure the trials and the shock, which will be unavoidable if you come, I should be most glad to see you once more," he wrote. Even so, he wondered if she knew what she was getting into. "When I think of your being insulted on the road, and perhaps while here, and of only seeing your wretchedness made complete, I shrink from it. Your composure and fortitude of mind may be quite equal to it all; but I am in dreadful doubt of it."

Perhaps he wasn't sure *his* composure could stand the visit. He had begun to take his leave of the earth; to be reminded of the affection and other good things the earth held for him might be more than he could bear. "Do consider the matter well before you make the plunge," he repeated. "I think I had better say no more on this most painful subject."

Mary made the trip. Governor Wise gave her a special pass, and on the afternoon of November 30 she saw her husband. They spoke of the children, of their education, of the farm at North Elba. The governor had allowed her a few hours; Brown, feeling the bonds of affection as he hadn't for a long time, asked the governor's representative if Mary could spend the night. The answer was a regretful no. With a final embrace they parted for the last time.

A letter he wrote the same day followed her as she left. "I am waiting the hour of my public murder with great composure of mind and cheerfulness, feeling the strong assurance that in no other possible way could I be used to so much advantage to the cause of good and of humanity, and that nothing that either I or all my family have sacrificed or suffered will be lost," he said. "I have now no doubt but that our seeming disaster will ultimately result in the most glorious success; so, my dear shattered and broken family, be of good cheer, and believe and trust in God with all your heart, and with all your soul; for He doeth all things well. Do not feel ashamed on my account, nor for one moment despair of the cause or grow weary of well doing. I bless God I never felt stronger confidence in the certain and near approach of a bright morning and a glorious day than I have felt, and do now feel, since my confinement here." The end was near. To them, and to himself, he urged, "Be faithful unto death."

DECEMBER 2, 1859, dawned clear and, for the season, quite warm. A haze set in by nine o'clock, but the temperature continued to climb. Residents of Charles Town threw open their windows to keep their houses from overheating. Early risers heard the sounds of hammers and saws coming from a field at the edge of the town; carpenters were building the platform for John Brown's farewell to earth. All morning, troops from local militias marched from their bivouacs outside town to take up positions surrounding the field. Their inexpertise caused the maneuvers to drag on for hours, until they got it almost right.

At half past ten the prisoner was summoned. A wagon carrying his coffin rolled up to the door of the jail. John Brown walked out, climbed into the wagon and sat upon the coffin. With a military escort leading the way, the wagon moved slowly toward the execution field. As the wagon crested a high point, Brown looked across the land, and his jailer, seated next to him, heard him say, "This is beautiful country." The wagon halted at the scaffold. Brown stepped from the wagon. He turned to the jailer. "I have no words to thank you for all your kindness to me," he said.

He mounted the scaffold. His arms were tied behind his back, and his ankles were bound. In a steady voice, betraying no sign of fear, he requested of the sheriff and the captain of the guard, "Let there be no more delay than is necessary."

His dark, dirty hat was removed; a fresh white hood was placed over his head. The sheriff helped him to his spot on the scaffold's trapdoor. A noose was fitted around his neck. The sheriff awaited the signal that the troops were at last in position. They were still shuffling when the captain of the guard decided to honor Brown's request. He nodded to the sheriff, who swung a hatchet that severed the rope holding the trapdoor.

The door fell away beneath the prisoner. The noose caught his fall but didn't snap his neck. He slowly strangled, his body twitching for several minutes before the motion finally stopped. Two doctors examined the hanging body and pronounced John Brown dead.

PART IV

The Telegraph Office

J OHN BROWN WAS hung today," Thomas Jackson wrote to his wife. "He behaved with unflinching firmness." Jackson had yet to win the nickname Stonewall; in 1859 he taught at the Virginia Military Institute and commanded cadets from the school assigned to Charles Town for the execution. Jackson was an ardent defender of Virginia against all its enemies; he believed Brown deserved his sentence. But Jackson was also a pious Christian who feared for the fate of Brown's soul. "I was much impressed with the thought that before me stood a man, in the full vigor of health, who must in a few minutes be in eternity. I sent up a petition that he might be saved. Awful was the thought that he might in a few minutes receive the sentence 'Depart ye wicked into everlasting fire.' I hope that he was prepared to die, but I am very doubtful—he wouldn't have a minister with him."

Also present at the hanging was a twenty-one-year-old actor named John Wilkes Booth. The Maryland-born Booth agreed with Jackson that Brown deserved to die. Yet the boldness of Brown appealed to his sense of the dramatic. He joined one of the militia regiments for the sole purpose of seeing the execution; he later declared, "John Brown was a man inspired, the grandest character of the century!"

Robert E. Lee had returned to his home on the Potomac after the storming of the engine house, but he was back in western Virginia for the execution. Lee supervised federal troops who provided security beyond that afforded by the militia. His preparations were thorough; he expected no trouble. "Tomorrow will probably be the last of Captain Brown," Lee wrote to his wife on December 1.

HE COULDN'T HAVE been more wrong. The hanging was not the end of John Brown but a new beginning. Brown's parting testament shortly surfaced, scribbled on a scrap of paper passed to a sympathetic guard before he left the jail. "I, John Brown, am now quite certain that the crimes of this guilty land will never be purged away but with blood," he declared.

The dreadful forecast made the martyr into a prophet as well. Or so it seemed to those who commenced the apotheosis of John Brown. Henry Thoreau praised Brown as the model of what every American should aspire to be. "He was a superior man," Thoreau told a crowd in Concord. "He did not value his bodily life in comparison with ideal things. He did not recognize unjust human laws, but resisted them as he was bid." Thoreau rejected the authority of the Virginia court—or any human court—over one like Brown. "He could not have been tried by a jury of his peers, because his peers did not exist." Some antislavery men criticized Brown for launching his assault on bondage with so few men; Thoreau rejoined, "When were the good and the brave ever in a majority?" Brown's foes called the raid on Harpers Ferry a failure; they didn't understand the nature of history, Thoreau said. Failures could portend the greatest success. "I see now that it was necessary that the bravest and humanest man in all the country should be hung." Thoreau called upon his state to honor such a man. "I would rather see the statue of Captain Brown in the Massachusetts State House yard than that of any other man whom I know. I rejoice that I live in this age, that I am his contemporary."

Henry Beecher joined Thoreau in blessing Brown. Beecher traced Brown's antislavery struggle from Kansas—where, Beecher reminded his flock, Brown had lost a son to slavery's partisans—to Harpers Ferry. The struggle had pushed him to extremes, perhaps even unbalanced him slightly, but it also brought out traits honest men could only admire. "Bold, unflinching, honest, without deceit or dodge, refusing to take technical advantages of any sort, but openly avowing his principles and motives, glorying in them in danger and death as much as when in security—that wounded old father is the most remarkable figure in this whole drama. The governor, the officers of the state, and all the attorneys are pygmies compared to him." Beecher didn't condone all of Brown's actions, yet he could not but praise the man.

"By and by, when men look back and see without prejudice that whole scene, they will not be able to avoid saying: 'What must be the measure of manhood in a scene where a crazed old man stood head and shoulders above those who had their whole reason? What is average citizenship when a lunatic is a hero?'"

Wendell Phillips spoke at the funeral. John Brown's body was taken to North Elba; the Boston abolitionist gave the eulogy. "He has abolished slavery in Virginia," Phillips asserted, surprisingly. He explained, "History will date Virginia emancipation from Harpers Ferry. True, the slave is still there. So, when the tempest uproots a pine on your hills, it looks green for months, a year or two. Still, it is timber, not a tree. John Brown has loosened the roots of the slave system. It only breathes, it does not live, hereafter." Virginia had tried and convicted John Brown, Phillips said, but now Virginia was called to account. "Virginia stands at the bar of the civilized world on trial. Round her victim crowd the apostles and martyrs, all the brave, high souls who have said, 'God is God,' and trodden wicked laws under their feet." The Almighty had blessed slavery's opponents by sending them John Brown. "Could we have asked for a nobler representative of the Christian North putting her foot on the accursed system of slavery?"

JOHN BROWN'S ARREST and execution had a different effect on those who had been his closest allies and material supporters. Several feared being swept up in Brown's prosecution. "On the evening when the news came that John Brown had taken and was then holding the town of Harper's Ferry, it so happened that I was speaking to a large audience in National Hall, Philadelphia," Frederick Douglass recalled. "The announcement came upon us with the startling effect of an earthquake. It was something to make the boldest hold his breath. I saw at once that my old friend had attempted what he had long ago resolved to do, and I felt certain that the result must be his capture and destruction." The subsequent news of Brown's arrest therefore came as no surprise.

What *did* surprise—and alarm—Douglass was the discovery that he himself might be implicated in Brown's actions. "His carpet-bag had been secured by Governor Wise, and it was found to contain numerous letters and documents which directly implicated Gerrit Smith, Joshua R. Giddings, Samuel G. Howe, Frank P. Sanborn, and myself. This intelligence was soon followed by a telegram saying that we were all to be arrested." Douglass's presence in Philadelphia had been well advertised; he could only assume that those seeking his arrest would look for him there. He sought the help of friends, but his friends made themselves scarce. "Upon one ground or another, they all thought it best not to be found in my company at such a time," Douglass observed. He couldn't fault them. "The truth is that in the excitement which prevailed my friends had reason to fear that the very fact that they were with me would be a sufficient reason for their arrest with me."

Douglass judged he would be safer the greater distance he placed between himself and Virginia. He headed for the Delaware River wharf, where he could catch a boat for New York. The boat was behind schedule, and Douglass grew tenser with each minute's delay. Finally the boat came and he made his escape. "I reached New York at night, still under the apprehension of arrest at any moment, but no signs of such an event being made, I went at once to the Barclay Street ferry, took the boat across the river." He spent the night—"an *anxious* night," he said—with a friend in Hoboken.

Things looked no better in the morning. The papers reported that the government was sparing no effort to seize all those behind the Harpers Ferry raid, and any documents they might have. "I was now somewhat uneasy from the fact that sundry letters and a constitution written by John Brown were locked up in my desk in Rochester," Douglass related. To keep the papers from being discovered, he sent an unsigned telegram to the telegraph operator in Rochester, a friend who would know what it meant: "Tell Lewis"—Douglass's eldest son—"to secure all the important papers in my high desk." The message arrived none too soon, for agents of the Virginia state government arrived shortly thereafter. "The mark of the chisel with which the desk was opened is still on the drawer, and is one of the traces of the John Brown raid," Douglass later wrote.

What to do with *himself* was now the problem. "To stay in Hoboken was out of the question, and to go to Rochester was to all appearance to go into the hands of the hunters, for they would naturally seek me at my home if they sought me at all," Douglass reflected. "I, however, resolved to go home and risk my safety there. I felt sure that, once in the city, I could not be easily taken from there without a preliminary hearing upon the requisition, and not then if the people could be made aware of what was in progress." But getting to Rochester was no small detail. "It would not do to go to New York City and take the train, for that city was not less incensed against John Brown conspirators than many parts of the South." Instead he sneaked by night to Paterson, New Jersey, where he caught an Erie Railroad train for Rochester.

Home proved no refuge. He had been there only moments when a neighbor, the lieutenant governor of New York, informed him that the governor would be obliged to honor an extradition request from the governor of Virginia. The people of Rochester might defend him, but in the interest of civil peace the lieutenant governor urged him to continue north, to Canada. Off Douglass went. And just in time. "Several United States marshals were in Rochester in search of me within six hours after my departure," he said.

Douglass realized he hadn't covered himself in glory by high-tailing it out of the country. He tried to explain in a letter he sent from Canada to a Rochester newspaper. John Brown's lieutenant John Cook had escaped Harpers Ferry ahead of the storming of the engine house but been captured while fleeing north; he had been quoted in the press as calling Douglass a coward for having promised to take part in the raid and then backing out. "Mr. Cook may be perfectly right in denouncing me as a coward," Douglass wrote. "I have not one word to say in defense or vindication of my character for courage; I have always been more distinguished for running than fighting, and, tried by the Harper's-Ferry-Insurrection test, I am most miserably deficient in courage, even more so than Cook when he deserted his brave old captain and fled to the mountains." But Cook was quite wrong to assert that Douglass had promised to take part in the raid. "Of whatever other imprudence and indiscretion I may have been guilty, I have never made a promise so rash and wild as this. The taking of Harper's Ferry was a measure never encouraged by my word or by my vote. At any time or place, my wisdom or my cowardice has not only kept me from Harper's Ferry, but has equally kept me from making any promise to go there. I desire to be quite emphatic here, for of all guilty men, he is the guiltiest who lures his fellow-men to an undertaking of this sort, under promise of assistance which he afterwards fails to render. I therefore declare that there is no man living, and no man dead, who, if living, could truthfully say that I ever promised him, or anybody else, either conditionally, or otherwise, that I would be present in person at the Harper's Ferry insurrection."

Douglass said that no man hated slavery more than he did. So why had he not joined Brown? "My answer to this has already been given; at least impliedly given—'The tools to those who can use them!' Let every man work for the abolition of slavery in his own way. I would help all and hinder none." Moreover, as an escaped slave himself, he stood in a peculiarly delicate position. "A government recognizing the validity of the *Dred Scott* decision at such a time as this is not likely to have any very charitable feelings towards me, and if I am to meet its representatives I prefer to do so at least upon equal terms." Douglass was willing to face a jury in New York, but a former slave would get no justice in Virginia. This was why he had fled. "I have quite insuperable objections to being caught by the hounds of Mr. Buchanan, and 'bagged' by Gov. Wise. For this appears to be the arrangement. Buchanan does the fighting and hunting, and Wise 'bags' the game."

THE NEWS FROM Harpers Ferry caught Frank Sanborn as unprepared as it did Frederick Douglass. The young man taught school when he wasn't agitating for abolition. "Arrangements had been made for the annual chestnuting excursion of my pupils," he recalled of the week of the raid. The field trip proceeded even as the raid story unfolded. "The interval gave me the information that an indefinite number of my letters, with those of Gerrit Smith, Dr. Howe and others, had been captured at the Kennedy Farm; and nobody knew to what extent the records of our conspiracy were in the hands of the slaveholding authorities," Sanborn wrote. He consulted the other members of the secret committee, who emphatically agreed that they must cover their tracks. "I therefore spent hours Tuesday and Wednesday nights searching my papers to destroy such as might compromise other persons." With George Stearns he obtained legal advice from a Boston lawyer of their acquaintance, John Andrew. "We put our case before our friend Andrew, without stating to him the full particulars of our complicity with Brown." Andrew said they stood a good chance of being seized by agents of the Virginia government and hustled out of the state.

Sanborn had already packed a bag, and he chose not to tarry. "After leaving Andrew's office, therefore, I took my slight luggage on board the steamboat for Portland, leaving letters and instructions with my sister Sarah, who was then my housekeeper at Concord, for her action in case I should find it expedient not to return home after a few days. The whole matter was so uncertain, and the action to be taken by the national authorities, and by the mass of the people, was so much in the dark, that it was impossible to say what might be the best course."

He reached Quebec City the evening of the next day and lay low. After most of a week he got a letter from Wendell Phillips containing a revised opinion by John Andrew. The lawyer now thought that Massachusetts law would shield Sanborn and the others from extradition to Virginia, assuming they could get to a Massachusetts court before being carried out of the state. Phillips explained that he had asked Andrew point-blank whether Sanborn should return. Andrew replied, "Send him what I have written, and let him decide for himself." To Sanborn, Phillips said, "You know better than we what the precise contents of your letters were, and so can better judge."

Sanborn chanced the return. He learned that George Stearns and Samuel Howe had taken refuge in Canada, and that Gerrit Smith was in a Utica insane asylum, undone by nerves. Sanborn's friend Edwin Morton, who knew as much about the conspiracy as he did, had sailed for England.

For a time no one molested Sanborn. He began to think he was safe. He let down his guard. His was sitting in his study one evening when the doorbell rang. His servant had gone to bed and his sister was in her room. "I went down into the front hall and answered the bell. A young man presented himself and handed me a note, which I stepped back to read by the light of the hall lamp. It said that the bearer was a person deserving charity." Sanborn pondered how to answer. "When I looked up from reading the note, four men had entered my hall, and one of them, Silas Carleton by name, a Boston tipstaff"—bailiff—"as I afterward learned, came forward and laid his hand on me, saying, 'I arrest you.'"

"By what authority?" demanded Sanborn.

Carleton read an order of the U.S. Senate for Sanborn's arrest. At the insistence of Virginia's Senator Mason, the Senate had commenced investigation of the Harpers Ferry raid and had summoned Sanborn to testify. Fearing for his safety on slave soil, Sanborn had refused to go. The Senate had engaged Carleton to fetch him.

Sanborn's sister, hearing the voices in the hallway and sensing their meaning, threw on clothes, ran to the door and began shouting to the neighbors for help.

Sanborn's captors handcuffed him before he could move. He decided to fight nonetheless. "I was young and strong and resented this indignity," he recalled. "They had to raise me from the floor and began to carry me (four of them) to the door where my sister stood, raising a constant alarm. My hands were powerless, but as they approached the door I braced my feet against the posts and delayed them. I did the same at the posts of the veranda, and it was some minutes before they got me on the gravel walk at the foot of my stone steps. Meanwhile, the church bells were ringing a fire alarm, and the people were gathering by tens. At the stone posts of the gateway I checked their progress once more, and again, when the four rascals lifted me to insert me, feet foremost in their carriage (a covered hack with a driver on the box), I braced myself against the sides of the carriage door and broke them in."

By this time Sanborn's captors realized they needed to secure his feet. One, a fellow with a long beard, grabbed Sanborn's feet and held them together. But when the four had almost gotten Sanborn into the carriage, his sister yanked on the man's beard, causing him to lose his grip, and Sanborn began to kick again.

The gathering crowd joined the fight. An elderly gentleman took his walking cane and beat the horses of the carriage to get them to pull away. The horses jerked the carriage several paces forward, leaving Sanborn and the four behind.

A lawyer neighbor came up to Sanborn. He asked if Sanborn petitioned for habeas corpus, to stay the arrest.

"By all means!" said Sanborn.

The lawyer hurried the short distance to the home of a judge who in the years since passage of the Fugitive Slave Act had grown accustomed to such emergency appeals. His form book was handy in his library, and he at once filled in the blanks. He handed the writ to the sheriff, also familiar with the practice, and the sheriff ordered Sanborn's captors to stand down.

They objected, claiming that their mandate superseded that of the judge. The sheriff at once enlisted the crowd that had surrounded the carriage as his *posse comitatus*. "I was forcibly snatched from senatorial custody," Sanborn recounted. "At the same time my Irish neighbors rushed upon them and forced them to take their broken carriage and make off toward Lexington, the way they had driven up in the early evening. They were pursued by twenty or thirty of my townsmen, some of them as far as Lexington."

AT THE TIME of John Brown's death, Abraham Lincoln could congratulate himself on the progress of his campaign for president. He remained coy about his goal, lest he draw premature criticism, yet he could tell he was winning support. His swing around the West, from Ohio to Kansas, had introduced him to thousands of Republicans who had heard his name but never encountered him in person. Moncure Conway was one of the many who liked what they saw. "One warm evening in 1859, passing through the market-place in Cincinnati, I found there a crowd listening to a political speech in the open air," Conway remembered. He was a Virginian whose religious faith had led him to the ministry and to abolitionism. By the 1850s this combination was untenable below the Mason-Dixon Line, and Conway was driven from his pulpit in Washington to Ohio, where he preached to Unitarians and worked against slavery. "The speaker stood in the balcony of a small brick house, some lamps assisting the moonlight," he continued. "I had not heard of any meeting, and paused on the skirts of the crowd from curiosity, meaning to stay only a few moments. Something about the speaker, however, and some words that reached me, led me to press nearer. I asked the speaker's name and learned that it was Abraham Lincoln."

Conway studied Lincoln in the half-light. "The face had a battered and bronzed look, without being hard. His nose was prominent and buttressed a strong and high forehead; his eyes were high-vaulted and had an expression of sadness; his mouth and chin were too close together, the cheeks hollow. On the whole Lincoln's appearance was not attractive until one heard his voice, which possessed variety of expression, earnestness, and shrewdness in every tone. The charm of his manner was that he had no manner. He was simple, direct, humorous. He pleasantly repeated a mannerism of his opponent— 'This is what Stephen Douglas calls his gur-reat perrinciple'; but the next words I remember were these: 'Slavery is wrong!'"

Such conviction was what Conway wanted to hear, and what he had *not* been hearing from politicians in his vicinity. Cincinnati was separated from slave-state Kentucky by the Ohio River, narrow in this region and well ferried. Resident Ohioans could look across the river and see slaves laboring away; Kentuckians regularly crossed to take part in events in Cincinnati. Many Kentuckians had come to hear Lincoln; they booed and hissed when he said slavery was wrong. Lincoln was undeterred, and Conway was more impressed. "Slavery is wrong," Lincoln repeated. "No compromise, no political arrangement with slavery, will ever last which does not deal with it as wrong."

Conway's reaction was repeated everywhere Lincoln went. Republicans in Kansas had favored William Seward as the most forthright of their party on the slavery question, but Lincoln won many over on his visit to the territory. They were gratified that he had come to Kansas at all. "There are but few statesmen who could have been forced to do the work in which Abraham Lincoln *volunteered*," one recounted. "In the dead of winter he left the comforts of an attractive home to couple his energies with those of a young people in a distant territory battling for the right." Lincoln's words and actions earned him enthusiastic followers. "Here comes the next president of the United States," a Leavenworth Republican proclaimed on introducing Lincoln. Another Kansan said the same thing to a group of Republicans gathered to meet the visitor. "Gentlemen, I tell you Mr. Lincoln will be our next president," he declared. Lincoln tried to deflect the praise, to no avail. "I feel it, and I mean it," his host said.

BUT KANSAS WASN'T the country, not by a long way. Lincoln appealed to fellow westerners; the question was: Could he find support in the East?

He got a chance to find out in early 1860. The Young Men's Republican Union of New York invited him to come to the city and speak at the Cooper Institute. Some of the host group were simply curious; others opposed William Seward and hoped Lincoln might head him off. If nothing else, the rustic westerner would afford the city folk an evening's entertainment.

Lincoln took the opportunity most seriously. His political future hinged on this audition. He prepared for his speech by reviewing the arguments he had made against Stephen Douglas during the past several years. He couldn't assume that many of his listeners had read his remarks, but on the other hand he didn't want simply to repeat what he'd said earlier and annoy those who had.

He took as his text a statement in which Douglas claimed to be guided by America's founders on the question of slavery in the territories. "Our fathers," Douglas had said, "when they framed the government under which we live, understood this question just as well, and even better, than we do now."

To which Lincoln responded, to the Cooper audience, "I fully endorse this." The point at dispute was *what* the founders had understood on slavery in the territories, and what they intended for the institution there.

At lawyerly length Lincoln argued that the framers of the Constitution fully intended that Congress should have control of slavery in the territories. He noted that the same summer that witnessed the Constitutional Convention saw the passage of the Northwest Ordinance barring slavery north of the Ohio River. He remarked that of the thirty-nine signers of the Constitution, four were members of the Congress that approved the ordinance, and three of the four voted in favor. He observed that sixteen of the thirty-nine were members of the first Congress under the Constitution, which unanimously approved a bill implementing the ordinance. George Washington, another of the thirty-nine, signed the bill. During the first decades under the Constitution, while most of the framers still lived, Congress routinely regulated slavery in the territories.

The historical record was incontrovertible, Lincoln declared. "I defy any man to show that any one of them ever, in his whole life, declared that, in his understanding, any proper division of local from federal authority, or any part of the Constitution, forbade the federal government to control as to slavery in the federal territories." He went further: "I defy anyone to show that any living man in the whole world ever did, prior to the beginning of the present century (and I might almost say prior to the beginning of the last half of the present century) declare that, in his understanding, any proper division of local from federal authority, or any part of the Constitution, forbade the federal government to control as to slavery in the federal territories." Stephen Douglas claimed the founders for his side, but he was simply wrong. He should admit as much.

The Republicans were more than happy to embrace a correct reading of the founders' intentions. "This is all Republicans ask—all Republicans desire—in relation to slavery," Lincoln said. "As those fathers marked it, so let it be again marked, as an evil not to be extended, but to be tolerated and protected only because of and so far as its actual presence among us makes that toleration and protection a necessity."

Lincoln addressed the people of the South, as if they were present. "You consider yourselves a reasonable and a just people; and I consider that in the general qualities of reason and justice you are not inferior to any other people. Still, when you speak of us Republicans, you do so only to denounce us as reptiles, or, at the best, as no better than outlaws. You will grant a hearing to pirates or murderers, but nothing like it to 'Black Republicans.'" Such language poisoned political discourse, Lincoln said, and jeopardized the interests of the South as well as the North. He made a modest request: "Bring forward your charges and specifications, and then be patient long enough to hear us deny or justify."

Southerners called themselves conservatives while branding Republicans radicals, Lincoln said. He rejected the charge. "What is conservatism? Is it not adherence to the old and tried, against the new and untried? We stick to, contend for, the identical old policy on the point in controversy"—slavery in the territories—"while you with one accord reject, and scout, and spit upon that old policy, and insist upon substituting something new."

Southerners blamed Republicans for agitating the slavery question in politics. Lincoln rejected this charge too. "We admit that it is more prominent, but we deny that we made it so. It was not we, but you, who discarded the old policy of the fathers. We resisted, and still resist, your innovation; and thence comes the greater prominence of the question."

Southerners said Republicans encouraged insurrection among the slaves. "What is your proof?" asked Lincoln. He supplied the most recent answer given by Southerners: "Harper's Ferry! John Brown!!" Lincoln rejected this allegation as well, most vehemently. "John Brown was no Republican, and you have failed to implicate a single Republican in his Harpers Ferry enterprise." Lincoln dismissed the raid as the work of an unbalanced mind. "John Brown's effort was peculiar. It was not a slave insurrection. It was an attempt by white men to get up a revolt among slaves, in which the slaves refused to participate. In fact, it was so absurd that the slaves, with all their ignorance, saw plainly enough it could not succeed. That affair, in its philosophy, corresponds with the many attempts, related in history, at the assassination of kings and emperors. An enthusiast broods over the oppression of a people till he fancies himself commissioned by Heaven to liberate them. He ventures the attempt, which ends in little else than his own execution."

Southerners were getting carried away by their own rhetoric, Lincoln said. Many were calling for secession. "You will destroy the government, unless you be allowed to construe and enforce the Constitution as you please, on all points in dispute between you and us. You will rule or ruin." Lincoln noted that some Southerners were threatening to disregard the result of the coming presidential contest. "You will not abide the election of a Republican president! In that supposed event, you say, you will destroy the Union; and then, you say, the great crime of having destroyed it will be upon us! That is cool. A highwayman holds a pistol to my ear, and mutters through his teeth, 'Stand and deliver, or I shall kill you, and then you will be a murderer!'"

Lincoln now spoke to his fellow Republicans. "It is exceedingly desirable that all parts of this great confederacy shall be at peace, and in harmony, one with another. Let us Republicans do our part to have it so. Even though much provoked, let us do nothing through passion and ill temper. Even though the Southern people will not so much as listen to us, let us calmly consider their demands, and yield to them if, in our deliberate view of our duty, we possibly can."

But *could* Republicans yield, in good conscience? What *were* those Southern demands? Lincoln observed that with each concession by the North, Southern demands had increased. For decades Southerners had demanded the repeal of the Missouri Compromise; having achieved this in the Kansas-Nebraska Act, they insisted on repudiation of the congressional authority underlying the compromise, which the Dred Scott decision delivered. So what *would* satisfy the South? What must Republicans do? "Simply this: We must not only let them alone, but we must, somehow, convince them that we do let them alone. This, we know by experience, is no easy task. We have been so trying to convince them from the very beginning of our organization, but with no success. In all our platforms and speeches we have constantly protested our purpose to let them alone; but this has had no tendency to convince them."

What *would* convince the South? "This, and this only: Cease to call slavery wrong, and join them in calling it right. And this must be done thoroughly, done in acts as well as in words. Silence will not be tolerated; we must place ourselves avowedly with them." Republicans must join Southerners as apologists for slavery. "Holding, as they do, that slavery is morally right, and socially elevating, they cannot cease to demand a full national recognition of it, as a legal right, and a social blessing."

This, of course, the Republicans could not do, and would not do. Slavery was wrong, and they would continue to call it wrong. But they might still be circumspect. "Wrong as we think slavery is, we can yet afford to let it alone where it is, because that much is due to the necessity arising from its actual presence in the nation."

Conscience and circumspection were the true path forward for the Republican party and for the country, Lincoln concluded. "Neither let us be slandered from our duty by false accusations against us, nor frightened from it by menaces of destruction to the government nor of dungeons to ourselves. Let us have faith that right makes might, and in that faith let us, to the end, dare to do our duty as we understand it."

LINCOLN'S LISTENERS DIDN'T know what to make of him at first. "When Lincoln rose to speak I was greatly disappointed," recalled one. "He was tall, tall—oh, how tall! and so angular and awkward that I had, for an instant, a feeling of pity for so ungainly a man. His clothes were black and ill-fitting, badly wrinkled—as if they had been jammed carelessly into a small trunk. His bushy head, with the stiff black hair thrown back, was balanced on a long and lean head-stalk, and when he raised his hands in an opening gesture, I noticed that they were very large. He began in a low tone of voice—as if he were used to speaking out-doors and was afraid of speaking too loud. He said, 'Mr. *Cheerman*,' instead of 'Mr. Chairman,' and employed many other words with an old-fashioned pronunciation. I said to myself, 'Old fellow, you won't do. It's all very well for the wild West, but this will never go down in New York.'"

Yet Lincoln kept on, and the mood in the hall changed—slowly at first, then in a rush. "He began to get into his subject," the skeptical New Yorker recounted. "He straightened up, made regular and graceful gestures; his face lighted up as with an inward fire; the whole man was transfigured. I forgot his clothes, his personal appearance, and his individual peculiarities. Presently, forgetting myself, I was on my feet with the rest, yelling like a wild Indian, cheering this wonderful man. In the close parts of his argument, you could hear the gentle sizzling of the gas-burners. When he reached a climax, the thunders of applause were terrific. It was a great speech. When I came out of the hall, my face glowing with excitement and my frame all aquiver, a friend, with his eyes aglow, asked me what I thought of Abe Lincoln, the rail-splitter. I said: 'He's the greatest man since St. Paul.'"

L INCOLN HADN'T EXPECTED to make a tour of the East, but
his New York speech won such plaudits that Republicans nearby
insisted he come stump for them. To Connecticut he went, rack-
ing his brain to discover new ways of saying the same things he had
been saying for months or years. In New Haven he reiterated that he
and the Republicans had no designs against slavery in the South. "If
we were to form a government anew, in view of the actual presence of
slavery, we should find it necessary to frame just such a government
as our fathers did, giving to the slaveholder the entire control where
the system was established," he said. "From the necessities of the case
we should be compelled to form just such a government as our blessed
fathers gave us; and, surely, if they have so made it, that adds another
reason why we should let slavery alone where it exists." To this refrain
he added a new verse. "If I saw a venomous snake crawling in the
road, any man would say I might seize the nearest stick and kill it; but
if I found that snake in bed with my children, that would be another
question." Lincoln's audience laughed, but he wasn't joking. "I might
hurt the children more than the snake, and it might bite them." His
listeners applauded. "Much more, if I found it in bed with my neighbor's children, and I had bound myself by a solemn compact not to
meddle with his children under any circumstances, it would become
me to let that particular mode of getting rid of the gentleman alone."
More laughter. "But if there was a bed newly made up, to which the
children were to be taken, and it was proposed to take a batch of
young snakes and put them there with them, I take it no man would
say there was any question how I ought to decide!" Much laughter
and cheering. Lest anyone miss his point, Lincoln concluded, "That

is just the case! The new territories are the newly made bed to which our children are to go, and it lies with the nation to say whether they shall have snakes mixed up with them or not. It does not seem as if there could be much hesitation what our policy should be!" Applause all around.

AS LINCOLN GREW more visible, he took greater care not to become *too* visible. He shunned controversy whenever possible. "My name is new in the field, and I suppose I am not the *first* choice of a very great many," he wrote to an Ohio supporter. But he might be the second choice of a majority, and at the convention that could be enough. "Our policy, then, is to give no offence to others—leave them in a mood to come to us, if they shall be compelled to give up their first love."

This was the key. Lincoln would let the bigger names in the party fight to a draw, leaving the convention to turn to a man no one much objected to—himself.

But it wasn't easy, for as his star continued to rise, *he* became a bigger name. Illinois Republicans gathered in Decatur to make their choice of the party's hopefuls. "It was a very large and spirited body, comprising an immense number of delegates, among whom were the most brilliant, as well as the shrewdest men in the party," recalled Ward Lamon, a Lincoln friend. "It was evident that something of more than usual importance was expected to transpire." Lincoln sat in the back of the Wigwam, as the temporary meeting hall was called, trying to be inconspicuous. He failed. The convention's chairman rose, commanded the attention of the crowd, and said, "I am informed that a distinguished citizen of Illinois, and one whom Illinois will ever delight to honor, is present; and I wish to move that this body invite him to a seat on the stand." He pointed toward the back and pronounced the name: "Abraham Lincoln!"

"Not a shout, but a roar of applause, long and deep, shook every board and joist of the Wigwam," Lamon continued. "The motion was seconded and passed. A rush was made for the hero that sat on his heels. He was seized, and jerked to his feet. An effort was made to jam him through the crowd to his place of honor on the stage; but the crowd was too dense, and it failed. Then he was boosted—lifted up bodily—and lay for a few seconds sprawling and kicking upon the heads and shoulders of the great throng. In this manner he was gradually pushed toward the stand, and finally reached it, doubtless to his great relief, in the arms of some half-dozen gentlemen, who set him down in full view of his clamorous admirers." The commotion grew louder. "The cheering was like the roar of the sea. Hats were thrown up by the Chicago delegation, as if hats were no longer useful."

The chairman silenced the delegates in order to speak. "There is an old Democrat outside who has something he wishes to present to this convention," he said. Delegates were puzzled. What could a Democrat bring to a Republican convention? Some feared a trick.

"The door of the Wigwam opened," Lamon recalled, "and a fine, robust old fellow, with an open countenance and bronzed cheeks, marched into the midst of the assemblage, bearing on his shoulder two small triangular heart rails, surmounted by a banner with this inscription: 'TWO RAILS, FROM A LOT MADE BY ABRAHAM LINCOLN AND JOHN HANKS, IN THE SANGAMON BOTTOM, IN THE YEAR 1830.' The sturdy bearer was old John Hanks himself"—a Lincoln cousin— "enjoying the great field-day of his life. He was met with wild and tumultuous cheers, prolonged through several minutes."

The delegates demanded a speech from Lincoln. Blushing but shaking with laughter, he acceded. "Gentlemen," he said, "I suppose you want to know something about those things." He pointed to the rails. "Well, the truth is, John Hanks and I did make rails in the Sangamon Bottom. I don't know whether we made those rails or not." He examined them more closely. "Fact is, I don't think they are a credit to the makers." He laughed the more. "But I do know this: I made rails then, and I think I could make better ones than these now."

The delegates couldn't contain their enthusiasm. Unanimously they declared, "Abraham Lincoln is the first choice of the Republican party of Illinois for the presidency." They instructed the Illinois delegates to the national convention to vote as a unit for Lincoln and employ all honorable means to win his nomination.

THE DECATUR GROUNDSWELL for Lincoln rolled north to Chicago as the national party gathered there. The convention marked a coming-out for the booming city on the lake; Republican leaders sought to capture the votes of the region of which Chicago served as the commercial hub. Railroads linked Chicago to every part of the country, but the distance to New York hindered the ability of the backers of William Seward to arrange the ostensibly spontaneous outbursts of support expected of candidates. Lincoln's Illinois friends, by contrast, manipulated the seating charts in the meeting hall—another purpose-built structure, also called the Wigwam—in a manner to magnify their own influence and minimize collusion among delegations that might try to block his advance.

Lincoln directed his supporters to be discreet. "Be careful to give no offence, and keep cool under all circumstances," he urged a Kansas ally. The convention would deal with issues besides slavery; of these the tariff was one with roots in the party's Whig prehistory. Lincoln adopted the most uncontroversial stance possible for a Republican. "In the days of Henry Clay I was a Henry Clay-tariff-man, and my views have undergone no material change upon that subject," he wrote to a supportive delegate. Yet even here he counseled discretion. "Save me from the appearance of obtrusion." In a scribbled note to Edward Baker, an old friend now serving as a lieutenant at the convention, Lincoln stressed, "*Make no contracts that will bind me.*"

The strategy worked admirably. William Seward was the favorite as the convention opened, and he led on the first ballot, with Lincoln far behind. But Seward fell short of a majority, and his failure to win outright was seen as evidence of underlying weakness. Lincoln's men inside the Wigwam bargained with Simon Cameron of Pennsylvania, suggesting that Cameron would receive a cabinet post in a Lincoln administration if Pennsylvania put him over the top. Cameron duly delivered Pennsylvania, whose votes created a bandwagon effect that propelled Lincoln past Seward on the second ballot. A third ballot completed the shift, giving Lincoln the nomination. The party balanced the ticket geographically by tapping Hannibal Hamlin of Maine for vice president.

THE LOSERS WERE disconsolate. "Dear Seward," wrote Thurlow Weed, an Albany editor who served as the New York senator's floor leader, "I do not know that you care to learn by what means our expectations have been disappointed." Weed had labored on Seward's behalf for years, and he could hardly bear the result. "I have slight inclination to think, or speak or write, still less to go where I shall be seen or questioned." Yet Seward deserved an explanation for his defeat. "We were beaten by a combination of all the disappointed, whose diligent assertions (sustained by the delegates from these states) were that you would lose New Jersey, Pennsylvania, Indiana and Connecticut." The Pennsylvania delegation, in particular, "were violent and denunciatory, all saying that you could not carry the state." Seward's reputation for arrogance had cost him. Weed observed that many of those who worked with him in Washington had sabotaged his chances. "Much of this mischief has been doing for months by members of Congress."

But the villain of the piece was Horace Greeley, the *New York Tribune* editor. "Greeley was malignant," Weed wrote. "He misled many fair minded men. He was not scrupulous. He said to some that you could not carry New York and that 20 of our delegates were against you." Weed disputed Greeley's head count but not his entire message. "The traitors from New York were few in number but most violent and unscrupulous."

Weed mourned the loss. "We have all been to church this morning"—a Sunday—"but the sadness deepens." Even so, he encouraged Seward to accept the result graciously. "A prompt and cheerful acquiescence in the nomination," he said, "is not only wise but a duty." As for Weed himself: "Lincoln's confidential friends ask me to go to Springfield."

HIS DISAPPOINTED RIVALS ASIDE, the Republicans as a party were thrilled at Lincoln's nomination. "The enthusiasm with which the result was received was immense," wrote Greeley's Chicago correspondent. "The Wigwam, packed with some 12,000 people, resounded with shouts and calls of satisfaction for five or ten minutes. There was no repressing the irrepressible enthusiasm, and it only subsided when everybody was tired. There was never such another scene in America." The reaction was even stronger outside the Wigwam. "Chicago is in a blaze of glory tonight. Bonfires, processions, torchlights, fireworks, illuminations and salutes have filled the air with noise and the eye with beauty. 'Honest Abe' is the cry in every mouth, and the 'irrepressible conflict' against slavery and corruptions opens with great promise and immense enthusiasm. It is impossible to exaggerate the good feeling and joy that prevail here. The Illinois delegation resolved that the millennium has come." Some of the Illinoisans wept tears of joy. "They say it is a triumph of the people over politicians."

Republicans across the country—which was to say, outside the South—joined the celebration. "A grand torchlight procession is now marching the streets," declared a dispatch from Philadelphia. Detroit weighed in: "A salute of 100 guns was fired here this afternoon, and bonfires and illuminations were the order of the evening." From Newark: "A large, spontaneous and enthusiastic meeting of Republicans was held here this evening, ratifying and congratulating themselves on the Chicago nomination." Bangor, Maine: "One hundred guns were fired, and the Republicans are jubilant for the Chicago nomination." Boston, being Boston, was slightly more restrained: "Mr. Lincoln's nomination for president caused some surprise, but was well received generally by the Republicans, who hailed the announcement with a salute of 100 guns." Buffalo, mindful of its upstate New York neighbor Seward, was polite: "A salute was fired here this afternoon upon the receipt of the news of the nomination of Lincoln and Hamlin. No other evidences of mad enthusiasm, however, were witnessed."

P ARTIES ALWAYS CHEER their newly anointed champions, but the Republicans had special reason to celebrate, for by the time they chose Lincoln, they could imagine they were not simply selecting a nominee but naming a president. Slavery had split the Whigs; now it cleaved the Democrats. Stephen Douglas's party had gathered ahead of the Republicans, in Charleston, with Douglas the front-runner. But Douglas's popular-sovereignty approach to slavery in the territories, and especially his Freeport Doctrine of territorial nullification of the Dred Scott decision, alienated uncompromising Southerners. Decades earlier, in the interest of party unity, the Democrats had adopted a rule requiring a two-thirds supermajority for nomination. This year it had the opposite effect. Douglas garnered a simple majority on the first ballot, but not two-thirds. He improved his total only marginally in more than fifty additional ballots. At length, exhausted, the convention voted to recess for six weeks and reconvene in Baltimore, where, Douglas partisans hoped, the influence of the Southern diehards would be diminished.

The Republican convention took place during the Democratic recess. Republicans indulged the not unreasonable hope that the Democrats would *never* agree on a candidate, clearing the Republican path to the White House; this hope was what inspired the giddiness that greeted the selection of Lincoln.

Stephen Douglas received the news of Lincoln's nomination via telegram at the Capitol at Washington. Several Republicans happened to be around him when he read the news. He reflected for a moment, nodded his head as though he had expected it, and said, "Gentlemen, you have nominated a very able and a very honest man."

And one even more likely to become the next president after the Democrats failed to mend their breach. The Baltimore reprise of the Charleston convention collapsed almost at once, with several Southern delegations walking out. While the remainers nominated Douglas, the bolters chose John Breckinridge of Kentucky.

LINCOLN COULD READ the evolving political landscape, and he understood what it required of him. The presidency was his to lose. He should speak as little as possible; when speech could not be avoided, he should strive to say nothing. And even then he should cover his tracks. At the end of a letter vaguely describing an utterly noncommittal conversation with Thurlow Weed, William Seward's man, Lincoln instructed the recipient, "Burn this; not that there is anything wrong in it, but because it is best not to be known that I write at all."

He refused to promise jobs in a Lincoln administration. Aspiring officeholders made their availability known; he ignored them. "Remembering that Peter denied his Lord with an oath, after most solemnly protesting that he never would, I will not swear I will make no committals; but I do think I will not," Lincoln told Lyman Trumbull.

He declined to affirm even things he believed in. Temperance societies heard he wasn't a drinker and tried to get him to take the pledge publicly. He begged off. "I think it would be improper for me to write, or say anything to, or for, the public, upon the subject of which you inquire," he wrote to the representative of one anti-liquor committee. Newspapers had reported that Lincoln hosted a dry reception for a visiting group of dignitaries; Lincoln acknowledged the truth of the report. "Having kept house sixteen years, and having never held the 'cup' to the lips of my friends then, my judgment was that I should not, in my new position, change my habit in this respect." But he wouldn't translate his personal preference into a political statement, and he hoped others wouldn't either. "I therefore wish the letter I do write"—the present letter—"to be held as strictly confidential."

He avoided those who wanted to make him famous. Reporters and instant authors produced biographies of the little-known nominee. Some sought Lincoln's cooperation and even approval. He refused.

While urging Republican allies to examine the manuscripts for errors that might reflect ill on the party, he said he would have nothing to do with any life story. "I *authorize nothing*—will be *responsible* for *nothing.*"

Silence and opaqueness didn't come easily to one who loved to talk and tell revealing stories. Occasionally he slipped. A newsman trolling for an article tried to get Lincoln to visit his Kentucky birthplace. Lincoln demurred. "You suggest that a visit to the place of my nativity might be pleasant to me," he said. "Indeed it would. But would it be safe? Would not the people lynch me?" He meant this to be funny, yet it didn't seem so when he read himself quoted in the *New York Herald.* He tried to wriggle out. "This is decidedly wrong," Lincoln declared of the article. As to the statement ascribed to him: "I did not say it." But then he essentially admitted he *had* said it. "I have, *playfully,* (and never otherwise) related this incident"—of writing the letter—"several times; and I suppose I did so to the *Herald* correspondent, though I do not remember it. If I did, it is all that I did say from which the correspondent could have inferred his statement." He didn't want to be held responsible for a misinterpretation of his joke. "I dislike exceedingly for Kentuckians to understand that I am charging them with a purpose to inveigle me, and do violence to me," he wrote to a friend. Yet he wouldn't take the responsibility of addressing the matter himself. "I cannot go into the newspapers," he told the friend, who, he hoped, *would* go to the papers. He sent the friend a proposed correction. "Would not the editor of the *Herald,* upon being shown this letter, insert the short correction, which you find upon the enclosed scrap? Please try him, unless you perceive some sufficient reason to the contrary. In no event, let my name be publicly used."

HIS INSCRUTABILITY APPEARED to pay off. "We know not what a day may bring forth," he wrote to a Republican ally on July 4. "But today it looks as if the Chicago ticket will be elected. I think the chances were more than equal that we could have beaten the Democracy *united.* Divided, as it is, its chance appears indeed very slim." Lincoln knew things could change. "Great is the Democracy in resources; and it may yet give its fortunes a turn. It is under great temptation to do something." But he didn't think Stephen Douglas's party had many options left. "What can it do which was not thought of, and found impracticable, at Charleston and Baltimore? The signs now are that Douglas and Breckinridge will each have a ticket in every state. They are driven to this to keep up their bombastic claims of *nationality*, and to avoid the charge of *sectionalism* which they have so much lavished upon us." Lincoln appreciated the irony in this situation. "It is an amusing fact, after all Douglas has said about *nationality*, and *sectionalism*, that I had more votes from the Southern section at Chicago, than he had at Baltimore! In fact, there was more of the Southern section represented at Chicago, than in the Douglas rump concern at Baltimore!!"

As the Democrats' chances dwindled, they tried to flush Lincoln out by increasingly personal attacks. He was said to be a Know-Nothing in disguise, an allegation intended to weaken Lincoln among immigrants. One article in a Democratic paper placed Lincoln at a gathering at a Know-Nothing lodge in Quincy, Illinois.

He felt obliged to answer, but off the record. "I suppose as good, or even better, men than I may have been in American, or Know-Nothing lodges, but in point of fact, I never was in one, at Quincy, or elsewhere," he wrote to a friend who had been with him at the time in question. "It was in 1854, when I spoke in some hall there, and after the speaking, you, with others, took me to an oyster saloon, passed an hour there, and you walked with me to, and parted with me at, the Quincy House, quite late at night. I left by stage for Naples before daylight in the morning, having come in by the same route, after dark, the evening previous to the speaking, when I found you waiting at the Quincy House to meet me." Lincoln urged his friend to back him up. "That I never was in a Know-Nothing lodge in Quincy, I should expect, could be easily proved, by respectable men who were always in the lodges and never saw me there. An affidavit of one or two such would put the matter at rest." But again he had to stay out of it himself. "Our adversaries think they can gain a point, if they could force me to openly deny this charge, by which some degree of offence would be given to the Americans. For this reason, it must not publicly appear that I am paying any attention to the charge."

A potentially more explosive slander connected Lincoln to John

Brown. Democratic papers asserted that Lincoln had been part of Brown's secret network, giving fifty dollars to the author of the Harpers Ferry insurrection. Lincoln denied the charge most vigorously. "I never gave fifty dollars, nor one dollar, nor one cent, for the object you mention, or any such object," he replied to a correspondent who had asked about the story. He *had* subscribed twenty-five dollars toward a Kansas defense fund, on the condition that the overseer of the fund, a distinguished judge, confirm that the money was needed to keep the Missouri ruffians at bay. But this was late in the fight for Kansas, and the judge had decided the money wasn't needed. "I never paid a dollar on the subscription," Lincoln said. He certainly had never sent money to John Brown.

IN EARLY AUGUST victory looked closer than ever. "I hesitate to say it, but it really appears now as if the success of the Republican ticket is inevitable," Lincoln wrote to a Republican friend. "We have no reason to doubt any of the states which voted for Fremont. Add to these Minnesota, Pennsylvania, and New Jersey, and the thing is done."

His Republican neighbors in Springfield shared his anticipation and held a rally that included a stop at his front door. He felt compelled to come out but not to speak. "I appear among you upon this occasion with no intention of making a speech," he declared. "It has been my purpose, since I have been placed in my present position, to make no speeches." He would let people look at him, but that was all. After a few minutes he bowed out. "You will kindly let me be silent," he said.

Sometimes silence required more justification. He developed a stock answer: "My published speeches contain nearly all I could willingly say," he told one questioner, among many. In this case he added, "*Justice* and *fairness* to *all,* is the utmost I have said, or will say."

Yet he couldn't ignore the possible consequences of his election. Southern fire-eaters insisted that their states would secede if Lincoln won. He said he didn't believe them. "The people of the South have too much of good sense, and good temper, to attempt the ruin of the government," he replied to a New York Republican who had raised the issue. "At least, so I hope and believe." Lincoln's answer was labeled

"Private," but he didn't ask the recipient to burn it. Without challenging the separatists directly, he wanted to let out that he had confidence in the ordinary people of the South.

The question of the South's reaction grew more pressing as November approached. One writer after another urged him to reassure the South he had no designs against slavery there. He steadfastly refused. With the election just weeks away, he was more determined than ever to keep silent on matters of substance. "I appreciate your motive when you suggest the propriety of my writing for the public something disclaiming all intention to interfere with slaves or slavery in the States," he responded to a questioner from Tennessee. "But in my judgment, it would do no good. I have already done this many, many, times; and it is in print, and open to all who will read. Those who will not read, or heed, what I have already publicly said, would not read, or heed, a repetition of it." Wrapping his caution in the words of the Gospel, he said, "If they hear not Moses and the prophets, neither will they be persuaded though one rose from the dead."

To another correspondent, also seeking a statement of reassurance to the South, Lincoln asked, "What is it I could say which would quiet alarm? Is it that no interference by the government, with slaves or slavery within the states, is intended? I have said this so often already that a repetition of it is but mockery, bearing an appearance of weakness and cowardice, which perhaps should be avoided. Why do not uneasy men *read* what I have already said? And what our *platform* says? If they will not read, or heed, these, would they read, or heed, a repetition of them? Of course the declaration that there is no intention to interfere with slaves or slavery in the states, with all that is fairly implied in such declaration, is true; and I should have no objection to make, and repeat the declaration a thousand times, if there were no danger of encouraging bold bad men to believe they are dealing with one who can be scared into anything." Such bad men must receive no encouragement, and they would get none from Abraham Lincoln.

LINCOLN'S STRATEGY of silence paid off on election day. His ticket swept the Northern states, giving him a decisive majority of the electors. The Republicans, the antislavery party, had captured the White

House in only their second try. They celebrated again, this time with the assurance of victory achieved.

Lincoln himself was of two minds about the result. He was pleased to have won, to have achieved his highest ambition. But he had been given nothing like the mandate a president-elect hopes for. He had lost every Southern state, and in the country at large, half again as many people had voted against him as for him. He would be the sixteenth president of the republic fashioned by America's founders, but if the angry voices already rising in the South were to be credited, he might be the last.

ROBERT BARNWELL RHETT WASN'T angry at the outcome of the election; he was delighted. Rhett was the most torrid of South Carolina fire-eaters, having been hoping and working for secession for more than a decade. The *Charleston Mercury*, the paper he owned, had amplified every argument in favor of secession and dismissed every argument against. For many months Rhett and the paper had portrayed the "Black Republicans" as an imminent threat to slavery and the Southern way of life, and insisted that the election of a Republican president must finally force South Carolina to do what it should have done years before. As Lincoln's victory became inevitable, Rhett's paper grew breathless that Southern freedom was at hand. "The issue before the country is the extinction of slavery," the *Mercury* proclaimed on November 3. "No man of common sense, who has observed the progress of events, and who is not prepared to surrender the institution, with the safety and independence of the South, can doubt that the time for action has come—now or never. The Southern States are now in the crisis of their fate; and, if we read aright the signs of the times, nothing is needed for our deliverance but that the ball of revolution be set in motion."

Some in the South were arguing that secession should await agreement among the slave states on when and how the break might best occur. Rhett blasted such caution as the counsel of timidity. Secession would never come if every state waited on the slowest. Cooperation would *follow* individual secession; it need not precede it. "The example of a forward movement only is requisite to unite Southern states in a common cause." And South Carolina was the state to provide the example. "Other states are torn and divided, to a greater or less extent, by old party issues. South Carolina alone is not. Any practical move"—by South Carolina—"would enable the people of other states to rise above their past divisions, and lock shields on the broad ground of Southern security."

Delay would strengthen the enemies of the South. "In the position in which the South will be placed by the election of an Abolition-ist white man as President of the United States, and an Abolitionist colored man as Vice President of the United States"—the attacks on the Republican ticket had included assertions of black ancestry for Hannibal Hamlin—"we should not hesitate," Rhett and the *Mer-cury* declared. "The evils of submission are too terrible for us to risk them."

South Carolina took Rhett's advice. Upon the confirmation of the electoral vote, state leaders summoned a convention, which swiftly approved an ordinance of secession. A declaration of the causes—a manifesto of secession—accompanied the ordinance. The declara-tion noted that a previous convention, in 1852, had proclaimed South Carolina's sovereign right to secede from the Union, a right that followed from the nature of the Constitution as a compact among independent states. But the earlier convention had forborne to act on that right. South Carolina was acting now because its grievances against the Union had grown intolerable. First was the failure of the federal government to enforce the constitutional obligation of other states to return fugitive slaves. Nearly all the Northern states by law or practice materially obstructed the return of fugitives. "Thus the constituted compact has been deliberately broken and disregarded by the non-slaveholding states, and the consequence follows that South Carolina is released from her obligation." Beyond this, the Northern states actively discriminated against the property rights of the South and conspired to attack its institutions. "Those states have assumed the right of deciding upon the propriety of our domestic institutions; and have denied the rights of property established in fifteen of the states and recognized by the Constitution; they have denounced as sinful the institution of slavery; they have permitted open establish-ment among them of societies whose avowed object is to disturb the peace and to eloign"—carry off—"the property of the citizens of other states. They have encouraged and assisted thousands of our slaves to leave their homes; and those who remain, have been incited by emissaries, books and pictures to servile insurrection."

The agitation against the South had been growing for a quarter century, during which South Carolina had patiently hoped for better, the declaration continued. The recent election revealed that such hope was misplaced. "Observing the forms of the Constitution, a sectional party has found within that article establishing the executive department the means of subverting the Constitution itself. A geographical line has been drawn across the Union, and all the states north of that line have united in the election of a man to the high office of President of the United States, whose opinions and purposes are hostile to slavery. He is to be entrusted with the administration of the common government, because he has declared that that 'Government cannot endure permanently half slave, half free,' and that the public mind must rest in the belief that slavery is in the course of ultimate extinction."

The victory of the antislavery party placed South Carolina's interests in grave peril. "On the 4th day of March next, this party will take possession of the government," the declaration said. "The guaranties of the Constitution will then no longer exist; the equal rights of the states will be lost. The slaveholding states will no longer have the power of self-government, or self-protection, and the federal government will have become their enemy." South Carolina had chosen to preempt this fate. "The Union heretofore existing between this state and the other states of North America is dissolved."

WENDELL PHILLIPS WAS twice happy. The abolitionist orator had applauded Lincoln's election, and now he cheered South Carolina's secession—not for South Carolina's sake, but for the Union's. He hoped the other slave states would join South Carolina in leaving. For Phillips, Southern secession would allow the free states to rid themselves of the moral burden they had been carrying for decades. "After drifting a dreary night of thirty years before the hurricane, our ship of state is going to pieces on the lee shore of slavery," Phillips said. And none too soon. He likened the present moment to 1776. Just as the American colonies had broken free from Britain, so the North was about to break free from the South. Anyone who placed Union over honor now should be ostracized as the Loyalists had been ostracized then. "Suppose at that moment John Adams had cried out, 'Now let the people everywhere forget independence, and remember only 'God save the king'!" Phillips's audience hooted appreciatively.

Phillips granted the Southern right to secede, on moral and practical grounds. "A Union is made up of willing states, not of conquered provinces," he said. Perhaps the Constitution forbade secession; perhaps the North had a legal right to keep the South in the Union. This didn't matter. "There are some rights, quite perfect, yet wholly incapable of being enforced. A husband or a wife who can only keep the other partner within the bond by locking the doors and standing armed before them, had better submit to peaceable separation." Phillips's listeners nodded.

Some would mourn the breakup of the Union as the failure of a noble experiment. Not Phillips. "Real unions are not made; they grow. This was made, like an artificial waterfall or a Connecticut nutmeg. It was not an oak which today a tempest shatters. It was a wall hastily built, in hard times, of round boulders; the cement has crumbled, and the smooth stones, obeying the law of gravity, tumble here and there. Why should we seek to stop them, merely to show that we have a right and can?" Better to start work on the successor to this doomed thing. "Let us build, like the pyramids, a fabric which every natural law guarantees; or, better still, *plant* a Union whose life survives the ages."

Abolitionists who endorsed secession had to answer a troubling question: Would it not entrench Southern slavery the more? Phillips said no. On the contrary, it would guarantee the end of Southern slavery. He quoted Senator Andrew Johnson of Tennessee, an opponent of secession. "If I were an abolitionist," Johnson had recently said, "and wanted to accomplish the abolition of slavery in the Southern states, the first step I would take would be to break the bonds of this Union. I believe the continuance of slavery depends on the preservation of this Union, and a compliance with all the guarantees of the Constitution." Phillips agreed. Outside the Union, he said, slavery would confront the growing hostility of the world without the protection of the Constitution and of the North. Outside the Union, no

Fugitive Slave Act would compel the return of escaped slaves. John Brown had had to take the slaves he rescued from Missouri all the way to Canada; once the South left the Union, the next John Brown's destination would be Illinois or Ohio.

The civilized nations were paying close attention, Phillips said. What they wanted to see was where Americans stood on the issue of the hour. "Let the world distinctly understand why they go—to save slavery," he said of the secessionists, "and why we rejoice in their departure—because we know their declaration of independence is the jubilee of the slave." Yes, the Union of 1787 would have failed. But it had been doomed from the start. "All lies bear bitter fruit. Today is the inevitable fruit of our fathers' faithless compromise in 1787." Other countries must see that Americans had finally come to their senses. "For the sake of the future, in freedom's name, let thinking Europe understand clearly why we sever."

Phillips asked himself, rhetorically, why he placed so little value on the Union. "Because I consider it a failure," he answered. "Certainly, so far as slavery is concerned, it is a failure." The number of slaves had quintupled under the aegis of the Union; this hardly recommended the Union as a promoter of freedom. American values and morality had suffered commensurately since the founding of the Union. "At its outset, nine men out of ten were proud to be called abolitionists; now, nine out of ten would deem it not only an insult but a pecuniary injury to be charged with being so." Freedom of speech had been sacrificed to slavery, lest slaveholders take offense. "Before the Union existed, Washington and Jefferson uttered the boldest antislavery opinions; today they would be lynched in their own homes, and their sentiments have been mobbed this very year in every great city of the North."

Having failed, the Union must give way. The slaveholders doomed themselves by secession, Phillips said, but they gave liberty a second chance in America. "All hail, then, Disunion!"

WILLIAM LLOYD GARRISON THOUGHT the South had gone mad. "The election of the Republican candidate, Abraham Lincoln, to the presidency of the United States has operated upon the whole slave-holding South in a manner indicative of the torments of the damned,"

Garrison wrote in *The Liberator.* "The brutal dastards and bloody-minded tyrants who have so long ruled the country with impunity are now furiously foaming at the mouth, gnawing their tongues for pain, indulging in the most horrid blasphemies, uttering the wildest threats, and avowing the most treasonable designs. Their passions, 'set on fire of hell,' are leading them into every kind of excess, and they are inspired by a demoniacal phrenzy." Garrison quoted from the Book of Revelation to mark the South as the modern Babylon; he turned to the ancient Greeks—and John Brown—to declare, "Whom the gods intend to destroy, they first make mad." This was the condition of Southern leaders, he said. "They are insane from their fears, their guilty forebodings, the lust of power and rule, their hatred of free institutions, their consciousness of merited judgments; so that they may be properly classed with the inmates of a lunatic asylum."

Abraham Lincoln's pledges not to touch slavery in the states were lost on the Southern firebrands, said Garrison. "In vain does the Republican party present but one point of antagonism to slavery—to wit, no more territorial expansion—and exhibit the utmost cautiousness not to give offence in any other direction, and make itself hoarse in uttering professions of loyalty to the Constitution and the Union. Still they protest that its designs are infernal, and for them there is 'sleep no more'! Are not these the signs of a demented people?"

How should the rest of the country deal with these lunatics? "The question in its simplest form is, What is the value to the free states of their federal connection with the slave states?" asked Garrison. His answer was: very little. Slavery was an embarrassment to the United States in world affairs. Slavery, like all forms of bound labor, was a drag on a modern economy. Slavery discredited hard work and manual labor. Slavery debauched democracy. The conclusion was inescapable. "The free states not only derive no advantage from their Union with the slave states but positive injury."

The North should welcome separation from the South, Garrison said. If the South didn't separate from the North, the North should separate from the South. At the very least, the North should not resist separation. "When any of the slave states are bent upon secession, it should not be opposed by others but permitted peaceably and cheerfully, as a happier revolution than that which delivered us from

British domination. Every slaveholding state which secedes from the Union cuts off a decayed branch from its"—the Union's—"growth and accelerates its advance to power, respect, virtue and prosperity."

HORACE GREELEY DIDN'T PUSH the South away, but neither did he dispute secession's legitimacy. "We hold, with Jefferson, to the inalienable right of communities to alter or abolish forms of government that have become oppressive or injurious," the New York editor declared. "And if the Cotton States shall decide that they can do better out of the Union than in it, we insist on letting them go in peace. The right to secede may be a revolutionary one, but it exists nevertheless; and we do not see how one party can have a right to what another party has a right to prevent. We must ever resist the asserted right of any state to remain in the Union and nullify or defy the laws thereof; to withdraw from the Union is quite another matter. And whenever a considerable section of our Union shall deliberately resolve to go out, we shall resist all coercive measures designed to keep it in. We hope never to live in a republic whereof one section is pinned to the residue by bayonets."

Yet Greeley didn't want the South to act in haste. "We must insist that the step be taken, if it ever shall be, with the deliberation and gravity befitting so momentous an issue." Time should be allowed for tempers to cool and calmness return. Both sides of the question should be thoroughly aired. The people, in their democratic authority, should be consulted. "Let the act of secession be the echo of an unmistakable popular fiat," Greeley said. "A judgment thus rendered, a demand for separation so backed, would either be acquiesced in without the effusion of blood, or those who rushed upon carnage to defy and defeat it, would place themselves clearly in the wrong."

To date, Greeley said, the demands for secession didn't meet these criteria of deliberation. "They bear the unmistakable impress of haste—of passion—of distrust of the popular judgment. They seem clearly intended to precipitate the South into rebellion before the baselessness of the clamors which have misled and excited her can be ascertained by the great body of her people." Greeley hoped a prudent pause would ease the jitters and set things right. "We trust that they will be confronted with calmness, with dignity, and with unwavering trust in the inherent strength of the Union and the loyalty of the American people."

Greeley's editorial was much quoted—too much for his later comfort. It was taken, not surprisingly, as a permission for Southern states to leave the Union. "If the Cotton States shall decide that they can do better out of the Union than in it, we insist on letting them go in peace"—these words seemed quite clear. Greeley later claimed his purpose was to put the onus on the South; by opening the door, he would allay their claustrophobia. Perhaps that was his intent, but it was lost on most of those who read his excerpted words.

WHAT DISTINGUISHED the responses of Phillips, Garrison and Greeley to Southern secession was the irresponsibility of the authors, in the sense that they had no legal or political responsibility for the government's response to secession. Phillips and the others obviously hoped their words would shape government policy, but their hands had no grip on the levers of power.

William Seward was different. He was a senator, and he was being talked of as the next secretary of state. Seward's words had heft outsiders like Phillips and the others could only envy. Seward put the present moment in historical context. Self-government on republican lines was the invention of America, he said, and it was the destiny of America. Every state in the Union had a republican form of government, and each state depended on the others. "No republican state on this continent or any other can stand alone," Seward said. "That is an impossibility. And the reason is a simple one. So much liberty, so much personal independence, such scope to emulation and ambition as a free republic gives, where universal suffrage exists, are too much for any one state, standing alone, to maintain." Seward drew an analogy. "Republican states are like the sheaves in the harvest field. Put them up singly and every gust blows them down; stack them together and they defy all the winds of heaven." Seward cited Texas, which had tried independence and suffered in the experiment. The Texans couldn't wait to join the Union, once the Union allowed them in.

At a moment when radicals on both sides were rejecting compromise, Seward embraced it. He admired the Constitution but didn't revere it. The Union's charter had worked well but could stand tinker-ing. "Is it strange," he asked, "that this complex system of our govern-ment should be found, after a lapse of seventy years, to work a little rough, a little unequal, and that it should require that the engineer should look at the machinery to see where the gudgeon is worn out, and to see that the main wheel is kept in motion?" A minor adjust-ment and the machine would be running as well as ever.

Seward observed that the South wasn't the first part of the country to consider secession. New England had done so amid the War of 1812. But New Englanders had pulled back before taking any fatal steps. Seward supposed the South would pull back too. Yes, South Carolina had voted for secession, but exposure to the cold world outside the Union would cause a change of mind. Seward professed nothing but goodwill for South Carolina. "There is not a state on earth, outside the American Union, which I like half so well as I do the state of South Carolina, neither England, nor Ireland, nor Scotland, nor France, nor Turkey—although from Turkey they sent me Arab horses, and from South Carolina they send me nothing but curses." Seward's audience of New Yorkers chuckled. "And I have the presumption and vanity to believe that if there were nobody to overhear the state of South Carolina when she is talking, she would confess that she liked us tol-erably well. I am very sure that if anybody were to make a descent on New York tomorrow—whether Louis Napoleon, or the Prince of Wales, or his mother"—more chuckles—"or the emperor of Russia, or the emperor of Austria, all the hills of South Carolina would pour forth their populations for the rescue of New York." Much applause. Seward added, "If any of those powers were to make a descent on South Carolina, I know who would go to her rescue." A voice from the crowd: "We'd all go!" Seward nodded, "We'd all go—everybody." Audience: "That's so," and much applause.

"Therefore they do not humbug me with their secession," he con-tinued. "And I do not think they will humbug you. And I do not believe that if they do not humbug you and me, they will much longer succeed in humbugging themselves." Laughter. "Now, fellow citizens, this is the ultimate truth of all this business. These states are always to be together—always shall. Talk of striking down a star from that constellation—it is a thing which cannot be done." Loud applause.

What should be done? "I do not know any better rule than the rule which every good father of a family observes," Seward said. Children were sometimes rambunctious, but the father kept a steady course. And so should the national government with respect to the secessionists. "That is, be patient, kind, paternal, forbearing, and wait until they come to reflect for themselves."

Seward, speaking in late December, said he noticed improvement already in the outlook for the Union. "I believe that secession was stronger on the night of the 6th of November last, when a president and vice-president who were unacceptable to the slave states were elected, than it is now. That is now some fifty days since, and I believe that every day's sun which set since that time has set on mollified passions and prejudices, and that if you will only give it time, sixty days' more suns will give you a much brighter and more cheerful atmosphere." Great applause and cheering.

STEPHEN DOUGLAS HAD a unique perspective on the events of that winter. In a decade he had ascended from obscurity to the apex of the most powerful party in America. More than anyone else he had set the agenda of American politics. The debates of the era were debates Douglas had started and in which he took a central part. Yet now his career lay in ruins. His party was riven, his country was fracturing, and the man whose career he had resurrected was pushing past him into the White House.

"No man in America regrets the election of Mr. Lincoln more than I do," Douglas told a group from New Orleans who had solicited his views in the aftermath of the balloting. "None made more strenuous exertions to defeat him; none differ with him more radically and irreconcilably upon all the great issues involved in the contest. No man living is more prepared to resist, by all the legitimate means sanctioned by the Constitution and laws of our country, the aggressive party which he and his party are understood to represent."

Yet Douglas had no doubt where his ultimate responsibility lay, and hence his true loyalty. "I am bound, as a good citizen and law-abiding man, to declare my conscientious conviction that the mere election of any man to the presidency by the American people, in accordance with the Constitution and laws, does not of itself furnish any just cause or reasonable ground for dissolving our federal Union."

Douglas observed that even the proponents of secession found no fault with the election itself, alleging no corruption or miscounting. Nor did any of them claim that Lincoln had done anything yet to endanger slavery. Rather, they *apprehended* that he would do something. "Is this apprehension well founded?" asked Douglas. He thought not. "The president can do nothing except what the law authorizes. His duty is to see the laws faithfully executed. If he fails to perform this duty he will soon find himself a prisoner before the high court of impeachment." Douglas remarked that the Democratic party, though defeated and broken, still lived. It included many Northern conservatives on the slave question, who would hold Lincoln to account.

Present laws protected the South, Douglas said. They had been enacted with the participation of the South. Congressional arithmetic ensured that they would not be overturned without the complicity of the South. This unarguable fact made talk of secession not merely pernicious but rashly counterproductive. Douglas underlined this point: "No bill can pass either house of Congress impairing or disturbing the rights or institutions of the Southern people in any manner whatever, unless *a portion of the Southern Senators and Representatives absent themselves so as to give an Abolition majority in consequence of their absence.*"

The appropriate response to Lincoln's election was not secession but patience, Douglas said—patience and confidence in the American system. "Four years will soon pass away, when the ballot-box will furnish a peaceful, legal and constitutional remedy for all the evils and grievances with which the country may be afflicted."

Douglas suspected that for some Southerners the complaints against Lincoln were red herrings. These men—"who look upon disunion and a Southern confederacy as a thing desirable in itself, and are only waiting for an opportunity to accomplish that which had been previously resolved upon"—were as deceitful as they were wrong. They would drive the South to revolution under false pretenses. They deserved nothing but scorn.

Honest Southerners—the majority, Douglas hoped—would see things differently. "To those who regard the Union under the

Constitution, as our fathers made it, the most precious legacy ever bequeathed to a free people by a patriotic ancestry, and are determined to maintain it as long as their rights and liberties, equality and honor are protected by it, the election of Mr. Lincoln, in my humble opinion, presents no just cause, no reasonable excuse for disunion."

T HE PERSON EVERYONE wanted to hear from remained silent. Lincoln had watched the reaction to his victory, which included distress in financial markets as well as the political turmoil, and concluded he could do little constructive about it. Editors sought a statement; reporters darkened his Springfield doorstep. He disappointed them, going no further than a few scribbled lines he let a news correspondent carry back to his boss. "I find Mr. Lincoln is not insensible to any uneasiness in the minds of candid men, nor to any commercial, or financial, depression, or disturbance, in the country if there be such," Lincoln wrote. "Still he does not, so far as at present advised, deem it necessary, or proper for him to make, or authorize, any public declaration. He thinks candid men need only to examine his views already before the public."

This wasn't much, and it failed the obvious test. What Lincoln had said before the election he had said as a candidate. Candidates are tempted to tailor their remarks to what they think voters want to hear. Lincoln was a candidate no longer, but the president-elect. His words would now carry weight beyond anything he had said before. Even for him simply to repeat those words as president-elect would reinforce them in a way an admonition to read the earlier speeches couldn't.

Lincoln soon realized that if he wouldn't speak, he at least had to explain his silence. He did so with the same caution that had marked the campaign. A former senator from Connecticut implored Lincoln to "disarm the mischief makers" by means of a public statement. Lincoln commenced his response with the disclaimer "This is intended as a strictly private letter to you." He continued, "It is with the most profound appreciation of your motive, and highest respect for your judgment too, that I feel constrained, for the present, at least, to make no declaration for the public." Why not? "First, I could say nothing which I have not already said, and which is in print, and open for the inspection of all. To press a repetition of this upon those who *have* listened, is useless; to press it upon those who have *refused* to listen, and still refuse, would be wanting in self-respect, and would have an appearance of sycophancy and timidity, which would excite the contempt of good men, and encourage bad ones to clamor the more loudly. I am not insensible to any commercial or financial depression that may exist; but nothing is to be gained by fawning around the 'respectable scoundrels' who got it up. Let them go to work and repair the mischief of their own making; and then perhaps they will be less greedy to do the like again."

A Missouri editor, a Democrat, taxed Lincoln for his silence; Lincoln responded with greater acerbity. "I could say nothing which I have not already said, and which is in print and accessible to the public. Please pardon me for suggesting that if the papers, like yours, which heretofore have persistently garbled, and misrepresented what I have said, will now fully and fairly place it before their readers, there can be no further misunderstanding. I beg you to believe me sincere when I declare I do not say this in a spirit of complaint or resentment; but that I urge it as the true cure for any real uneasiness in the country that my course may be other than conservative. The Republican newspapers now, and for some time past, are and have been republishing copious extracts from my many published speeches, which would at once reach the whole public if your class of papers would also publish them. I am not at liberty to shift my ground—that is out of the question. If I thought a *repetition* would do any good I would make it. But my judgment is it would do positive harm. The secessionists *per se*, believing they had alarmed me, would clamor all the louder."

The pressure nonetheless intensified. Lincoln yielded slightly. Lyman Trumbull was scheduled to speak in Springfield; he was known to have Lincoln's ear, and Lincoln his. Trumbull's words would be listened to carefully. Lincoln drafted a passage for Trumbull to insert in his speech. "I have labored in, and for, the Republican organization with entire confidence that whenever it shall be in power, each and all of the states will be left in as complete control of their own affairs respectively, and at as perfect liberty to choose, and employ, their own means of protecting property, and preserving peace and order within their respective limits, as they have ever been under any administration," Trumbull should say. "Those who have voted for Mr. Lincoln, have expected, and still expect this; and they would not have voted for him had they expected otherwise. I regard it as extremely fortunate for the peace of the whole country that this point, upon which the Republicans have been so long and so persistently misrepresented, is now to be brought to a practical test and placed beyond the possibility of doubt. Disunionists *per se* are now in hot haste to get out of the Union, precisely because they perceive they cannot much longer maintain apprehension among the Southern people that their homes and firesides and lives are to be endangered by the action of the Federal Government. With such '*Now, or never*' is the maxim."

Trumbull delivered the message, and the response reinforced Lincoln's distrust of words. "The Boston Courier, and its class, hold me responsible for the speech, and endeavor to inflame the North with the belief that it foreshadows an abandonment of Republican ground by the incoming administration," he wrote to an Illinois editor, "while the Washington Constitution and its class hold the same speech up to the South as an open declaration of war against them. This is just as I expected, and just what would happen with any declaration I could make. These political fiends are not half sick enough yet. Party malice and not public good possesses them entirely." Quoting Jesus against the Pharisees, he said, "They seek a sign, and no sign shall be given them." Yet he softened slightly at the end: "At least such is my present feeling and purpose."

EVENTS COMPELLED further revelations. Amid the developing crisis, Congress named committees to seek a formula that might hold the Union together. Lincoln advised his allies in Washington how they should conduct themselves. "Let there be no compromise on the question of *extending* slavery," he wrote to Lyman Trumbull for the benefit of Republicans in the Senate. "If there be, all our labor is lost, and, ere long, must be done again. The dangerous ground—that into which some of our friends have a hankering to run—is Popular Sovereignty. Have none of it. Stand firm. The tug has to come, and better now, than any time hereafter." To Illinois Republican Elihu Washburne, in the House, which was considering both popular sovereignty and an extension of the old Missouri Compromise line, he urged similar resistance. "Let either be done, and immediately filibustering and extending slavery recommences," Lincoln said. "On that point hold firm, as with a chain of steel."

The compromisers gained momentum even so. Lincoln decided he had to speak up a bit more. He wrote to Thurlow Weed, who had arranged a meeting of governors. "Tell them you judge from my speeches that I will be inflexible on the territorial question; that I probably think either the Missouri line extended, or Douglas' and Eli Thayer's Popular Sovereignty would lose us everything we gained by the election," Lincoln said. As for the immediate question: "I believe you can pretend to find but little, if anything, in my speeches, about secession; but my opinion is that no state can, in any way lawfully, get out of the Union, without the consent of the others; and that it is the duty of the president, and other government functionaries to run the machine as it is."

Congress continued its work, prompting Lincoln to engage more directly. A Senate "Committee of Thirteen" began crafting a grand compromise on the order of the Missouri Compromise and the Compromise of 1850. Lincoln warned against anything that hinted at retreat from the Republican platform. *He* certainly wouldn't endorse any such thing. "It would make me appear as if I repented for the crime of having been elected, and was anxious to apologize and beg forgiveness," he said in a confidential letter to John Gilmer, a North Carolina congressman. Yet lest the committee run away without him, he outlined three acceptable provisions of a compromise: "That the fugitive slave clause of the Constitution ought to be enforced by a law of Congress, with efficient provisions for that object, not obliging private persons to assist in its execution, but punishing all who resist it, and with the usual safeguards to liberty, securing free men against being surrendered as slaves. That all state laws, if there be such, really, or apparently, in conflict with such law of Congress, ought to be repealed; and no opposition to the execution of such law of Congress ought to be made. That the federal Union must be preserved."

HE REACHED tentatively across the growing rift between North and South. Newspapers brought word that Alexander Stephens of Georgia had given an anti-secession speech in his state's legislature. Lincoln knew Stephens from Congress in the 1840s. They were both Whigs then, and both had opposed the war against Mexico. Of Stephens, Lincoln had written to William Herndon, "I take up my pen to say that Mr. Stephens of Georgia, a little, slim, pale-faced consumptive man, with a voice like Logan's"—Stephen Logan was an eminent Springfield lawyer—"has just concluded the very best speech of an hour's length I ever heard. My old, withered, dry eyes are full of tears yet." A dozen years later Lincoln hoped he and Stephens still shared an approach to national issues; the reports of the recent speech suggested they did. He sent a query to Stephens about the speech. "If you have revised it, as is probable, I shall be much obliged if you will send me a copy," he said.

Stephens replied that he had not had time to revise the speech but that the version reported in the papers was accurate enough. Lincoln hadn't really cared about the wording of the speech; he wanted an excuse to strike up a correspondence. "Your obliging answer to my short note is just received, and for which please accept my thanks," he responded. "I fully appreciate the present peril the country is in, and the weight of responsibility on me." Crucial to Lincoln's calculations about the South was an accurate estimate of Southern sentiment. He knew that the hotheads commanded the headlines at present, but what about the ordinary people of the South? What did they think? "Do the people of the South really entertain fears that a Republican administration would, *directly, or indirectly,* interfere with their slaves, or with them, about their slaves?" asked Lincoln. "If they do, I wish to assure you, as once a friend, and still, I hope, not an enemy, that there is no cause for such fears. The South would be in no more danger in this respect than it was in the days of Washington. I suppose, however, this does not meet the case. You think slavery is *right* and ought to be extended; while we think it is *wrong* and ought to be restricted. That I suppose is the rub. It certainly is the only substantial difference between us."

Stephens answered in similar vein. "Personally, I am not your enemy—far from it; and however widely we may differ politically, yet I trust we both have an earnest desire to preserve and maintain the Union," he said. "When men come under the influence of fanaticism, there is no telling where their impulses or passions may drive them. This is what creates our discontent and apprehensions." As evidence of the fanaticism, Stephens cited "such reckless exhibitions of madness as the John Brown raid into Virginia, which has received so much sympathy from many, and no open condemnation from any of the leading members of the dominant party." Stephens urged Lincoln to calm what passions he could. "In addressing you thus, I would have you understand me as being not a personal enemy, but as one who would have you do what you can to save our common country. A word fitly spoken by you now would be like 'apples of gold in pictures of silver.'"

THIS ENCOURAGEMENT FROM Stephens, a Southern friend of the Union, caused Lincoln to reconsider his reticence. Two long months now stood between him and his inauguration; until then he had no authority. But his power grew by the day. He wasn't yet president, but he *would be* president. His promises—or threats—mattered.

This was especially true given the vacuum of power in the White House in the meantime. No lame-duck president was ever lamer than James Buchanan, whose party and policies had been rejected at the ballot, and who himself pronounced secession unconstitutional but disclaimed executive authority to resist it. "Secession is neither more nor less than revolution," Buchanan declared. Yet only Congress, and not the president, possessed the authority to act against secession. "Apart from the execution of the laws, so far as this may be practicable, the executive has no authority to decide what shall be the relations between the federal government and South Carolina. He has been invested with no such discretion."

Lincoln read Buchanan's statement and realized the wreck of the Union might be a fait accompli by the time he was inaugurated. Alexander Stephens's plea for "a word fitly spoken by you now" was a signal to say something before it was too late.

But what could he say? That had been the problem, and it remained the problem. He took another small step toward a public statement following a secret visit by Duff Green, a onetime Jacksonian who had broken with Jackson to side with John Calhoun in the nullification crisis of the early 1830s and eventually became an intimate of James Buchanan. Green was nearly seventy, with white hair and a long beard that made him look like Father Time; apparently the journalists who had staked out Lincoln's home and office mistook him for an old farmer. At any rate they ignored him. The question Green brought to Lincoln was how far the president-elect might go toward reassuring the South that his administration didn't intend the destruction of slavery.

"My dear Sir," Lincoln responded in a letter addressed to Green but meant for moderate Southerners. "I do not desire any amendment of the Constitution. Recognizing, however, that questions of such amendment rightfully belong to the American people, I should not feel justified nor inclined to withhold from them, if I could, a fair opportunity of expressing their will thereon." In other words, Lincoln wouldn't support an amendment guaranteeing the future of slavery in the slave states, but neither would he oppose it. He went further. "I declare that the maintenance inviolate of the rights of the states, and especially the right of each state to order and control its own domestic institutions according to its own judgment exclusively, is essential to that balance of powers on which the perfection and endurance of our political fabric depends. And I denounce the lawless invasion by armed force of the soil of any state or territory, no matter under what pretext, as the gravest of crimes." This last was the condemnation of John Brown that Alexander Stephens had asked for.

Yet Lincoln remained cautious. "I am greatly averse to writing anything for the public at this time, and I consent to the publication of this only upon the condition that six of the twelve United States senators for the states of Georgia, Alabama, Mississippi, Louisiana, Florida, and Texas"—the states thought likeliest to join South Carolina in secession—"shall sign their names to what is written on this sheet below my name, and allow the whole to be published together." The statement Lincoln stipulated read, "We recommend to the people of the states we represent respectively to suspend all action for dismemberment of the Union at least until some act deemed to be violative of our rights shall be done by the incoming administration."

Nothing came of Lincoln's offer. "I regret your unwillingness to recommend an amendment to the constitution which will arrest the progress of secession," Green answered, after returning to Washington and consulting those to whom Lincoln's proposal was aimed. "The fact of my having been to Springfield having been published"—the reporters had eventually caught on—"I have deemed it expedient to publish a statement which will probably appear in the New York Herald of tomorrow. I have endeavored to so frame my remarks as to give no offense to you." Green was as good as his word; the statement in the *Herald* registered Green's understanding that Lincoln intended to "administer the government in such a manner as to satisfy the South." But Southern senators had no wish to align themselves openly with the leader of the Republicans, and Lincoln's letter never appeared in public.

THE FAILURE OF his effort at compromise caused Lincoln to dig in his heels. "What is our present condition?" he asked rhetorically in a letter to a Pennsylvania Republican congressman. "We have just carried an election on principles fairly stated to the people. Now we are told in advance the government shall be broken up unless we surrender to those we have beaten, before we take the offices. In this they are either attempting to play upon us, or they are in dead earnest. Either way, if we surrender, it is the end of us, and of the government. They will repeat the experiment upon us *ad libitum*. A year will not pass till we shall have to take Cuba as a condition upon which they will stay in the Union. They now have the Constitution, under which we have lived over seventy years, and acts of Congress of their own framing, with no prospect of their being changed; and they can never have a more shallow pretext for breaking up the government, or extorting a compromise, than now. There is, in my judgment, but one compromise which would really settle the slavery question, and that would be a prohibition against acquiring any more territory."

Lincoln's tone suggested that such a prohibition was out of the question. In fact Daniel Webster had recommended precisely this approach during the war with Mexico in the 1840s: no new territory, no debate over whether the new territory would be slave or free.

But Lincoln wasn't going to be the one to make such an offer. He had won, he was going to be president, and he wasn't going to be blackmailed by the losers. Lest his position be misinterpreted, he told a visitor, in words intended for publication, "I will suffer death before I will consent or will advise my friends to consent to any concession or compromise which looks like buying the privilege of taking possession of this government to which we have a constitutional right; because, whatever I might think of the merit of the various propositions before Congress, I should regard any concession in the face of menace the destruction of the government itself."

THIS REMAINED LINCOLN'S POSITION through the time he left Springfield for Washington. His route would serve as a victory lap through states that had elected him. But first he bade Springfield farewell. "My friends," he said. "No one not in my situation can appreciate my feeling of sadness at this parting. To this place, and the kindness of these people, I owe everything. Here I have lived a quarter of a century, and have passed from a young to an old man. Here my children have been born, and one is buried. I now leave, not knowing when, or whether ever, I may return, with a task before me greater than that which rested upon Washington. Without the assistance of that Divine Being who ever attended him, I cannot succeed. With that assistance I cannot fail. Trusting in Him, who can go with me and remain with you and be everywhere for good, let us confidently hope that all will yet be well. To His care commending you, as I hope in your prayers you will commend me, I bid you an affectionate farewell."

Lincoln traveled by train across Indiana, Ohio, Pennsylvania, Ohio again—including Hudson, where John Brown had his antislavery epiphany—Pennsylvania, New York, New Jersey, Pennsylvania and Maryland. He addressed the crowds that gathered at every stop. He spoke himself hoarse without conveying anything but thanks and determined optimism. "Let us believe, as some poet has expressed it, 'Behind the cloud, the sun is still shining,'" he told one whistle-stop gathering.

The optimism came hard. On the last leg of the trip he learned from Allan Pinkerton, a detective hired by the railroad that carried him, of an assassination plot in Baltimore. On his own time Pinkerton was an abolitionist and an admirer of John Brown. Pinkerton's Chicago home had sheltered Brown and the slaves Brown liberated from Missouri on their way to Canada. Pinkerton raised money for Brown, and according to family lore had told his son, on Brown's departure,

"Look well upon that man! He is greater than Napoleon and just as great as George Washington."

Pinkerton held Lincoln in less esteem, for now at any rate. But his job was to get the president-elect to Washington alive. Secessionists were rife in slave-state Maryland, and some appeared determined to kill Lincoln before he could be inaugurated. Lincoln agreed to a secret change to his published travel plans and slipped through Baltimore in disguise.

After the story broke, Lincoln second-guessed his decision as suggesting a lack of courage, at a moment when courage was most needed. Allan Pinkerton, despite having orchestrated the ruse, thought John Brown would have acted more boldly.

FINALLY LINCOLN COULD SPEAK openly. Finally he *must* speak openly. Inauguration day started early for Lincoln, who woke at five at Willard's Hotel. He ate breakfast and then had his son Robert read aloud the draft address Lincoln had written. He adjusted the prose to suit his ear and set the draft aside. From the windows of the hotel he could see the preparations that had been made to ensure that the transfer of power went smoothly. Lincoln had received the word of Winfield Scott, the commanding general of the army, that there would be no trouble. "Present my compliments to Mr. Lincoln when you return to Springfield," Scott had told an envoy Lincoln had sent to Washington to inquire about security arrangements. Lincoln had gotten threats from paramilitary types in Maryland and Virginia he judged Scott should know about. Scott listened and told the envoy Lincoln needn't worry. "Say to him that I'll look after those Maryland and Virginia rangers myself. I'll plant cannon at both ends of Pennsylvania Avenue, and if any of them show their heads or raise a finger I'll blow them to hell."

Lincoln didn't see cannons this morning, but he did see soldiers. Scott had mustered several companies of troops who now stood armed beside their horses, ready to leap into the saddle at the moment trouble surfaced. Other cavalrymen patrolled the streets and avenues, scanning the crowds for malcontents. Special policemen lined Pennsylvania Avenue, the route Lincoln would take to and from the ceremony.

No less conspicuous were roving gangs of "Wide Awakes," young men who had joined Republican clubs around the country and rallied for Lincoln and other Republican candidates. Being young and male, they not infrequently tangled with Democratic counterparts, bloodying noses, breaking bones and occasionally inflicting and receiving more serious wounds. They liked to think they had elected Lincoln in November, and now in March thousands had come to see him installed—and to *fore*stall any shenanigans by Democrats. On their heads they wore black caps; over their shoulders they threw capes that left their arms free for what arms might have to do. If this had not been their party's day, they would have seemed more than a little threatening; as it was, the police and soldiers watched them carefully.

A few drops of rain fell in the early morning, but the approach of noon brought a northwest wind that cleared the sky even as it stirred the dust of the many streets that remained unpaved. The air was cool without being cold. It would be a fine day to inaugurate a new president.

James Buchanan thought so. Buchanan left the White House for the last time shortly before noon; his open carriage drove the quarter mile to Willard's, where Lincoln got in. Mounted troops surrounded the vehicle, shielding the president-elect from possible snipers. Buchanan's only worry for himself was that he might be hit by a stray bullet; no one cared enough to want him dead. He claimed some credit for having held the Union together as long as he had, but the last three months had been a disaster. The six states Lincoln had tried to negotiate with had left the Union; the seven seceding states—including South Carolina—had formed the Confederate States of America. Buchanan couldn't transfer authority to Lincoln soon enough.

Lincoln impressed few with the figure he cut. An observer who had met him previously detected a change for the worse. "He was completely metamorphosed—partly by his own fault, and partly through the efforts of injudicious friends and ambitious tailors," the observer said. "He was raising (to gratify a very young lady, it is said) a crop of whiskers, of the blacking-brush variety, coarse, stiff and ungraceful; and in so doing spoiled, or at least seriously impaired, a face which, though never handsome, had in its original state a peculiar power and pathos. On the present occasion the whiskers were reinforced by brand-new clothes from top to toe; black dress-coat, instead of the usual frock, black cloth or satin vest, black pantaloons and a glossy hat evidently just out of the box. To cap the climax of novelty, he carried a huge ebony cane, with a gold head the size of an egg. In these, to him strange, habiliments, he looked so miserably uncomfortable that I could not help pitying him."

The military escort kept close around Lincoln and Buchanan on the mile's drive to the Capitol; they guarded the passage by which the two men walked from the carriage into the building. The pair proceeded to the Senate chamber. "Mr. Buchanan and Mr. Lincoln entered, arm in arm, the former pale, sad, nervous; the latter's face slightly flushed, with compressed lips," a reporter recounted. They sat and watched while a new senator was sworn in. "Mr. Buchanan sighed audibly and frequently, but whether from reflection upon the failure of his administration, I can't say," the reporter remarked. "Mr. Lincoln was grave and impassive as an Indian martyr."

The group moved outdoors, to a platform erected at the east portico of the Capitol. The tall figure of Lincoln was recognized even by those far from the platform; a cheer rose from the thousands on the grounds and beyond. Several minutes were required for the various dignitaries to take their seats; finally Edward Baker, Lincoln's friend and now a senator from Oregon, stepped forward. "Fellow citizens!" he said in a booming voice. "I introduce to you Abraham Lincoln, the president-elect of the United States of America."

Another cheer from the crowd. Lincoln stood, approached the small table that served as a lectern, and acknowledged his audience. A logistical problem emerged. In one hand was his hat, in the other his cane, and in his pocket was his speech. He looked around for a place to put the cane, and settled on balancing it on the table. This freed up one hand to find the speech, but he couldn't deliver the speech with the hat in his hand. The table being too small to accommodate it and the cane and the speech manuscript, he was about to bend over and put the hat on the floor of the platform when his old foe came to his rescue. Stephen Douglas, who remained a leader of Senate Democrats despite having been abandoned by much of his party, held out a hand and offered to hold Lincoln's hat. Lincoln gratefully accepted the offer.

The audience fell silent as Lincoln produced his written remarks. They had been waiting months to hear from the man who would guide their country through its greatest crisis. They seemed to hold their breath.

Lincoln wasted no time on formalities. He went straight to the issue at hand. "Apprehension seems to exist among the people of the Southern states that by the accession of a Republican administration their property and their peace and personal security are to be endangered," he said. He denied this supposition categorically. "There has never been any reasonable cause for such apprehension. Indeed, the most ample evidence to the contrary has all the while existed and been open to their inspection. It is found in nearly all the published speeches of him who now addresses you. I do but quote from one of those speeches when I declare that 'I have no purpose, directly or indirectly, to interfere with the institution of slavery in the states where it exists. I believe I have no lawful right to do so, and I have no inclination to do so.'"

Nor was this sentiment his alone. "Those who nominated and elected me did so with full knowledge that I had made this and many similar declarations and had never recanted them; and more than this, they placed in the platform for my acceptance, and as a law to themselves and to me, the clear and emphatic resolution which I now read: 'Resolved, That the maintenance inviolate of the rights of the states, and especially the right of each state to order and control its own domestic institutions according to its own judgment exclusively, is essential to that balance of power on which the perfection and endurance of our political fabric depend.'"

Republicans had been charged with abetting John Brown. Lincoln denied this categorically too. Nor would there be any new John Browns, not while Abraham Lincoln was president. "We denounce the lawless invasion by armed force of the soil of any state or territory, no matter what pretext, as among the gravest of crimes."

Lincoln promised to enforce the constitutional provision mandating the return of fugitive slaves. The same promise would bind others in the government. "All members of Congress swear their support to the whole Constitution—to this provision as much as to any other. To the proposition, then, that slaves whose cases come within the terms of this clause 'shall be delivered up' their oaths are unanimous." He would support new legislation to that effect and would take all appropriate measures to ensure its enforcement.

He realized this might not be enough. It hadn't been enough for the seven states that had approved ordinances of secession. Lincoln lamented their action for what it portended for the American republic. "It is seventy-two years since the first inauguration of a president under our national Constitution. During that period fifteen different and greatly distinguished citizens have in succession administered the executive branch of the government. They have conducted it through many perils, and generally with great success. Yet, with all this scope of precedent, I now enter upon the same task for the brief constitutional term of four years under great and peculiar difficulty. A disruption of the federal Union, heretofore only menaced, is now formidably attempted."

The disruption was without moral or constitutional basis, Lincoln said. "I hold that in contemplation of universal law and of the Constitution the Union of these states is perpetual." Perpetuity was the essence of government. "It is safe to assert that no government proper ever had a provision in its organic law for its own termination. Continue to execute all the express provisions of our national Constitution, and the Union will endure forever, it being impossible to destroy it except by some action not provided for in the instrument itself."

Even supposing the Constitution a contract, or compact, as Southerners did, unilateral secession was illegal. "Can it, as a contract, be peaceably unmade by less than all the parties who made it? One party to a contract may violate it—break it, so to speak—but does it not require all to lawfully rescind it?"

Yet the Constitution wasn't the final word—or, rather, it wasn't the original word. "The Union is much older than the Constitution. It was formed, in fact, by the Articles of Association in 1774. It was matured and continued by the Declaration of Independence in 1776. It was further matured, and the faith of all the then thirteen states expressly plighted and engaged that it should be perpetual, by the Articles of Confederation in 1778. And finally, in 1787, one of the declared objects for ordaining and establishing the Constitution was 'to form a more perfect Union.' But if destruction of the Union by one or by a part only of the states be lawfully possible, the Union is *less* perfect than before the Constitution, having lost the vital element of perpetuity."

Lincoln paused for effect. "It follows from these views that no state upon its own mere motion can lawfully get out of the Union;

that 'resolves' and 'ordinances' to that effect are legally void, and that acts of violence within any state or states against the authority of the United States are insurrectionary or revolutionary."

Another pause. "I therefore consider that in view of the Constitution and the laws the Union is unbroken, and to the extent of my ability, I shall take care, as the Constitution itself expressly enjoins upon me, that the laws of the Union be faithfully executed in all the states."

Lincoln made clear he wasn't declaring war on the seven states. "There needs to be no bloodshed or violence, and there shall be none unless it be forced upon the national authority. The power confided to me will be used to hold, occupy, and possess the property and places belonging to the government and to collect the duties and imposts; but beyond what may be necessary for these objects, there will be no invasion, no using of force against or among the people anywhere." The mails would be delivered, unless turned back by force. Federal offices would be filled by local residents; if local residents refused the offices, Lincoln said, he would not impose outsiders, though he had a right to do so. "So far as possible the people everywhere shall have that sense of perfect security which is most favorable to calm thought and reflection."

Lincoln reiterated that secession would not be tolerated. "The central idea of secession is the essence of anarchy. A majority held in restraint by constitutional checks and limitations, and always changing easily with deliberate changes of popular opinions and sentiments, is the only true sovereign of a free people. Whoever rejects it does of necessity fly to anarchy or to despotism. Unanimity is impossible. The rule of a minority, as a permanent arrangement, is wholly inadmissible; so that, rejecting the majority principle, anarchy or despotism in some form is all that is left."

What was the secessionists' complaint? "One section of our country believes slavery is right and ought to be extended, while the other believes it is wrong and ought not to be extended. This is the only substantial dispute." Other complaints were matters of detail. "The fugitive-slave clause of the Constitution and the law for the suppression of the foreign slave trade are each as well enforced, perhaps, as any law can ever be in a community where the moral sense of the people imperfectly supports the law itself. The great body of the people abide by the dry legal obligation in both cases, and a few break over in each. This, I think, cannot be perfectly cured, and it would be worse in both cases after the separation of the sections than before. The foreign slave trade, now imperfectly suppressed, would be ultimately revived without restriction in one section, while fugitive slaves, now only partially surrendered, would not be surrendered at all by the other."

The secessionists sought something that could not be. "Physically speaking, we cannot separate. We cannot remove our respective sections from each other nor build an impassable wall between them. A husband and wife may be divorced and go out of the presence and beyond the reach of each other, but the different parts of our country cannot do this. They cannot but remain face to face, and intercourse, either amicable or hostile, must continue between them. Is it possible, then, to make that intercourse more advantageous or more satisfactory after separation than before? Can aliens make treaties easier than friends can make laws? Can treaties be more faithfully enforced between aliens than laws can among friends?" Suppose the two sides went to war. "You cannot fight always; and when, after much loss on both sides and no gain on either, you cease fighting, the identical old questions, as to terms of intercourse, are again upon you."

Lincoln spoke directly to the secessionists. "In your hands, my dissatisfied fellow-countrymen, and not in mine, is the momentous issue of civil war. The government will not assail you. You can have no conflict without being yourselves the aggressors. You have no oath registered in heaven to destroy the government, while I shall have the most solemn one to preserve, protect and defend it."

He looked up from his papers and out across the crowd. "I am loath to close," he resumed. "We are not enemies, but friends. We must not *be* enemies. Though passion may have strained, it must not break, our bonds of affection. The mystic chords of memory, stretching from every battlefield and patriot grave to every living heart and hearthstone all over this broad land, will yet swell the chorus of the Union, when again touched, as surely they will be, by the better angels of our nature."

L INCOLN'S VOICE WAS clear and reasonably powerful. But even a stentor would have had difficulty being heard in the open air on that windy day. Not all caught the grace note at the end; many in the sprawling audience didn't realize he had finished until he turned away from the lectern.

Chief Justice Roger Taney, looking older and more cadaverous than ever, stepped forward to administer the oath of office. Possibly reflecting, doubtless ruefully, that he had done as much as any other person to make Lincoln president, the author of the Dred Scott decision instructed Lincoln that he should repeat the inaugural oath, phrase by phrase. Lincoln did so, laying special stress on the final words: "to preserve, protect and defend the Constitution of the United States."

Taney was the first to shake his hand. James Buchanan came next. Stephen Douglas, who had been listening carefully and nodding agreement, followed. Reporters asked Buchanan and Douglas what they made of Lincoln's remarks. Buchanan begged off, saying he would have to read the address carefully. Douglas answered forthrightly, and with satisfaction: "He does not mean coercion; he says nothing about retaking the forts or federal property—he's all right." Subsequently Douglas reconsidered. "I hardly know what he means," Douglas then said. "Every point in the address is susceptible of a double construction." Yet he added, "I think he does not mean coercion."

FREDERICK DOUGLASS HAD expected more—much more. After all the waiting, after everything Douglass and the other opponents of slavery had done to make it possible for an antislavery man to become president, Lincoln's words left Douglass disappointed and angry.

Douglass acknowledged the peculiar circumstances under which Lincoln spoke, starting with the assassination plots prepared against him. "The manner in which Mr. Lincoln entered the capital was in keeping with the menacing and troubled state of the times," Douglass told the readers of his eponymous monthly. "He reached the capital as the poor, hunted fugitive slave reaches the North, in disguise, seeking concealment, evading pursuers." Douglass didn't censure Lincoln for this. "He only did what braver men have done."

But Lincoln had failed to employ the moment to make the moral statement the country required. "The occasion required the utmost frankness and decision," Douglass said. "Overlooking the whole field of disturbing elements, he should have boldly rebuked them. He saw seven states in open rebellion, the Constitution set at naught, the national flag insulted, and his own life murderously sought by slave-holding assassins. Does he expose and rebuke the enemies of his country, the men who are bent upon ruling or ruining the country? Not a bit of it."

What did Lincoln do instead? "At the very start he seeks to court their favor, to explain himself where nobody misunderstands him, and to deny intentions of which nobody had accused him," Douglass wrote. "He knew full well that the grand objection to him and his party respected the one great question of slavery extension. The South wants to extend slavery, and the North wants to confine it where it is, where the public mind shall rest in the belief of its ultimate extinction. This was the question which carried the North and defeated the South in the election which made Mr. Abraham Lincoln president. Mr. Lincoln knew this, and the South has known it all along; and yet this subject only gets the faintest allusion, while others, never seriously in dispute, are dwelt upon at length."

Lincoln might as well have surrendered to the South, Douglass said. "Mr. Lincoln opens his address by announcing his complete loyalty to slavery in the slave states, and quotes from the Chicago platform a resolution affirming the rights of property in slaves, in the slave states. He is not content with declaring that he has no lawful power to interfere with slavery in the states, but he also denies having the least '*inclination*' to interfere with slavery in the states. This denial of all feeling against slavery, at such a time and in such circumstances, is wholly discreditable to the head and heart of Mr. Lincoln. Aside from the inhuman coldness of the sentiment, it was a weak and inappropriate utterance to such an audience, since it could neither appease nor check the wild fury of the rebel slave power. Any but a blind man can see that the disunion sentiment of the South does not arise from any misapprehension of the disposition of the party represented by Mr. Lincoln. The very opposite is the fact. The difficulty is, the slaveholders understand the position of the Republican party too well."

Lincoln had spoken like a lawyer when he should have spoken like a prophet, or at least a man of moral courage. "Weakness, timidity and conciliation towards the tyrants and traitors had emboldened them to a pitch of insolence which demanded an instant check," Douglass said of the secessionists. "Mr. Lincoln was in a position that enabled him to wither at a single blast their high-blown pride. The occasion was one for honest rebuke, not for palliations and apologies. The slaveholders should have been told that their barbarous system of robbery is contrary to the spirit of the age, and to the principles of liberty in which the federal government was founded." Lincoln had failed the test utterly. "Some thought we had in Mr. Lincoln the nerve and decision of an Oliver Cromwell; but the result shows that we merely have a continuation of the Pierces and Buchanans, and that the Republican president bends the knee to slavery as readily as any of his infamous predecessors."

Douglass, after hearing Lincoln, wondered what the government in Washington was good for. "It remains to be seen whether the federal government is really able to do more than hand over some John Brown to be hanged, suppress a slave insurrection, or catch a runaway slave—whether it is powerless for liberty, and only powerful for slavery."

WHAT DOUGLASS COMPLAINED of in Lincoln's response to secession was exactly what Lincoln took pride in. Douglass wanted the conflict between the secessionists and the Union to be about slavery; Lincoln wanted it to be about states' rights—which, in his view, included the right to permit slavery but *not* the right to secede. Douglass saw the struggle as essentially moral; Lincoln saw it as political. Douglass was an idealist; Lincoln, a pragmatist.

And the pragmatic issue that pressed on Lincoln during his first weeks in office was what to do about Fort Sumter. The island post in the harbor at Charleston was one of the last federal properties not occupied by local forces in the seceded states. It had little military value, lying under the guns of the South Carolina militia. But it had great symbolic value, as a test of Lincoln's resolve. Would the new president fight to defend Fort Sumter? The South was watching; the North was watching; the world was watching.

Lincoln put the matter to Winfield Scott, asking how long Fort Sumter could hold out in the absence of fresh supplies, and what would be required to reinforce and defend it. Scott wasn't optimistic. The fort might hold out for six weeks, he said, but securing the place would require twenty-five thousand men, a fleet of ships, new acts of Congress and six to eight months. Until then, the South Carolinians could take the fort at their leisure.

William Seward, now secretary of state, agreed that Fort Sumter was indefensible. On April 1, Seward sketched what he called "Some Thoughts for the President's Consideration." He began with a chiding: "We are at the end of a month's administration and yet without a policy either domestic or foreign." Seward granted the need for dealing with appointments and other tasks faced by any new administration. "But further delay to adopt and prosecute our policies for both domestic and foreign affairs would not only bring scandal on the Administration, but danger upon the country," Seward continued.

What to do? "*Change the question before the public from one upon slavery, or about slavery* for a question upon *Union or disunion*. In other words, from what would be regarded as a party question to one of *patriotism or Union*." Seward recommended evacuating Fort Sumter, indefensible anyway, and reinforcing the remaining federal forts in the South. Navy ships in foreign waters should be recalled and readied for a blockade of the rebel states. "This will raise distinctly the question of *Union* or *disunion*," Seward asserted.

To this point in Seward's memorandum, Lincoln couldn't disagree, though he might dislike the secretary's tone. What came next convinced Lincoln that Seward had a screw loose. "I would demand explanations from Spain and France, categorically, at once," he said, presumably referring to explanations as to how they proposed to treat secession. "I would seek explanations from Great Britain and Russia, and send agents into Canada, Mexico and Central America, to rouse a vigorous continental spirit of independence on this continent against European intervention. And if satisfactory explanations are not received from Spain and France, would convene Congress and declare war against them."

Seward wasn't finished. "But whatever policy we adopt, there must be an energetic prosecution of it. For this purpose it must be somebody's business to pursue and direct it incessantly. Either the President must do it himself, and be all the while active in it; or devolve it on some member of his Cabinet. Once adopted, debates on it must end, and all agree and abide. It is not in my especial province. But I neither seek to evade nor assume responsibility."

Lincoln hardly knew where to start in responding to Seward. He rejected the assertion that his administration lacked a policy; had the secretary not been listening at the inaugural address? Lincoln evinced puzzlement as to why abandoning Fort Sumter and defending other posts would shift the debate from slavery to disunion. He didn't respond directly to Seward's desire to foment a foreign crisis, even a war; Lincoln doubtless reckoned he had his hands full with one incipient war. As for Seward's offer to crack the cabinet into line and pursue an energetic policy—thereby making Seward an assistant president, apparently—Lincoln said simply, "If this must be done, *I* must do it."

IN THE END Lincoln ordered the resupply of Fort Sumter. He didn't expect the operation to succeed; rather he wanted to put the rebels in the position of firing the first shot. It came on April 12 and was followed by round after round of cannon fire upon the fort, which surrendered the next day.

Thus the war began. Lincoln hadn't sought it; indeed he had taken pains—far too many for the likes of Frederick Douglass—to prevent it. But now that it had begun, by hostile action of the South Carolinians, he would match force with force, and then some. He called on the militias of the loyal states to rally to the Union and suppress the rebellion. Asking for seventy-five thousand volunteers, he said, "I appeal to all loyal citizens to favor, facilitate, and aid this effort to maintain the honor, the integrity, and the existence of our national Union and the perpetuity of popular government."

MONG THOSE ANSWERING Lincoln's call was George Kimball of Boston, who enrolled in the Second Massachusetts Infantry Battalion, nicknamed the Tigers. Boston felt a special ownership interest in the American republic, with roots running to the Boston Tea Party and the Battle of Bunker Hill. And as the hotbed of abolitionism, Boston took particular issue with a rebellion by slaveholders.

Shortly after George Kimball enlisted, the Tigers were repositioned to Fort Warren, an unfinished facility on one of the islands that guarded the entrance to Boston's harbor. "We found the great fortress in a wretched state, very much as its builders had left it, with huge piles of earth, brick and stone encumbering its broad parade-ground and filling many of its casements," Kimball recounted afterward. He and his comrades were put to work readying the place for war. "This involved a great deal of hard labor, which, the young men of the battalion being mainly of good social standing, was in strange contrast to former employments." Yet President Lincoln had called and they would do their part. "They were a light-hearted, whole-souled set of fellows, and therefore accepted the situation without reservations of any kind, although it did not seem to be exactly that kind of military glory they were just then so thirsty for."

To ease their labors, they did what people in comparable circumstances had done from time out of mind: they sang. "We had many good singers among us," said Kimball, "and as nothing so effectually drives away weariness, particularly among soldiers and sailors, as a cheerful spirit and a joyous song, we constantly worked under the inspiration of these blessed agencies. We lustily sang all the popular songs of the day, whether wielding the shovel, swinging the pick, trundling the wheelbarrow, or rolling the heavy stones away. During our long evenings in quarters, too, we sang almost constantly."

They ran through drinking songs to ballads and marches and hymns from church and revival meetings. A favorite from revivals was a tune called "Say, Brothers, Will You Meet Us?" The melody was easy to learn, the words even more so, consisting of a single line repeated three times, followed by a new line and then the chorus.

As it happened, one of the battalion members was a fun-loving Scotsman named John Brown. Bearing the same name as the martyred abolitionist, this John Brown was deliberately confused with the other. "If he made his appearance a few minutes late among the working squad, or was a little tardy in falling into the company line, he was sure to be greeted with such expressions as 'Come, old fellow, you ought to be at it if you are going to help us free the slaves'; or, 'This can't be John Brown—why, John Brown is dead.'" At some point one of the teasers, to emphasize that this John Brown couldn't be the other, declared, "Yes, yes, poor old John Brown is dead; his body lies mouldering in the grave."

It wasn't long before one of the songsters matched the John Brown line to the "Say, Brothers" tune. The result became a favorite among the Tigers at Fort Warren, who sang it among themselves and for visitors. An enterprising music publisher of Charlestown, Massachusetts, heard it; he printed and sold lyrics sheets, with new verses added. The gist, the part everyone heard and remembered and that soldiers for the Union subsequently sang as they marched off to battle, was

> *John Brown's body lies a-mouldering in the grave*
> *John Brown's body lies a-mouldering in the grave*
> *John Brown's body lies a-mouldering in the grave*
> *His soul is marching on!*

ABRAHAM LINCOLN GROANED anew when he heard the song. Lincoln had kept his distance from John Brown from the moment he learned of the Harpers Ferry raid; the last thing he wanted now was for his struggle to save the Union to be treated as an abolitionist crusade. Four more slave states had joined the original seven seceders after Fort Sumter and his call for volunteers, yet the remaining four—Delaware, Maryland, Kentucky and Missouri—were still loyal. To keep these border states loyal, and to keep the Union's capital from becoming an island in a Confederate sea, Lincoln needed to reassure them he wasn't going to take away their slaves. Soldiers singing about John Brown did nothing but make his job harder.

It was plenty hard as things were. Enlistments proceeded apace; Lincoln's request for seventy-five thousand volunteers was quickly oversubscribed by eager patriots like George Kimball, most of whom expected the conquest of the South to be a summer's outing, if that. They, and everyone else on the Union side, discovered the grim truth in July when a Confederate army met an advancing Union force on the banks of a creek called Bull Run near Manassas, Virginia. The Federals had the better of the first hour of fighting but fell apart under Confederate counterattack. "It is now generally admitted that it was one of the best-planned battles of the war, but one of the worst-fought," wrote William Sherman, who was wounded at Bull Run. "Our men had been told so often at home that all they had to do was make a bold appearance, and the rebels would run; and nearly all of us for the first time then heard the sound of cannon and muskets in anger, and saw the bloody scenes common to all battles, with which we were soon to be familiar. We had good organization, good men, but no cohesion, no real discipline, no respect for authority, no real knowledge of war. Both armies were fairly defeated, and whichever stood fast, the other would have run. Though the North was overwhelmed with mortification and shame, the South really had not much to boast of, for in the three or four hours of fighting their organization was so broken up that they did not and could not follow our army, when it was known to be in a state of disgraceful and causeless flight."

The defeat at Bull Run sobered all on the Union side. The South would not be intimidated by show nor beaten in a summer. Lincoln looked for a new general and found George McClellan. He got Congress to approve the enlistment of half a million troops, for three years rather than the three months of the first volunteers. When Confederate president Jefferson Davis responded with a similar call for an expansion of Southern forces, both sides began preparing for a long conflict.

BULL RUN AND its consequences cast a new light on the slavery question. Lincoln had hoped to suppress the rebellion quickly, without reference to slavery. When the rebellion persisted, and indeed thrived, the slavery question became harder to avoid. The abolitionists continued to hector him for not attacking the root cause of the conflict; even some of his generals thought they knew better than their commander in chief what to do about slavery. A month after Bull Run, John Frémont, now the general in charge of the Union's western theater, declared martial law in Missouri. Frémont had always been impetuous, and having married into the family of Thomas Benton, he felt a special responsibility for Missouri. As a career soldier, he possessed far more military experience than Lincoln. Finally, and not least, as the initial standard-bearer of the Republican party, he thought he was as attuned as Lincoln to what the newly governing party stood for. Unlike Lincoln, who sought to keep slavery out of the discussion of war aims, Frémont sought to bring it front and center—to force Lincoln's hand. And so, in declaring martial law in Missouri, he proclaimed the confiscation of the property of all who had taken arms against the Union, and added, "Their slaves, if any they have, are hereby declared free."

Lincoln didn't anger easily, but Frémont's attempted coup set him off. The president immediately jerked the general back. "There is great danger that the closing paragraph, in relation to the confiscation of property and the liberating slaves of traitorous owners, will alarm our Southern Union friends and turn them against us," he wrote to Frémont. To avoid embarrassment—for Frémont and for himself—he asked the general to modify that part of his decree so as to make it conform to a recent act by Congress allowing the emancipation of only those slaves employed in hostile service against the United States.

Frémont wasn't to be rebuked so easily. He replied to Lincoln that he had thought his policy appropriate when he announced it, and he still did. He would rescind the emancipation proclamation if the president directly ordered him to do so, but not otherwise.

Lincoln wasted no time and gave the order. When the president's letter was released to the press—by Frémont or, possibly, his ambitious wife—the general was widely perceived as fearless and the president as timid.

Lincoln ignored most of the criticism. But he thought Orville Browning, an Illinois Republican, should have known better. Browning had taken Stephen Douglas's seat in the Senate after Douglas suddenly fell ill and died. "Coming from you, I confess it astonishes me," Lincoln wrote to Browning. "That you should object to my adhering to a law which you had assisted in making, and presenting to me, less than a month before, is odd enough. But this is a very small part. Genl. Fremont's proclamation, as to confiscation of property, and the liberation of slaves, is *purely political,* and not within the range of *military* law, or necessity. If a commanding general finds a necessity to seize the farm of a private owner, for a pasture, an encampment, or a fortification, he has the right to do so, and to so hold it, as long as the necessity lasts; and this is within military law, because within military necessity. But to say the farm shall no longer belong to the owner or his heirs forever, and this as well when the farm is not needed for military purposes as when it is, is purely political, without the savor of military law about it. And the same is true of slaves. If the general needs them, he can seize them, and use them; but when the need is past, it is not for him to fix their permanent future condition. That must be settled according to laws made by law-makers, and not by military proclamations."

Frémont had gone dangerously far, Lincoln said. "The proclamation in the point in question, is simply 'dictatorship.' It assumes that the general may do *anything* he pleases—confiscate the lands and free the slaves of *loyal* people, as well as of disloyal ones. And going the whole figure I have no doubt would be more popular with some thoughtless people than that which has been done. But I cannot assume this reckless position, nor allow others to assume it on my responsibility. You speak of it as being the only means of *saving* the government. On the contrary it is itself the surrender of the government. Can it be pretended that it is any longer the government of the U.S.—any government of Constitution and laws—wherein a general, or a president, may make permanent rules of property by proclamation?"

Frémont's decree, ungrounded in law, was equally misguided as policy, Lincoln said. "No doubt the thing was popular in some quarters, and would have been more so if it had been a general declaration of emancipation." But it threw the administration's efforts in the border states into disarray. "The Kentucky legislature"—then considering a vote of confidence in the Union—"would not budge till that proclamation was modified; and Gen. Anderson telegraphed me that on the news of Gen. Fremont having actually issued deeds of manumission, a whole company of our volunteers threw down their arms and disbanded. I was so assured as to think it probable that the very arms we had furnished Kentucky would be turned against us. I think to lose Kentucky is nearly the same as to lose the whole game. Kentucky gone, we cannot hold Missouri, nor, as I think, Maryland. These all against us, and the job on our hands is too large for us. We would as well consent to separation at once, including the surrender of this capital."

FRÉMONT WASN'T the only general trying to force the president's hand. David Hunter tested Lincoln's patience on an almost-daily basis, complaining of being passed over for command positions to which he felt himself entitled. Lincoln declined to respond to most of the complaints but got fed up. "It is difficult to answer so ugly a letter in good temper," he replied to Hunter's latest screed, about what the general considered exile in Kansas. "I am, as you intimate, losing much of the great confidence I placed in you, not from any act or omission of yours touching the public service, up to the time you were sent to Leavenworth, but from the flood of grumbling despatches and letters I have seen from you since." Hunter was grousing that other officers had more troops under them than he did; to which Lincoln responded, "You are adopting the best possible way to ruin yourself. 'Act well your part, there all the honor lies.' He who does *something* at the head of one regiment, will eclipse him who does *nothing* at the head of a hundred."

Yet Hunter's carping, and his political connections, had an effect, and eventually Lincoln gave him a larger command, nominally including the states of South Carolina, Georgia and Florida. Hunter proceeded to provoke Lincoln once again, this time by proclaiming the emancipation of slaves in those states.

Angered but not entirely surprised, Lincoln at once rescinded the proclamation and disavowed Hunter. "I, Abraham Lincoln, President of the United States, proclaim and declare that the Government of the United States had no knowledge, information, or belief of an intention on the part of General Hunter to issue such a proclamation," Lincoln said. Emancipation was no part of the administration's agenda. "Neither General Hunter nor any other commander or person has been authorized by the government of the United States to make proclamations declaring the slaves of any state free."

YET THE PRESSURE on Lincoln to do something about slavery didn't ease. If anything, it grew stronger with each month the war went on. Lincoln could assert that the war was about the Union, not about slavery, and for him it was. But everyone, including Lincoln, knew that slavery was the underlying cause of the sectional division that had produced secession and the war. He had intended to save the Union first and deal with slavery later, if at all; with this strategy floundering, he tried to reverse the order.

But he had to do so constitutionally, which meant with the concurrence of the slave states. In early 1862, Lincoln resurrected the scheme he had proposed while in the House of Representatives for compensated emancipation. Then he had targeted the District of Columbia; now he aimed at the border states. The idea was to show a peaceful path to a post-slavery South, a path that might be trodden by the border states initially and the rebel states in time.

He moved gingerly. The initiative on emancipation, he said, would remain with the states, per the Constitution. But the federal government would provide money "to compensate for the inconveniences, public and private, produced by such change of system." Lincoln conceded congressional prerogatives. "If the proposition contained in the resolution does not meet the approval of Congress and the country, there is the end," he said. But he hoped Congress and the country would respond positively, and he explained why they should do so. "The federal government would find its highest interest in such a measure, as one of the most efficient means of self-preservation. The leaders of the existing insurrection entertain the hope that this government will ultimately be forced to acknowledge the independence of some part of the disaffected region, and that all the slave states north of such part will then say, 'The Union for which we have struggled being already gone, we now choose to go with the Southern section.' To deprive them of this hope substantially ends the rebellion, and the initiation of emancipation completely deprives them of it as to all the states initiating it."

Lincoln made clear he was not expecting miracles. "The point is not that all the states tolerating slavery would very soon, if at all, initiate emancipation; but that while the offer is equally made to all, the more northern shall by such initiation make it certain to the more southern that in no event will the former ever join the latter in their proposed confederacy." He stressed he was not proposing an overnight revolution. "I say 'initiation' because, in my judgment, gradual and not sudden emancipation is better for all. In the mere financial or pecuniary view any member of Congress with the census tables and Treasury reports before him can readily see for himself how very soon the current expenditures of this war would purchase, at fair valuation, all the slaves in any named state." Another nod to the Constitution: "Such a proposition on the part of the general government sets up no claim of a right by federal authority to interfere with slavery within state limits, referring, as it does, the absolute control of the subject in each case to the state and its people immediately interested. It is proposed as a matter of perfectly free choice with them."

But the choice wasn't *perfectly* free. Lincoln for the first time hinted that if measures like the one he proposed were not adopted, more drastic consequences might follow. "The Union must be preserved, and hence all indispensable means must be employed," he said. "War has been made and continues to be an indispensable means to this end." The states in rebellion could end the war at once, simply by acknowledging the authority of the federal government. "If, however, resistance continues, the war must also continue; and it is impossible to foresee all the incidents which may attend and all the ruin which may follow it. Such as may seem indispensable or may obviously promise great efficiency toward ending the struggle must and will come." Speaking to slaveholders, he added, "I hope it may be esteemed no offense to ask whether the pecuniary consideration tendered would not be of more value to the states and private persons concerned than are the institution and property in it in the present aspect of affairs."

Lincoln didn't expect a swift embrace of his proposal, and he didn't get it. Congress endorsed his resolution as a statement of purpose but provided no money to fund it. Members weren't eager to ask their constituents, many of whom cared little about slavery, to reward the slaveholders for having started the war. More than a few skeptics simply worried at the expense.

Answering the expense complaint, Lincoln elaborated on the arithmetic lesson he had given. "Have you noticed the facts that less than one half-day's cost of this war would pay for all the slaves in Delaware, at four hundred dollars per head?" he inquired of one cost-counter. "That eighty-seven days cost of this war would pay for all in Delaware, Maryland, District of Columbia, Kentucky, and Missouri at the same price? Were those states to take the step, do you doubt that it would shorten the war more than eighty-seven days, and thus be an actual saving of expense."

Legislators from the border states, whose support would be crucial to the success of any paid-emancipation scheme, were adamantly opposed. To them Lincoln made a personal plea. "Gentlemen," he said, "after the adjournment of Congress, now very near, I shall have no opportunity of seeing you for several months. Believing that you of the border-states hold more power for good than any other equal number of members, I feel it a duty which I cannot justifiably waive, to make this appeal to you." He reiterated that compensated emancipation, if only in the border states, could end the war. "Let the states which are in rebellion see, definitely and certainly, that, in no event, will the states you represent ever join their proposed confederacy, and they cannot much longer maintain the contest. But you cannot divest them of their hope to ultimately have you with them so long as you show a determination to perpetuate the institution within your own states. Beat them at elections, as you have overwhelmingly done, and, nothing daunted, they still claim you as their own. You and I know what the lever of their power is. Break that lever before their faces, and they can shake you no more forever."

Lincoln appealed to the border-staters' self-interest. "Can you, for your states, do better than to take the course I urge?" he asked. "Discarding punctilio and maxims adapted to more manageable times, and looking only to the unprecedentedly stern facts of our case, can you do better in any possible event?" The border states must face reality. "If the war continue long, as it must, if the object be not sooner attained, the institution in your states will be extinguished by mere friction and abrasion—by the mere incidents of the war. It will be gone, and you will have nothing valuable in lieu of it."

Lincoln spoke softly, but his words carried a warning his listeners couldn't miss. "How much better for you, and for your people, to take the step which at once shortens the war and secures substantial compensation for that which is sure to be wholly lost in any other event. How much better to thus save the money which else we sink forever in the war. How much better to do it while we can, lest the war ere long render us pecuniarily unable to do it. How much better for you, as seller, and the nation, as buyer, to sell out and buy out that without which the war could never have been, than to sink both the thing to be sold and the price of it in cutting one another's throats."

Lincoln remarked that for more than a year he had resisted demands to strike directly at slavery. He couldn't resist forever. "The pressure in this direction is still upon me, and is increasing." There was yet time for men of vision to do the right thing. "You are patriots and statesmen; and, as such, I pray you, consider this proposition; and, at the least, commend it to the consideration of your states and people." The fate of democracy was in their hands. "Our common country is in great peril, demanding the loftiest views and boldest action to bring it speedy relief. Once relieved, its form of government is saved to the world; its beloved history and cherished memories are vindicated; and its happy future fully assured and rendered inconceivably grand. To you, more than to any others, the privilege is given, to assure that happiness and swell that grandeur, and to link your own names therewith forever."

LEAVING THE BORDER MEN to ponder, Lincoln sent a draft bill to the Senate and House spelling out a program of compensated emancipation. Any state that accepted his offer would receive 6 percent bonds from the U.S. government in amount equal to the number of slaves in that state, according to the 1860 census, multiplied by a dollar figure per slave to be established by Congress—probably around four hundred dollars. A state that adopted immediate emancipation would receive the full amount at once; a state that chose gradual emancipation would receive its bonds by installments. Should any state renege and reinstitute slavery, its bonds would be declared null and void.

Lincoln's bill was received, read and printed. And then it was set aside to gather dust. Congress remained to be convinced.

Yet the effort wasn't wholly in vain. The legislature approved and funded a program for compensated emancipation in the District of Columbia. The few thousand slaves freed as a result were small in number beside the millions on the plantations of the Deep South, but Lincoln was pleased at the symbolism. "I have never doubted the constitutional authority of Congress to abolish slavery in this District," he declared on signing the measure. "And I have ever desired to see the national capital freed from the institution in some satisfactory way." He recalled that he had proposed this very thing during his time in Congress many years earlier; now the deed was done.

A STUMBLING BLOCK in the politics of emancipation, even among many abolitionists, had long been the question of what to do with the freed slaves. No example existed of a successful biracial republic, and most Americans found such an entity hard to imagine. Lincoln, with many others, supported colonization in Africa or perhaps Central America—anywhere outside the United States. He persuaded Congress to appropriate money to encourage colonization; the emancipation law for the District of Columbia granted one hundred dollars to each former slave who emigrated. Colonization wasn't popular among blacks, who had little desire to leave the only country they had ever known. So Lincoln tried to change their minds. He summoned leaders of the free black community to the White House.

"Why should the people of your race be colonized?" he asked rhetorically. "Why should they leave this country?" His answer was straightforward. "You and we are different races. We have between us a broader difference than exists between almost any other two races.

Whether it is right or wrong I need not discuss, but this physical difference is a great disadvantage to us both, as I think your race suffer very greatly, many of them by living among us, while ours suffer from your presence. In a word, we suffer on each side. If this is admitted, it affords a reason at least why we should be separated."

Lincoln acknowledged the evil done to Americans of African descent. "Your race are suffering, in my judgment, the greatest wrong inflicted on any people." The wrong began with slavery, but it didn't end there. "Even when you cease to be slaves, you are yet far removed from being placed on an equality with the white race. You are cut off from many of the advantages which the other race enjoy. The aspiration of men is to enjoy equality with the best when free, but on this broad continent, not a single man of your race is made the equal of a single man of ours. Go where you are treated the best, and the ban is still upon you."

Blacks weren't the only ones who suffered. "I need not recount to you the effects upon white men growing out of the institution of slavery," Lincoln said. "See our present condition—the country engaged in war!—our white men cutting one another's throats, none knowing how far it will extend." Blacks weren't at fault for the war, yet they were deeply involved in its origin. "But for your race among us there could not be war, although many men engaged on either side do not care for you one way or the other." Lincoln reiterated for emphasis, "Without the institution of slavery and the colored race as a basis, the war could not have an existence."

"It is better for us both, therefore, to be separated," he went on. "I know that there are free men among you who, even if they could better their condition, are not as much inclined to go out of the country as those who, being slaves, could obtain their freedom on this condition. I suppose one of the principal difficulties in the way of colonization is that the free colored man cannot see that his comfort would be advanced by it. You may believe you can live in Washington or elsewhere in the United States the remainder of your life as easily, perhaps more so, than you can in any foreign country, and hence you may come to the conclusion that you have nothing to do with the idea of going to a foreign country."

Lincoln paused. "This is—I speak in no unkind sense—an extremely selfish view of the case," he said. "You ought to do something to help those who are not so fortunate as yourselves." Lincoln asserted that most whites wouldn't support emancipation if they thought it meant having to live side by side with free blacks. By emigrating, therefore, black people already free would render emancipation easier. "You would open a wide door for many to be made free." They meanwhile would increase colonization's chances of success. "If we deal with those who are not free at the beginning, and whose intellects are clouded by slavery, we have very poor materials to start with. If intelligent colored men, such as are before me, would move in this matter, much might be accomplished."

N EITHER COMPENSATED emancipation nor colonization answered the basic demand of the abolitionists. They wanted Lincoln to cut the Gordian knot and abolish slavery at once. Congress
handed the president Alexander's sword in the form of legislation per-
mitting the confiscation of rebel property, including slaves. The first
Confiscation Act, of August 1861, specified slaves in the actual service
of the Confederate military; the second, of July 1862, broadened the
permission to include all slaves of Confederate civilian and military
officials.

Yet Lincoln still had reservations, which he expressed to the
numerous individuals and groups who urged him to declare war on
slavery. To a delegation of Quakers who came to the White House,
Lincoln said he agreed with them that slavery was wrong. But proclaiming emancipation might do no good. "If a decree of emancipation could abolish slavery, John Brown would have done the work
effectually," he said. "Such a decree surely could not be more binding
upon the South than the Constitution, and that cannot be enforced
in that part of the country now. Would a proclamation of freedom be
any more effective?"

The Quakers rejoined that it would have a positive moral effect.
Lincoln allowed that it might, but it would create practical problems,
of which he had too many as things stood. The Quakers persisted,
saying they hoped God would guide him to issue a proclamation soon.

Lincoln acknowledged his need for divine guidance. He said he
sometimes felt he might be an instrument in God's hands for the
accomplishment of a great work. He certainly was not unwilling to

be that instrument. But he wasn't sure God saw things the way the Quakers did.

To a group of Presbyterians, Lincoln declared that there was no difference between them and him on the immorality of slavery. "Had slavery no existence among us, and were the question asked, Shall we adopt such an institution?, we should agree as to the reply which should be made," he said. He went on, "If there be any diversity in our views it is not as to whether we should receive slavery when free from it, but as to how we may best get rid of it already amongst us. Were an individual asked whether he would wish to have a wen on his neck, he could not hesitate as to the reply; but were it asked whether a man who has such a wen should at once be relieved of it by the application of the surgeon's knife, there might be diversity of opinion; perhaps the man might bleed to death as the result of such an operation."

FREDERICK DOUGLASS GREW more infuriated with Lincoln by the month. It was bad enough that the president had tried to appease the South when secession was simply a matter of words, but now the slave masters were at open war with the Union, and still he refused to strike at the source of their power. Douglass took the occasion of the Fourth of July in 1862 to excoriate Lincoln for his failure to confront the central challenge of the war. "It is by what President Lincoln has done in reference to slavery since he assumed the reins of government that we are to know what he is likely to do, and deems best to do," Douglass told his audience. "We all know how he came into power. He was elected and inaugurated as the representative of the antislavery policy of the Republican party. He had laid down and maintained the doctrine that liberty and slavery were the great antagonistic political elements in this country. That the Union of these states could not long continue half free and half slave, that they must in the end be all free or all slave." Lincoln at that time had made the right and honorable choice. "In the conflict between these two elements he arrayed himself on the side of freedom, and was elected with a view to the ascendancy of free principles."

This made the current Lincoln harder to understand. "I do not hesitate to say that whatever may have been his intentions, the action of President Lincoln has been calculated in a marked and decided way to shield and protect slavery from the very blows which its horrible crimes have loudly and persistently invited," Douglass said. The administration's policy regarding the Union and slavery was woefully misguided. "That policy is simply and solely to reconstruct the Union on the old and corrupting basis of compromise, by which slavery shall retain all the power that it ever had, with the full assurance of gaining more, according to its future necessities."

Nothing could be more fatuous or repugnant, Douglass said. "What does this policy of bringing back the Union imply? It implies, first of all, that the slave states will promptly and cordially, and without the presence of compulsory and extraneous force, cooperate with the free states under the very Constitution which they have openly repudiated and attempted to destroy." And it would leave unaddressed the problem that had split the Union in the first place. "While slavery lasts at the South, it will remain hereafter as heretofore the great dominating interest, overtopping all others, and shaping the sentiments, and opinions of the people in accordance with itself. We are not to flatter ourselves that because slavery has brought great troubles upon the South by this war that therefore the people of the South will be stirred up against it. If we can bear with slavery after the calamities it has brought upon us, we may expect that the South will be no less patient. Indeed we may rationally expect that the South will be more devoted to slavery than ever. The blood and treasure poured out in its defense will tend to increase its sacredness in the eyes of Southern people, and if slavery comes out of this struggle, and is retaken under the forms of old compromises, the country will witness a greater amount of insolence and bluster in favor of the slave system, than was ever shown before in or out of Congress."

Lincoln must come to see what the rest of the world saw so clearly. "Recognize the fact, for it is the great fact, and never more palpable than at the present moment, that the only choice left to this nation, is abolition or destruction. You must abolish slavery or abandon the Union. It is plain that there can never be any union between the North and the South while the South values slavery more than nationality. A union of interest is essential to a union of ideas, and without this union of ideas, the outward form of the union will be but as a rope of sand."

The president said that the Union came first, that he must suppress the rebellion before he could reach slavery. This stood things on their head, Douglass retorted. "It is far more true to say that we cannot reach the rebellion until we have suppressed slavery. For slavery is the life of the rebellion. Let the loyal army but inscribe upon its banner Emancipation and Protection to all who will rally under it, and no power could prevent a stampede from slavery, such as the world has not witnessed since the Hebrews crossed the Red Sea. I am convinced that this rebellion and slavery are twin monsters, and that they must fall or flourish together, and that all attempts at upholding one while putting down the other, will be followed by continued trains of darkening calamities."

The president must come to a decision. "This slavery-begotten and slavery-sustained and slavery-animated war has now cost this nation more than a hundred thousand lives, and more than five hundred millions of treasure," Douglass reminded Lincoln. "The question is, shall this stupendous and most outrageous war be finally and forever ended? Or shall it be merely suspended for a time, and again revived with increased and aggravated fury in the future?" The choice was stark. "By urging upon the nation the necessity and duty of putting an end to slavery, you put an end to the war, and put an end to the cause of the war, and make any repetition of it impossible. But just take back the pet monster again into the bosom of the nation, proclaim an amnesty to the slaveholders, let them have their slaves, and command your services in helping to catch and hold them, and so sure as like causes will ever produce like effects, you will hand down to your children here, and hereafter, born and to be born all the horrors through which you are now passing."

HORACE GREELEY'S AUDIENCE WAS larger than that of Frederick Douglass. The *New York Tribune* was the most popular paper in the nation's most populous city, and it gave Greeley the nation's largest platform for registering his dismay at Lincoln's failure to challenge slavery directly. "Dear sir," he wrote in an open letter in August

1862, "I do not intrude to tell you—for you must know already—
that a great proportion of those who triumphed in your election, and
of all who desire the unqualified suppression of the rebellion now
devastating our country, are sorely disappointed and deeply pained
by the policy you seem to be pursuing with regard to the slaves of
rebels. I write only to set succinctly and unmistakably before you what
we require, what we think we have a right to expect, and of what we
complain."

The president must "EXECUTE THE LAWS," Greeley stressed. These
included the most recent confiscation law. "We think you are strangely
and disastrously remiss in the discharge of your official and imperative
duty with regard to the emancipating provisions of the new Confiscation Act. Those provisions were designed to fight slavery with liberty. They prescribe that men loyal to the Union, and willing to shed
their blood in her behalf, shall no longer be held, with the nation's
consent, in bondage to persistent, malignant traitors, who for twenty
years have been plotting and for sixteen months have been fighting to
divide and destroy our country. Why these traitors should be treated
with tenderness by you, to the prejudice of the dearest rights of loyal
men, we cannot conceive."

Another group did almost as much damage. "We think you are
unduly influenced by the counsels, the representations, the menaces,
of certain fossil politicians hailing from the border slave states," Greeley said. These planters and their lackeys did not represent the people
of those states generally, and they abetted the Confederacy. By tip-
toeing around them, Lincoln damaged the Union cause. "Whatever
strengthens or fortifies slavery in the border states strengthens also
treason," Greeley said.

Greeley demanded decisive action. "It is the duty of a government
so wantonly, wickedly assailed by rebellion as ours has been to oppose
force to force in a defiant, dauntless spirit. It cannot afford to temporize
with traitors nor with semi-traitors. It must not bribe them to behave
themselves, nor make them fair promises in the hope of disarming
their causeless hostility." Lincoln should have dealt with slavery from
the start. "Had you, sir, in your inaugural address, unmistakably given
notice that in case the rebellion already commenced were persisted in,
and your efforts to preserve the Union and enforce the laws should be

resisted by armed force, *you would recognize no loyal person as rightfully held in slavery by a traitor,* we believe the rebellion would therein have received a staggering if not fatal blow." Most Southerners at that time were Unionists at heart, Greeley contended. But they needed support from the president of the Union. Instead they got hesitation and bumbling. The secessionists took courage, the Unionists warning. "Every coward in the South soon became a traitor from fear, for loyalty was perilous, while treason seemed comparatively safe."

Yet it wasn't too late. The president should now say what he hadn't said at the start: that slaves held by rebels were no longer slaves at all. The Confiscation Act gave him the authority; he simply had to use it.

The cause of the country demanded no less. "On the face of this wide earth, Mr. President, there is not one disinterested, determined, intelligent champion of the Union cause who does not feel that all attempts to put down the rebellion and at the same time uphold its inciting cause are preposterous and futile—that the rebellion, if crushed out tomorrow, would be renewed within a year if slavery were left in full vigor—that army officers who remain to this day devoted to slavery can at best be but half-way loyal to the Union—and that every hour of deference to slavery is an hour of added and deepened peril to the Union."

LINCOLN OWED GREELEY thanks for sabotaging Seward at the Chicago convention, and he recognized the reach of the *Tribune.* He also understood Greeley's generous self-regard. And so even as he gave the editor an exclusive story, in the form of a written response, he twitted Greeley's pomposity. "I have just read yours of the 19th addressed to myself through the New-York Tribune," he wrote in a letter for publication. "If there be in it any statements, or assumptions of fact, which I may know to be erroneous, I do not, now and here, controvert them. If there be in it any inferences which I may believe to be falsely drawn, I do not now and here, argue against them. If there be perceptible in it an impatient and dictatorial tone, I waive it in deference to an old friend, whose heart I have always supposed to be right."

Lincoln turned to the central issue. "As to the policy I 'seem to be pursuing,' as you say, I have not meant to leave anyone in doubt. I would save the Union. I would save it the shortest way under the Constitution. The sooner the national authority can be restored, the nearer the Union will be the Union as it was. Broken eggs can never be mended, and the longer the breaking proceeds, the more will be broken." Reconsidering, Lincoln backtracked and crossed out the last sentence. This would be read as a state paper; he didn't want to sound colloquial.

Greeley had linked slavery to the struggle for the Union. Lincoln tried to disentangle the questions. "If there be those who would not save the Union unless they could at the same time *save* slavery, I do not agree with them. If there be those who would not save the Union unless they could at the same time *destroy* slavery, I do not agree with them. My paramount object in this struggle *is* to save the Union, and is *not* either to save or to destroy slavery."

Realizing his letter would be excerpted, Lincoln put the matter more succinctly. "If I could save the Union without freeing *any* slave, I would do it; and if I could save it by freeing *all* the slaves I would do it; and if I could save it by freeing some and leaving others alone I would also do that." He reemphasized his priorities. "What I do about slavery, and the colored race, I do because I believe it helps to save the Union; and what I forbear, I forbear because I do *not* believe it would help to save the Union. I shall do *less* whenever I shall believe what I am doing hurts the cause, and I shall do *more* whenever I shall believe doing more will help the cause. I shall try to correct errors when shown to be errors; and I shall adopt new views so fast as they shall appear to be true views."

Yet Lincoln didn't want Greeley's readers to think him an agnostic on slavery. "I have here stated my purpose according to my view of *official* duty," he closed. "I intend no modification of my oft-expressed *personal* wish that all men everywhere could be free."

LINCOLN'S RESPONSE GAVE the abolitionists nothing. Sixteen months into the war, the president seemed no closer to striking at the root of the conflict. A delegation of clergymen from Chicago delivered a memorial, or petition, imploring him to change course.

Lincoln read their paper and listened to their arguments. He assured them he had thought the slavery question over very carefully for many months. Yet he could find no easy solution. "I am approached with the most opposite opinions and advice, and that by religious men, who are equally certain that they represent the divine will," he said. "I am sure that either the one or the other class is mistaken in that belief, and perhaps in some respects both. I hope it will not be irreverent for me to say that if it is probable that God would reveal his will to others, on a point so connected with my duty, it might be supposed he would reveal it directly to me, for, unless I am more deceived in myself than I often am, it is my earnest desire to know the will of Providence in this matter. And if I can learn what it is I will do it."

He smiled sadly. "These are not, however, the days of miracles, and I suppose it will be granted that I am not to expect a direct revelation. I must study the plain physical facts of the case, ascertain what is possible and learn what appears to be wise and right. The subject is difficult, and good men do not agree. For instance, the other day four gentlemen of standing and intelligence from New York called, as a delegation, on business connected with the war, but before leaving, two of them earnestly beset me to proclaim general emancipation, upon which the other two at once attacked them! You know, also, that the last session of Congress had a decided majority of antislavery men, yet they could not unite on this policy. And the same is true of the religious people. Why, the rebel soldiers are praying with a great deal more earnestness, I fear, than our own troops, and expecting God to favor their side, for one of our soldiers who had been taken prisoner told Senator Wilson a few days since that he met with nothing so discouraging as the evident sincerity of those he was among in their prayers."

But Lincoln's visitors, having coming all the way to Washington, deserved more than this. "We will talk over the merits of the case," he said. "What *good* would a proclamation of emancipation from me do, especially as we are now situated? I do not want to issue a document that the whole world will see must necessarily be inoperative, like the Pope's bull against the comet! Would my *word* free the slaves, when I cannot even enforce the Constitution in the rebel states? Is there a single court, or magistrate, or individual that would be influenced by it there? And what reason is there to think it would have any greater effect upon the slaves than the late law of Congress, which I approved, and which offers protection and freedom to the slaves of rebel masters who come within our lines? Yet I cannot learn that that law has caused a single slave to come over to us. And suppose they could be induced by a proclamation of freedom from me to throw themselves upon us—*what should we do with them?* How can we feed and care for such a multitude?"

He asked his visitors to think carefully about the course they advocated. "Tell me, if you please, what possible result of good would follow the issuing of such a proclamation as you desire? Understand, I raise no objections against it on legal or constitutional grounds, for as commander-in-chief of the army and navy in time of war, I suppose I have a right to take any measure which may best subdue the enemy. Nor do I urge objections of a moral nature in view of possible consequences of insurrection and massacre at the South." Lincoln let his visitors mull these consequences for a moment. He resumed: "I view the matter as a practical war measure, to be decided upon according to the advantages or disadvantages it may offer to the suppression of the rebellion."

Lincoln's guests said again that the rebellion was about slavery and that until he challenged slavery he'd never defeat it. They emphasized the moral effect in Europe of an emancipation proclamation. Such a proclamation would energize the North and weaken the South.

Lincoln listened patiently. "I admit that slavery is the root of the rebellion, or at least its *sine qua non*," he said. "The ambition of politicians may have instigated them to act, but they would have been impotent without slavery as their instrument. I will also concede that emancipation would help us in Europe, and convince them that we are incited by something more than ambition." Britain had close commercial ties to the South, yet it was adamantly opposed to slavery. Emancipation would all but guarantee that the British—and the French, who were following Britain's lead on the American conflict—would not back the Confederacy against the Union. Lincoln continued, "I grant further that it would help *somewhat* at the North, though not so much, I fear, as you and those you represent imagine. Still, some additional strength would be added in that way to the war. And then unquestionably it would weaken the rebels by drawing off their laborers, which is of great importance."

Yet he couldn't get past the problems. "I am not so sure we could do much with the blacks. If we were to arm them, I fear that in a few weeks the arms would be in the hands of the rebels; and indeed thus far we have not had arms enough to equip our white troops. I will mention another thing, though it meet only your scorn and contempt: There are fifty thousand bayonets in the Union armies from the border slave states. It would be a serious matter if, in consequence of a proclamation such as you desire, they should go over to the rebels."

He refused to yield the moral ground to his visitors. "Let me say one thing more: I think you should admit that we already have an important principle to rally and unite the people in the fact that constitutional government is at stake. This is a fundamental idea, going down about as deep as anything."

But he didn't want to leave them bereft. "Do not misunderstand me because I have mentioned these objections," he concluded. "They indicate the difficulties that have thus far prevented my action in some such way as you desire. I have not decided against a proclamation of liberty to the slaves, but hold the matter under advisement. And I can assure you that the subject is on my mind, by day and night, more than any other. Whatever shall appear to be God's will I will do."

LINCOLN'S REFERENCE to God wasn't simply for the benefit of the visiting clergy. He had never been conspicuously religious, but as the casualties mounted, he couldn't help wondering if Providence had ordained America's struggle. "The will of God prevails," he mused in a note to himself. "In great contests each party claims to act in accordance with the will of God. Both *may* be, and one *must* be wrong. God cannot be *for* and *against* the same thing at the same time. In the present civil war it is quite possible that God's purpose is something different from the purpose of either party—and yet the human instrumentalities, working just as they do, are of the best adaptation to effect His purpose. I am almost ready to say this is probably true—

that God wills this contest, and wills that it shall not end yet. By his mere quiet power, on the minds of the now contestants, He could have either *saved* or *destroyed* the Union without a human contest. Yet the contest began. And having begun He could give the final victory to either side any day. Yet the contest proceeds."

WITHOUT TELLING Frederick Douglass, Horace Greeley or the
visiting clerics, Lincoln prepared for the moment when his policy might change. The hectic pace of the war had transformed
the White House from a quiet residence to a cockpit of command,
with staff and messengers coming and going constantly. To escape the
frenzy, Lincoln took refuge in the telegraph office of the war department, a short distance away. One morning in the summer of 1862
he asked Major Thomas Eckert, whose desk he commandeered, for
writing paper. "I procured some foolscap and handed it to him," Eckert recalled. "He then sat down and began to write." Eckert watched
discreetly. "He would look out of the window a while and then put
his pen to paper, but he did not write much at once. He would study
between times and when he had made up his mind he would put
down a line or two, and then sit quiet for a few minutes."

Even in this hideaway the war intruded. Couriers brought messages and carried messages away. Another distraction was less weighty.
An extensive spiderweb filled part of the interstice between one set of
the double-paned windows. Eckert had informally enlisted the builders. "Lincoln commented on the web and I told him that my lieutenants would soon report and pay their respects to the president," he
recounted. "Not long after, a big spider appeared at the crossroads and
tapped several times on the strands, whereupon five or six others came
out from different directions. Then what seemed to be a great confab
took place, after which they separated, each on a separate strand of
the web."

The president returned to his writing, yet didn't appear to accomplish much. "On the first day Lincoln did not cover one sheet of his

special writing paper," Eckert recalled. "When ready to leave, he asked me to take charge of what he had written and not allow anyone to see it." Eckert said he certainly would.

Lincoln returned the next day, and nearly every day for weeks. "Sometimes he would not write more than a line or two, and once I observed that he had put question marks on the margin of what he had written. He would read over each day all the matter he had previously written and revise it, studying carefully each sentence."

Eckert's curiosity rose with each presidential visit. But he resisted the temptation to read Lincoln's draft, and his curiosity wasn't assuaged until Lincoln put down his pen with an air of finality. "For the first time he told me that he had been writing an order giving freedom to the slaves in the South, for the purpose of hastening the end of the war," Eckert said.

LINCOLN WAS FAR from sure his idea would work. "Things had gone from bad to worse, until I felt that we had reached the end of our rope on the plan of operations we had been pursuing; that we had about played our last card, and must change our tactics or lose the game," Lincoln later explained to Francis Carpenter, a portrait painter for whom Lincoln was then sitting. "I now determined upon the adoption of the emancipation policy; and without consultation with or the knowledge of the cabinet, I prepared the original draft of the proclamation, and after much anxious thought called a cabinet meeting upon the subject."

The meeting went about as Lincoln anticipated. "I said to the cabinet that I had resolved upon this step, and had not called them together to seek their advice but to lay the subject matter of a proclamation before them." He read the proclamation and asked for comments. He heard nothing he hadn't already thought of—the proclamation might disturb the congressional elections; it should say something about arming the slaves who came to Union lines—until William Seward spoke up. "Mr. President," said Seward, "I approve of the proclamation, but I question the expediency of its issue at this juncture. The depression of the public mind, consequent upon our repeated reverses, is so great that I fear the effect of so important a step. It may be viewed as the last measure of an exhausted government, a cry for help—the government stretching forth its hands to Ethiopia instead of Ethiopia stretching forth her hands to the government." Lincoln afterward summarized Seward's view: "It would be considered our last shriek in the retreat." Seward recommended holding off until Union forces won an important victory.

"The wisdom of the view of the secretary of state struck me with very great force," Lincoln recounted. "It was an aspect of the case that in all my thought upon the subject I had entirely overlooked." The president agreed to put the proclamation aside, awaiting a battlefield turn for the better.

BUT THINGS GOT WORSE. In the last days of August a Union army under John Pope attempted to regain the honor lost at Bull Run the previous summer, in the same locale. The second Battle of Bull Run proved even more disastrous than the first as the Confederates under Robert E. Lee and Thomas Jackson—now called Stonewall for his stout resistance at Bull Run the year before—routed the Federals and sent them running again.

Lincoln took the news hard. "The President was in deep distress," wrote Edward Bates, the attorney general, following a cabinet meeting after the battle. "He seemed wrung by the bitterest anguish—said he felt almost ready to hang himself."

"Things looked darker than ever," Lincoln himself recalled, according to Francis Carpenter. The president wasn't sure if he'd ever get the victory he needed to release his emancipation proclamation. Lee followed his victory at Bull Run with a strike into Maryland. Congressional elections were approaching, and Lee hoped, by carrying the war into Union territory and threatening the Union capital, to shake the confidence of Northern voters in Lincoln.

It was a risky move. Union commander George McClellan, whose reluctance to fight had frustrated Lincoln so far, now had no choice. And he had nearly twice as many troops as Lee, with the advantages of interior lines of supply and communication. The battle could go either way, with the war perhaps in the balance.

The contest, fought on the banks of Antietam Creek, proved a bloodbath. The two sides together suffered more than twenty thousand casualties, about equally divided. It was the most savage day in American military history, before or after. Because the invaders required a victory to maintain their momentum, the draw amounted to a defeat, and Lee was forced to head back to Virginia. Lincoln hoped for news that McClellan was pursuing Lee to seal the victory and crush the rebellion.

He meanwhile decided the time had come. "I determined to wait no longer," he recalled. He made a few final corrections to his draft and regathered the cabinet. He read his proclamation and published it two days later. Citing his authority as president of the United States and, conspicuously, as "Commander in Chief of the Army and Navy thereof," Lincoln reiterated that his primary goal remained the preservation of the Union. He said he would again urge Congress to approve a program for compensated emancipation. He would continue to encourage colonization of American blacks abroad.

And then the crucial part: "On the 1st day of January, A.D. 1863, all persons held as slaves within any state or designated part of state the people whereof shall then be in rebellion against the United States shall be then, thenceforward, and forever free; and the executive government of the United States, including the military and naval authority thereof, will recognize and maintain the freedom of such persons and will do no act or acts to repress such persons, or any of them, in any efforts they may make for their actual freedom."

FOR A STATEMENT so eagerly awaited by so many, Lincoln's proclamation was off-puttingly dry, scarcely befitting the momentous decision it announced. Readers would hardly guess at the hours Lincoln had spent in its drafting.

Yet that dryness hadn't come easily; aridity was the aim of the effort expended. Lincoln characterized emancipation as a technical matter, a matter of military necessity. He understood that his words freed few slaves at once, for it exempted slaves in places *not* in rebellion, where his power matched his authority. Even saying as much as he did, in the operative paragraph, came hard. "When I finished reading this paragraph," he told Francis Carpenter, referring to the pre-proclamation cabinet meeting, "Mr. Seward stopped me and said, 'I think, Mr. President, that you should insert after the word "recognize," in that sentence, the words "and maintain."' I replied that I had already fully considered the import of that expression in this connection, but I had not introduced it, because it was not my way to promise what I was not entirely sure that I could perform, and I was not prepared to say that I thought we were exactly able to 'maintain' this. But Seward insisted that we ought to take this ground, and the words finally went in."

FREDERICK DOUGLASS AT LAST had something to praise Lincoln for. "We shout for joy that we live to record this righteous decree," he declared. "'Free forever' oh! long enslaved millions, whose cries have so vexed the air and sky, suffer on a few more days in sorrow, the hour of your great deliverance draws nigh! oh! ye millions of free and loyal men who have earnestly sought to free your bleeding country from the dreadful ravages of revolution and anarchy, lift up now your voices with joy and thanksgivings for with freedom to the slave will come peace and safety to your country."

Douglass appreciated the problems ahead. "Opinions will widely differ as to the practical effect of this measure upon the war. All that class at the North who have not lost their affection for slavery will regard the measure as the very worst that could be devised, and as likely to lead to endless mischief. All their plans for the future have been projected with a view to a reconstruction of the American government upon the basis of compromise between slaveholding and non-slaveholding states." They would urge Lincoln to retract the proclamation or at least ignore its implications.

Douglass hadn't lost his distrust of Lincoln, but he thought the president would resist such pressure. "Abraham Lincoln may be slow, Abraham Lincoln may desire peace even at the price of leaving our terrible national sore untouched to fester on for generations, but Abraham Lincoln is not the man to reconsider, retract and contradict words and purposes solemnly proclaimed over his official signature."

Emancipation brought the world to the Union side, Douglass declared. "The effect of this paper upon the disposition of Europe will be great and increasing. It changes the character of the war in European eyes and gives it an important principle as an object, instead of national pride and interest. It recognizes, and declares the real nature of the contest, and places the North on the side of justice and civilization, and the rebels on the side of robbery and barbarism. It will disarm all purpose on the part of European Government to intervene in favor of the rebels and thus cast off at a blow one source of rebel power."

Whether the proclamation actually abolished slavery depended on two things, Douglass said. "The first is that the slave states shall be in rebellion on and after the first day of January 1863, and the second is we must have the ability to put down that rebellion." The Confederates could still frustrate emancipation by suspending military operations. Douglass hoped they would not, and didn't think they would. "The South is thoroughly in earnest and confident. It has staked everything upon the rebellion. Its experience thus far in the field has rather increased its hopes of final success than diminished them. Its armies now hold us at bay at all points, and the war is confined to the border states, slave and free." This wouldn't change in the next few months. "Whoever therefore, lives to see the first day of next January, should Abraham Lincoln be then alive and president of the United States, may confidently look in the morning papers for the final proclamation, granting freedom, and freedom forever, to all slaves within the rebel states."

As to the ability of the Union to defeat the rebellion, Douglass was even more confident, now that the North had right on its side. "We have full power to put down the rebellion. Unless one man is more than a match for four, unless the South breeds braver and better men than the North, unless slavery is more precious than liberty, unless a just cause kindles a feebler enthusiasm than a wicked and villainous one, the men of the loyal states will put down this rebellion and slavery, and all the sooner will they put down that rebellion by coupling slavery with that object. Tenderness towards slavery has been the loyal weakness during the war. Fighting the slaveholders with one hand and holding the slaves with the other has been fairly tried and has failed. We have now inaugurated a wiser and better policy, a policy which is better for the loyal cause than an hundred thousand armed men."

LINCOLN'S PROCLAMATION BROUGHT a crowd of celebrants to the White House. They gathered beneath his window and shouted hurrahs for the proclamation and its author. Lincoln had never liked to speak extemporaneously, and he didn't want to speak now, but the throng wouldn't leave until he made at least a modest statement. "I appear before you to do little more than acknowledge the courtesy you pay me, and to thank you for it," he said. "I have not been distinctly informed why it is this occasion you appear to do me this honor, though I suppose it is because of the proclamation."

Loud applause and shouts confirmed his supposition.

"What I did, I did after very full deliberation, and under a very heavy and solemn sense of responsibility," Lincoln continued.

More cheers, and shouts of "Good! God bless you!"

"I can only trust in God I have made no mistake."

"No mistake! . . . Go ahead, you're right!"

"I shall make no attempt on this occasion to sustain what I have done or said by any comment," Lincoln said.

"That's unnecessary; we understand it!"

"It is now for the country and the world to pass judgment on it, and, maybe, to take action on it."

"That's so!"

Lincoln segued to praise the soldiers who waged the battles that made the proclamation possible. "I only ask you, at the conclusion of these few remarks, to give three hearty cheers to all good and brave officers and men who fought those successful battles."

Three cheers echoed off the walls of the White House and into the city.

Lincoln wished the revelers good night and ducked back inside.

The crowd then marched to the nearby home of Salmon Chase, the treasury secretary, who came out to second their support for the president. "It is the dawn of a new era," Chase said. "The latest generations will celebrate it. The world will pay homage to the man who has performed it."

Tremendous applause from the crowd.

Cassius Clay, a Kentucky kinsman of Henry Clay and an ardent supporter of the proclamation, was with Chase that evening. He joined the praise for Lincoln and the proclamation, which he called "the great act which will make Abraham Lincoln immortal among men." He added, "The issue between liberty and slavery, thanks be to God, has come at last."

Loud applause from the crowd.

Clay shouted a question: "Does anyone fear the result?"

"No! No!"

LINCOLN TOOK the hosannas with a grain of salt. "While I hope something from the proclamation, my expectations are not as sanguine as are those of some friends," he confided to Hannibal Hamlin a short while later. "It is six days old, and while commendation in newspapers and by distinguished individuals is all that a vain man could wish, the stocks"—corporate shares—"have declined, and troops come forward more slowly than ever. This, looked soberly in the face, is not very satisfactory. We have fewer troops in the field at the end of six days than we had at the beginning, the attrition among the old outnumbering the addition by the new. The North responds to the proclamation sufficiently in breath, but breath alone kills no rebels."

H E HOPED NOT to have to kill many more rebels. The carnage of Antietam shocked even those who thought they had become inured to what modern weapons could do to mortal flesh. Lincoln appreciated irony, the mischief life plays on human designs; doubtless he noted the irony that increasingly tied him to John Brown. The Kansas slayer and Harpers Ferry raider had embraced violence in the struggle against slavery, while Lincoln had condemned it. Lincoln chose instead the peaceful path of democratic politics. But Lincoln's path had by now led to slaughter a thousand times greater than anything John Brown ever committed. And unless the South experienced a sudden change of heart, the slaughter would only continue.

Desperate to ease the mayhem, Lincoln once more appealed to Congress to fund his program of compensated emancipation. His annual message in December 1862 reiterated his conviction that the free Union and a slave Confederacy could never coexist. "There is no line, straight or crooked, suitable for a national boundary upon which to divide," he said. "Trace through, from east to west, upon the line between the free and slave country, and we shall find a little more than one-third of its length are rivers, easy to be crossed, and populated, or soon to be populated, thickly upon both sides; while nearly all its remaining length are merely surveyors' lines, over which people may walk back and forth without any consciousness of their presence." Inhabitants of the heartland of North America, of the valleys of the Mississippi, Ohio and Missouri Rivers, would never allow themselves to be separated from their natural sea outlets, which must happen if the Confederacy survived. "Separate our common country into two nations, as designed by the present rebellion, and every man of this great interior region is thereby cut off." Suppose the war somehow ended with the Confederacy intact. The peace would not last; the geography of North America would compel a resumption of hostilities. "It demands union and abhors separation," Lincoln said. "It would ere long force reunion, however much of blood and treasure the separation might have cost."

Lincoln offered more detail about his proposal than on previous occasions. He recommended that every state be given until January 1, 1900, to abolish slavery. Those that did so before then would be eligible for compensation from the federal government proportional to the number of slaves freed, in amounts to be determined by Congress. Lincoln's plan exempted slaves freed by "the chances of war" during the current rebellion; their owners would not receive compensation. Meanwhile, Congress would provide new funds for colonizing free blacks on foreign soil.

"Without slavery the rebellion could never have existed; without slavery it could not continue," Lincoln said. He observed that even on the Union side there was a great diversity of views on slavery and black people. "Some would perpetuate slavery; some would abolish it suddenly and without compensation; some would abolish it gradually and with compensation: some would remove the freed people from us, and some would retain them with us." He acknowledged that different people would fault different aspects of his plan. Yet the plan had answers to their objections. "The emancipation will be unsatisfactory to the advocates of perpetual slavery, but the length of time should greatly mitigate their dissatisfaction. The time spares both races from the evils of sudden derangement—in fact, from the necessity of any derangement—while most of those whose habitual course of thought will be disturbed by the measure will have passed away before its consummation. They will never see it. Another class will hail the prospect of emancipation, but will deprecate the length of time. They will feel that it gives too little to the now living slaves. But it really gives them much. It saves them from the vagrant destitution which must largely attend immediate emancipation in localities where their numbers are very great, and it gives the inspiring assurance that their posterity shall be free forever."

Northerners might complain that Lincoln's plan made them pay

Southern slaveholders while receiving nothing in exchange. "Yet the measure is both just and economical," Lincoln rejoined. "In a certain sense the liberation of slaves is the destruction of property—property acquired by descent or by purchase, the same as any other property." Northerners were hardly blameless in the matter of slavery. "The people of the South are not more responsible for the original introduction of this property than are the people of the North; and when it is remembered how unhesitatingly we all use cotton and sugar and share the profits of dealing in them, it may not be quite safe to say that the South has been more responsible than the North for its continuance. If, then, for a common object this property is to be sacrificed, is it not just that it be done at a common charge?"

Lincoln again pointed out that his plan would *save* Northerners money, by shortening the war, which was burning through money at a rate that would pay for all the slaves in the country in a matter of months. Moreover, the discounting effect of growth in the American population and economy made a dollar today more expensive than a dollar years or decades in the future. "A dollar will be much harder to pay for the war than will be a dollar for emancipation on the proposed plan. And then the latter will cost no blood, no precious life. It will be a saving of both."

Lincoln granted that he was asking a lot. But the moment demanded a lot. "The dogmas of the quiet past are inadequate to the stormy present. The occasion is piled high with difficulty, and we must rise with the occasion. As our case is new, so we must think anew and act anew. We must disenthrall ourselves, and then we shall save our country."

In language unusually emotional for him in a written message, Lincoln concluded, "Fellow citizens, we cannot escape history. We of this Congress and this administration will be remembered in spite of ourselves. No personal significance or insignificance can spare one or another of us. The fiery trial through which we pass will light us down in honor or dishonor to the latest generation. We say we are for the Union. The world will not forget that we say this. We know how to save the Union. The world knows we do know how to save it. We, even we here, hold the power and bear the responsibility. In giving freedom to the slave we assure freedom to the free—honorable alike in what we give and what we preserve. We shall nobly save or meanly lose the last best hope of earth. Other means may succeed; this could not fail. The way is plain, peaceful, generous, just—a way which if followed the world will forever applaud and God must forever bless."

BUT HIS WAY WAS not followed; Congress once again ignored Lincoln's plea. And so, on January 1, 1863, he took the fateful step. He repeated the language of the preliminary proclamation, listed the states then in rebellion, excepting the counties that had fallen under Union control, and said, "I do order and declare that all persons held as slaves within said designated states and parts of states are and henceforward shall be free, and that the executive government of the United States, including the military and naval authorities thereof, will recognize and maintain the freedom of said persons." He cautioned the newly freed men and women to refrain from violence, unless in self-defense, and he encouraged them to seek paid work.

He continued, "I further declare and make known that such persons of suitable condition will be received into the armed service of the United States to garrison forts, positions, stations, and other places and to man vessels of all sorts in said service."

He closed, "Upon this act, sincerely believed to be an act of justice, warranted by the Constitution upon military necessity, I invoke the considerate judgment of mankind and the gracious favor of Almighty God."

JEFFERSON DAVIS READ the Emancipation Proclamation as a cry of Union despair. Or so he told the Confederate legislature, which was inclined to agree. As mightily as Lincoln had struggled to keep slavery out of his public discussion of war aims, Confederate leaders had put slavery at the center of what they said they were fighting for. Alexander Stephens, Lincoln's hope for Georgia, had abandoned his Unionism when his state fell in line with the other seceders, and he had identified slavery as the fundamental issue on which the Confederacy rested. Stephens noted that Thomas Jefferson and the other founders had labored under the assumption that all men were created equal. "This was an error," Stephens said. The Confederacy had gotten things right. "Our new government is founded upon exactly the opposite idea; its foundations are laid, its cornerstone rests, upon the great truth that the negro is not equal to the white man; that slavery—subordination to the superior race—is his natural and normal condition. This, our new government, is the first in the history of the world based upon this great physical, philosophical and moral truth." Most people in America hadn't seen the light. "Those at the North who still cling to these errors, with a zeal above knowledge, we justly denominate fanatics. All fanaticism springs from an aberration of the mind, from a defect in reasoning. It is a species of insanity." The Confederacy stood against this insanity. And the Confederacy would prevail because it stood on the truth of white supremacy and black subordination. "It is upon this," said Stephens, "our social fabric is firmly planted; and I cannot permit myself to doubt the ultimate success of a full recognition of this principle throughout the civilized and enlightened world."

On the strength of such views, Stephens became vice president of the Confederacy, sitting beside Jefferson Davis, the president. Davis had been one of the three members of the Senate committee that investigated John Brown's raid on Harpers Ferry; he signed his name to the committee report that called the raid "the act of lawless ruffians, under the sanction of no public or political authority—distinguishable only from ordinary felonies by the ulterior ends in contemplation by them, and by the fact that the money to maintain the expedition, and the large armament they brought with them, had been contributed and furnished by citizens of other states of the Union under circumstances that must continue to jeopard the safety and peace of the Southern states, and against which Congress has no power to legislate." Davis and the committee urged Congress to remedy this deficiency. Until it did—until federal law allowed the slave states protection against future John Browns—the Union would be in mortal peril. "The committee can find no guarantee elsewhere for the security of peace between the states of the Union."

Davis sponsored a Senate resolution affording the South protection against other Browns. His resolution asserted that slavery was essential to the welfare of the South; that its existence had been endorsed by the Constitution, which had been ratified by all thirteen states; that "no change of opinion or feeling on the part of the non-slaveholding states of the Union in relation to this institution can justify them or their citizens in open or covert attacks thereon"; and that "all such attacks are in manifest violation of the mutual and solemn pledge to protect and defend each other, given by the states respectively, on entering into the constitutional compact which formed the Union."

The Senate approved Davis's resolution, albeit on a party-line vote, with Democrats in favor and Republicans against or abstaining. The failure of the party of Lincoln, who had just won the Republican nomination, to support the resolution disposed Davis to doubt the Republicans' devotion to constitutional principles. He subsequently refused to believe Lincoln's claims as candidate and then as president that he had no designs against slavery in the states.

And in January 1863 he wasn't surprised by Lincoln's Emancipation Proclamation, which he condemned as a monstrous assault on the people of the South—"the most execrable measure recorded in the history of guilty man." It was a cry of "impotent rage" on the part of Lincoln and the North. The Confederacy must and would respond. Davis declared that any Union officers captured while leading black troops would be delivered to state authorities for punishment according to the state laws against fomenting slave revolts. These typically mandated capital punishment. Union enlisted men would be treated as unwilling accomplices in said crimes.

Beyond its furious impotence, the Union proclamation revealed the fundamental duplicity of Lincoln and the Republicans, Davis said. The Confederate president quoted the passages from Lincoln's inaugural address disavowing both the authority and the inclination to interfere with slavery in the states. The new proclamation gave the lie to Lincoln's words. "The people of this Confederacy, then, cannot fail to receive this proclamation as the fullest vindication of their own sagacity in foreseeing the uses to which the dominant party in the United States intended from the beginning to apply their power; nor can they cease to remember with devout thankfulness that it is to their own vigilance in resisting the first stealthy progress of approaching despotism that they owe their escape from consequences now apparent to the most skeptical."

Davis took comfort from the fact, as he saw it, that the proclamation rendered impossible any reconciliation with the United States. "It has established a state of things which can lead to but one of three possible consequences—the extermination of the slaves, the exile of the whole white population of the Confederacy, or absolute and total separation of these states from the United States." The first possibility, the extermination of the slaves, might result from the race war to which Lincoln and the Republicans were goading the slaves of the South. The second would occur if Union arms so assisted the slaves as to make a victory for whites impossible; whites would not consent to live in a black country and would emigrate. The third—the most likely—would follow from the rallying of the white South to the banner of the Confederacy and the defeat of the Union.

Davis predicted that Lincoln's proclamation would be read by the world as an admission of Northern weakness—"an authentic statement by the government of the United States of its inability to subjugate the South by force of arms." Britain and other foreign countries would accord the Confederacy the diplomatic recognition it deserved. Davis predicted that Northerners themselves would perceive it as the last gasp of a failing administration. "That people are too acute not to understand that a restitution of the Union has been rendered forever impossible by the adoption of a measure which, from its very nature, neither admits of retraction nor can coexist with union."

THE SATISFACTION OF feeling that he had been right all along about Lincoln—that the Republican president was John Brown in a frock coat—didn't much help Jefferson Davis or the Confederate cause. Lincoln indeed was now waging war against slavery, as Brown had done, but where Brown's war had failed miserably to win the support of its intended beneficiaries, Lincoln's succeeded famously. Slaves had been fleeing their homes for Union lines for some time; the Emancipation Proclamation caused their numbers to increase dramatically, and Lincoln's invitation to the former slaves to join the fight for freedom prompted a substantial portion of them to do just that.

Frederick Douglass couldn't resist an I-told-you-so at Lincoln's expense. "When first the rebel cannon shattered the walls of Sumter and drove away its starving garrison, I predicted that the war then and there inaugurated would not be fought out entirely by white men," Douglass declared. Others should have realized the same thing. "Only a moderate share of sagacity was needed to see that the arm of the slave was the best defense against the arm of the slaveholder."

But finally Lincoln had acted, and it was up to black men to respond. "From East to West, from North to South, the sky is written all over 'NOW OR NEVER,'" Douglas said. "Liberty won by white men would lose half its luster. Who would be free themselves must strike the blow. Better even to die free than to live slaves."

Few slaves read Douglass's paper, being mostly illiterate. But males of military age responded to the sentiment he expressed and took up arms for their freedom. Eventually some hundred thousand joined the Union ranks. The Union war department initially envisioned employing the freedmen in support of white troops, on account of both their inexperience and the peculiar hazards they encountered in battle. Where white troops who were captured were treated as prisoners of war, former slaves might be re-enslaved or simply shot. But plans changed amid the fighting, and before long freedmen found themselves in the thick of battle.

An early engagement took place at Milliken's Bend on the Mississippi, where a Union garrison was supporting Ulysses Grant's siege of Vicksburg. A Confederate force under Henry McCulloch received orders to drive the Federals into the river. McCulloch maneuvered his men close to the Union lines and turned them loose. "The troops charged the breastworks, carrying it instantly, killing and wounding many of the enemy by their deadly fire, as well as the bayonet," McCulloch reported afterward. He added, with some surprise, "This charge was resisted by the negro portion of the enemy's force with considerable obstinacy." Their white comrades had shown no such courage. "The white or true Yankee portion ran like whipped curs almost as soon as the charge was ordered."

McCulloch wasn't the most reliable of witnesses; his report read as though the Confederates won the battle, which in fact they lost. But it revealed the fighting ability of the former slaves. Their own white officers asserted the same thing. "We were attacked here on June 7, about 3 o'clock in the morning, by a brigade of Texas troops, about 2,500 in number," reported Matthew Miller, a captain of a black Louisiana regiment. "We had about 600 men to withstand them, 500 of them negroes." Of the company Miller commanded, half were killed in the battle and all but one of the rest were wounded. "I never felt more grieved and sick at heart than when I saw how my brave soldiers had been slaughtered, one with six wounds, all the rest with two or three, none less than two wounds. Two of my colored sergeants were killed, both brave, noble men; always prompt, vigilant, and ready for the fray. I never more wish to hear the expression, 'The niggers won't fight.' Come with me 100 yards from where I sit and I can show you the wounds that cover the bodies of 16 as brave, loyal, and patriotic soldiers as ever drew bead on a rebel."

A Union general who witnessed the same battle told Charles Dana, the assistant war secretary, "It is impossible for men to show greater gallantry than the negro troops in that fight." This view quickly pervaded Union thinking about black soldiers. "The bravery of the blacks in the battle at Milliken's Bend completely revolutionized the sentiment of the army with regard to the employment of negro troops," Dana observed. "I heard prominent officers who formerly in private had sneered at the idea of the negroes fighting express themselves after that as heartily in favor of it."

DURING THE MONTHS after the Emancipation Proclamation, the war as a whole turned in the Union's favor. Grant took Vicksburg, reclaiming the Mississippi for the North and cutting the Confederacy in two. George Meade's Army of the Potomac defeated Robert E. Lee's Army of Northern Virginia at Gettysburg, neutralizing a threat to Washington and dealing the entire Confederate project a demoralizing blow.

Washington hailed the thrilling news. A large crowd gathered in front of the National Hotel and shouted itself hoarse before heading west on Pennsylvania Avenue. The Marine Band joined them, playing exuberant airs. On reaching the White House, the happy mob called for the president to come out. Lincoln appeared at the window. "Fellow citizens," he said. "I am very glad indeed to see you tonight, and yet I will not say I thank you for this call, but I do most sincerely thank Almighty God for the occasion on which you have called."

Great cheers from the crowd.

Many others had noted the coincidence between the recent Union victories and America's Independence Day; Lincoln took this as his theme. "How long ago is it?—eighty odd years—since on the Fourth of July for the first time in the history of the world a nation by its representatives, assembled and declared as a self-evident truth that 'all men are created equal.'" Lincoln rambled through a brief history of the Fourth of July before thinking better of the effort. "Gentlemen, this is a glorious theme, and the occasion for a speech, but I am not prepared to make one worthy of the occasion." Maybe at another time. Seeking escape, he nodded toward the band: "I will now take the music."

LINCOLN HAD HARDLY ABSORBED the meaning of Vicksburg and Gettysburg when a new and alarming front in the war developed. New York City had never liked the Union war effort. The commercial hub of the North had long-standing ties to the South, with cotton coming into the city, often for transshipment elsewhere, and loans flowing back to the planters. Other parts of the state were friendly to the likes of John Brown and Frederick Douglass, but the city preferred slaveholders to slaves. As secession carried off the South, the mayor of New York, Fernando Wood, recommended that his city secede from his state and the Union to form a de facto alliance with the slaveholders. "With our aggrieved brethren of the slave states, we have friendly relations and a common sympathy," Wood said. "While other portions of our state have unfortunately been imbued with the fanatical spirit which actuates a portion of the people of New England, the city of New York has unfalteringly preserved the integrity of its principles of adherence to the compromises of the Constitution and the equal rights of the people of all the states. We have respected the local interests of every section, at no time oppressing but all the while aiding in the development of the resources of the whole country. Our ships have penetrated to every clime, and so have New York capital, energy and enterprise found their way to every state, and, indeed, to almost every county and town of the American Union. If we have derived sustenance from the Union, so have we in return disseminated blessings for the common benefit of all. Therefore, New York has a right to expect and should endeavor to preserve a continuance of uninterrupted intercourse with every section." Wood predicted that the secession spirit would catch on across the country. "California and her sisters of the Pacific will no doubt set up an independent republic and husband their own rich mineral resources. The western states, equally rich in cereals and other agricultural products, will probably do the same." What was good for the other sections would be good for New York City, which had been consistently ill-used by both the federal government and the state government of New York. "Why should not New York City, instead of supporting by her contributions in revenue two-thirds of the expenses of the United States, become also equally independent? As a free city, with but nominal duty on imports, her local government could be supported without taxation upon her people. Thus we could live free from taxes, and have cheap goods nearly duty free. In this she would have the whole and united support of the Southern states, as well as all the other states to whose interests and rights under the Constitution she has always been true."

Wood didn't get his way. He wasn't ready to take up arms for his city's independence, and Albany wouldn't let the city go without a fight. But as the war unfolded, New Yorkers were conspicuously unenthusiastic for the Union, and the city became a haven for Southern sympathizers.

It was also a magnet for immigrants, who arrived with no attachment to the Union and no feeling of responsibility for slavery. To the degree that the immigrants—many of them Irish, and most uneducated and unskilled—had opinions on the race question, they viewed blacks as potential competitors in the job market. Emancipation promised the immigrants little but a harder scramble to reach the lowest rungs of the economic ladder. Many opposed emancipation, some quite bitterly.

The immigrants' attitude would have counted little had native Northerners remained eager to enlist in the Union army. But after two years of the war, their devotion was flagging. Congress resorted to conscription, for the first time compelling young men into the national army. The Enrollment Act was unpopular from the start. It required male citizens, and immigrants who had filed for citizenship, between the ages of twenty and forty-five to register for a draft lottery, which would fill quotas set by the federal government. The draft effectively exempted the wealthy, who were allowed to pay others to take their places. It also exempted blacks, who had been barred from citizenship by the Dred Scott decision. The result was that poor whites, often immigrants, were dragooned to fight a war in which they might get killed or maimed and which, if successful, would flood the labor market with people they feared and despised.

The draft provoked riots in several cities of the North; in New York the riots became a kind of urban warfare America had never experienced. John Torrey was a botanist and chemist who lived on

Forty-Ninth Street and worked in the federal Assay Office in the Wall Street district of lower Manhattan. "We have had great riots today and they are still in progress," he wrote to a friend on Monday, July 13. "They were reported to us at the Assay Office about noon, but I thought they were exaggerated." A new eyewitness report from a colleague showed them to be all too true. "Mr. Mason came in and said that he saw a mob stop two 3rd Ave. cars to take out some negroes and maltreat them." Manhattan had a large community of African Americans, who since the war's beginning had been blamed by the city's dominant Democratic party—the party of Fernando Wood—for the conflict. The draft added to their woes. The assault on the blacks on the streetcars made John Torrey think of his black housekeepers; he headed home to protect them. The cars he normally rode had been stopped by the rioters; he tried another line, on Fourth Avenue. "I found the streets full of people, and when I reached the terminus (now 34th Street) I found the whole road way and sidewalks filled with rough fellows (and some equally rough women) who were tearing up rails, cutting down telegraph poles, and setting fire to buildings."

Torrey walked the remaining fifteen blocks toward his house. The rioters were too busy to pay him any mind. He thought he had seen the worst of the violence. But as he entered Forty-Ninth Street, the mob grew thick and angry. His house and others on the street were better appointed and maintained than many of those in the neighborhoods he had passed through; adjacent to Columbia College, the street was home to abolitionists and other Republicans. The rioters started in on a house at one end of the street; Torrey feared they would work their way along to his. He stepped up his pace and got there first. "I found Jane and Maggie"—his daughters—"a little alarmed but not frightened. The mob had been in the College Grounds and came to our house wishing to know if a Republican lived there." Torrey's daughters denied it; their father was a scientist, not a politician, they said. The mob didn't debate the point, and moved on. "They were going to burn President King's house, as he was rich and a decided Republican."

That particular arson was averted by some Catholic priests who appealed to the Irish rioters to consider their immortal souls. The mob returned to Torrey's house. "The furious bareheaded and coatless men assembled under our windows and shouted aloud for Jeff Davis!" Torrey wrote. He kept his servants out of sight and prepared his daughters to flee at a moment's notice.

The rioters became distracted by a more appealing target. "The mob, furious as demons, went yelling over to the Colored-Orphan Asylum in 5th Ave. a little below where we live. And rolling a barrel of kerosene in it, the whole structure was soon in a blaze, and is now a smoking ruin. What has become of the 300 poor innocent orphans I could not learn." He later discovered that the children had escaped ahead of the flames. But the burning of the orphanage revealed how far out of control the rioting had gone. "Before this fire was extinguished—or rather burned out, for the wicked wretches who caused it would not permit the engines to be used—the northern sky was brilliantly illuminated, probably by the burning of the Aged Colored-Women's Home in 65th Street, or the Harlem Rail Road Bridge."

Torrey ventured out as night was falling. "I took a walk a short distance down 5th Avenue, and seeing a group of rowdies in the grounds of Dr. Ward's large and superb mansion, I found they had gone there with the intention of setting fire to the building." The doctor and his family had come out front to plead for their home. They swore they were Democrats and opposed the draft. The rioters left the house standing. "But they may return before morning," Torrey remarked.

Torrey's curiosity caused him to question the rioters on their plans. "I conversed with one of the ringleaders, who told me they would burn the whole city before they were through. He said they were to take Wall Street in hand tomorrow."

Torrey and his household slept in street clothes that night, with ears cocked for the tramp of the mob's feet. They were spared, but the city the next day looked like a war zone. Militia troops from Gettysburg, weary after saving Washington from the rebels, were brought in to save New York from itself. Citizens and government workers armed themselves for battle. Torrey arrived at the Assay Office and discovered an arsenal. "The people there were spoiling for a fight," he said. "They had a battery of about 25 rifle barrels, carrying three balls each and mounted on a gun-carriage. It could be loaded and fired with rapidity. We also had 10-inch shells, to be lighted and thrown out of the windows. Likewise quantities of SO_3"—sulfur trioxide, used in the assay process and capable of producing a poison gas—"with arrangements for projecting it on the mob." Perhaps the mob got wind of what awaited them, for they left the Assay Office alone.

They found plenty of other victims. "The worst mobs are on the 1st and 2nd and 7th Avenues," Torrey wrote on Wednesday, July 15. "Many have been killed there. They are very hostile to the negroes, and scarcely one of them is to be seen. A person who called at our house this afternoon saw three of them hanging together. The Central Park has been a kind of refuge to them. Hundreds were there today, with no protection in a very severe shower. The station houses of the police are crowded with them."

The purposeful rioting descended into arrant hooliganism. "Walking out on 5th Ave. near 48th St., a man who lives there told me that a few minutes before, in broad sunlight, three ruffians seized the horses of a gentleman's carriage and demanded money," Torrey said. "By whipping up, they barely escaped. Immediately afterwards, they stopped another carriage, turned the persons out of it, and then got in themselves, shouting and brandishing their clubs." The extortion escalated. "Thieves are going about in gangs, calling at houses, and demanding money—threatening the torch if denied."

By Thursday the militia and the police had managed to restore order. But the toll of the violence was deeply disturbing. More than one hundred people had been killed and some two thousand injured. Several blacks were hanged; hundreds were burned out of their homes; thousands fled Manhattan never to return. The damage to property would take years to repair.

T HE SMOKE FROM the fires dissipated beyond the Hudson, but the gloom was felt as far as the Potomac. Lincoln had expected his Emancipation Proclamation to be controversial, but he hadn't expected its opponents to incinerate New York. In the aftermath of the riots he concluded he needed to do a better job explaining what the proclamation meant and how it enhanced the war effort.

His opportunity arrived a few weeks later in the form of an invitation from Springfield to address a gathering there. Lincoln likely had solicited the invitation, which gave him, in declining, a chance to speak his mind. "It would be very agreeable to me to thus meet my old friends at my own home," he said in a letter addressed to James Conkling, one of the organizers, yet intended for publication. "But I cannot, just now, be absent from here so long as a visit there would require." He proceeded, "There are those who are dissatisfied with me. To such I would say: You desire peace; and you blame me that we do not have it. But how can we attain it?" He identified three possible courses. "First, to suppress the rebellion by force of arms. This, I am trying to do. Are you for it? If you are, so far we are agreed. If you are not for it, a second way is, to give up the Union. I am against this. Are you for it? If you are, you should say so plainly. If you are not for *force*, nor yet for *dissolution*, there only remains some imaginable *compromise*."

But what would the compromise be? "I do not believe any compromise embracing the maintenance of the Union is now possible," Lincoln said. "All I learn leads to a directly opposite belief. The strength of the rebellion, is its military—its army. That army dominates all the country, and all the people, within its range. Any offer of terms made by any man or men within that range, in opposition to that army, is simply nothing for the present; because such man or men have no power whatever to enforce their side of a compromise, if one were made with them."

Lincoln admitted that the unhappiness with his administration wasn't merely about the Union's slow progress at arms. "To be plain, you are dissatisfied with me about the negro. Quite likely there is a difference of opinion between you and myself upon that subject. I certainly wish that all men could be free, while I suppose you do not. Yet I have neither adopted nor proposed any measure which is not consistent with even your view, provided you are for the Union. I suggested compensated emancipation, to which you replied you wished not to be taxed to buy negroes. But I had not asked you to be taxed to buy negroes except in such way as to save you from greater taxation to save the Union exclusively by other means."

So he had taken action on his own, and incurred additional anger. "You dislike the emancipation proclamation; and, perhaps, would have it retracted. You say it is unconstitutional. I think differently. I think the Constitution invests its commander-in-chief with the law of war in time of war. The most that can be said, if so much, is, that slaves are property. Is there—has there ever been—any question that by the law of war property, both of enemies and friends, may be taken when needed? And is it not needed whenever taking it helps us or hurts the enemy? Armies, the world over, destroy enemies' property when they cannot use it; and even destroy their own to keep it from the enemy."

In any event, the proclamation had been issued. What to do now? "The proclamation, as law, either is valid or is not valid. If it is not valid, it needs no retraction. If it is valid, it cannot be retracted, any more than the dead can be brought to life. Some of you profess to think its retraction would operate favorably for the Union. Why better *after* the retraction, than *before* the issue? There was more than a year and a half of trial to suppress the rebellion before the proclamation issued, the last one hundred days of which passed under an explicit notice that it was coming, unless averted by those in revolt returning to their allegiance." The war had gone well in the months since the proclamation was issued, Lincoln said. And he thought the proclamation had much to do with it. "Some of the commanders of our armies in the field who have given us our most important successes believe the emancipation policy and the use of colored troops constitute the heaviest blow yet dealt to the rebellion."

Critics said the proclamation had damaged Union morale. Lincoln addressed those in his reading audience who felt that way. "You say you will not fight to free negroes." This was ungenerous. "Some of them seem willing to fight for you—but no matter. Fight you, then, exclusively to save the Union. I issued the proclamation on purpose to aid you in saving the Union. Whenever you shall have conquered all resistance to the Union, if I shall urge you to continue fighting, it will be an apt time then for you to declare you will not fight to free negroes."

Lincoln repeated his rationale for the proclamation. "I thought that in your struggle for the Union, to whatever extent the negroes should cease helping the enemy, to that extent it weakened the enemy in his resistance to you." Was there something wrong with this logic? The error had not been shown to him. "I thought that whatever negroes can be got to do as soldiers leaves just so much less for white soldiers to do in saving the Union." From this followed emancipation. "Negroes, like other people, act upon motives. Why should they do anything for us if we will do nothing for them? If they stake their lives for us, they must be prompted by the strongest motive—even the promise of freedom. And the promise being made, must be kept."

Lincoln asked his readers to take courage from recent events. "The signs look better," he said. Referring to the capture of Vicksburg, he declared, "The Father of Waters again goes unvexed to the sea." Victories in the East were having a cumulative effect. "It is hard to say that anything has been more bravely and well done than at Antietam, Murfreesboro, Gettysburg, and on many fields of lesser note." The end wasn't yet near, but it was getting closer. "Peace does not appear so distant as it did. I hope it will come soon, and come to stay; and so come as to be worth the keeping in all future time. It will then have been proved that among free men there can be no successful appeal from the ballot to the bullet, and that they who take such appeal are sure to lose their case and pay the cost. And then there will be some black men who can remember that, with silent tongue and clenched teeth, and steady eye and well-poised bayonet, they have helped mankind on to this great consummation; while, I fear, there will be some white ones, unable to forget that, with malignant heart, and deceitful speech, they have strove to hinder it."

He didn't want to get ahead of himself. "Let us not be over-sanguine of a speedy final triumph. Let us be quite sober. Let us diligently apply the means, never doubting that a just God, in his own good time, will give us the rightful result."

LINCOLN'S LETTER TO James Conkling fell short of its target. He had wanted it to be published but not in the mutilated form it first took in the papers. "I am mortified this morning to find the letter to you, botched up, in the Eastern papers, telegraphed from Chicago," he wrote to Conkling. "How did this happen?"

Conkling explained that he was mortified too, but the cause was an honest mistake. He noted that the full letter had been published the next day, and he was confident no lasting harm was done.

Lincoln had reason to be sensitive, for during this period he was stretching the Constitution to the breaking point. In mid-September he suspended the writ of habeas corpus for individuals arrested as "spies or aiders or abettors of the enemy." The suspension was broad, applying throughout the country, and it was open-ended, lasting for the duration of the war or until it was explicitly revoked.

Lincoln's critics grew apoplectic. The Emancipation Proclamation was bad enough, they said, depriving citizens of their property. But suspending habeas corpus deprived Americans of their liberty. The proscription might seem narrow on paper, but there was little to prevent corrupt officials from arresting their enemies as spies, locking them up and never having to bring them before a judge.

Lincoln wasn't finished. The next day he issued instructions to federal tax officials in South Carolina regarding the disposal of plantations on the Sea Islands abandoned by their rebel owners and seized for nonpayment of taxes. He gave various orders about the surveying and recording of lots and parcels of land, and then declared, "You are further directed to issue certificates for the said lots and parcels of land to the heads of families of the African race, one only to each, preferring such as by their good conduct, meritorious services or exemplary character, will be examples of moral propriety and industry to those of the same race." The plots set aside for African Americans weren't without cost; the price was pegged at the going rate for federal land of $1.25 per acre. Yet neither were they large: twenty acres. For $25 a former slave could become a landowner.

Lincoln's policy for the Sea Islands suggested a broader approach to the conundrum of what to do about the freedmen—the former slaves—after the war. He had long favored emigration to Africa or colonies in some other foreign land, but he wasn't finding many takers. So why not internal colonies, on land the slaves had been working for generations? There were problems with this approach, starting with the fact that most Southern plantations had not been abandoned and weren't likely to be. Yet there would be problems with any approach to such a difficult issue. One had to start somewhere.

AFTER THE FOUL-UP with his letter to James Conkling, Lincoln sought another opportunity to air his ideas on the war and emancipation. The conflict had started, on the Northern side, as a narrow effort to preserve the Union, but it had grown into a broader crusade for freedom. Lincoln gave the transformation much thought, and in November 1863 he put his thoughts into public words.

A cemetery had been created for the thousands killed at Gettysburg; Lincoln was invited to the dedication. His staff laid plans for him to leave the capital early in the morning, transfer trains at Baltimore and arrive at Gettysburg by noon for the two o'clock ceremony. He would return to Washington afterward.

Lincoln vetoed the schedule. "I do not like this arrangement," he said. "I do not wish to so go that by the slightest accident we fail entirely, and, at the best, the whole to be a mere breathless running of the gauntlet." He had something important to say, and he didn't want to be rushed or prevented entirely.

The itinerary was changed to get him to Gettysburg the day before the ceremony. The locals put on a dinner with patriotic music. They naturally asked Lincoln to speak. He declined—"for several substantial reasons," he said. "The most substantial of these is that I have no speech to make."

The audience laughed.

"In my position it is somewhat important that I should not say any foolish things."

"If you can help it!" a voice shouted.

"It very often happens that the only way to help it is to say nothing at all."

More laughter.

"Believing that is my present condition this evening, I must beg of you to excuse me from addressing you further."

The next day a great crowd converged to hear a moving oration by Edward Everett, a Bostonian famed for his command of Greek, Latin and the other well-springs of high rhetoric. He recounted the battle, memorialized the fallen and prayed for reconciliation between North and South. The audience wept, laughed and cheered, convinced after two hours that they had heard a speech for the ages.

As the applause for Everett died down, Lincoln was introduced. The audience hoped he wouldn't speak long, after all they had sat through. He didn't. But he spoke profoundly. In less than three minutes he recast his original war aim in a fresh mold, fusing freedom and equality to Union as the triadic core of a new vision of what should come out of the conflict. "Four score and seven years ago our fathers brought forth on this continent, a new nation, conceived in liberty, and dedicated to the proposition that all men are created equal," Lincoln said. "Now we are engaged in a great civil war, testing whether that nation, or any nation so conceived and so dedicated, can long endure." He praised the fallen, and he summoned his listeners to dedicate themselves to the cause the soldiers had so gallantly served— "that this nation, under God, shall have a new birth of freedom; and that government of the people, by the people, for the people, shall not perish from the earth."

U NION SOLDIERS HAD BEEN carrying the Constitution in their haversacks since the war began, so to speak; with his Gettysburg Address, Lincoln added the Declaration of Independence. His opening "four score and seven years ago" was the first clue; quick calculators immediately arrived at 1776, rather than the Constitution's 1789. The Declaration's—and now Lincoln's—emphasis on liberty and equality made his new war aims far more ambitious than simply preserving the Union. Months after the Emancipation Proclamation, Lincoln was promising no less than the revolutionizing of Southern— and American—society.

If the Union won the war, that is. Lincoln believed he had found his winning general in the relentless Grant, whom he brought east to handle the clever Lee. And he thought Grant had discovered a winning strategy in loosing the implacable William Sherman against Georgia. Other Union generals and admirals would attack the Confederacy elsewhere, exploiting the advantages of the North in men and resources, with all to culminate in the collapse of the rebellion.

The final offensive—or so Lincoln hoped it would be—commenced in May 1864. Sherman drove toward Atlanta, Grant toward Richmond. Sherman's campaign proceeded as planned, but Grant's bogged down in the convoluted region called the Wilderness, where Lee capitalized on his local knowledge and dealt Grant daunting blows. Grant never wavered; he continued to pound forward. But any hope of a quick end to the fighting vanished in the humid Virginia air.

Francis Carpenter was painting Lincoln's portrait during this period, and he saw the president's spirits sag. "Absorbed in his papers, he would become unconscious of my presence, while I intently studied every line and shade of expression in that furrowed face," Carpenter recalled. "In repose, it was the saddest face I ever knew. There were days when I could scarcely look into it without crying. During the first week of the battles of the Wilderness he scarcely slept at all. Passing through the main hall of the domestic apartment on one of these days, I met him, clad in a long morning wrapper, pacing back and forth a narrow passage leading to one of the windows, his hands behind him, great black rings under his eyes, his head bent forward upon his breast—altogether such a picture of the effects of sorrow, care, and anxiety as would have melted the hearts of the worst of his adversaries."

It wasn't simply the war that weighed on Lincoln's soul. He and Mary had lost another son, Willie, two years earlier, to disease, and the gloom that settled upon them at that time had never lifted. Lincoln had his work to distract him, but the effect was only fleeting. As for Mary, Willie's death seems to have caused a kind of nervous breakdown. Elizabeth Keckley, a former slave who became a successful dressmaker in Washington and a member of the Lincoln household, recalled Lincoln urging Mary to pull herself together. "Mother, do you see that large white building yonder?" he said, pointing to the insane asylum. "Try and control your grief, or it will drive you mad, and we may have to send you there." When the war went well, Lincoln's personal sorrow lightened; when it went badly, the background heartache returned.

And then there was the political opposition. Grant's setback bolstered Lincoln's critics, not least within his own party. A group of Radical Republicans, as the most antislavery Republicans called themselves, plotted a break with the administration. The Radicals resented Lincoln's slowness to issue the Emancipation Proclamation, and they feared backsliding should progress toward victory stall, as it was doing. Some of the resentment was personal: John Frémont still smarted from being overruled by Lincoln on slavery in Missouri, and from subsequent relief from command. Frémont let out that he'd be happy to reprise his role as presidential nominee from eight years earlier. The Radicals called a convention ahead of the regular Republican convention; in the company of disaffected pro-war Democrats they made Frémont the nominee of the Radical Democracy party.

The nomination won the support of many Republican abolitionists, including Frederick Douglass.

The regular Republicans met a week later under a new banner of their own. Inviting pro-war and Southern Unionist Democrats, they branded themselves the National Union party. Their nomination of Lincoln was no surprise, but the replacement of Hannibal Hamlin in the vice presidential slot by Tennessean Andrew Johnson raised eyebrows among those unfamiliar with Hamlin's Radical affinities. The maneuver elicited jeers from Radicals who said Lincoln was going soft on the South, in that Johnson was a slaveholder. But then the convention adopted a hard-line position on slavery. "Resolved," the platform declared, "that as slavery was the cause, and now constitutes the strength of this rebellion, and as it must be, always and every-where, hostile to the principles of republican government, justice and the national safety demand its utter and complete extirpation from the soil of the republic." The convention applauded Lincoln's policy toward slavery and the slaves. "We approve, especially, the Proclama-tion of Emancipation, and the employment as Union soldiers of men heretofore held in slavery." Finally, the platform insisted that emanci-pation be written into the Constitution. "While we uphold and main-tain the acts and proclamations by which the government, in its own defense, has aimed a deathblow at this gigantic evil, we are in favor, furthermore, of such an amendment to the Constitution, to be made by the people in conformity with its provisions, as shall terminate and forever prohibit the existence of slavery within the limits of the juris-diction of the United States."

THE PLATFORM DIDN'T SATISFY Horace Greeley, who remained a regular Republican but hectored Lincoln throughout the summer of 1864. The voluble editor asserted that the people of the North were crying out for peace and that the president must convince them he was seeking it. The alternative was a Democratic victory in the fall elections, which would doom the war effort and mortally wound the Republican party—not to mention Greeley's Republican *Tribune*. As full of himself as ever, Greeley offered to move things along. During the summer of 1864 he heard of two men at Niagara Falls who claimed to have contacts with the Confederate government; these contacts were interested in facilitating peace negotiations between the Union and the Confederacy. Greeley urged Lincoln to respond to this overture and tendered his own services in the venture.

Lincoln doubted that the contacts, if they existed, had any standing with the Confederate government. But he did *not* doubt that Greeley would excoriate him if he failed to pursue the possibility. So he sent Greeley a letter, via his personal secretary John Hay, stipulating his conditions. "To Whom It May Concern," Lincoln wrote. "Any proposition which embraces the restoration of peace, the integrity of the whole Union, and the abandonment of slavery, and which comes by and with an authority that can control the armies now at war against the United States, will be received and considered by the Executive government of the United States, and will be met by liberal terms on other substantial and collateral points; and the bearer, or bearers thereof shall have safe-conduct both ways."

Lincoln expected this letter to be published, as it was. He knew there was no chance it would lead to anything, for it required the Confederacy to sign its own death warrant and Southern slaveholders to give up their slaves. The South would have to be beaten on the battlefield before this would happen. But at least Lincoln got credit for making an offer.

Yet he didn't get *much* credit. *The New York Herald*, the nation's leading Democratic paper, accused Lincoln of rank partisanship. "What is the sine qua non demanded by Mr. Lincoln of the rebellious states as a condition precedent to the re-establishment of peace and the Union?" the paper cried. "Nothing less than the abolition of slavery. The rebellious states must make good his emancipation proclamation before Abraham Lincoln can agree to any peace with them." Until recently Lincoln had declared the restoration of federal control in the Southern states to be his primary goal, with slavery a secondary matter. Why the change? "We can only conclude that, without requiring the abolition of slavery therein as an essential condition, Mr. Lincoln is afraid that peace and reunion may come too soon to suit his ambitious purposes and the grasping designs of his party." The war had been the making of the Republican party, the *Herald* said; peace would be its unmaking. Hence Lincoln's embrace of emancipation, which made peace impossible.

Jefferson Davis had recently been quoted as saying the war was not about slavery. "This war must go on till the last of this generation falls in his tracks, and his children seize his musket and fight our battle, unless you acknowledge our right to self-government," Davis had said. "We are not fighting for slavery. We are fighting for independence, and that, or extermination, we will have."

The editors of the *Herald* took Davis at his word. "Jeff Davis was perfectly right," they said. The war was *not* about slavery, on either side. "The Southern politicians are merely fighting for power. They employed the slavery question to induce the Southern people to sustain them, just as they used the tariff question in Jackson's time. With the same truth it may be said that the Northern people are not fighting for anti-slavery. Anti-slavery was the pretext used by Northern politicians to get office and to turn the Southerners out of office."

Republicans as a party were culpable, the *Herald* said, but Lincoln was the most culpable, and his policy of arming slaves the most cynical. "Niggers are not fit for soldiers. They can dig, and drive mules; they cannot and will not fight." News reporting to the contrary was one big partisan lie. "They never have fought well in any battle. To insist that the niggers should be in the army was to insist that there should be a weak point in every line of battle with which we faced the enemy." For the recent troubles of the Union army, Lincoln had only himself to blame. "Abolitionism is, therefore, the real difficulty now; and unless the President soon finds out how to do away with this difficulty he may be sure that the people will find out how to do away with him."

The New York Times cut Lincoln more slack than the *Herald* did, but even the *Times* thought Lincoln pushed things too far by making abolition a requirement for peace. "The President has a right, and it is his duty, to insist upon the integrity of the Union as a *sine qua non*," the paper declared. "But it is not so with slavery." Lincoln had no constitutional mandate to free slaves, nor did he have constitutional authority to do so, beyond his authority as commander in chief. Yet that authority was a consequence of the war, and it would vanish with the war's end. To confiscate slaves for employment by the Union army was one thing, not unlike the confiscation of mules. But at war's end the mules would revert to their owners, and so would the slaves. The *Times* urged Lincoln to return to his original justification for the war. "The South should understand that the one thing and the only thing which shuts them away from us, which builds up between us and them an impassable wall of separation, which shuts our ears to every claim or demand they can make upon us, which steels our hearts against them and strengthens our arms for their destruction, is that they are waging war for the destruction of the Union."

Some of Lincoln's own military officers joined the chorus against making abolition a condition of peace. George Meade, the hero of Gettysburg, read the president's "To Whom It May Concern" letter with dismay, believing it would lengthen the war. "It is a pity Mr. Lincoln employed the term 'abandonment of slavery,' as it implies its immediate abolition or extinction, to which the South will never agree, at least not until our military successes have been greater than they have hitherto been, or than they now seem likely to be," Meade wrote to his wife. "Whereas had he said the *final adjustment* of the slavery question, leaving the door open to gradual emancipation, I really believe the South would listen and agree to terms." Perhaps the president would change his mind. "God grant it may be so, and that it will not be long before this terrible war is brought to a close."

L INCOLN HEARD the complaints but refused to heed them. Alexander Randall was a former governor of Wisconsin; Joseph Mills was his friend and fellow Republican. The two visited Lincoln in the White House in August 1864. Mills was favorably surprised by Lincoln. "The President appeared to be not the pleasant joker I had expected to see, but a man of deep convictions and an unutterable yearning for the success of the Union cause," he noted in his diary. "His voice was pleasant—his manner earnest and cordial. As I heard a vindication of his policy from his own lips, I could not but feel that his mind grew in stature like his body, and that I stood in the presence of the great guiding intellect of the age, and that those huge Atlantian shoulders were fit to bear the weight of mightiest monarchies. His transparent honesty, his republican simplicity, his gushing sympathy for those who offered their lives for their country, his utter forgetfulness of self in his concern for his country, could not but inspire me with confidence that he was Heaven's instrument to conduct his people through this red sea of blood to a Canaan of peace and freedom."

Alexander Randall thought Lincoln looked tired. He suggested the president take a summer holiday. A few weeks would do him good.

Lincoln replied that he could leave Washington but Washington wouldn't leave him. "My thoughts, my solicitude for this great country follow me where ever I go," he said. The looming election compounded the problem. "I don't think it is personal vanity, or ambition, but I cannot but feel that the weal or woe of this great nation will be decided in the approaching canvas. My own experience has proven to me that there is no program intended by the Democratic party but that will result in the dismemberment of the Union." The Democrats wanted to appease the South by restoring slaves to their masters. "There are now between one and two hundred thousand black men now in the service of the Union," Lincoln said. "These men will be disbanded and returned to slavery and we will have to fight two nations instead of one." Lincoln shook his head. "You cannot conciliate the South when the mastery and control of millions of blacks makes them sure of ultimate success." The Democrats didn't understand, or wouldn't admit, how fully the fortunes of the Union now depended on the military service of the former slaves. "Abandon all the posts now possessed by black men, surrender all these advantages to the enemy, and we would be compelled to abandon the war in three weeks."

Lincoln remarked that some Democrats had urged him to show good faith toward the South. "There have been men who have proposed to me to return to slavery the black warriors of Port Hudson and Olustee"—where former slaves had performed with conspicuous gallantry—"to their masters to conciliate the South." He would do no such thing. "I should be damned in time and in eternity." Some Democrats were alleging that abolition had supplanted the Union as Lincoln's chief war aim. This was not true, he said; the Union remained his guiding star. "But no human power can subdue this rebellion without using the emancipation lever as I have done. Freedom has given us the control of two hundred thousand able-bodied men, born and raised on Southern soil. It will give us more yet. Just so much it has subtracted from the strength of our enemies." The Democrats were full of bluster. "My enemies condemn my emancipation policy. Let them prove by the history of this war that we can restore the Union without it."

THE BLUSTER OF the Democrats reflected a new division in their party. The sectional division of 1860 had put Lincoln in the White House; the new division, between peace Democrats and war Democrats, might put him back there if they weren't careful. The peace Democrats were ready to abandon the war effort, leaving the Confederacy and slavery intact. The war Democrats wanted to keep fighting but demanded more effective leadership than Lincoln was giving the country. The split could easily have produced another bolt from the convention if the leaders of the party hadn't been so desperate to prevent it. "Let us, at the very outset of our proceedings, bear in mind that the dissensions of the last Democratic convention were one of the principal causes which gave the reins of government into the hands of our opponents, and let us beware not to fall into the same fatal error," the chairman of the convention chided his colleagues.

The error was avoided by giving the platform to the peace faction and the nomination to the warriors. George McClellan, the thirty-seven-year-old "Young Napoleon," still looked the part of a military hero despite having been sacked by Lincoln, and the Democrats were more than happy to blame Lincoln rather than McClellan for the demotion. They placed McClellan, fully uniformed, at the head of their ticket, where he vowed to fight the war to victory. In doing so, he contradicted the platform, which resolved that "justice, humanity, liberty and the public welfare demand that immediate efforts be made for a cessation of hostilities."

The finesse might have worked to elect McClellan. Lincoln thought it would, though he was certain it couldn't win the war. Should the Democrats win, the pressure for a cease-fire, at least, would be overwhelming. The South would use the time to replenish, while the North would become accustomed to peace. The peace party in the North would grow, and the war would likely never be resumed. The Union would be permanently lost.

August began dismally for Lincoln. Grant still struggled to find traction in Virginia; Atlanta stubbornly defied Sherman. Thurlow Weed, as astute an observer of politics as existed in the North, visited the White House to deliver a bleak forecast. "I told Mr. Lincoln that his reelection was an impossibility," Weed afterward informed William Seward. "Nobody here doubts it"—Weed was writing from New York—"nor do I see anybody from other states who authorizes the slightest hope of success." Lincoln's insistence on emancipation was an anchor dragging the party down. "The people are wild for peace. They are told that the President will only listen to terms of peace on condition that slavery be abandoned." Weed's confidants were imploring him to get the president to soften his stance. "Commissioners should be immediately sent to Richmond offering to treat for peace on the basis of Union." Weed endorsed the idea. "That something should be done and promptly done to give the administration a chance for its life is certain."

Others brought the same message. Alexander Hamilton was a grandson of the famous treasury secretary, a general in the Union army, and a man of sound political instincts and solid connections. He answered a summons from Lincoln, who requested that he give speeches on behalf of the war effort and the administration. "No, sir," Hamilton replied. "As things stand at present I don't know what in the name of God I could say, as an honest man, that would help you." Lincoln needed to make drastic changes. "Unless you clean these men away who surround you, and do something with your army, you will be beaten overwhelmingly."

Lincoln responded that this was plain talk. But it was nothing he hadn't thought of himself. "You think I don't know I am going to be beaten," he said. *"But I do,* and unless some great change takes place, *badly beaten."* He reflected on public disappointment with the war. "The people promised themselves when General Grant started out that he would take Richmond in June. He didn't take it, and they blame me. But I promised them no such thing. And yet they hold me responsible."

Hamilton reiterated that big changes had to be made. He recommended tossing out nearly the entire cabinet. "No matter whether you like the men or not. You must send them away at once. If they are friends, they'll go cheerfully for your sake. If they are enemies, what the hell do you care what they think?"

"That's very plain talk," Lincoln repeated.

"Regular backwoods," Hamilton acknowledged. "But I do not mean to deceive you."

Lincoln asked again whether Hamilton would speak on the administration's behalf.

Hamilton once more declined. "It would not look well for me to go out canvassing for you in uniform, and I think if I take it off it will be to make speeches against you." He looked directly at Lincoln. "If I tender you my resignation you will know what it means."

"Yes, I'll not misunderstand you," Lincoln said.

———

FREDERICK DOUGLASS MET with Lincoln during the dark days. "The President's '*To whom it may concern*' frightened his party and his party in return frightened the President," Douglass wrote in a letter to an abolitionist ally. "The country was struck with one of those bewilderments which dethrone reason for the moment. Everybody was thinking and dreaming of peace, and the impression had gone abroad that the President's antislavery policy was about the only thing which prevented a peaceful settlement with the rebels. McClellan was nominated and at that time his prospects were bright as Mr. Lincoln's were gloomy." From every side the president was pressed to modify his policy. He invited Douglass to the White House and sought his counsel. "He showed me a letter written with a view to meet the peace clamor raised against him. The first point made in it was the important fact that no man or set of men authorized to speak for the Confederate government had ever submitted a proposition for peace to him. Hence the charge that he had in some way stood in the way of peace fell to the ground. He had always stood ready to listen to any such propositions. The next point referred to was the charge that he had in his Niagara letter committed himself and the country to an abolition war rather than a war for the Union, so that even if the latter could be attained by negotiation, the war would go on for abolition. The President did not propose to take back what he had said in his Niagara letter but wished to relieve the fears of his peace friends by making it appear that the thing which they feared could not happen and was wholly beyond his power."

Lincoln explained his reasoning to Douglass. "Even if I would, I could not carry on the war for the abolition of slavery," he said. "The country would not sustain such a war, and I could do nothing without the support of Congress. I could not make the abolition of slavery an absolute prior condition to the reestablishment of the Union." He asked Douglass directly, "Shall I send forth this letter?"

"Certainly not," Douglass answered. "It would be given a broader meaning than you intend to convey. It would be taken as a complete surrender of your antislavery policy and do you serious damage."

Commenting to his abolitionist friend, Douglass wrote, "I have looked and feared that Mr. Lincoln would say something of the sort, but he has been perfectly silent on that point and I think will remain so. But the thing which alarmed me most was this: The President said he wanted some plan devised by which we could get more of the slaves within our lines. He thought that now was their time—and *that such only of them as succeeded in getting within our lines would be free after the war is over.* This shows that the President only has faith in his proclamations of freedom during the war and that he believes their operation will cease with the war."

Douglass went on to say to his friend that he himself was lying low during the election campaign. "I am not doing much in this presidential canvass for the reason that Republican committees do not wish to expose themselves to the charge of being the 'Niggar' party. The negro is the deformed child which is put out of the room when company comes. I hope to speak some after the election, though not much before, and I am inclined to think I shall be able to speak all the more usefully because I have had so little to say during the present canvass." Douglass supported Lincoln, but ambivalently. "When there was any shadow of a hope that a man of more decided antislavery convictions and policy could be elected, I was not for Mr. Lincoln, but as soon as the Chicago convention my mind was made up and it is made up still."

LINCOLN DIDN'T SEND the letter. Instead, on August 23 he wrote what amounted to an obituary for his administration and its hopes. "This morning, as for some days past, it seems exceedingly probable that this Administration will not be re-elected," he said. "Then it will be my duty to so co-operate with the President elect as to save the Union between the election and the inauguration, as he will have secured his election on such ground that he cannot possibly save it afterwards."

Lincoln signed, folded and sealed the note. He carried it to a meeting of the cabinet and, without divulging the contents, had each of the members sign its back. Lincoln intended to unseal the note after McClellan's victory, as an explanation of the course he would then follow. He would invite the president-elect to the White House. "I would say, 'General, the election has demonstrated that you are stronger, have more influence with the American people than I. Now let us together, you with your influence and I with all the executive power of the government, try to save the country. You raise as many troops as you possibly can for this final trial, and I will devote all my energies to assisting and finishing the war.'"

William Seward, on hearing this, objected, "And the general would answer you 'Yes, yes,' and the next day when you saw him again and pressed these views upon him, he would say, 'Yes, yes,' and so on forever, and would have done nothing at all."

"At least," replied Lincoln, "I should have done my duty and have stood clear before my own conscience."

T O LINCOLN'S SURPRISE, it didn't come to that. The president thought William Sherman had fallen off the map, so little did he hear from Georgia. The Confederate commander John Bell Hood couldn't find Sherman either—until Sherman showed up on the back side of Atlanta, having severed the last rail link to the city. Hood had to scramble simply to save his army; he left to Sherman the Georgia capital. At nearly the same moment David Farragut and his Union gunboats took Mobile, essentially closing Confederate access to the Gulf of Mexico.

After months of bad news from the battlefront, the good news bathed the North in relief and gratitude. Lincoln formally thanked God and the Union's gallant soldiers. The recent victories, he said, called for "devout acknowledgment to the Supreme Being in whose hands are the destinies of nations." The president declared a day of remembrance, requesting "that on next Sunday, in all places of public worship in the United States, thanksgiving be offered to Him for His mercy in preserving our national existence against the insurgent rebels who so long have been waging a cruel war against the government of the United States, for its overthrow, and also that prayer be made for the Divine protection to our brave soldiers and their leaders in the field."

In private Lincoln recalculated the likely votes in the coming election. The Union victories cut the legs from beneath McClellan's candidacy. McClellan's complaint against Lincoln had been that the Union wasn't winning the war. Suddenly it *was* winning, and McClellan's challenge to the president—by a general, no less—appeared unseemly at best, unpatriotic at worst. Voters and then states that had looked certain to reject the president now embraced him. When Union cavalry commander Phil Sheridan rolled up Confederate forces in the Shenandoah Valley, the turn of the tide was complete. "It does look as if the people wanted me to stay here a little longer," Lincoln told a visitor. "And I suppose I shall have to, if they do."

THEY DID, and he did. Lincoln defeated McClellan handily in the popular vote and overwhelmingly in the electoral vote. The victory brought supporters to the White House to cheer for the reelected president. Lincoln was in a thoughtful mood. "It has long been a grave question whether any government, not *too* strong for the liberties of its people, can be strong *enough* to maintain its own existence in great emergencies," he said. The election had been held, the war notwithstanding, and the people had delivered their verdict. "But the rebellion continues; and now that the election is over, may not all, having a common interest, reunite in a common effort to save our common country?"

Amid the campaign, Maryland had decided to abolish slavery. Maryland Unionists, whose numbers had grown with the rising fortunes of the Union army, made emancipation a central issue in efforts to revise the state's constitution, and with the help of Union soldiers given leave to vote, they carried the day. A delegation personally delivered the good news to Lincoln at the White House.

"Most heartily do I congratulate you, and Maryland, and the nation, and the world, upon the event," Lincoln declared in response. "I regret that it did not occur two years sooner, which I am sure would have saved to the nation more money than would have met all the private loss incident to the measure. But it has come at last, and I sincerely hope its friends may fully realize all their anticipations of good from it, and that its opponents may, by its effects, be agreeably and profitably disappointed."

A few weeks later another group of Maryland Unionists paid him a visit. Lincoln congratulated them anew on their accomplishment, saying it was more significant that Maryland had voted to end slavery than that it had voted to retain him in office. Presidential elections came every four years, he said, but emancipation was permanent.

The outcome of the war was nearly certain, though the end was not yet in sight, when Lincoln issued his fourth annual message in early December. He urged Congress to deliver the final blow to slavery. An emancipation amendment had been introduced by Republicans in the Senate earlier that year. The senators debated the form and wording of the measure before approving it by the necessary two-thirds majority. The House of Representatives balked, however; with every seat up for grabs in the approaching election—not just a third of the seats, as in the Senate—proportionately fewer members were willing to make the irretrievable step. The outcome of the election, in which the Republicans gained fifty House seats, changed the reckoning. The pro-amendment forces took heart, and the antis, many now lame ducks, saw little reason to stand in the way of history.

Lincoln gave the process a nudge. Almost certainly the next Congress would approve the amendment if the present one did not, he said. "Hence there is only a question of time as to when the proposed amendment will go to the states for their action. And as it is to so go at all events, may we not agree that the sooner the better?" He conceded that the recent elections did not bind the current members of Congress. But it did reveal the sense of the country. "It is the voice of the people now for the first time heard upon the question. In a great national crisis like ours, unanimity of action among those seeking a common end is very desirable, almost indispensable." The people had spoken; Congress must listen. Lincoln didn't presume to dictate; the Constitution gave no role to the president in amendments. Nor did he propose to make emancipation an explicit condition of peace. Yet he repeated what he had said earlier: "While I remain in my present position I shall not attempt to retract or modify the emancipation proclamation, nor shall I return to slavery any person who is free by the terms of that proclamation or by any of the acts of Congress." He now added, "If the people should, by whatever mode or means, make it an executive duty to re-enslave such persons, another, and not I, must be their instrument to perform it."

WHEN THE HOLDOVER House took up the measure in January 1865, the president prodded wavering members, despite his disclaimer of an executive role in amending the Constitution. He buttonholed a Democrat whose brother had been mortally wounded in the Battle of Chancellorsville. Lincoln had visited the dying man in the hospital and done what he could to ease his pain. "Your brother died to save the republic from death by the slaveholders' rebellion," he now observed to the lawmaker. "I wish you could see it to be your duty to vote for the constitutional amendment ending slavery." The member voted in favor.

Officials of Lincoln's administration and certain of his allies in Congress employed methods of persuasion common to the era, sometimes with Lincoln's knowledge, typically with his tacit approval. Offices were promised; reciprocal support was pledged for unrelated measures; quite possibly money exchanged hands. Whether the inducements swayed votes was difficult to know; in the murky dawn of the Gilded Age, lawmakers often expected to be rewarded for doing what they had intended to do anyway.

The final vote was close, but positive. Celebrants again swept to the White House, where Lincoln was finally getting the hang of responding. The moment, he said, called for congratulation to the country and the whole world. But the work was not yet finished. "There is a task yet before us—to go forward and consummate by the votes of the states that which Congress so nobly began yesterday." Loud applause. Lincoln reported that his own state, Illinois, had ratified the amendment that very day. More applause. He claimed some credit for himself in having issued the Emancipation Proclamation. More applause. "But that proclamation falls far short of what the amendment will be when fully consummated." Lincoln acknowledged the questions that had been raised about the proclamation. Some people doubted its legal validity; others had said it didn't go far enough. Those questions were now moot. "This amendment is a king's cure for all the evils. It winds the whole thing up." Tremendous applause.

T HERE REMAINED the matter of the war. The Confederates were in dire straits but weren't quite defeated. Their principal problem was manpower, for where Northern numbers allowed Grant to replace each soldier lost, the slimmer Southern population left Lee to watch his ranks dwindle. In desperation Confederate leaders considered a measure unthinkable to most only months before: making soldiers of their slaves. As Lee explained to Andrew Hunter, a Virginia friend and legislator—and the prosecutor of John Brown—Lincoln's Emancipation Proclamation was having precisely the military effect its advocates had forecast. It augmented the Union army even as it deprived the South of essential labor. The situation would get worse if the South continued to rely on white soldiers alone. "Should the war continue under existing circumstances, the enemy may in course of time penetrate our country and get access to a large part of our negro population. It is his avowed policy to convert the able-bodied men among them into soldiers, and to emancipate all." The South faced a stark choice. "We must decide whether slavery shall be extinguished by our enemies and the slaves be used against us, or use them ourselves at the risk of the effects which may be produced upon our social institutions." Lee preferred the latter. "My own opinion is that we should employ them without delay. I believe that with proper regulations they can be made efficient soldiers. They possess the physical qualifications in an eminent degree. Long habits of obedience and subordination, coupled with the moral influence which in our country the white man possesses over the black, furnish an excellent foundation for that discipline which is the best guaranty of military efficiency."

Lee acknowledged that the slaves must be offered an incentive to fight for the South; they needed to have an interest in the outcome. "Such an interest we can give our negroes by giving immediate freedom to all who enlist, and freedom at the end of the war to the families of those who discharge their duties faithfully (whether they survive or not), together with the privilege of residing at the South. To this might be added a bounty for faithful service." Immediate freedom for enlistees was essential. "We should not expect slaves to fight for prospective freedom when they can secure it at once by going to the enemy, in whose service they will incur no greater risk than in ours." Eventual freedom for all slaves would be the logical, and acceptable, consequence. "The best means of securing the efficiency and fidelity of this auxiliary force would be to accompany the measure with a well-digested plan of gradual and general emancipation. As that will be the result of the continuance of the war, and will certainly occur if the enemy succeed, it seems most advisable to adopt it at once, and thereby obtain all the benefits that will accrue to our cause."

Lee's proposal was an abomination to others among the Confederate leaders. "I think that the proposition to make soldiers of our slaves is the most pernicious idea that has been suggested since the war began," declared Howell Cobb, a former governor of Georgia and currently a Confederate general. "It is to me a source of deep mortification and regret to see the name of that good and great man and soldier, General R. E. Lee, given as authority for such a policy. My first hour of despondency will be the one in which such a policy shall be adopted. You cannot make soldiers of slaves, nor slaves of soldiers. The moment you resort to negro soldiers your white soldiers will be lost to you; and one secret of the favor with which the proposition has been received in portions of the Army is the hope that when negroes go into the Army they will be permitted to retire. It is simply a proposition to fight the balance of the war with negro troops. You can't keep white and black troops together, and you can't trust negroes by themselves." Cobb allowed that slaves might be manual laborers in support of the army. "Use all the negroes you can get, for all the purposes for which you need them, but don't arm them. The day you make soldiers of them is the beginning of the end of the revolution. If slaves will make good soldiers our whole theory of slavery is wrong."

The Confederate congress split the difference. In March 1865 it passed a law allowing the enlistment of slaves in the Confederate military, to serve in "whatever capacity" the Confederate president directed. That is, the black soldiers could be armed. But the measure was silent on emancipation. "Nothing in this act shall be construed to authorize a change in the relation which the said slaves shall bear toward their owners, except by consent of the owners and of the states in which they may reside," it declared.

THIS LAST—and unavailing—gasp of the Confederacy shortly followed Lincoln's first words of his second term. They were few but carefully chosen. "At this second appearing to take the oath of the presidential office there is less occasion for an extended address than there was at the first," he explained to the audience on the muddy Capitol grounds. "Then a statement somewhat in detail of a course to be pursued seemed fitting and proper. Now, at the expiration of four years, during which public declarations have been constantly called forth on every point and phase of the great contest which still absorbs the attention and engrosses the energies of the nation, little that is new could be presented. The progress of our arms, upon which all else chiefly depends, is as well known to the public as to myself, and it is, I trust, reasonably satisfactory and encouraging to all."

Lincoln considered that earlier inauguration. "Four years ago all thoughts were anxiously directed to an impending civil war. All dreaded it, all sought to avert it. While the inaugural address was being delivered from this place, devoted altogether to *saving* the Union without war, insurgent agents were in the city seeking to *destroy* it without war, seeking to dissolve the Union and divide effects by negotiation. Both parties deprecated war, but one of them would *make* war rather than let the nation survive, and the other would *accept* war rather than let it perish, and the war came."

He reflected on the cause of the war. "One-eighth of the whole population were colored slaves, not distributed generally over the Union, but localized in the southern part of it. These slaves consti-tuted a peculiar and powerful interest. All knew that this interest was somehow the cause of the war. To strengthen, perpetuate and extend this interest was the object for which the insurgents would rend the

Union even by war, while the government claimed no right to do more than to restrict the territorial enlargement of it."

The course of the war had surprised both sides. "Neither party expected for the war the magnitude or the duration which it has already attained. Neither anticipated that the cause of the conflict might cease with or even before the conflict itself should cease. Each looked for an easier triumph, and a result less fundamental and astounding."

Lincoln referred to God more freely these days, perhaps because the weight of the war had become too much for him to bear alone. But he did so modestly, appreciating that appeals to the Almighty weren't a monopoly of either side in the conflict. "Both read the same Bible and pray to the same God," he said. "And each invokes His aid against the other. It may seem strange that any men should dare to ask a just God's assistance in wringing their bread from the sweat of other men's faces, but let us judge not, that we be not judged. The prayers of both could not be answered. That of neither has been answered fully. The Almighty has His own purposes."

He quoted the evangelist Matthew: "Woe unto the world because of offenses, for it must needs be that offenses come, but woe to that man by whom the offense cometh." In his own voice he said, "If we shall suppose that American slavery is one of those offenses which, in the providence of God, must needs come, but which, having continued through His appointed time, He now wills to remove, and that He gives to both North and South this terrible war as the woe due to those by whom the offense came, shall we discern therein any departure from those divine attributes which the believers in a living God always ascribe to Him?"

He was approaching his end. "Fondly do we hope, fervently do we pray, that this mighty scourge of war may speedily pass away. Yet if God wills that it continue until all the wealth piled by the bondsman's two hundred and fifty years of unrequited toil shall be sunk, and until every drop of blood drawn with the lash shall be paid by another drawn with the sword, as was said three thousand years ago so still it must be said, 'The judgments of the Lord are true and righteous altogether.'"

It was a sobering thought: that there might be much more blood to shed. He closed on a more promising note. "With malice toward none, with charity for all, with firmness in the right as God gives us to see the right, let us strive on to finish the work we are in, to bind up the nation's wounds, to care for him who shall have borne the battle and for his widow and his orphan, to do all which may achieve and cherish a just and lasting peace among ourselves and with all nations."

FREDERICK DOUGLASS ATTENDED Lincoln's inauguration, and while he recognized how far the country had come since the first inauguration, he sensed some unnerving similarities between the two moments. "There was murder in the air then, and there was murder in the air now," Douglass wrote. "His first inauguration arrested the fall of the republic, and the second was to restore it to enduring foundations. At the time of the second inauguration the rebellion was apparently vigorous, defiant, and formidable, but in reality, weak, dejected, and desperate. It had reached that verge of madness when it had called upon the negro for help to fight against the freedom which he so longed to find, for the bondage he would escape—against Lincoln the emancipator, for Davis the enslaver. But desperation discards logic as well as law, and the South was desperate." Grant was at the gates of Richmond, and Sherman had reached the sea. The days of the Confederacy were numbered. "This condition of things made the air at Washington dark and lowering. The friends of the Confederate cause here were neither few nor insignificant. They were among the rich and influential. A wink or a nod from such men might unchain the hand of violence and set order and law at defiance. To those who saw beneath the surface it was clearly perceived that there was danger abroad, and as the procession passed down Pennsylvania Avenue I for one felt an instinctive apprehension that at any moment a shot from some assassin in the crowd might end the glittering pageant and throw the country into the depths of anarchy."

Douglass suppressed his grim thoughts for the moment. Lincoln had won; the Union was being secured; slavery's days were numbered. He joined the throng gathered to witness the new beginning. "Reaching the Capitol, I took my place in the crowd where I could see the presidential procession as it came upon the east portico, and where I could hear and see all that took place." Little of celebration infused the moment. "The whole proceeding was wonderfully quiet, earnest, and solemn. From the oath as administered by Chief Justice Chase"— Salmon Chase had succeeded Roger Taney, who had died the previous autumn after twenty-eight years in office—"to the brief but weighty address delivered by Mr. Lincoln, there was a leaden stillness about the crowd. The address sounded more like a sermon than like a state paper. In the fewest words possible he referred to the condition of the country four years before on his first accession to the presidency, to the causes of the war, and the reasons on both sides for which it had been waged."

Douglass deemed the words well suited to the occasion. "They struck me at the time, and have seemed to me ever since, to contain more vital substance than I have ever seen compressed in a space so narrow." Yet this judgment wasn't universally shared. "When I clapped my hands in gladness and thanksgiving at their utterance, I saw in the faces of many about me expressions of widely different emotion." Already the course of reconstruction was being contested; by no means did all of Lincoln's listeners take pleasure in his call for reconciliation.

On that day Douglass encountered the new vice president, who intensified his foreboding. "I was standing in the crowd by the side of Mrs. Thomas J. Dorsey, when Mr. Lincoln"—who had seen Douglass in the audience—"touched Mr. Johnson and pointed me out to him. The first expression which came to his face, and which I think was the true index of his heart, was one of bitter contempt and aversion. Seeing that I observed him, he tried to assume a more friendly appearance, but it was too late; it is useless to close the door when all within has been seen. His first glance was the frown of the man; the second was the bland and sickly smile of the demagogue. I turned to Mrs. Dorsey"—the wife of a prominent black man of Philadelphia—"and said, 'Whatever Andrew Johnson may be, he certainly is no friend of our race.'"

Douglass remained in the capital through the evening. "The usual reception was given at the executive mansion, and though no colored persons had ever ventured to present themselves on such occasions, it seemed, now that freedom had become the law of the republic, and colored men were on the battlefield mingling their blood with that of white men in one common effort to save the country, that it was not too great an assumption for a colored man to offer his congratulations to the President with those of other citizens. I decided to go." He tried to get other black men to go with him, but all begged off, not wishing to share the embarrassment they felt sure Douglass would experience. "It was finally arranged that Mrs. Dorsey should bear me company, so together we joined in the grand procession of citizens from all parts of the country, and moved slowly towards the executive mansion. I had for some time looked upon myself as a man, but now in this multitude of the elite of the land, I felt myself a man among men."

His pride took a blow when he reached the door. "Two policemen stationed there took me rudely by the arm and ordered me to stand back, for their directions were to admit no persons of my color." Douglass instantly objected. "I told the officers I was quite sure there must be some mistake, for no such order could have emanated from President Lincoln; and that if he knew I was at the door he would desire my admission." The officers, not wishing a scene, escorted him in. But instead of taking him to the main reception room, they hustled him toward a side exit. As soon as he realized what was afoot, Douglass stopped and stood his ground. "You have deceived me," he declared. "I shall not go out of this building till I see President Lincoln." Just then a white man Douglass knew passed by on the way in. Douglass got his attention. "Be so kind as to say to Mr. Lincoln that Frederick Douglass is detained by officers at the door," he said. Shortly there came back orders that Douglass and his friend were to be admitted. "Mrs. Dorsey and I walked into the spacious East Room, amid a scene of elegance such as in this country I had never before witnessed. Like a mountain pine high above all others, Mr. Lincoln stood, in his grand simplicity and home-like beauty. Recognizing me, even before I reached him, he exclaimed, so that all around could hear him, 'Here comes my friend Douglass.'"

Lincoln drew Douglass aside. "I am glad to see you," he said. "I saw you in the crowd today, listening to my inaugural address. How did you like it?"

"Mr. Lincoln, I must not detain you with my poor opinion, when there are thousands waiting to shake hands with you," Douglass replied.

"No, no, you must stop a little, Douglass. There is no man in the country whose opinion I value more than yours. I want to know what you think of it."

"Mr. Lincoln, that was a sacred effort," Douglass said.

"I am glad you liked it," Lincoln said.

IF FREDERICK DOUGLASS HEARD an echo of John Brown in Lincoln's second inaugural address, he didn't mention it. But as one who had known Brown well, Douglass—then or later—must have reflected that Lincoln's suggestion that "every drop of blood drawn with the lash shall be paid by another drawn with the sword" sounded chillingly like Brown's final prediction that "the crimes of this guilty land will never be purged away but with blood."

John Wilkes Booth hadn't known Brown, although he had made a point of attending his execution. Nor did he know Abraham Lincoln, though he watched and listened at Lincoln's second inauguration. Booth had come to his own conclusion about blood and guilt, and he intended to act on it, in a way not unlike Brown's. "John Brown was a man inspired, the grandest character of the century!" he had said then. He now cast himself in a similar role. Booth's identification with the South had intensified since Harpers Ferry. As the secession crisis unfolded in the weeks after Lincoln's first election, Booth composed a dramatic soliloquy supporting the South. "I will fight with all my heart and soul, even if there's not a man to back me, for equal rights and justice to the South," he vowed. Those who disagreed should not be let to live. "Such men I call traitors, and treason should be stamped to death and not allowed to stalk abroad in any land. So deep is my hatred for such men that I could wish I had them in my grasp and I the power to crush. I'd grind them into dust!" Booth valued the small part he had played against treason. "I saw John Brown hung, and I blessed the justice of my country's laws. I may say I helped to hang John Brown, and while I live, I shall think with joy upon the day when I saw the sun go down upon one traitor less within our land."

Booth didn't deliver this speech in public, but its themes festered as the war developed. Lincoln became the arch villain in Booth's drama. "*He* is Bonaparte in one great move," Booth told his sister in 1864. "That is, by overturning this blind republic and making himself a king. This man's reelection which will follow his success, I tell you, will be a reign!" After Lincoln indeed was reelected, Booth harked back to his moment with John Brown. The story improved in Booth's telling. "When I aided in the capture and execution of John Brown— who was a murderer on our Western border, and who was fairly tried and convicted before an impartial judge and jury of treason, and who, by the way, has since been made a god—I was proud of my little share in the transaction, for I deemed it my duty and that I was helping our common country to perform an act of justice. But what was a crime in poor John Brown is considered (by themselves) as the greatest and only virtue of the whole Republican party. Strange transmigration, *vice* to become a *virtue*, simply because more indulge in it. I thought then, as now, that the abolitionists were the only traitors in the land. And that the entire party deserved the fate of poor old Brown."

Booth plotted his—and the South's, as he saw it—revenge against Lincoln. He conspired to kidnap Lincoln and carry him off to the South. But as Confederate forces lost ground in the months after Lincoln's reelection, the difficulty of reaching Confederate territory increased, and the conspiracy shifted to assassination. Booth now likened Lincoln to Julius Caesar, and himself to Brutus. "If the South is to be aided it must be done quickly," he wrote. "It may already be too late. When Caesar had conquered the enemies of Rome and the power that was his menaced the liberties of the people, Brutus arose and slew him. The stroke of his dagger was guided by his love of Rome."

Booth's dagger was in fact a pistol. On the evening of April 14— five days after Robert E. Lee surrendered to Ulysses Grant at Appomattox Court House, effectively ending the war—he shot Lincoln in the back of the head at Ford's Theatre in Washington.

Booth escaped the theater on horseback and fled Washington through Maryland and Virginia. A broken leg, from landing awkwardly on the stage, slowed him and then compelled him to find a doctor. A manhunt filled several days; at last he was cornered in a barn in Virginia.

Perhaps his memory of John Brown made him hope for arrest and trial; with his dramatic training he could imagine delivering a speech as memorable as Brown's closing statement to the Charles Town court. Or maybe Booth didn't think about that at all, or changed his mind, for when soldiers closed in, he refused their demand that he surrender, and was fatally shot.

L INCOLN DIED the day after he was shot. And death linked him
to John Brown in a way their lives never had.

Some in the South, sharing Booth's bitterness, applauded the
killing, but many others feared Union reprisals for the murder. Jefferson Davis, on learning the news, remarked, "I certainly have no
special regard for Mr. Lincoln, but there are a great many men of
whose end I would much rather hear than his."

Southern blacks had special cause for worry. Effective emancipation for slaves in the Confederacy awaited the arrival of Union forces.
And even then it didn't always come at once. William Sherman
recalled a moment on the march through Georgia when his soldiers
were pitching camp. "I walked up to a plantation house close by, where
were assembled many negroes, among them an old, gray-haired man,
of as fine a head as I ever saw," Sherman wrote. "I asked him if he
understood about the war and its progress. He said he did; that he had
been looking for the 'angel of the Lord' ever since he was knee-high,
and, though we professed to be fighting for the Union, he supposed
slavery was the cause, and that our success was to be his freedom."
Sherman asked the man if the other slaves in that area held the same
view. "He said they surely did. I then explained to him that we wanted
the slaves to remain where they were, and not to load us down with
useless mouths, which would eat up the food needed for our fighting
men; that our success was their assured freedom; that we could receive
a few of their young, hearty men as pioneers; but that, if they followed
us in swarms of old and young, feeble and helpless, it would simply
load us down and cripple us in our great task." Sherman recalled the
result. "I believe that old man spread this message to the slaves, which

was carried from mouth to mouth, to the very end of our journey, and that it in part saved us from the great danger we incurred of swelling our numbers so that famine would have attended our progress."

A consequence of the forbearance of the slaves was that at war's end their hopes for the arrival of the "angel of the Lord" were greater than ever. But suddenly, with Lincoln's killing, their freedom was in doubt. Few slaves knew more than a smattering about Andrew Johnson, but a white slave-owner from Tennessee couldn't be expected to have much sympathy for black folks. "The colored people express their sorrow and sense of loss in many cases with sobs and loud lamentations!" a South Carolina schoolteacher wrote in her diary. "Secesh come back; we're going to be slaves again," recently liberated black men and women were heard saying.

The laments in the North were less personal but more openly aired. In meeting halls and churches across the North, Lincoln was eulogized by hundreds of speakers. He was shot on Good Friday and died on Saturday; on Easter Sunday preachers drew the connection to Jesus, whose resurrection they were celebrating. None suggested that Lincoln would rise from the dead, but many prayed that his death might foreshadow the rebirth of the nation after its searing trial. "Without the shedding of blood is no remission," said a Cincinnati divine, in words borrowed from Saint Paul and echoed by many that day.

Lincoln himself had raised the issue of blood atonement in his second inaugural address. Now his own blood was part of the reckoning, and his link to John Brown more compelling. Brown had foretold blood atonement while becoming one of the first sacrifices; Lincoln at the time had resisted the concept for his country and scarcely imagined it for himself. But he made decisions whose consequences included a bloodletting far greater than anything Brown had envisioned, and finally his own death. Brown was a first martyr in the war that freed the slaves, Lincoln one of the last.

More slowly than Brown and more tentatively, Lincoln had summoned heaven to justify his actions. Brown professed to know that God was on his side; Lincoln only hoped He was. "If God wills" was Lincoln's preferred construction; the president didn't presume to commit the Almighty. But over the course of the war, as the carnage mounted, he felt compelled to call on heaven for moral support.

Did he question his own actions? Did he ask if there could have been another way? Almost constantly, and until the end. No one tried harder and more persistently than Lincoln to find a nonviolent path to freedom for the slaves. From his first call for compensated emancipation in the District of Columbia, while a member of Congress, to his last offer of the same to the Southern states, even on the verge of congressional approval of the Thirteenth Amendment, he fondly hoped and fervently prayed that money might spare blood in expiating America's original sin. But those who hadn't heeded John Brown wouldn't heed Brown's reluctant successor, and the slaughter continued, until the last drops of blood—including Lincoln's own—were shed.

IN ONE OF LINCOLN'S final speeches, to the crowd applauding the approval of the Thirteenth Amendment by Congress, the president reminded his listeners that the work of emancipation wouldn't be finished until the amendment had been ratified by the states. The war had made emancipation possible, but the peace might yet make it unconstitutional, if the Constitution itself weren't changed.

Ratification arrived more swiftly, and by different means, than he guessed. Lincoln's martyrdom imbued ratification with an irresistible urgency, and within eight months of his death the required three-quarters of the states had approved. American slavery was no more.

The end of slavery didn't imply full black freedom. Southern states enacted "black codes" that reinstituted slavery in all but name. The Radical Republicans who took control of Reconstruction after Lincoln's death overturned these, but violence by the Ku Klux Klan and kindred groups and the oppressive system of sharecropping kept most blacks from enjoying anything like the freedoms taken for granted by whites. W. E. B. Du Bois, writing decades later, declared, "Slavery was not abolished even after the Thirteenth Amendment. There were four million freedmen and most of them on the same plantation, doing the same work that they did before emancipation."

Frederick Douglass saw things differently, not least because he had been a slave. Douglass appreciated the injustice black men and women still suffered in the South, but he understood the monumental importance of removing them from the realm of property and remaking them, with the additional help of the Fourteenth Amendment, into citizens. The basic law of the land had long been against them; now it was on their side, even if its promises too frequently went unenforced.

Douglass traveled to Harpers Ferry in 1881, to speak at Storer College, an institute for former slaves and their children, which had recently established a John Brown Professorship. The mere existence of such a college, not to mention the naming of a professorship for John Brown, reminded Douglass what progress had been made in the years since he had tried to talk Brown out of his suicidal mission to this very place. Douglass recounted the violent deeds of that time, to an audience who knew Brown by name but not much more. "It certainly is not a story to please, but to pain," Douglass acknowledged. "It is not a story to increase our sense of social safety and security, but to fill the imagination with wild and troubled fancies of doubt and danger." Yet it could not have been otherwise. "The bloody harvest of Harper's Ferry was ripened by the heat and moisture of merciless bondage of more than two hundred years. That startling cry of alarm on the banks of the Potomac was but the answering back of the avenging angel to the midnight invasions of Christian slave traders on the sleeping hamlets of Africa." Douglass candidly recalled his own refusal to join Brown's mission. "His zeal in the cause of my race was far greater than mine. It was as the burning sun to my taper light. Mine was bounded by time; his stretched away to the boundless shores of eternity. I could live for the slave, but he could die for him."

Brown's incandescence had kindled the nation, Douglass said. "The armies of the nation have found it necessary to do on a large scale what John Brown attempted to do on a small one." Yet opinion on Brown was still divided. He had subverted a state; innocent people had been killed. "Brown assumed tremendous responsibility in making war upon the peaceful people of Harper's Ferry," Douglass said.

But Brown had his reasons. "In his eye a slave-holding community could not be peaceable but was, in the nature of the case, in one incessant state of war. To him such a community was not more sacred than a band of robbers; it was the right of any one to assault it by day or night." Brown saw no hope for change by moral or political means. "He knew the proud and hard hearts of the slave-holders, and that they never would consent to give up their slaves till they felt a big stick about their heads."

The raid on Harpers Ferry had freed no slaves. "Did John Brown fail?" asked Douglass. He considered the matter. "He certainly did fail to get out of Harper's Ferry before being beaten down by United States soldiers. He did fail to save his own life, and to lead a liberating army into the mountains of Virginia."

But this posed the wrong question. John Brown did not go to Harpers Ferry to save his life. "The true question is, Did John Brown draw his sword against slavery and thereby lose his life *in vain*? And to this I answer ten thousand times: No! No man fails, or can fail who so grandly gives himself and all he has to a righteous cause." John Brown, in losing his life, set in motion events that succeeded better than he ever dreamed. "If John Brown did not end the war that ended slavery, he did at least begin the war that ended slavery," Douglass said. "John Brown began the war that ended American slavery and made this a free republic. Until this blow was struck, the prospect for freedom was dim, shadowy and uncertain. The irrepressible conflict was one of words, votes and compromises. When John Brown stretched forth his arm the sky was cleared. The time for compromises was gone; the armed hosts of freedom stood face to face over the chasm of a broken Union; and the clash of arms was at hand. The South staked all upon getting possession of the federal government, and failing to do that, drew the sword of rebellion and thus made her own, and not Brown's, the lost cause of the century."

THE QUESTION HAD BEEN: What does a good man do when his country commits a great evil? John Brown chose the path of violence, Lincoln of politics. Yet the two paths wound up leading to the same place: the most terrible war in American history. Brown aimed at slavery and shattered the Union; Lincoln defended the Union and destroyed slavery.

Was one path more right, or more righteous, than the other? Brown's path had the advantage of immediacy; it was soul-satisfying to him, perhaps to his followers who lost their lives pursuing his vision, and definitely to those who praised him from a safe distance. Lincoln's path had the advantage of legitimacy; cloaked in the Constitution, even when he stretched that venerable fabric, Lincoln's accomplishment possessed authority that could come only from America's founding document, now amended.

Constitutional authority wasn't everything, as the postwar experience of the former slaves showed. Most Southern slaveholders weren't any more convinced of the evil of their ways by Lincoln than they had been by Brown. Union arms, not Union arguments, overthrew slavery. Brown was perhaps right, by the time he said it, that only blood would purge America of slavery. The South was not to be talked out of slavery. Yet Lincoln was certainly right in making violence a last resort. It mattered to the North, if not to the South, that Lincoln fought for the Union first and for emancipation only later. A war begun to end slavery would likely have lost the Union, by failing to engage Northern Democrats and other skeptics on the race question. But a war begun to save the Union could, and did, end by destroying slavery.

Frederick Douglass never warmed to Lincoln the way he did to John Brown. "He was preeminently the white man's president, entirely devoted to the welfare of white men," Douglass told an audience at a ceremony marking the eleventh anniversary of Lincoln's death. "He was ready and willing at any time during the first years of his administration to deny, postpone and sacrifice the rights of humanity in the colored people to promote the welfare of the white people of this country." Lincoln opposed the extension of slavery into the federal territories, but he did so for the good of whites, not of slaves. And he protected slavery in the South during the early part of the war. "He was ready to execute all the supposed guarantees of the United States Constitution in favor of the slave system anywhere inside the slave states. He was willing to pursue, recapture and send back the fugitive slave to his master, and to suppress a slave rising for liberty, though his guilty master was already in arms against the government." Speaking to the whites in his mixed audience, Douglass declared, "First, midst and last, you and yours were the objects of his deepest affection and his most earnest solicitude. You are the children of Abraham Lincoln." Turning to the blacks: "We are at best only his step-children, children by adoption, children by forces of circumstances and necessity."

And yet Lincoln did more good for the black race than any American before him. "Though the Union was more to him than our free-dom or our future, under his wise and beneficent rule we saw ourselves gradually lifted from the depths of slavery to the heights of liberty and manhood." Lincoln could not have done other than he had done—he could not have *been* other than he was—and served the black race so well. "Had he put the abolition of slavery before the salvation of the Union, he would have inevitably driven from him a powerful class of the American people and rendered resistance to rebellion impos-sible. Viewed from the genuine abolition ground, Mr. Lincoln seemed tardy, cold, dull and indifferent; but measuring him by the sentiment of his country, a sentiment he was bound as a statesman to consult, he was swift, zealous, radical and determined."

And at the crucial moment Lincoln dealt the decisive blow for liberty. "Can any colored man, or any white man friendly to the free-dom of all men, ever forget the night which followed the first day of January, 1863, when the world was to see if Abraham Lincoln would prove to be as good as his word? I shall never forget that memorable night, when in a distant city"—Boston—"I waited and watched at a public meeting, with three thousand others not less anxious than myself, for the word of deliverance." Thousands of heads in Doug-lass's audience nodded agreement, recalling where they had been on that historic evening. "Nor shall I ever forget the outburst of joy and thanksgiving that rent the air when the lightning brought to us the Emancipation Proclamation. In that happy hour we forgot all delay, and forgot all tardiness." The only thing that mattered was the historic deed. "We were thenceforward willing to allow the president all the latitude of time, phraseology and every honorable device that states-manship might require for the achievement of a great and beneficent measure of liberty and progress."

The work wasn't finished. The work of freedom never would be. In Douglass's audience this day were the most distinguished members of the United States government—the president, the chief justice, sena-tors and representatives—as well as leaders of the African American community, which had funded a statue of Lincoln, standing by a slave at the moment of emancipation. It was the first memorial to Lincoln in the nation's capital, and it hadn't come without controversy. The broader turmoil of Reconstruction, too, reminded all present that the struggle never ceased. Yet Douglass asked his audience to recall what Lincoln had accomplished for the two races together. "While Abraham Lincoln saved for you a country, he delivered us from a bondage, according to Jefferson, one hour of which was worse than ages of the oppression your fathers rose in rebellion to oppose." Without Lincoln's first accomplishment, the second couldn't have come. God worked in mysterious ways; Lincoln wasn't perfect, but he was perfectly suited to his task. "Taking him for all in all, measuring the tremendous magnitude of the work before him, considering the necessary means to ends, and surveying the end from the beginning, infinite wisdom has seldom sent any man into the world better fitted for his mission than Abraham Lincoln."

Douglass closed with a comment to his black audience. They knew full well that the struggle for freedom continued, for they suffered slights every day. But they could take collective pride in what they now saw before them. "When now it shall be said that the colored man is soulless, that he has no appreciation of benefits or benefactors; when the foul reproach of ingratitude is hurled at us, and it is attempted to scourge us beyond the range of human brotherhood, we may calmly point to the monument we have this day erected to the memory of Abraham Lincoln."

Acknowledgments

I have learned about the Civil War era from every author and editor whose works on the subject I have read since high school. The most pertinent of them for this book are identified in the source notes. But to all I am indebted.

Kris Puopolo and Bill Thomas at Doubleday kept nudging me to sharpen the focus; if anything is still blurry, it's not their fault. Ingrid Sterner continues to be a model copy editor.

My colleagues at the University of Texas at Austin are a generous repository of historical knowledge. My students pose a constant challenge to my storytelling skills: if I can hold their interest, I might be onto something. They can't get enough of John Brown.

Sources

The present book is based primarily on the words—written, spoken and remembered—of John Brown and Abraham Lincoln.

The best collection on Brown is *The Life and Letters of John Brown*, edited by Franklin Benjamin Sanborn (1885). A useful complement is "'His Soul Goes Marching On': The Life and Legacy of John Brown," West Virginia Archives and History, wvculture.org.

The outstanding Lincoln collection is *The Collected Works of Abraham Lincoln*, edited by Roy P. Basler et al. (1953–1955). The Abraham Lincoln Papers at the Library of Congress contain additional documents. Lincoln's presidential papers form part of the Papers of the Presidents, American Presidency Project, presidency.ucsb.edu.

Biographies of John Brown are numerous. The most useful for present purposes, balancing proximity to the subject and his times against historical perspective, is Oswald Garrison Villard, *John Brown* (1910).

Biographies of Lincoln are legion; several are cited in the notes. One worth particular mention is Michael Burlingame, *Abraham Lincoln: A Life* (2013), which is but a portion of a much larger manuscript the author has generously made available through the Lincoln Studies Center at Knox College, knox.edu.

Frederick Douglass plays an important role in the story of Brown and Lincoln. His *Narrative of the Life of Frederick Douglass* (1845) made him famous; his *Life and Times of Frederick Douglass* (1881) told what happened later. The finest biography of Douglass is David W. Blight, *Frederick Douglass: Prophet of Freedom* (2018).

Books on the period of the Civil War are too numerous to identify here even in the most summary manner. Yet two that deal especially with the central theme of the present work are Stephen B. Oates, *Our Fiery Trial: Abraham Lincoln, John Brown, and the Civil War Era* (1979), and Eric Foner, *The Fiery Trial: Abraham Lincoln and American Slavery* (2010).

Notes

Prologue

1 **"My Dear Wife"**: John Brown to Mary Brown, Oct. 31 and Nov. 3, 1859, in *The Life and Letters of John Brown*, comp. and ed. Franklin Benjamin Sanborn (1885), 579–80. This collection will be cited below as *Life and Letters*.

PART I · POTTAWATOMIE

Chapter 1

7 **"then a wilderness"**: Brown to Henry Stearns, July 15, 1857, in *Life and Letters*, 12–17.

10 **"The trouble is"**: Oswald Garrison Villard, *John Brown* (1910), 20, 58.

11 **"I have been trying to devise"**: Brown to Frederick Brown, Nov. 21, 1834, in *Life and Letters*, 40–41.

12 **"Instead of being"**: John Brown Jr. in *Life and Letters*, 88.

12 **"It is a Brown trait"**: Villard, *John Brown*, 28.

13 **"Here, before God"**: Recollection by Edward Brown in *Northwestern Congregationist*, Oct. 21, 1892, reprinted in *Nation*, Feb. 12, 1914.

Chapter 2

14 **"Thomas, the youngest son"**: Lincoln recollections for campaign biography, ca. June 1860, in *The Collected Works of Abraham Lincoln*, ed. Roy P. Basler et al. (1953), 4:61–62. This collection will be cited as *Collected Works*.

15 **"Oh, now, Sarah"**: Manuscript of Michael Burlingame, "Abraham Lincoln: A Life," vol. 1, chap. 1, p. 14, at Lincoln Studies Center, Knox College, knox.edu. Portions of this lengthy manuscript were published as *Abraham Lincoln: A Life* (2013). This source will be identified as "Burlingame MS."

15 **"A. now thinks that the aggregate"**: Lincoln recollections, ca. June 1860, in *Collected Works*, 4:62.

16 **"I used to be a slave"**: Eric Foner, *The Fiery Trial: Abraham Lincoln and American Slavery* (2010), 36.

16 **"When he was nineteen"**: Lincoln recollections, ca. June 1860, in *Collected Works*, 4:63.

16 **"Here they built a log-cabin"**: Ibid., 4:64–65.

18 **"It is true"**: David Herbert Donald, *Lincoln* (1995), 55–58. Historians have debated the accuracy of the stories told about Lincoln and Ann Rutledge. Lincoln never mentioned her in letters, and no letters from her to him survive.

But most Lincoln biographers, including Donald, grant the essence of the accounts.

Chapter 3

20 **"We were worked in all weathers"**: Frederick Douglass, *Narrative of the Life of Frederick Douglass* (1849), 63–73.

21 **"I have often been asked"**: Frederick Douglass, *The Life and Times of Frederick Douglass* (1882), 170.

22 **"In person he was lean"**: Ibid., 237–40.

Chapter 4

26 **"I do not think I can come"**: Lincoln to Joshua Speed, July 4, 1842, in *Collected Works*, 1:289.

27 **"I had known Abraham Lincoln"**: Jesse W. Weik, "Lincoln and the Matson Negroes," *Arena* 17 (1897): 755–57.

29 **"The doctors say"**: Burlingame MS., 1:6:547.

29 **"They believe that the institution"**: Protest by Lincoln and Dan Stone, March 3, 1837, in *Collected Works*, 1:75.

29 **"It is sometimes called"**: Charles Dickens, *American Notes for General Circulation* (1842), 1:282–85, 292–95.

31 **"All the house"**: Lincoln to Mary Todd Lincoln, April 16, 1848, in *Collected Works*, 1:465.

31 **"The country bordering"**: Lincoln recollections, ca. June 1860, in *Collected Works*, 4:66.

31 **"Let him answer"**: Lincoln remarks in House of Representatives, Jan. 12, 1848, in *Collected Works*, 1:439.

32 **"There was not one"**: Lincoln remarks in House of Representatives, Jan. 10, 1849, in *Collected Works*, 2:22.

32 **"Finding that I was abandoned"**: Lincoln remarks, undated 1861, in *Collected Works*, 2:22n.

33 **"His profession had almost"**: Lincoln recollections, ca. June 1860, in *Collected Works*, 4:67.

Chapter 5

34 **"a covenant with death"**: *William Lloyd Garrison: The Story of His Life as Told by His Children* (1894), 3:88.

35 **"Nothing so charms"**: Brown, "Words of Advice," Jan. 15, 1851, in *Life and Letters*, 124–26.

Chapter 6

37 **"He ever was"**: Lincoln eulogy of Henry Clay, July 6, 1852, in *Collected Works*, 2:130–32.

38 **"He was a man of low stature"**: *The Reminiscences of Carl Schurz* (1907), 2:30–31.

40 **"I have determined"**: Douglas speech in Senate, Dec. 23, 1851, in *Congressional Globe*, 32nd Cong., 1st sess., app., 68.

41 **"To the states of Missouri and Iowa"**: Douglas to J. H. Crane et al., Dec. 17, 1853, in *The Letters of Stephen A. Douglas*, ed. Robert W. Johannsen (1961), 268–71.

42 **"I know it will raise"**: Mrs. Archibald Dixon, *History of Missouri Compromise and Slavery in American Politics* (1903), 445.

42 "The bill rests upon": Douglas to editor of *Concord (N.H.) State Capitol Reporter*, Feb. 16, 1854, in *Letters of Stephen A. Douglas*, 284.

43 "I could travel": Robert W. Johannsen, *Stephen A. Douglas* (1997 ed.), 451.

Chapter 7

44 "The farm was a mere recent clearing": Richard Henry Dana Jr., "How We Met John Brown," *Atlantic Monthly*, July 1871, 6–7.

46 "Before he came": *Life and Letters of John Brown*, 103–4.

47 "The people of Kansas": David Atchison speech in Platte County, Mo., Nov. 6, 1854, *Platte Argus*, Nov. 6, 1854, in Daniel W. Wilder, *The Annals of Kansas* (1857), 40.

48 "act to punish offences": *Annals of Kansas*, 57.

49 "I had just arrived": Thomas H. Gladstone, *Kansas; or, Squatter Life and Border Warfare in the Far West* (1857), 38–39, 94–95.

50 "During the years 1853 and 1854": *Life and Letters*, 188–91.

52 "If you or any": John Brown to John Brown Jr., Aug. 21, 1854, in *Life and Letters*, 191.

52 "John's two letters": John Brown to Mary Brown, June 28, 1855, in *Life and Letters*, 194.

52 "I am writing": John Brown to Mary Brown and children, Sept. 4, 1855, in *Life and Letters*, 199.

53 "We found our folks": John Brown to Mary Brown and children, Oct. 13–14, 1855, in *Life and Letters*, 200–201.

Chapter 8

54 "The repeal of the Missouri compromise": Lincoln recollections, ca. June 1860, in *Collected Works*, 4:67.

54 "A live issue was presented": William H. Herndon and Jesse William Weik, *Herndon's Lincoln* (1889), 2:366.

55 "It is now several minutes": Lincoln speech at Peoria, Oct. 16, 1854, in *Collected Works*, 2:247–83.

60 "After the evening meal": Horace White, *The Life of Lyman Trumbull* (1913), 40n.

Chapter 9

61 "I never saw him so dejected": Burlingame MS., 1:10:1150.

62 "He was always calculating": *Herndon's Lincoln*, 2:375–76.

62 "I think I am a Whig": Lincoln to Speed, Aug. 24, 1855, in *Collected Works*, 2:320–23.

65 "At Springfield we were energetic": *Herndon's Lincoln*, 2:380.

Chapter 10

68 "A battle is to be fought": Henry Ward Beecher, *Defence of Kansas* (1856), 1–6.

70 "*What!*" the friend replied: *Life and Letters of Harriet Beecher Stowe*, ed. Annie Fields (1897), 163–65.

71 "So this is the little lady": Donald, *Lincoln*, 542.

72 "crime against Kansas": *The Crime Against Kansas: Speech of Hon. Charles Sumner in the Senate of the United States, 19th and 20th May, 1856* (1856), 5–14, 85–86.

73 "That damn fool": David Herbert Donald, *Charles Sumner and the Coming of the Civil War* (1960), 239.

Chapter 11

75 "About three or four weeks ago": John Brown to Mary Brown and children, Dec. 16, 1855, in *Life and Letters*, 217–20.

76 "The weather continues": John Brown to Mary Brown and children, Feb. 1 and 6, 1856, in *Life and Letters*, 222–23.

77 "Camps were formed": Thomas Goodrich, *War to the Knife: Bleeding Kansas, 1854–1861* (2004 ed.), 112.

77 "Boys, this day": Ibid., 114–15.

78 "We here have passed": John Brown to Mary Brown and children, June 1856, in *Life and Letters*, 236–37.

Chapter 12

79 "A number of United States soldiers": Brown to Giddings, Feb. 20, 1856, in Villard, *John Brown*, 131.

79 "You need have no fear": Giddings to Brown, March 17, 1856, in Villard, *John Brown*, 132.

80 "We utterly repudiate": Villard, *John Brown*, 135.

80 "My father, in order to ascertain": Salmon Brown to William Connelly, May 28, 1913, in "'His Soul Goes Marching On': The Life and Legacy of John Brown," West Virginia Archives and History, wvculture.org. This collection will be cited as West Virginia Archives.

81 "Williams knew everybody": Ibid.

81 "Caution! Caution, sir!": Villard, *John Brown*, 153–54.

82 "The reason for taking the night": Salmon Brown to William Connelly, May 28, 1913.

82 "We were all in bed": Mahala Doyle affidavit, June 7, 1856, West Virginia Archives.

83 "The three Doyles": Salmon Brown to William Connelly, May 28, 1913.

83 "The next morning was Sunday": John Doyle affidavit, June 7, 1856, West Virginia Archives.

83 "We were disturbed": Louisa Jane Wilkinson affidavit, June 13, 1856, West Virginia Archives.

85 "We were aroused": James Harris affidavit, June 6, 1856, West Virginia Archives.

Chapter 13

87 "A man rode up": Jason Brown letter in *Lawrence (Kans.) Journal*, Feb. 8, 1880, West Virginia Archives.

87 "No one can defend": John Sedgwick to his sister, June 11, 1856, in *Correspondence of John Sedgwick, Major-General* (1903), 2:8–9.

88 "An outrage of the darkest": Villard, *John Brown*, 168.

88 "Brother Jason and I": John Brown Jr. to *Cleveland Leader*, Nov. 29, 1883, West Virginia Archives.

89 "WAR! WAR!": Villard, *John Brown*, 189.

90 "a state of civil war": *DeBow's Review*, Aug. 1856.

90 "We started about 4 o'clock": "Owen Brown's Account of the Fight at Black Jack, Kan.," *Springfield Republican*, Jan. 14, 1889, West Virginia Archives.

Chapter 14

94 "He exhibited at all times": August Bondi, "With John Brown in Kansas," *Transactions of the Kansas State Historical Society* 8 (1904): 282–83.

95   **"Suddenly, thirty paces before me"**: James Redpath, *The Public Life of Captain John Brown* (1860), 83–85.

97   **"During the day he stayed"**: W. A. Phillips, "Three Interviews with Old John Brown," *Atlantic Monthly*, Dec. 1879, 739–41.

99   **"We severally pledge"**: *Life and Letters*, 287–88.

100   **"Men, come on!"**: Villard, *John Brown*, 243–48.

PART II · SPRINGFIELD

Chapter 15

105   **"I understand you are"**: Lincoln to John Bennett, Aug. 4, 1856, in *Collected Works*, 2:358.

106   **"The question of slavery"**: Lincoln speech at Kalamazoo, Aug. 27, 1856, in *Collected Works*, 2:361–66.

106   **"All this talk"**: Lincoln speech at Galena, Ill., July 23, 1856, in *Collected Works*, 2:355.

106   **"All of us who did not vote"**: Lincoln speech at Chicago, Dec. 10, 1856, in *Collected Works*, 2:385.

107   **"Having devoted the most"**: Lincoln to C. D. Gilfillan, May 9, 1857, in *Collected Works*, 2:395.

107   **"too old, when they became"**: Timothy S. Huebner, "Roger B. Taney and the Slavery Issue: Looking Beyond—and Before—*Dred Scott*," *Journal of American History* 97, no. 1 (June 2010): 20–25.

109   **"I never speak upon political issues"**: Taney quoted in Don E. Fehrenbacher, *The Dred Scott Case: Its Significance in American Law and Politics* (1978), 552, 557–58.

109   **"Lovely and comely"**: Walker Lewis, *Without Fear or Favor: A Biography of Chief Justice Roger Brooke Taney* (1965), 380.

110   **"Times now are not"**: Austin Allen, *Origins of the Dred Scott Case: Jacksonian Jurisprudence and the Supreme Court, 1837–1856* (2006), 146.

111   **"They had for more than a century"**: Taney in *Dred Scott v. Sandford*, 60 U.S. 393 (1856).

112   **"positive good"**: John Calhoun speech in Senate, Feb. 6, 1837, in *The Works of John C. Calhoun* (1864), 2:631.

112   **"The rights of property"**: Taney in *Dred Scott v. Sandford*, 60 U.S. 393 (1856).

Chapter 16

114   **"The Congress, the Executive"**: Jackson veto message, July 10, 1832, in Papers of the Presidents, American Presidency Project, presidency.ucsb.edu. This collection will be cited as Papers of the Presidents.

115   **"It would be interesting"**: Lincoln speech at Springfield, June 26, 1857, in *Collected Works*, 2:398–410.

Chapter 17

121   **"I desire to know"**: J. N. Holloway, *History of Kansas* (1868), 399.

122   **"The Lecompton constitution"**: Douglas to John W. Forney et al., Feb. 6, 1858, in *Letters of Douglas*, 408–10.

123   **"By God, sir"**: Johannsen, *Stephen A. Douglas*, 585–86.

123   **"What think you"**: Lincoln to Trumbull, Nov. 30, 1857, in *Collected Works*, 2:427.

124 "He wrote on stray envelopes": *Herndon's Lincoln*, 2:396–97n.
125 "If we could first know": Lincoln speech at Springfield, June 16, 1858, in *Collected Works*, 2:461–69.

Chapter 18

129 "John, isn't it dreadful": Villard, *John Brown*, 270n.
130 "'Old Brown' of Kansas": Ibid., 271.
130 "A man of rare common-sense": Henry David Thoreau, "A Plea for Captain John Brown," Oct. 30, 1859, gutenberg.org.
131 "He used to take out": *Life and Letters*, 512.
131 "Captain John Brown, the old partisan": William Lawrence, *Life of Amos A. Lawrence, with Extracts from His Diary and Correspondence* (1888), 124–28.
132 "If you get the arms and money": Villard, *John Brown*, 275.
133 "Old Brown's *Farewell*": Ibid., 288.

Chapter 19

134 "It is true": *Herndon's Lincoln*, 2:398–400.
134 "I had thought": Burlingame MS., 1:12:1297.
134 "I have never professed": Lincoln fragment, ca. July 1858, in *Collected Works*, 2:482.
135 "I clearly see": Lincoln fragment, ca. Aug. 21, 1858, in *Collected Works*, 2:548–49.
135 "I am much flattered": Lincoln to John L. Scripps, June 23, 1858, in *Collected Works*, 2:471.
136 "Will it be agreeable": Lincoln to Douglas, July 24, 1858, in *Collected Works*, 2:522.
136 "Recent events have interposed": Douglas to Lincoln, July 24, 1858, in *Papers of Douglas*, 423–24.
137 "I can only say": Lincoln to Douglas, July 29, 1858, in *Collected Works*, 2:528–30.

Chapter 20

140 "Prior to 1854 this country": "First Joint Debate, at Ottawa: Mr. Douglas's Speech," in *Political Debates Between Abraham Lincoln and Stephen A. Douglas* (1897), at bartleby.com. This collection will be cited as *Political Debates*.

Chapter 21

147 "When a man hears himself": "First Joint Debate, at Ottawa: Mr. Lincoln's Reply," in *Political Debates*.

Chapter 22

151 "All at once, after the train": *Reminiscences of Carl Schurz*, 2:89–96.

Chapter 23

156 "I desire to know": "Second Joint Debate, at Freeport: Mr. Lincoln's Speech," in *Political Debates*.
157 "a hundred times": "Second Joint Debate, at Freeport: Mr. Douglas's Speech," in *Political Debates*.
158 "There was, in no sense": Smith D. Atkins, "Patriotism of Northern Illinois," *Transactions of the Illinois State Historical Society* (1911): 80.
159 Southern newspapers blasted the Freeport formula: Burlingame MS., 1:13:1396.

159 **"The fight must go on"**: Lincoln to Henry Asbury, Nov. 19, 1858, in *Collected Works*, 3:339.

PART III · HARPERS FERRY

Chapter 24

163 **"It seems as though"**: Villard, *John Brown*, 290–91.
164 **"He was exhibiting"**: Charles Blair testimony, West Virginia Archives.
165 **"One of U.S. Hounds"**: Villard, *John Brown*, 287.
165 **"I am much confused"**: Brown to Mary Brown et al., May 27, 1857, in *Life and Letters*, 410–11.
166 **"I am (praised be God!)"**: Brown to wife and children, Jan. 30, 1858, in *Life and Letters*, 440–41.
167 **"Dear father, you have asked"**: Ruth Thompson to Brown, Feb. 20, 1858, in *Life and Letters*, 441–42.
167 **"I am here with our good friends"**: F. B. Sanborn, *Recollections of Seventy Years* (1909), 144–47.
169 **"My dear Friend"**: Brown to Sanborn, Feb. 24, 1858, in *Life and Letters*, 444–45.

Chapter 25

170 **"I had been a protégé"**: Richard Realf testimony, Jan. 21, 1860, in *Report of the Select Committee of the Senate Appointed to Inquire into the Late Invasion and Seizure of the Public Property at Harper's Ferry* (1860), Testimony: 90–98. This report will be cited as Mason Report, for its chairman, James Mason.
173 **"Whereas slavery, throughout its entire"**: "Provisional Constitution and Ordinances for the People of the United States," in Mason Report, 48–59.

Chapter 26

176 **"I have great faith"**: Smith to Sanborn, July 26, 1858, in *Life and Letters*, 466.
176 **"We were at supper"**: Sanborn, *Life and Letters*, 471.
177 **"It seems to me"**: Smith to Sanborn, May 7, 1858, in *Life and Letters*, 458.
177 **"Have been down with the ague"**: Brown to Sanborn, Aug. 6, 1858, in *Life and Letters*, 476.
177 **"I am still very weak"**: Brown to wife and children, Sept. 13, 1858, in *Life and Letters*, 478.
177 **"My health is some improved"**: Brown to children, Dec. 2, 1858, in *Life and Letters*, 480–81.
178 **"Two small companies"**: "John Brown's Parallels," Jan. 1859, in *Life and Letters*, 481–82.
178 **"A short distance from our road"**: *Life and Letters*, 486–87.
179 **"I am once more in Iowa"**: Brown to wife and children, Feb. 10, 1859, in *Life and Letters*, 490.
179 **"While we sympathize"**: Villard, *John Brown*, 385.
179 **"1st. Whole party"**: "Reception of Brown and Party at Grinnell, Iowa," in Villard, *John Brown*, 387.
180 **"My friend, you talk very brave"**: *Life and Letters*, 490–91.
180 **"We might be held"**: Villard, *John Brown*, 390.

Chapter 27

181 **"He tells his story"**: Alcott diary, May 8, 1859, in *Life and Letters*, 504–5.
182 **"From the time of my visit"**: *Life and Times of Frederick Douglass*, 274–79.

Chapter 28

186 **"I have been on expenses"**: Lincoln to Norman Judd, Nov. 16, 1858, in *Collected Works,* 3:337.

186 **"No man knows"**: Burlingame MS., 1:14:1523.

186 **"It is bad to be poor"**: Lincoln to Hawkins Taylor, Sept. 6, 1859, in *Collected Works,* 3:400.

187 **"Douglas has gone South"**: Lincoln to Trumbull, Dec. 11, 1858, in *Collected Works,* 3:344–45.

187 **"You must not let"**: Lincoln to Chase, Sept. 21, 1859, in *Collected Works,* 3:471.

187 **"Besides a strong desire"**: Lincoln to Colfax, July 6, 1859, in *Collected Works,* 3:390–91.

188 **"Please pardon the liberty"**: Lincoln to Chase, June 9, 1859, in *Collected Works,* 3:384.

189 **"Of course I would be pleased"**: Lincoln to Sargent, June 23, 1859, in *Collected Works,* 3:387–88.

189 **"Never forget that we"**: Lincoln speech, March 1, 1859, in *Collected Works,* 3:369–70.

190 **"This will never do"**: *Recollected Words of Abraham Lincoln,* comp. and ed. Don E. Fehrenbacher and Virginia Fehrenbacher (1996), 204.

190 **"Slavery is wrong"**: Lincoln speech at Cincinnati, Sept. 17, 1859, in *Collected Works,* 3:440, 460.

190 **"I hold that if there is"**: Lincoln speech at Cincinnati, Sept. 17, 1859, in *Abraham Lincoln: Speeches and Writings, 1859–1865* (1989), 85–86.

192 **"How would you feel"**: Burlingame MS., 1:14:1550.

192 **"Just think of such a sucker"**: Ibid., 1523–24.

Chapter 29

193 **"Good morning, gentlemen"**: John Unseld testimony, in Mason Report: Testimony, 1–4.

195 **"To a passer-by, the house"**: Osborne P. Anderson, *A Voice from Harpers Ferry* (1861), 24–31.

197 **"I heard the noise"**: Daniel Whelan testimony, in Mason Report: Testimony, 21–22.

199 **"They appeared at my chamber"**: Lewis Washington testimony, in Mason Report: Testimony, 29–35.

202 **"Col. Washington opened"**: Anderson, *Voice from Harpers Ferry,* 34–37.

203 **"About half past one o'clock"**: John Starry testimony, in Mason Report: Testimony, 23–25.

Chapter 30

205 **"Express train bound east"**: Phelps to W. P. Smith, Oct. 17, 1859, in *Correspondence Relating to the Insurgency at Harpers Ferry* (1860), 5.

205 **"Your dispatch is evidently"**: Smith to Phelps, Oct. 17, 1859, in *Correspondence Relating to the Insurgency at Harpers Ferry,* 5–6.

206 **"My dispatch was not exaggerated"**: Phelps to Smith, Oct. 17, 1859, in *Correspondence Relating to the Insurgency at Harpers Ferry,* 6.

206 **"Matter is probably much exaggerated"**: Smith to J. B. Ford, Oct. 17, 1859, in *Correspondence Relating to the Insurgency at Harpers Ferry,* 7.

206 **"Daylight revealed"**: Anderson, *Voice from Harpers Ferry,* 36–37.

206 **"Information has been received"**: "To the Baltimore Newspaper Press," Oct. 17, 1859, in *Correspondence Relating to the Insurrection at Harpers Ferry,* 5.

207   "It was about twelve o'clock": Anderson, *Voice from Harpers Ferry*, 39–42.
209   "I said to them": John Starry testimony, in Mason Report: Testimony, 27.
210   "We then caught hold of him": Hunter testimony, in *The Life, Trial and Execution of Capt. John Brown* (1859), 76.
211   "In consideration of all my men": *Governor's Message and Reports of the Public Officers of the State . . . of Virginia* (1859), 65.
211   "In the quiet of the night": Villard, *John Brown*, 448.
212   "The United States armory": John Garrett to James Buchanan, Oct. 17, 1859, in *Correspondence Relating to the Insurrection at Harpers Ferry*, 9.
212   "Their safety was the subject": Lee report, Oct. 19, 1859, in Mason Report: Appendix, 41–44.
213   "I approached the door": John S. Mosby, "Personal Recollections of General J. E. B. Stuart," *Munsey's Magazine*, April 1913, 36.
213   "My object was": Lee report, Oct. 19, 1859, in Mason Report: Appendix, 41.
213   "Colonel Lee gave me orders": Israel Green, "The Capture of John Brown," *North American Review*, Dec. 1885, 564–69.

Chapter 31

216   "Insurrectionary Outbreak": *Richmond Daily Dispatch*, Oct. 18, 1859.
216   "Fearful and Exciting Intelligence": *New York Herald*, Oct. 18, 1859.
217   "Who is Brown": *New York Herald*, Oct. 19, 1859.
217   "misguided, wild and apparently insane": *William Lloyd Garrison: The Story of His Life as Told by His Children*, 3:486.
218   "We are damnably exercised": Charles Ray to Lincoln, Oct. 20, 1859, Abraham Lincoln Papers, Library of Congress.
218   "a higher law": William Seward speech in the Senate, March 11, 1850, in *Speech of William H. Seward on the Admission of California* (1850), 27–28.
218   "He has forgotten": Burlingame MS., 1:14:1567.
218   "Since the humbug insurrection": William Frazer to Lincoln, Nov. 12, 1859, Lincoln Papers.
219   "John Brown has shown": Lincoln remarks at Elwood, Kans., Nov. 30 or Dec. 1, 1859, in *Collected Works*, 3:495–97.

Chapter 32

220   "Are you Captain Brown": *Life, Trial and Execution of John Brown*, 35–36.
221   "I immediately examined the leader": Barton H. Wise, *The Life of Henry A. Wise of Virginia, 1806–1876* (1899), 245–47.
222   "He is a wiry, active man": *Life, Trial and Execution of John Brown*, 44–49.

Chapter 33

229   "Brown seemed weak and haggard": *Life, Trial and Execution of John Brown*, 55–93.

Chapter 34

238   "My dear Wife, and Children": John Brown to Mary Brown and children, Oct. 31, 1859, in *Life and Letters*, 579–80.
241   "positively refused his consent": Villard, *John Brown*, 512.
241   "I am, besides, quite cheerful": John Brown to Mary Brown and children, Nov. 8, 1859, in *Life and Letters*, 585–87.
242   "If you feel sure": Brown to Mary Brown and children, Nov. 16, 1859, in *Life and Letters*, 591–93.

243 "I am waiting the hour": John Brown to Mary Brown and children, Nov. 30, 1859, in *Life and Letters*, 613–15.

244 "This is beautiful country": *New York Daily Tribune*, Dec. 5, 1859.

PART IV · THE TELEGRAPH OFFICE

Chapter 35

247 "John Brown was hung today": *Life and Letters of General Thomas J. Jackson*, ed. Mary Anna Jackson (1892), 130–31.

247 "John Brown was a man inspired": *"Right or Wrong, God Judge Me": The Writings of John Wilkes Booth*, ed. John Rhodehamel and Louise Taper (1997), 53.

247 "Tomorrow will probably be": Lee to Mary Lee, Dec. 1, 1859, in *Recollections and Letters of General Robert E. Lee*, ed. Robert E. Lee (son), (1904), 22.

248 "I, John Brown": Villard, *John Brown*, 554.

248 "He was a superior man": Thoreau, "Plea for Captain John Brown."

248 "Bold, unflinching, honest": William C. Beecher and Samuel Scoville, *A Biography of Rev. Henry Ward Beecher* (1888), 301–2.

249 "He has abolished slavery": Phillips eulogy of Brown, Dec. 8, 1859, in *American Patriotism: Speeches, Letters and Other Papers Which Illustrate the Foundation, the Development and the Preservation of the United States of America*, comp. Selim H. Peabody (1880), 504–7.

249 "On the evening when the news": *Life and Times of Frederick Douglass*, 268–73.

252 "Arrangements had been made": Sanborn, *Recollections of Seventy Years*, 187–90, 208–11.

Chapter 36

256 "One warm evening in 1859": Moncure Daniel Conway, *Autobiography* (1905), 1:317–18.

257 "There are but few": Burlingame MS., 1:14:1573–75, 1580–82.

258 "Our fathers," Douglas had said: Lincoln address at Cooper Institute, Feb. 27, 1860, in *Collected Works*, 3:522–50.

261 "When Lincoln rose to speak": Noah Brooks, *The Life of Lincoln*, in *The Writings of Abraham Lincoln*, ed. Arthur Brooks Lapsley (1906), 8:186–87.

Chapter 37

263 "If we were to form": Lincoln speech at New Haven, March 6, 1860, in *Collected Works*, 4:17–18.

264 "My name is new": Lincoln to Samuel Galloway, March 24, 1860, in *Collected Works*, 4:33–34.

264 "It was a very large": Ward H. Lamon, *The Life of Abraham Lincoln* (1872), 444–46.

266 "Be careful to give": Lincoln to Mark Delahay, May 12, 1860, in *Collected Works*, 4:49.

266 "In the days of Henry Clay": Lincoln to Edward Wallace, May 12, 1860, in *Collected Works*, 4:49.

266 *"Make no contracts"*: Marginal note on *Missouri Democrat*, May 17, 1860, in *Collected Works*, 4:50.

266 "Dear Seward," wrote Thurlow Weed: Weed to Seward, May 20, 1860, *Mississippi Valley Historical Review* (June 1947): 103–4.

267 "The enthusiasm with which the result": *New York Daily Tribune,* May 19, 1860.

Chapter 38

269 "Gentlemen, you have nominated": John B. Alley recollection, in *Reminiscences of Abraham Lincoln,* ed. Allen Thorndike Rice (1886), 575.
270 "Burn this": Lincoln to Leonard Swett, May 30, 1860, in *Collected Works,* 4:57.
270 "Remembering that Peter": Lincoln to Trumbull, June 5, 1860, in *Collected Works,* 4:71.
270 "I think it would be improper": Lincoln to J. Mason Haight, June 11, 1860, in *Collected Works,* 4:75.
271 "I *authorize nothing*": Lincoln to Samuel Galloway, June 19, 1860, in *Collected Works,* 4:79–80.
271 "You suggest that a visit": Lincoln to Samuel Haycraft, June 4, 1860, in *Collected Works,* 4:69–70.
271 "This is decidedly wrong": Lincoln to George Fogg, Aug. 16, 1880, in *Collected Works,* 4:96.
271 "We know not": Lincoln to Anson Henry, July 4, 1860, in *Collected Works,* 4:81–82.
272 "I suppose as good": Lincoln to Abraham Jonas, July 21, 1860, in *Collected Works,* 4:85–86.
273 "I never gave fifty dollars": Lincoln to J. C. Lee, Oct. 24, 1860, in *Collected Works,* 4:131.
273 "I hesitate to say it": Lincoln to Simeon Francis, Aug. 4, 1860, in *Collected Works,* 4:89–90.
273 "I appear among you": Lincoln remarks, Aug. 8, 1860, in *Collected Works,* 4:91.
273 "My published speeches": Lincoln to Apolion Cheney, Aug. 14, 1860, in *Collected Works,* 4:93.
273 "The people of the South": Lincoln to John Fry, Aug. 15, 1860, in *Collected Works,* 4:95.
274 "I appreciate your motive": Lincoln to William Speer, Oct. 23, 1860, in *Collected Works,* 4:130.
274 "What is it I could say": Lincoln to George Davis, Oct. 27, 1860, in *Collected Works,* 4:132–33.

Chapter 39

276 "The issue before the country": *Charleston Mercury,* Nov. 3, 1860.
277 "Thus the constituted compact": "Declaration of the Immediate Causes Which Induce and Justify the Secession of South Carolina from the Federal Union," Dec. 24, 1860, Avalon Project, avalon.law.yale.edu.
278 "After drifting a dreary night": Wendell Phillips, "The Lesson of the Hour," in *Disunion* (1861), 5–25.
280 "The election of the Republican": William Lloyd Garrison, "Southern Desperation," *Liberator,* Nov. 16, 1860.
281 "The question in its simplest form": J. P. B., "Value of the Union," *Liberator,* Dec. 28, 1860.
282 "We hold, with Jefferson": Greeley in *New York Daily Tribune,* Nov. 9, 1860, reproduced in Horace Greeley, *The American Conflict: A History of the Great Rebellion in the United States of America* (1865), 1:358–59.
283 Perhaps that was his intent: See David M. Potter, "Horace Greeley and Peaceable Secession," *Journal of Southern History* 7, no. 2 (May 1941): 145–59.

283 "No republican state": Seward address, Dec. 22, 1860, in *The Rebellion Record,* ed. Frank Moore, vol. 1 (1861), "Documents and Narratives," 5–7.
285 "No man in America": Douglas to Ninety-Six New Orleans Citizens, Nov. 13, 1860, in *Letters of Stephen A. Douglas,* 499–503.

Chapter 40

288 "I find Mr. Lincoln": Lincoln statement, ca. Nov. 9, 1860, in *Collected Works,* 4:138.
288 "disarm the mischief makers": Truman Smith to Lincoln, Nov. 7, 1860, in *Collected Works,* 4:138–39.
288 "This is intended": Lincoln to Truman Smith, Nov. 10, 1860, in *Collected Works,* 4:138.
289 "I could say nothing": Lincoln to Nathaniel Paschall, Nov. 16, 1860, in *Collected Works,* 4:139–40.
289 "I have labored": Lincoln draft for Trumbull, Nov. 20, 1860, in *Collected Works,* 4:141–42.
290 "The Boston Courier": Lincoln to Henry Raymond, Nov. 28, 1860, in *Collected Works,* 4:146.
290 "Let there be no compromise": Lincoln to Trumbull, Dec. 10, 1860, in *Collected Works,* 4:149–50.
291 "Let either be done": Lincoln to Washburne, Dec. 13, 1860, in *Collected Works,* 4:151.
291 "Tell them you judge": Lincoln to Weed, Dec. 17, 1860, in *Collected Works,* 4:154.
291 "It would make me appear": Lincoln to Gilmer, Dec. 15, 1860, in *Collected Works,* 4:151–52.
291 "That the fugitive slave clause": Lincoln draft resolutions, Dec. 20, 1860, in *Collected Works,* 4:156–57.
292 "I take up my pen": Lincoln to Herndon, Feb. 2, 1848, in *Collected Works,* 1:448.
292 "If you have revised it": Lincoln to Stephens, Nov. 30, 1860, in *Collected Works,* 4:146.
292 "Your obliging answer": Lincoln to Stephens, Dec. 22, 1860, in *Collected Works,* 4:160.
293 "Personally, I am not your enemy": Stephens to Lincoln, Dec. 30, 1860, in *Recollections of Alexander H. Stephens,* ed. Myrta Lockett Avary (1910), 60.

Chapter 41

294 "Secession is neither": Buchanan annual message, Dec. 3, 1860, in Papers of the Presidents.
295 "My dear Sir": Lincoln to Green, Dec. 28, 1860, in *Collected Works,* 4:162–63.
295 "I regret your unwillingness": Green to Lincoln, Jan. 7, 1861, Lincoln Papers.
296 "administer the government": *New York Herald,* Jan. 8, 1861, in *Collected Works,* 4:163n.
296 "What is our present condition?": Lincoln to James Hale, Jan. 11, 1861, in *Collected Works,* 4:172.
296 "I will suffer death": Lincoln remarks, ca. Jan. 19–21, 1861, in *Collected Works,* 4:175–76.
297 "My friends": Lincoln farewell address, Feb. 11, 1861, in *Collected Works,* 4:190.
297 "Let us believe": Lincoln remarks at Tolono, Ill., Feb. 11, 1861, in *Collected Works,* 4:191.
298 "Look well upon that man!": Lewis Lloyd, "Lincoln and Pinkerton," *Journal of the Illinois State Historical Society* (1948): 376.

Chapter 42

299 **"Present my compliments"**: *Herndon's Lincoln,* 3:493.
300 **"He was completely metamorphosed"**: Unidentified eyewitness in ibid., 3:495–96.
301 **"Mr. Buchanan and Mr. Lincoln"**: *New York Times,* March 5, 1861.
302 **"Apprehension seems to exist"**: Lincoln inaugural address, March 4, 1861, in Papers of the Presidents.

Chapter 43

306 **"He does not mean coercion"**: *New York Times,* March 5, 1861.
307 **"The manner in which Mr. Lincoln"**: "The Inaugural Address," *Douglass' Monthly,* April 1861.
309 **"Some Thoughts for the President's Consideration"**: Seward to Lincoln, April 1, 1861, in *Collected Works,* 4:317–18n.
310 **"If this must be done"**: Lincoln to Seward, April 1, 1861, in *Collected Works,* 4:316–17.
311 **"I appeal to all loyal citizens"**: Proclamation 80, April 15, 1861, in Papers of the Presidents.

Chapter 44

312 **"We found the great fortress"**: George Kimball, "Origin of the John Brown Song," *New England Magazine,* Dec. 1889, 371–76.
314 **"It is now generally admitted"**: *Memoirs of General William T. Sherman* (1876), 1:181–82.
315 **"Their slaves, if any they have"**: Frémont proclamation, Aug. 31, 1861, *Harper's Weekly,* Sept. 14, 1861.
315 **"There is great danger"**: Lincoln to Frémont, Sept. 2, 1861, in *Collected Works,* 4:506.
316 **"Coming from you"**: Lincoln to Browning, Sept. 22, 1861, in *Collected Works,* 4:531–33.
317 **"It is difficult to answer"**: Lincoln to Hunter, Dec. 31, 1861, in *Collected Works,* 5:84–85.
318 **"I, Abraham Lincoln"**: Proclamation 90, May 19, 1862, in Papers of the Presidents.

Chapter 45

319 **"to compensate for the inconveniences"**: Lincoln special message to Congress, March 6, 1862, in Papers of the Presidents.
321 **"Have you noticed"**: Lincoln to Henry Raymond, March 9, 1862, in *Collected Works,* 5:152–53.
321 **"Gentlemen," he said**: Lincoln remarks, July 12, 1862, in *Collected Works,* 5:317–19.
322 **Lincoln sent a draft bill**: Special message, July 14, 1862, in Papers of the Presidents.
323 **"I have never doubted"**: Lincoln signing statement, April 16, 1862, in Papers of the Presidents.
323 **"Why should the people"**: Lincoln remarks, Aug. 14, 1862, in *Collected Works,* 5:370–75.

Chapter 46

326 "If a decree": Remarks to a Delegation of Progressive Friends, June 20, 1862, in *Collected Works*, 5:278–79.

327 "Had slavery no existence": Lincoln remarks, July 17, 1862, in *Collected Works*, 5:327.

327 "It is by what President Lincoln": Frederick Douglass, "The Slaveholders' Rebellion," speech, July 4, 1862, *Douglass' Monthly*, Aug. 1862.

329 "Dear Sir," he wrote: *New York Daily Tribune*, Aug. 20, 1862.

331 "I have just read yours": Lincoln to Greeley, Aug. 22, 1862, in *Collected Works*, 5:388–89.

333 "I am approached": Reply to Emancipation Memorial Presented by Chicago Christians of All Denominations, Sept. 13, 1862, in *Collected Works*, 5:419–25.

335 "The will of God prevails": Lincoln note, ca. Sept. 2, 1862, in *Collected Works*, 5:403–4.

Chapter 47

337 "I procured some foolscap": Eckert quoted in David Homer Bates, "Lincoln in Everyday Humor: Part III—Lincoln in the Telegraph Office," *Century Illustrated Monthly*, July 1907, 371–72.

338 "Things had gone from bad to worse": F. B. Carpenter, *Six Months at the White House with Abraham Lincoln* (1866), 20–22.

339 "The President was in deep distress": Bates note in *Collected Works*, 5:486n.

339 "Things looked darker": Carpenter, *Six Months at the White House*, 22.

340 "Commander in Chief of the Army": Proclamation 93 (Preliminary Emancipation Proclamation), Sept. 22, 1862, in Papers of the Presidents.

340 "When I finished reading": Carpenter, *Six Months at the White House*, 23–24.

341 "We shout for joy": "Emancipation Proclaimed," *Douglass' Monthly*, Oct. 1862.

343 "I appear before you": *New York Daily Tribune*, Sept. 25, 1862.

344 "While I hope": Lincoln to Hamlin, Sept. 28, 1862, in *Collected Works*, 5:444.

Chapter 48

345 "There is no line": Lincoln annual message, Dec. 1, 1862, in Papers of the Presidents.

348 "I do order and declare": Emancipation Proclamation, Jan. 1, 1863, in Papers of the Presidents.

349 "This was an error": Stephens speech, March 21, 1861, in *Alexander H. Stephens in Public and Private*, ed. Henry Cleveland (1866), 721–22.

349 "the act of lawless ruffians": Mason Report, 18.

350 "no change of opinion": Jefferson Davis, resolution, in *The Rise and Fall of the Confederate Government* (1912), 1:42.

350 "the most execrable measure": Davis message to Confederate senate and house of representatives, Jan. 12, 1863, in *Rebellion Record*, 6:380–81.

Chapter 49

352 "When first the rebel cannon": *Douglass' Monthly*, March 1863.

353 "The troops charged the breastworks": Henry McCulloch report, June 8, 1863, in *The War of the Rebellion: A Compilation of the Official Records of the Union and Confederate Armies* (1889), ser. 1, vol. 24, pt. 2, 467–70.

353 "We were attacked": Matthew M. Miller to his aunt, June 10, 1863, in *War of the Rebellion*, ser. 3, 3:452–53n. See also Martha M. Bigelow, "The Significance of Milliken's Bend in the Civil War," *Journal of Negro History* 45 (1960): 156–63.

353 "It is impossible for men": Charles A. Dana, *Recollections of the Civil War* (1898), 86.

354 "Fellow citizens," he said: Lincoln response to a serenade, July 7, 1863, in *Collected Works*, 6:319–20.

355 "With our aggrieved brethren": Wood statement to New York City Council, Jan. 6, 1861, in *The Political History of the United States of America During the Great Rebellion*, comp. and ed. Edward McPherson (1865), 42–44.

357 "We have had great riots": Torrey to Asa Gray, July 13–16, 1863, in "An Eye-witness Account of the New York City Draft Riots, July, 1863," ed. A. Hunter Dupree and Leslie H. Fishel Jr., *Mississippi Valley Historical Review* 47, no. 3 (Dec. 1960): 472–79.

Chapter 50

360 "It would be very agreeable": Lincoln to Conkling, Aug. 26, 1863, in *Collected Works*, 6:406–10.

363 "I am mortified": Lincoln to Conkling, Sept. 3, 1863, in *Collected Works*, 6:430.

363 "spies or aiders": Proclamation 104, Sept. 15, 1863, in Papers of the Presidents.

363 "You are further directed": Lincoln instructions to tax commissioners, Sept. 16, 1863, in *Collected Works*, 6:457.

364 "I do not like this arrangement": Lincoln to Edwin Stanton, Nov. 17, 1863, in *Collected Works*, 7:16.

364 "for several substantial reasons": Lincoln remarks, Nov. 18, 1863, in *Collected Works*, 7:16–17.

365 "Four score and seven years": Gettysburg Address, Nov. 19, 1863, in Papers of the Presidents.

Chapter 51

366 "Absorbed in his papers": Carpenter, *Six Months at the White House*, 30–31.

367 "Mother, do you see": Elizabeth Keckley, *Behind the Scenes; or, Thirty Years a Slave and Four Years in the White House* (1868), 104–5.

368 "Resolved," the platform declared: National Union party platform, June 7, 1864, American Presidency Project.

369 "To Whom It May Concern": Lincoln letter, July 18, 1864, in *Collected Works*, 7:451.

369 "What is the sine qua non": *New York Herald*, July 27, 1864.

370 "This war must go on": *New York Times*, July 24, 1864.

370 "Jeff Davis was perfectly right": *New York Herald*, Aug. 1, 1864.

370 "Niggers are not fit": *New York Herald*, Aug. 4, 1864.

370 "The President has a right": *New York Times*, July 23, 1864.

371 "It is a pity Mr. Lincoln": Meade to Mrs. Meade, July 26, 1864, in *The Life and Letters of George Gordon Meade*, ed. George Gordon Meade (1913), 2:215–16.

Chapter 52

372 "The President appeared to be": John T. Mills diary, Aug. 19, 1864, in *Collected Works*, 7:506–7.

374 "Let us, at the very outset": August Belmont opening remarks, Aug. 29, 1864, in *Official Proceedings of the Democratic National Convention Held in 1864 at Chicago* (1864), 3.

374 "justice, humanity, liberty": Democratic party platform, Aug. 29, 1864, at American Presidency Project.

374 "I told Mr. Lincoln": Weed to Seward, Aug. 22, 1864, *Century Magazine*, Aug. 1889, 548.

375 **"No, sir," Hamilton replied:** Hamilton quoted in J. K. Butler to Benjamin Butler, Aug. 11, 1864, in *Private and Official Correspondence of Gen. Benjamin F. Butler* (1917), 5:35–36.

376 **"The President's *'To whom it may concern'"*:** Douglass to Theodore Tilton, Oct. 15, 1864, in *Descriptive Catalogue of the Gluck Collection of Manuscripts and Autographs in the Buffalo Public Library* (1899), 35–36.

377 **"This morning, as for some days past":** Lincoln memo, Aug. 23, 1864, in *Collected Works,* 7:514.

377 **"I would say, 'General'":** John Hay diary, Nov. 11, 1864, in *Inside Lincoln's White House: The Complete Civil War Diary of John Hay,* ed. Michael Burlingame and John R. Turner Ettlinger (1997), 248.

Chapter 53

379 **"devout acknowledgment to the Supreme Being":** Lincoln proclamation, Sept. 3, 1864, in *Collected Works,* 7:533–34.

380 **"It does look":** From entry for Oct. 15, 1864, in *The Diary of George Templeton Strong,* ed. Allan Nevins and Milton Halsey Thomas (1988 ed.), 251.

380 **"It has long been":** Lincoln response to serenade, Nov. 10, 1864, in *Collected Works,* 8:100–101.

380 **"Most heartily do I congratulate":** Lincoln response to serenade, Oct. 19, 1864, in *Collected Works,* 8:52.

380 **emancipation was permanent:** Lincoln reply to Maryland Union Committee, Nov. 17, 1864, in *Collected Works,* 8:113–14.

381 **"Hence there is only a question":** Lincoln annual message, Dec. 6, 1864, in Papers of the Presidents.

382 **"Your brother died":** Isaac N. Arnold, *The History of Abraham Lincoln and the Overthrow of Slavery* (1866), 469.

382 **"There is a task":** Lincoln response to serenade, Feb. 1, 1865, in *Collected Works,* 8:254–55.

Chapter 54

383 **"Should the war continue":** Lee to Hunter, Jan. 11, 1865, *War of the Rebellion,* ser. 4, 3:1012–13.

384 **"I think that the proposition":** Cobb to James Seddon, Jan. 8, 1865, *War of the Rebellion,* ser. 4, 3:1009.

385 **"whatever capacity":** In General Orders No. 14, March 23, 1865, in *War of the Rebellion,* ser. 4, 3:1161.

385 **"At this second appearing":** Second inaugural address, March 4, 1865, in Papers of the Presidents.

Chapter 55

388 **"There was murder in the air":** *Life and Times of Frederick Douglass,* 440–45.

391 **"I will fight with all my heart":** Booth, *"Right or Wrong, God Judge Me,"* 55–60.

392 **"*He* is Bonaparte":** Ibid., 65n.

392 **"When I aided in the capture":** Ibid., 125.

392 **"If the South is to be aided":** Ibid., 149. This is the reconstruction of a letter written by Booth, handed to an associate for delivery and then destroyed by that associate before delivery. The associate later reproduced the letter from memory. Its wording might not be precisely accurate, but its gist seems to capture Booth's thinking.

Chapter 56

394   "I certainly have no": *Life and Reminiscences of Jefferson Davis by Distinguished Men of His Times* (1890), 50.

394   "I walked up to a plantation house": *Memoirs of Sherman*, 2:180–81.

395   "The colored people express": Carolyn L. Harrell, *When the Bells Tolled for Lincoln: Southern Reactions to the Assassination* (1997), 57–58.

396   "Slavery was not abolished": W. E. B. Du Bois, *Black Reconstruction in America* (1963 ed.), 188.

397   "It certainly is not a story": Douglass speech, May 30, 1881, West Virginia Archives.

399   "He was preeminently": Douglass address, April 14, 1876, in *Oration by Frederick Douglass Delivered on the Unveiling of the Freedmen's Monument in Memory of Abraham Lincoln* (1876).

Index

HEIRS OF THE FOUNDERS
Henry Clay, John Calhoun and Daniel Webster,
the Second Generation of American Giants

In the early 1800s, Daniel Webster, Henry Clay, and John Calhoun rose
to prominence in Congress when the Founding Fathers were beginning to
retire to their farms. Together these heirs of the founders took the country
to war, battled one another for the presidency, and set themselves the task
of finishing the work the founders had left undone. Their rise was marked
by dramatic duels, fierce debates, scandal, and political betrayal. Yet each
in his own way sought to remedy the two glaring flaws in the Constitution:
its refusal to specify where authority ultimately rested, with the states or
the nation, and its unwillingness to address the essential incompatibility
of republicanism and slavery. H. W. Brands thrillingly narrates an epic
American rivalry and the little-known drama of the dangerous early years
of our democracy.

History

REAGAN
The Life

H. W. Brands brilliantly establishes Ronald Reagan as one of the two great
presidents of the twentieth century, a true peer to Franklin Roosevelt.
Reagan conveys with sweep and vigor how the confident force of Reagan's
personality and the unwavering nature of his beliefs enabled him to engineer a conservative revolution in American politics and play a crucial role
in ending communism in the Soviet Union. Employing archival sources
not available to previous biographers and drawing on dozens of interviews
with surviving members of Reagan's administration, Brands has crafted a
richly detailed and fascinating narrative of the presidential years. *Reagan*
is a storytelling triumph, an irresistible portrait of an underestimated politician whose pragmatic leadership and steadfast vision transformed the
nation.

Biography

THE GENERAL VS. THE PRESIDENT
MacArthur and Truman at the Brink of Nuclear War

At the height of the Korean War, President Harry S. Truman committed a gaffe that sent shock waves around the world when he suggested that General Douglas MacArthur, the willful, fearless, and highly decorated commander of the American and UN forces, had his finger on the nuclear trigger. A correction quickly followed, but the damage was done. The contest of wills between these two titanic characters unfolds against the turbulent backdrop of a faraway war and terrors conjured at home by Joseph McCarthy. *The General vs. the President* vividly evokes the making of a new American era.

History

ALSO AVAILABLE
The Age of Gold
American Colossus
Andrew Jackson
The First American
The Heartbreak of Aaron Burr
Lone Star Nation
The Man Who Saved the Union
The Murder of Jim Fisk for the Love of Josie Mansfield
Traitor to His Class

ANCHOR BOOKS
Available wherever books are sold.
www.anchorbooks.com